ON STAGE
for
CHRISTMAS

ON STAGE
for
CHRISTMAS

A collection of royalty-free, one-act
Christmas plays for young people

Edited by

SYLVIA E. KAMERMAN

Publishers　　　　　PLAYS, INC.　　　　　*Boston*

Copyright © 1978

by

PLAYS, INC.

Reprinted 1979

Library of Congress Cataloging in Publication Data

Main entry under title:
   On stage for Christmas

   SUMMARY: Thirty-three plays on levels from lower grades through senior high. Production notes included.
   1. Christmas plays.   2. Children's plays.
   [1. Christmas plays.   2. Plays] I. Kamerman,
Sylvia E.
PN6120.C5063   808.82'41   78-15517
ISBN 0-8238-0226-4

Contents

Junior and Senior High

Middle Grades

Lower Grades

ON STAGE
for
CHRISTMAS

Reindeer on the Roof

By Mildred Hark and Noel McQueen

A blown fuse puts out the lights for the Stevens family, but the remaining glow reminds them of the true meaning of Christmas . . .

Characters

MR. STEVENS
MRS. STEVENS
EDDIE STEVENS, *16*
MARY STEVENS, *14*
OLIVER STEVENS, *8*
MR. BROWN
MRS. BROWN
CORA, *their teen-age daughter*
SALLY COOK, *a reporter*
BILL ROSS, *a photographer*

TIME: *Christmas Eve.*
SETTING: *The Stevens living room. An undecorated Christmas tree stands at one side. There is a large window on rear wall, with evergreen bushes visible above sill.*
AT RISE: MR. STEVENS *is seen outside upstage window*

looping a string of colored lights over bushes. MRS.
STEVENS *enters left carrying greens, box of ornaments
and package of tinsel. Humming a Christmas tune, she
hangs two or three balls on tree. Sound of hammering
is heard offstage, and* MRS. STEVENS *looks up and
shakes her head.* MR. STEVENS *moves out of view. In
a moment,* MR. STEVENS *enters, takes off coat and
tosses it on chair.*

MR. STEVENS (*Singing*): We wish you a Merry Christmas
and a Happy New Year! (*To* MRS. STEVENS) Jane, I've
just strung thirty-two more lights on the bushes out
front. That makes two hundred and eighty-two, not
counting the spotlights for the reindeer on the roof.

MRS. STEVENS: Yes, George, I know. The people up the
street had two hundred and fifty lights, so we had to
have more.

MR. STEVENS: But Jane, it looks wonderful.

MRS. STEVENS (*Sarcastically*): Yes, sunrise on the Arctic
was never like our front yard.

MR. STEVENS: Jane, that's the whole idea — to make our
whole place look like the North Pole. Santa sitting in
his sleigh, with reindeer pulling it across the roof. I
really want to win the prize this year, and I think
we've got a good chance. (*Sound of hammering is
heard.*) Eddie's nailing down the last reindeer now.

MRS. STEVENS: I know, George, I'm not deaf. (*The
phone rings and she starts toward it.*) I'll get it. (*She
hands box of ornaments to* MR. STEVENS.) Will you
please put some of the balls on the tree? I've been
trying to get it trimmed all afternoon. (*She picks up
phone.*) Hello? Oh, Edna. Merry Chrismtas Eve to you.
too. (*She sits.*) Oh, no, I'm glad to sit down for a
minute . . . . The usual things, trimming the tree,

cooking for tomorrow, pies, puddings, stuffing the turkey . . . . Help? I should say not. The rest of the
family are all working on the display. If you ask me,
this thing is going too far. . . . Everyone's trying to
outdo everybody else. When the *Daily News* first offered a prize for the best Christmas display, it was fun,
and the competition was good-natured. But now it's
really gotten out of hand. My whole family is on the
roof. Eddie is nailing down the last reindeer and
Mary's helping him. And Oliver is sitting in the sleigh
shouting, "Go Prancer, go Dancer!" I just hope they
don't all fall. We'll be using the sleigh to take them all
to the hospital.

EDDIE (*Offstage; shouting*): Hey, be careful! Look out!
(*Sound of loud crash is heard from offstage.* MR.
STEVENS *rushes out.*)

MRS. STEVENS (*Into phone*): Oh, Edna. I'll have to hang
up. Someone *has* fallen. I must see what's happened.
(*She hangs up phone and rushes right, calling.*) George,
what is it? Oliver's fallen off the roof! I know he has.
Oh, dear — oh, dear. (*She rushes back in and picks up
phone; dials*) Operator, operator (*Pause*) — I must get
the doctor! Why don't they answer? (MR. STEVENS
*rushes in right carrying large reindeer head, cut out of
plywood and painted.*)

MR. STEVENS: It's all right, Jane. It wasn't Oliver.

MRS. STEVENS (*Putting down phone*): Well, who was it,
then?

MR. STEVENS: Don't worry, Jane. See? It was one of the
reindeer. The head broke off.

MRS. STEVENS (*Sighing*): Thank goodness.

MR. STEVENS: Thank goodness? Jane, this is serious.(*Examining reindeer cut-out*)

MRS. STEVENS: George Stevens, you almost sound as though you wish it had been one of the children who had fallen off the roof instead.

MR. STEVENS: Don't be ridiculous! But we can't have a headless reindeer. We'll have to get this up again somehow.

MRS. STEVENS: I thought you'd be finished with that display by now.

MR. STEVENS: It's more than a display, Jane. It's a Christmas *spectacular.*

MRS. STEVENS: Spectacular, display — call it anything you like — you've been working on it since the Fourth of July. Now it's Christmas Eve, and nothing else has been done. The tree isn't trimmed, the presents aren't wrapped, the turkey isn't stuffed. *(Exasperated)* Why can't you just have seven reindeer?

MR. STEVENS *(Aghast)*: *Seven* reindeer? Why, it wouldn't be authentic. Santa Claus always has eight reindeer. *(Loud footsteps are heard offstage)* Here come the children.

MRS. STEVENS: I'll be glad when they don't have to climb up and down that ladder any more. It's dangerous.

MR. STEVENS: Oh, nonsense. (MARY *enters, followed by* EDDIE.)

MARY: Poor Prancer.

EDDIE *(Irritated)*: This is just great! We had everything all set, and then Mary leans on Prancer's head and knocks it off.

MARY *(Laughing)*: How was I to know you didn't have it nailed on tight?

MR. STEVENS: What do you think we should do, Eddie?

EDDIE: I can nail it on again, of course. *(Looking at head)* But some of the paint was nicked off. The least you can do, Mary, is touch up his nose.

MARY: But I'll get paint all over my hands again. Besides,

I have other things to do — wash my hair, hem my dress for tomorrow — and my presents aren't even wrapped.

MRS. STEVENS: Then you know how *I* feel, Mary. You've all been busy up on the roof, and no one's lifted a finger to help me. (*Putting another ornament on tree*) I can't do everything. I've been trying to trim the tree and stuff the turkey — (*Motioning toward candlestick on windowsill*) and I want to get that candlestick polished.

MR. STEVENS: What do you want to do that for, Jane?

MRS. STEVENS: Because I want a candle in the window, George. (*Determined*) You like your reindeer on the roof, and I like my candle in the window. My mother always had one when I was a little girl. She said it represented the Christmas star.

MR. STEVENS: That's very nice, Jane, but it isn't very spectacular.

EDDIE: Don't you want us to have the best Christmas display on the street, Mom? And how about you, Mary? You've been as excited as anyone, and now you don't even want to paint Prancer's nose.

MARY: All right! I'll get the paint. It's just that I've painted so *many* reindeer . . . . (*She goes out left.*)

MR. STEVENS (*Examining reindeer head again*): I'm glad there's not too much damage done. (*To* EDDIE) Wouldn't it be something if the *Daily News* chose our house as the prize winner? A special presentation by the Mayor, dinner for the whole family at the best restaurant in town — sounds good, doesn't it?

EDDIE: Sure, Dad, but I wouldn't count on our winning it.

MR. STEVENS: Why not? We have a real Christmas spectacular.

EDDIE: I know. But you should see some of the decorations on Cherry Street. One house has a Christmas tree fifty feet high on the roof.

MRS. STEVENS: We have a Christmas tree only six feet high, and we haven't finished trimming it yet.

EDDIE (*Laughing*): O.K., Mom. I'll help. (*He goes to her, and she hands him some decorations.*)

MRS. STEVENS: You, too, George. Put down that reindeer head and hang a few ornaments on the tree. I'm going to polish this candlestick. (*She takes polishing cloth from her pocket and rubs brass candlestick.* MR. STEVENS *puts reindeer head on a chair. He and* EDDIE *slowly hang decorations on tree.*)

MR. STEVENS (*Stopping with ornament in hand and looking up*): A Christmas tree fifty feet high. (*Sighs*) That's spectacular, all right.

EDDIE (*Sadly*): Yes, I guess the *Daily News* will choose that display. (*Then brightening*) But we'll have the best display on our street, anyway.

MR. STEVENS: Do you think so, Eddie?

EDDIE: I *know* so. I've seen 'em all. Nobody has anything like our reindeer on the roof.

MR. STEVENS: Of course, we don't know what the Browns next door are going to have. Jim Brown hasn't put his up yet. He could be planning something very big.

EDDIE: Cora did tell me that her father had to work late today. Maybe that's the reason.

MR. STEVENS: Eddie, you see a lot of Cora. Didn't you find out what her father's going to have as an outdoor display?

EDDIE: Of course not, Dad. Just because I've been dating Cora doesn't mean I'm going to pry into her family's affairs. Anyway, you always taught us to mind our own business.

MRS. STEVENS: Eddie is right, George. If you're so anxious to find out what Jim Brown is going to put on his roof, why haven't you asked him yourself?

MR. STEVENS: I haven't seen Jim in weeks.

MRS. STEVENS: And all because of this Christmas display business! We've been friends with Jim and Susan Brown for years, and now this silly rivalry is spoiling it.

MR. STEVENS: I didn't mean to spoil anything, Jane. I just thought Eddie might have heard — or Susan might have told you.

MRS. STEVENS: Well, she didn't, and I wouldn't ask her. In fact, we've steered clear of the subject altogether. But I've asked them over for Christmas afternoon, as we always have — and I don't want any boasting about the displays. All this fuss over a silly prize!

MR. STEVENS: O.K., but if I'd had more time, I could have thought of something more original. (*Thinking out loud*) We could have rigged up electric sleigh bells. That really would have been something . . . .

MRS. STEVENS (*Interrupting impatiently*): With the alarm clock and the smoke detector and the telephone and the doorbells, we have enough bells in this house without having Santa Claus clanging any on the roof.

EDDIE: O.K., Mom. (*He starts left.*) But I have an idea for something else we can do. (*He rushes off left.*)

MRS. STEVENS: Now, what's he going to do? Make Santa Claus sing "White Christmas" while the reindeer do a soft shoe?

MR. STEVENS: It doesn't seem to me there's time to do anything. (MARY *enters left with small paint can and brush. During next lines she dabs paint on head of reindeer.*)

MARY: Where's Eddie going in such a hurry? He almost knocked me over on the basement stairs.

MR. STEVENS: I don't know. He has a new idea for something else for the display.

MARY: I hope it doesn't involve any more painting. I've had enough.

MRS. STEVENS: I should think so. Painting eight reindeer is no small job.

MARY (*Laughing*): Not to mention Santa and his sleigh. Dad, that was quite a brainstorm you had — buying an old sleigh from that farmer.

MR. STEVENS (*Looking pleased*): Yes, I thought it was rather a good idea myself.

MRS. STEVENS: Well, I didn't. I felt like a fool when the men took it off the truck, and I told them you wanted it put in the garage so nobody would see it until Christmas.

MARY (*Laughing*): Poor Mom.

MRS. STEVENS: It wasn't funny. I'm sure they thought we were all crazy. And I don't blame them. That old wreck of a thing.

MR. STEVENS: But it looks fine now. All it needed was a coat of paint. (EDDIE *enters left with electric cord with eight bulbs attached to it.*)

MARY: Now, what?

EDDIE: Wait'll you hear. Look, Dad, how would you like to have the eyes on the reindeer light up?

MR. STEVENS: Eyes light up? You mean a separate light for each eye? It sounds terrific.

EDDIE (*Taking reindeer head*): I remembered we had this old cord in the basement. (*He hangs one bulb over reindeer head so bulb is in front of its eye.*) All we have to do is loop one bulb over the head of each reindeer. From the street it will look as if the eyes are lighted.

MR. STEVENS: That's a great idea, Eddie! But where are you going to plug in the cord? It's not long enough to reach the ground.

EDDIE (*Disappointed*): I never thought of that. Well, it was a good idea while it lasted.

MR. STEVENS (*Looking toward* MRS. STEVENS): I could drive down and buy an extension cord.

MRS. STEVENS: No, George, you can't. I don't want to be difficult on Christmas Eve, but this is too much.

MARY: Mom, you don't like having the display at all, do you?

MRS. STEVENS: I didn't say that, dear. It's just that I think it's getting a little out of hand. Now everybody in town tries to outdo his next-door neighbor.

EDDIE (*Laughing*): You have to be tough if you want to win, Mom. That's the good old competitive spirit.

MRS. STEVENS: Well, it's not the *Christmas* spirit. Edna Beatty told me over the phone that on her street some of the neighbors aren't speaking to each other because of the rivalry over their displays.

MR. STEVENS (*Smiling*): All right, Jane. We won't go out for a cord. But speaking of the neighbors, I wonder what Jim Brown is going to come up with. (*Sarcastically*) Knowing him, he probably has an acceptance speech for the prize all written.

MARY (*Teasing*): Eddie ought to know what the Browns are having.

MR. STEVENS (*Laughing*): That's what I said.

EDDIE: Cora hasn't told me anything, but then, I haven't asked her.

MARY: I'll bet you told her what we were having.

EDDIE: Why should I? Even if I told her, that doesn't mean she'd tell me what her family was doing.

MARY: I just know you told her, Eddie — you never could keep a secret!

MRS. STEVENS: Now, Mary, stop teasing your brother.

Whatever display the Browns have is their own business, and I for one am not going to let it cause any trouble between us.

EDDIE: I just hope it doesn't cause any trouble between Cora and me.

MARY (*Laughing*): I should hope not, after you spent a fortune on her Christmas present.

EDDIE: Yes, I'm going over later to give it to her. Hey, maybe I ought to go over right now and — and see if I can help them with their display.

MR. STEVENS: Eddie, what are you talking about? We haven't finished our own yet. What about that broken reindeer head?

EDDIE: I'll fix that. It'll only take a minute.

MRS. STEVENS: But there are still a lot of other things to do. Someone will have to help me get the food ready for the carolers.

EDDIE: When those carolers see Santa and his reindeer galloping across our roof, they'll probably forget all about food.

MRS. STEVENS: I hope not. After all, I think being hospitable is more a part of Christmas than reindeer on the roof. And who's going to put the tinsel on the tree?

MARY: Why can't Oliver do that?

EDDIE: Good idea. I'll call him down.

MRS. STEVENS: Down? Don't tell me you left that child up on the roof by himself.

EDDIE: He's all right. He's sitting in the sleigh beside Santa, having a wonderful time.

OLIVER (*Offstage*): Ouch — Oh-h-h . . .

MRS. STEVENS: That's Oliver. He's hurt. (*She starts right, as* OLIVER *appears in doorway, bundled up in jacket and scarf.*) Oliver, are you all right?

OLIVER: Sure. I slipped coming down the ladder, I was in

such a hurry. But I landed in a pile of snow. (*He removes his scarf and unbuttons his coat.*)

MRS. STEVENS: Thank goodness. Eddie, you mustn't ever let Oliver stay up there alone again.

EDDIE: O.K., Mom, but you let him climb trees all summer.

MARY: He climbs like a monkey.

MR. STEVENS: You worry too much, Jane.

OLIVER (*Starting off left*): I might as well have stayed up there. I guess nobody is interested.

MRS. STEVENS: Interested in what, Oliver?

OLIVER: Something I saw.

MARY: From up on the roof?

OLIVER: Uh-huh. I thought at least Dad would care.

MR. STEVENS: Oliver, stop beating around the bush. What is this all about?

OLIVER: About a half hour ago a truck drove into the Browns' yard.

MRS. STEVENS: What's so wonderful about that? It was probably delivering something.

OLIVER (*With a rush*): That's right. A sleigh and Santa Claus and eight reindeer and — and men with ladders put it right up on the roof. And it's all lighted up and the whole Brown family is out front looking at it.

MR. STEVENS: So that's it! Jim waited until the last minute because he was copying my idea.

EDDIE: He must have had the whole display made downtown somewhere.

MARY: It isn't fair, after the way we worked.

MR. STEVENS: Fair? (*Indignant*) Jim Brown doesn't know what the word means. (*He starts right.*) And I'm going to tell him so. (*He exits right.*)

MRS. STEVENS (*Calling*): George, don't — wait — come back here. Oh dear, this is terrible.

EDDIE: I *did* tell Cora.

MARY: I knew you did.

MRS. STEVENS: That doesn't mean that Cora told her father. There's nothing original about having Santa Claus and his reindeer for Christmas decorations even up on the roof.

MR. STEVENS (*Appearing outside at window with hands cupped, shouting toward left*): A fine display, Jim Brown . . . Very spectacular . . . Too bad you didn't have the idea yourself. . . . What's that? . . . Oh, really? Well, as far as I'm concerned, you never had an idea in your life! (*He moves out of view.*)

OLIVER (*Snickering*): I guess Dad told him.

MRS. STEVENS: Oliver, there is nothing to laugh about. All this shouting at neighbors on Christmas Eve. It's disgraceful!

MR. STEVENS (*Entering right*): Can you imagine Jim Brown doing a thing like that? The reindeer, the sleigh — everything — all just like ours. And he has the nerve to say he had his idea a year ago.

MRS. STEVENS: Maybe he did. After all, where did you get your idea?

MR. STEVENS: From the cover of that magazine of yours. The December issue last year.

MARY: That's right, Mom, we copied it.

MRS. STEVENS: That magazine has a circulation of three million copies — and Susan Brown gets it, too.

EDDIE: Maybe Cora didn't tell her father after all.

MRS. STEVENS: Of course not. It's just a coincidence. Why is everyone so excited?

MR. STEVENS (*Grudgingly*): I suppose you're right. A spectacular coincidence.

EDDIE: Wait a minute, Dad. We still have a chance to outdo the Browns. They don't have the eyes of their reindeer lighted up, do they?

MR. STEVENS: No, they don't. (*More cheerful*) Say, I think I'm getting your message, Eddie. (*To* MRS. STEVENS) Quite an enterprising son we have here, Jane. Looks as if we may all be meeting the Mayor tomorrow, after all.

MRS. STEVENS (*Warningly*): George . . .

MR. STEVENS: No, Eddie, we can't do it.

EDDIE: I know where we can attach those lights. I just figured it out. Give me a hand, Dad. (*He picks up cord.*) You bring Prancer's head.

MR. STEVENS: Anything you say. (*He grabs head.*)

EDDIE: Come on, it will only take five minutes. (*They exit right.* MR. STEVENS *grabs his coat on way out.*)

MARY: You have to hand it to Eddie. When things get tight, he gets good ideas.

MRS. STEVENS: I don't approve of doing something just to try to outdo the neighbors. And your father ought to go over and apologize to the Browns for the way he shouted.

MARY: I'm sorry everything's such a mess, Mom. Can I do anything to help?

MRS. STEVENS: For one thing you can put up those greens. I'll light the candles.

MARY: O.K. (*She picks up greens and puts them over pictures on wall.* MRS. STEVENS *takes matches from table and pretends to light candles on window and mantel. They can be electric, and she can turn them on as she puts match near them.*)

MRS. STEVENS: It would be nice to have a fire in the fireplace, but I don't suppose anyone will have time to get it ready. (*She opens box of tinsel.*) Oliver, here's the tinsel for the tree. Let's get that finished.

OLIVER: All right, Mom. (*Through next lines he puts tinsel on tree. There is sound of hammering.*)

MARY: It sounds as though Prancer's head is back on again.

MRS. STEVENS: That may be, but I think your father has his own head on backwards. I can't get over his shouting at the Browns like that.

MARY: He was just upset. (*Going to* MRS. STEVENS) I know how you feel, though. It is a shame for all this to happen at Christmas, when everything should be peaceful and happy.

MRS. STEVENS: That's just it. Whatever happened to good will toward men?

MARY: Maybe the Browns didn't take Dad seriously. (*Doorbell rings off right.*) Uh-oh, company at a time like this. (*She goes off right and re-enters with* CORA, *who carries a wrapped Christmas present.*)

MRS. STEVENS: Hello, Cora! Merry Christmas Eve. I'm so glad you've come.

CORA: I can only stay a minute, Mrs. Stevens. Is Eddie home?

MRS. STEVENS: Yes, but he's up on the roof. I'll call him.

CORA: There really isn't time. (*Holding up package*) I just wanted to give him this.

MRS. STEVENS: Why, how nice.

MARY: He said something about coming over to see you later.

MRS. STEVENS: Of course, you'll all be over here tomorrow, anyway.

CORA: That's the trouble, Mrs. Stevens. My father says we can't come. (*Uncomfortably*) It's all because of the way Mr. Stevens acted.

MRS. STEVENS (*Upset*): I was afraid something like this would happen. (EDDIE *enters, carrying a wrapped Christmas present.*)

EDDIE: Hi, Cora.

CORA: Hello, Eddie.

MARY: We thought you were up on the roof.

EDDIE: I was. I climbed in your bedroom window. Dad's coming down the ladder. (*Going to* CORA) I saw you come up the walk, and I didn't know when I'd have a chance to give you this.

CORA (*Taking package from* EDDIE): Thanks, it looks wonderful. Here is one for you. (*Handing package to* EDDIE) I didn't know when *I'd* have a chance either, with our families angry at each other.

EDDIE: Angry? Who's angry?

MARY: Mr. Brown is, Eddie. He says they can't come over tomorrow.

MRS. STEVENS: I don't know that I blame him — but I *am* so disappointed.

EDDIE: Mom, I think Mr. Brown is being kind of unreasonable.

CORA (*Angry*): Unreasonable? When you copied our idea?

EDDIE: *We* copied? We've had the idea for months.

CORA: So have we.

EDDIE: We're not the ones who copied.

CORA: And I suppose we are! Let me tell you, Eddie Stevens, my father doesn't have to copy any ideas from you or anyone else in your family. (*She starts right.*) And I don't want your old Christmas present either! (*She slams package down on table and rushes out right.* EDDIE *stands for moment with package in hand, then tosses it on top of other one.*)

EDDIE: What a mess!

MARY: What did you expect her to do? I'd be angry too.

EDDIE: But, Mary, having Santa on the roof was our idea.

MARY: Yes, and I'm beginning to think we'd all be better off if Santa had stayed at the North Pole. (MR. STEVENS *enters.*)

MR. STEVENS: What's going on? I've been waiting outside to see the eyes light up.

EDDIE: I'm sorry, Dad. I plugged the cord in, but then I
saw Cora and rushed down here. I guess I forgot to
turn on the switch.

MR. STEVENS: It's time to light them up.

EDDIE: Sure. Right away. (*He starts left.*)

MARY (*Suspiciously*): Eddie, wait a minute. (*He turns.*)
You said you climbed in my window and you were
plugging that cord in when you saw Cora. Eddie, where
did you plug in those lights?

EDDIE (*Trying to smile*): I figured the cord would reach
through your window and to the lamp on your dressing table. It worked out fine.

MARY: That's what you think! Well, it won't work at all,
because it's not going to be there. I need my dressing
table.

EDDIE: But what about the lights in the reindeers' eyes?

MARY: I don't want to hear any more about reindeer.
Think of my eyes. Think of my face, think of my hair.
I have to fix my hair tonight. (*Turning to* MRS. STE-
VENS) Oh, Mom, tell them they can't do this to me.

MRS. STEVENS: I'm sorry, dear, but I have nothing to do
with the spectacular.

EDDIE: Oh, come on, Mary. Think of what it means to
have those lights on. Think of that special presentation
by the Mayor!

MR. STEVENS (*Going to* MARY *and putting his arm
around her*): He's right, Mary. Think of all the work
we've done — those lights are the only thing that will
make it more spectacular than Jim Brown's.

MARY (*Half-smiling*): Oh, all right — but I think it's a
dirty trick.

EDDIE (*Patting her on back*): You're all right, Mary. (*He starts left.*) Get ready, everybody, for the light that lies in the reindeers' eyes. (*He exits left.*)

MR. STEVENS (*Excitedly*): I'm going out front to look. (*He starts right.*)

OLIVER: Me, too. (*He rushes out right.*)

MR. STEVENS (*Stopping*): Aren't you two coming?

MARY: I'm afraid I've lost my enthusiasm, Dad. I'll look at them later.

MRS. STEVENS: I don't care to see them. This whole thing has caused enough trouble.

MR. STEVENS: Come now, Jane. Cheer up. (*He tries to put his arm around her.*)

MRS. STEVENS (*Pulling away*): No, I mean it. (*All the lights except candles go out. There should be enough soft light on the stage so the rest of the action can be clearly seen.*)

MR. STEVENS: The lights!

MARY: Oh, no. (*Pause.*)

MRS. STEVENS: I guess my candles weren't such a bad idea after all.

MR. STEVENS (*Sadly*): They're out — every light in the house is out!

MARY: In the front yard, too. What happened?

MR. STEVENS: When Eddie turned on those eight extra lights, the main fuse blew!

MARY (*With a little laugh*): I guess it was the straw that broke the camel's back.

OLIVER (*Rushing in right*): Say, all the lights are off outside and in the house, too.

MARY: Yes, so we've noticed.

EDDIE (*Entering left*): I guess that's the end of our Christmas display.

MR. STEVENS: Is it the main fuse, Eddie?

EDDIE: Yes, and we can't replace it. We'll have to call the

electric company. They probably won't come for hours.

OLIVER: You mean we can't have any lights? Not even on the Christmas tree?

EDDIE (*Sadly*): Not even on the Christmas tree.

OLIVER: What'll we do?

MRS. STEVENS: There doesn't seem to be anything we *can* do, Oliver. (OLIVER *takes off his coat and sits down sadly.*)

MR. STEVENS: A fine Christmas this turned out to be. We might as well kiss the prize goodbye. Aren't you going to say anything, Jane?

MRS. STEVENS: I've been saying it all day. I've had a feeling all along that no good would come of this.

MR. STEVENS: All right, you don't have to say any more. (*He takes off his coat as he goes to phone.*) I'll call the electric company and see what they can do. (*He picks up phone book, backs upstage, and reads by candlelight. Carolers are heard off in distance.*)

EDDIE: Listen, the carolers are on their way to our street. Now everybody will be coming out to look at the displays.

MR. STEVENS (*Dejectedly*): Well, they won't see anything at our house. (*He dials.*) Hello . . . This is George Stevens, 124 Maple . . . All our lights are out . . . The main fuse . . . What's that? (*There is a knock off right.*)

OLIVER: Even the doorbell doesn't work.

MRS. STEVENS: See who it is, Oliver. (OLIVER *exits right.*)

MR. STEVENS (*Into phone*): But it's a desperate situation. This is Christmas Eve . . . . All right, if that's the best you can do. (*He hangs up phone.*) They can't send a repairman till late tonight or early tomorrow morning.

(OLIVER *enters, followed by* CORA *and* MR. *and* MRS. BROWN.)

OLIVER: It's the Browns, Mom.

MRS. BROWN (*Going to* MRS. STEVENS): Yes, we just had to come, Jane. Jim didn't want to at first, but I insisted — after all, when neighbors are in trouble —

MRS. STEVENS (*Warmly*): Oh, Susan, I'm so glad to see you. . . . George, isn't this wonderful? (*To* BROWNS) Let me take your coats. (*They remove coats and give them to* MRS. STEVENS.)

MR. STEVENS (*Embarrassed*): Why — um — yes. It certainly is. (*Going toward them*)

MR. BROWN: George, old man, when I saw your lights go out I thought it was a good joke.

MR. STEVENS (*Starting to get angry again*): Oh, you did, did you?

MR. BROWN: Now, take it easy, George. I know you must feel pretty upset.

MR. STEVENS (*Holding out his hand*): I guess I did sort of fly off the handle. I'm sorry, Jim.

MR. BROWN (*Shaking hands with* MR. STEVENS): That's all right, George. I was a bit hot under the collar, too. (*Reaches into his pocket and takes out two fuses, hands them to* MR. STEVENS.) I brought over a couple of fuses for you.

MR. STEVENS (*Looking at them quickly):* That's very thoughtful, Jim, but unfortunately, we blew a main fuse. (*As* MRS. STEVENS *hangs up coats in closet,* EDDIE *moves over to* CORA.)

EDDIE: I'm glad your father changed his mind about coming over here, Cora.

CORA: So am I, Eddie.

MRS. STEVENS (*Walking back to group*): Please sit down,

all of you. It's a little dark, but we do have candles. (*All sit.*)

MRS. BROWN: It's certainly good to be here. Jane, I just didn't feel right being angry with you on Christmas Eve.

MR. BROWN: Neither did I. I may have laughed when I saw those lights go out, but then I got to thinking how hard you'd worked, and . . .

MARY (*Disgruntled*): And now just when it's time for everyone to see the displays, what do we have? Zero.

MR. STEVENS: At least they'll see one Santa on the roof — yours, Jim. The Brown family is sure to win the *Daily News* prize. (*A bright flash of light is seen outside.*)

MRS. STEVENS: What was that?

OLIVER: It sure was bright! (MARY *walks to window.*)

EDDIE: At least we know it's not in our house. We don't have enough juice to light a night light.

MARY (*Looking out window*): There's a car out front and someone's coming up the walk . . . a young man and woman.

MR. STEVENS: For people in the dark, we're attracting a lot of company.

MARY (*Laughing*): I'll say. (*She goes off right.*)

MRS. STEVENS: It is too bad we lost our electricity. The tree looked so cheerful with the lights on.

MRS. BROWN: Don't worry about it, Jane. The house looks perfectly lovely. (MARY *enters, followed by* SALLY COOK *and* BILL ROSS. BILL *carries a camera and* SALLY *a notebook.* MR. *and* MRS. STEVENS *rise as they enter.*)

MARY: Mom, Dad, listen —

SALLY (*Quickly taking over*): Mr. and Mrs. Stevens, I'm Sally Cook from the *Daily News*, and this is Bill Ross, our photographer. We just took a picture of your house.

MR. STEVENS (*In disbelief*): Of *our* house?

BILL: It'll be on the front page tomorrow. We're happy to tell you that your house has been selected as the most attractively decorated in town. Congratulations!

ALL (*Astonished; ad lib*): But why? It's all dark! I can't believe it! You're kidding! (*Etc.*)

SALLY: We thought the darkness was a fine contrast to all the other brightly lighted places. Just the simple star in the window.

MR. STEVENS (*Confused*): Star?

SALLY: From the street the lighted candle looks like a star. It's the only display in town with the true feeling of Christmas.

MARY: You mean our little candle in the window is the best display?

BILL: Yes. You see, every year we've been choosing homes with more and more elaborate decorations as the prize-winners, but there gets to be a sameness about them.

MR. STEVENS: I know what you mean.

BILL: Then we came to your street and saw the light shining in the darkness like the Christmas star.

SALLY (*Continuing*): There was a beautiful simplicity about it — a welcome relief from the commercial effects everywhere else. (*She opens notebook.*) Who thought of it, may I ask?

MR. STEVENS: My wife did.

MRS. STEVENS: Well, yes . . . I suppose that's true. You see, when I was a child, my mother always put a candle in the window, so the idea's not really original . . .

SALLY: I see. But what made it so unusual and impressive was the darkness all around it. Quite unique.

MRS. STEVENS (*Smiling*): I can't take the credit for that. My husband and my son were responsible for the darkness.

SALLY: Great! Then the whole family shared in the idea! We can say, "Family plans unusual lighting effects together." (*Writes quickly*) We'll have to hurry to get this in the first edition, Bill — let's go. (*To* MR. *and* MRS. STEVENS) Someone from the paper will get in touch with you to let you know the particulars — the presentation, the dinner, all that. Good night, all, and Merry Christmas!

BILL: Merry Christmas. (*Exits with* SALLY)

MR. STEVENS (*Pleased*): Can you imagine that? Here I was, thinking that a lot of bright lights would win the prize, and it turns out that the electrical failure was to our advantage!

MARY: And don't forget Mom's little old candle.

EDDIE: That's right. Mom even tried to give all of us credit for the idea. I guess that's the old Christmas spirit!

MRS. STEVENS (*Laughing*): Nonsense! After all, the lights going out did create the "unusual" effect, as that reporter said.

MR. BROWN: The Browns may have had the biggest display, but the Stevenses have won the *Daily News* Christmas prize. Congratulations, folks! (MR. *and* MRS. STEVENS *sit down again as carolers are heard outside singing last line of a carol.*)

EDDIE: The carolers are right outside. (*To* MARY *and* CORA.) We ought to be out there with them.

MARY: O.K., let's go.

MRS. STEVENS (*Starting to rise*): We ought to ask them in — but there are no refreshments ready.

EDDIE: That's all right, Mom. We'll bring some of the carol singers back later.

MARY: Good idea. Don't worry, Mom. We can have some hot chocolate and cookies later.

EDDIE: I'm going to get them to sing "Hark the Herald Angels Sing." That's the one where I can really show off my singing style.

CORA: Goodbye, everyone. (CORA, EDDIE *and* MARY *rush off.*)

MRS. STEVENS (*Sitting back in chair*): After all the excitement, I, for one, am going to relax for a minute and enjoy Christmas Eve. Jim and Susan, I hope you'll stay and enjoy it with us.

MR. BROWN: It is so pleasant and cozy here with just the candlelight.

MRS. STEVENS: It would be even cozier if George would light a fire in the fireplace.

MR. STEVENS: Why not? At least I know I won't blow a fuse when I light the match. (*He goes to fireplace and takes a piece of wood from basket.*)

MRS. STEVENS (*Looking at* OLIVER, *who is yawning*): Oliver, you really should be in bed.

OLIVER: But, Mom —

MRS. STEVENS: No, dear, you'd better go to bed now. You look so sleepy, and you'll want to be up bright and early tomorrow morning. (*To* MR. STEVENS, *who is at fireplace, holding a piece of wood*) What's the matter, George?

MR. STEVENS: I can't light a fire. Santa Claus's sleigh is set right over the chimney.

MRS. STEVENS: Oh, dear. (*Shrugging*) Well, we really don't need it. (*To* OLIVER) Oliver, what are you looking so sad about?

OLIVER: I'm worried. (*Pause*) If that old sleigh is right over the chimney, how's the real Santa Claus going to get in?

MRS. STEVENS: Hm-m-m ... (*Sarcastically*) Well, George, we don't seem to be finished with your spectacular yet. Maybe you can explain this.

MR. STEVENS: I wouldn't worry about it, Oliver. Santa Claus will find a way.

OLIVER: But, Dad — how?

MRS. STEVENS (*Amused*): I'm afraid your answer doesn't seem very satisfactory, George.

MR. STEVENS: I suppose I could go up and take down the sleigh.

OLIVER (*Sadly*): Never mind, I don't really believe in Santa Claus anyhow . . . . Goodnight, everybody. (*He goes off.*)

MR. BROWN: He looked so sad.

MRS. STEVENS: George, we must do something.

MR. STEVENS: Yes, but I don't know what. (*There is a pause, then some loud footsteps are heard from off left.*) Sh-h — Oliver's coming back.

OLIVER (*Reappearing in doorway, holding something behind his back*): Mom, could you come here for a minute?

MRS. STEVENS: Why, of course, dear. (*She goes over and leans down as* OLIVER *whispers into her ear. She nods, and* OLIVER *hands her a stocking and goes out. She holds up stocking.*) Look, Oliver brought his stocking — and do you know what he said? Would I mind leaving the front door open a little — just in case?

MRS. BROWN: Down deep he really does believe in Santa Claus.

MRS. STEVENS (*Hanging stocking over fireplace*): Christmas is a good time for hoping, if not always believing . . . .

MR. STEVENS: That's what Christmas is all about! Merry Christmas to everyone. (*Sound of carolers is heard from offstage singing "Hark, the Herald Angels Sing" as curtain falls.*)

THE END

A Christmas Promise

By Helen Louise Miller

Since Greg is too shy to talk to girls, he's more surprised than anyone to find that he has four dates to the Christmas dance!

Characters

MRS. EMILY COLLINS
MRS. MAY SPENCER, *her neighbor*
PATTY COLLINS, *17*
JEFF RAMSEY, *Patty's boyfriend*
GREG COLLINS, *15*
MR. AL COLLINS

SETTING: *The Collins living room, decorated for Christmas with a lighted tree, etc. Exit right leads to rest of house; left exit leads to front door. There is a telephone onstage. Mrs. Spencer's coat is on a chair.*

AT RISE: MRS. COLLINS *is displaying a tuxedo to her friend,* MRS. SPENCER, *who is sewing on a white evening gown.*

MRS. COLLINS: Don't you think the tailor did a wonderful job of cutting down this old tuxedo?

MRS. SPENCER: Why, yes, Emily. It looks brand new.

MRS. COLLINS: I hope Greg likes it. He's growing so fast, we can't afford to buy him a new tux, but he really needs one for the Christmas dance tomorrow night.

MRS. SPENCER: This evening gown for Kathy has miles and miles of stitches in it. I want it to be a surprise for her. Thank goodness I can work on it here, so she won't see it.

MRS. COLLINS: Speaking of surprises, I don't know whether to hang this tux in my husband's closet or pack it in a box.

MRS. SPENCER: The closet sounds like the best bet to me. At Christmastime the kids look everywhere for presents, except in the obvious places. Even if Greg did see it, he'd probably pass right over it as one of his father's suits.

MRS. COLLINS: I think you're right. Oh, May, I can hardly wait to see him in it. Greg's never had any interest in girls, but this year I'm determined to get him to that dance. This (*Indicating the tuxedo*) ought to do it.

MRS. SPENCER: Kathy is just eating her heart out to go. That's why I decided to give her this gown for Christmas, so she'll have something to wear, just in case.

MRS. COLLINS: What do you mean, just in case? The dance is tomorrow night. Doesn't she have a date yet?

MRS. SPENCER: Not yet, but you know the old saying. "While there's life, there's hope."

MRS. COLLINS: Wouldn't it be sweet if Kathy and Greg could go together? They'd make a lovely couple, and it would be thrilling for us. My son — your daughter — their first big dance!

MRS. SPENCER: Why, Emily, it would be marvelous! But what about Greg? Maybe he has a date already.

MRS. COLLINS: Heavens, no! I know Greg. He's so shy.

Asking a girl out is the worst part of the whole thing for him. This way it will be easy. After all, he's known Kathy all his life.

MRS. SPENCER: Emily, it's a wonderful idea! Kathy will be dying to go with Greg.

MRS. COLLINS: Then it's all settled. Now I'd better get this suit upstairs before Greg comes popping in here.

MRS. SPENCER: You might as well take this dress along with you, Emily. I'll come over later to pick it up when I'm sure Kathy is out. By the way, where's your daughter?

MRS. COLLINS: Patty? She's probably out with Jeff. He usually brings her home from school.

MRS. SPENCER: Jeff is such a nice fellow.

MRS. COLLINS: Yes, he's over here morning, noon and night, but we really don't mind.

MRS. SPENCER: Of course not. Well, Emily, thanks for letting me sew over here. I know you have a thousand things to do the day before Christmas.

MRS. COLLINS (*With suit and dress over her arm*): You know I love to have you. Now remember, not too many hints to Kathy. Greg will probably come over right after supper to ask her.

MRS. SPENCER: I hope so. (*Puts on coat*)

MRS. COLLINS: And don't forget our Open House tomorrow night. It's the first big party we've given in years. I had to talk my husband into it, but now I think he's more excited than I am.

MRS. SPENCER: Your husband Al will be the life of the party. He always is. We wouldn't miss it for the world. Goodbye and don't forget to speak to Greg.

MRS. COLLINS: Don't worry, I won't. (MRS. SPENCER *exits left and* MRS. COLLINS *exits right with clothes. The phone rings.* MRS. COLLINS *re-enters without dress and suit to answer phone.*) Hello . . . Oh, Jeff . . . . Why,

no, Patty isn't here. I thought she was with you . . . .
I don't know when she'll be in . . . . Of course, I'll
tell her . . . . Why yes, if you want to. Sure, it's all
right. You can come over and wait for her . . . .
What's the matter? Is something wrong ? . . . Well,
you sound upset . . . . I'm glad to hear everything's
O.K. . . . Yes, I'll be sure to tell her you called, but
what difference does it make if you're coming over
anyhow? . . . All right, all right. Goodbye. (*Hangs up*)
Honestly, sometimes I think Jeff is missing a few
marbles!

PATTY (*Entering left, in coat, with an armload of pack-ages*): Look, Mom, I've got Jeff's Christmas present. I
can hardly wait to show it to you.

MRS. COLLINS: Are all those for Jeff?

PATTY (*Dumping her packages on sofa*): No, only one of
them, but wait till you see it. It's really super! It cost
me twice as much as I wanted to spend, but I guess
he's worth it, the big lug.

MRS. COLLINS: The big lug just called you.

PATTY: Jeff called? When?

MRS. COLLINS: Not more than two minutes ago. He
didn't say what he wanted, but he sounded upset, and
he wanted to come over and wait for you.

PATTY: Must be something important. (*Opens box*) Look,
Mom, isn't it perfectly beautiful? (*Holds up a brightly-colored shirt*) Won't this absolutely knock his eye out?

MRS. COLLINS: It certainly will! Anyone who looks at him
will need sunglasses. What are your other packages?

PATTY: Surprises! And no peeking! I'm taking these up-stairs before Greg barges in and starts snooping around.
(*Picks up her packages and starts to leave*)

MRS. COLLINS: Oh, Patty, you should see his tuxedo. It
looks perfect.

PATTY: When did it get here?

MRS. COLLINS: Just a little while ago. I hung it up in your father's closet. Take a look when you go up.

PATTY: I will. I hope Greg likes it.

MRS. COLLINS: Why wouldn't he like it? It looks as if it came right out of the store. You'd never dream it was a hand-me-down.

PATTY: Oh, I didn't mean that. I was just wondering if he wouldn't rather have had a different Christmas present — that backpack he's always talking about, for instance.

MRS. COLLINS: Well, he's getting the tuxedo whether he likes it or not. If he has a tux he has no excuse for not going to the Christmas dance. I have everything arranged. (*Doorbell rings.*) That's probably Jeff. (*Taking packages from* PATTY) Here, let me take those things.

PATTY: Thanks, Mother. Just stuff them into my closet. (MRS. COLLINS *exits. Doorbell rings again.*) O.K., I'm coming. I'm coming. (*Exits briefly, then re-enters with* JEFF)

JEFF: Where in the world were you? I was standing out there ringing the bell for ten minutes.

PATTY: Why didn't you barge right in the way you usually do?

JEFF: The door was locked. Pat, something terrible has happened.

PATTY: What? You do look funny. Mother said you sounded a little upset when you called.

JEFF: Not upset — frantic! Guess who arrived to spend the holidays with us — without a word of warning?

PATTY: From the way you sound it must be the Abominable Snowman!

JEFF: No, but you're close. It's Aunt Mabel and Cousin Millicent. (*Drops on sofa in tragic despair*) Can you believe it?

PATTY: That is pretty bad, but it could be worse. Isn't your cousin Millicent that stringy little kid who was here a couple of years ago — the one we used to call Pilly-Milly?

JEFF (*Groaning*): That's the one — Pilly-Milly! And to think she has to come *now*!

PATTY: Oh, well, it won't be so terrible. She's older now, probably has more sense and maybe even better looks. And besides you won't be seeing much of her, so why worry?

JEFF: But you don't understand. That's just the trouble. She *is* older, she *has* grown up, and I *will* be seeing her — especially tomorrow night.

PATTY: Tomorrow night! Why, tomorrow night is the Christmas dance. What are you talking about?

JEFF (*In agony*): Patty, sit down. This is going to be a shock. I don't even know how to tell you, but I can't take you to the dance.

PATTY (*Furious*): What? Jeff Ramsey, are you out of your mind? What are you talking about?

JEFF: I'm talking about my cousin Millicent. The family says I've got to take her to the dance.

PATTY: But that's impossible! You're taking me. We've had our date for ages.

JEFF: That's what I keep telling them. But they won't listen. My mother came up with this weird idea that the three of us could all go together, but I told her that was out.

PATTY: It sure is. I wouldn't be caught dead going with an extra girl. What got into your mother?

JEFF: It's Aunt Mabel. She seems to have her under a spell. There's no reasoning with her. She's determined to get Millicent to that dance.

PATTY: I still can't see why you have to be the victim. Why don't you get someone else to take her?

JEFF: At this late date? The day before the dance? Everybody has a date.

PATTY: Well, you'll have to get out of it some way, Jeff Ramsey, or I'll never speak to you again.

JEFF: I was afraid you'd take it like that.

PATTY: How did you expect me to take it? Standing me up the night before the big Christmas dance! Jeff, you're a spineless creature . . . you're a worm! You're worse than a worm — you're . . . you're an amoeba!

JEFF: Go ahead, call me all the names you can think of, but what can I do?

PATTY: What can you do? You can stand up and be a man. You can say you won't break your date with me. What can they do about it?

JEFF: Plenty! They can hold out on me.

PATTY: What do you mean?

JEFF: Money! I don't even have a nickel. I've spent every cent I own, and mostly on you. Mom promised to stake me to the dance as part of my Christmas present — flowers, tickets, dinner, the works! We're licked, I tell you, unless we can think of somebody else to take Millicent.

PATTY: What about Mark Miller?

JEFF: He's out. He's taking Judy Byers.

PATTY: I know! Pinky Hatfield! He never has a date. Come on, let's call him. He's a good friend of Greg's.

JEFF: Forget it! The Hatfields are out of town.

PATTY: We've got to find somebody.

JEFF: I tell you, it's no use. I've checked out everyone. There just isn't anybody. Our Christmas goose is cooked.

PATTY (*Jumping up in excitement*): Jeff, I've got it! I've got it! I know just the person.

JEFF (*Catching her excitement*): Who?

PATTY: Greg!

JEFF: Greg?

PATTY: Yes, Greg, my brother!

JEFF: But Greg doesn't go to dances.

PATTY: He's going to this one, my friend, and he's going with your cousin Millicent.

JEFF: But he's met Millicent. Unless he's lost his mind he'll never agree to take her to the dance.

PATTY: One girl's just like another to Greg. He doesn't care about any of them. He'll be glad enough to get a date without having to ask anyone.

JEFF: If he doesn't like girls, why would he go at all?

PATTY: It's Mother's idea. She thinks he should go this year and she's been working hard on him. He gave in about a week ago, and tomorrow she's giving him a tuxedo, so he can't back out.

JEFF: But maybe he has a date.

PATTY: Not Greg. He told me just last night he didn't have a date.

JEFF: Then you really think you can fix it?

PATTY: Just leave it to me. Now go home and tell Pilly-Milly she's going to the dance with the Don Juan of Hill Street.

JEFF: What a relief! Patty, you're one in a million. (*Nervously*) Suppose something goes wrong!

PATTY: Trust me, coward, nothing will go wrong. I've done plenty of favors for Greg in my time, and I know he'll do this for me.

JEFF: This calls for a celebration. Remind me to tell you sometime what I really think of you, Pat.

PATTY: I'll do that. Now move, and get things under control at your house while I take care of things here.

JEFF: O.K., Patty. Be sure to call me the minute you have Greg signed and sealed.

PATTY: Don't worry, I will. Oh, this is going to be a wonderful Christmas, Jeff! Even the weather seems right. There were little snowflakes when I was downtown.

JEFF: And they're getting bigger. Maybe we'll be having a white Christmas after all. See you later, Patty, and thanks for everything.

PATTY: Bye, Jeff. (JEFF *exits.*)

MRS. COLLINS (*Entering*): Has Jeff gone, Patty?

PATTY: Just left. And wait till you hear the awful mess he's in. His Aunt Mabel and that awful Cousin Millicent dropped in on them unexpectedly.

MRS. COLLINS: No wonder the poor boy was upset.

PATTY: But that's not all! Wait till I tell you!

MRS. COLLINS: I do want to hear about Jeff, dear, but right now I have other things on my mind. Your father, for instance — he doesn't have his boots with him, and it's beginning to snow. Would you mind taking the car and picking him up? The buses will be so crowded tonight.

PATTY: Sure, I'll go. (*Pulling on her coat*) I hardly get out of this coat, and I have to put it on again. Where are the keys?

MRS. COLLINS (*Handing keys to her*): Here they are. And be sure to finish your story about Jeff when you come back. I want to hear it.

PATTY: Believe me, it's right out of a T.V. comedy. By the way, if Greg comes home, tell him I want to see him.

MRS. COLLINS: I can't imagine where that boy is. I haven't seen him all day. Drive slowly, Pat. The streets are starting to get slippery.

PATTY: I will. Bye. (*She exits. Phone rings.*)

MRS. COLLINS: I wonder if that's Greg. (*On phone*) Hello . . . . Yes, this is Mrs. Collins . . . Who? Oh, Mr. Prentice, I've heard Al speak of you . . . . Why, no, he hasn't come home yet, but I'm expecting him shortly. My daughter just went to meet him . . . . Yes, I'll have him call you the minute he comes in. What's that number? . . . . Hotel Whitemarsh, 436-3347. Very well. . . . Thank you. Goodbye. (*She hangs up phone and writes number on pad; to herself*) I think he's one of the partners in Al's company. (GREG *enters left with an armful of packages.*)

GREG: Hi, Mom!

MRS. COLLINS: I'm so glad you're home, Greg. I have something very important to ask you. Why don't you come out to the kitchen and we can talk while I stuff the turkey.

GREG: I'll be right there. I have to take some things upstairs first. (*She exits. He puts down packages, takes off jacket and begins to open packages. First he pulls out a compact, opens it, and tries the powderpuff. Next he produces a bracelet which he puts on his own arm and admires. Finally he gets a perfume atomizer and squirts a little in the air. Meanwhile,* MR. COLLINS *enters left, wearing coat, and stands watching in amazement.*)

MR. COLLINS: What's this, Greg? Dress rehearsal for a beauty contest?

GREG: Oh, hi, Dad. Say, how do you think this smells? (*Sprays perfume*)

MR. COLLINS (*Sniffing*): Kind of exotic, I'd say. Is it hair tonic?

GREG: No! It's perfume. It costs a lot — five ninety-eight plus tax.

MR. COLLINS: I see. For your mother?

GREG: No. I bought some powder for Mom.

MR. COLLINS: Well, I'm sure Patty will like the perfume. (*Coming closer and seeing the bracelet*) I must say you outdid yourself. Perfume, a bracelet and a compact! Pat will be overcome.

GREG: They aren't for Pat.

MR. COLLINS: Don't tell me that at long last you've succumbed to the charms of a woman!

GREG: I guess you could say that. I met her today. I never thought any girl could be so great.

MR. COLLINS: Coming from you, Greg, that is quite an announcement. (*Takes off coat and moves toward phone table*)

GREG: Honest, Dad, I never knew it could happen like that.

MR. COLLINS: What could happen like what?

GREG: Love. It really knocks your socks off!

MR. COLLINS: That's nice, Greg. (*Noticing phone call memorandum on pad*) What's this? "Call J.P. Prentice at Hotel Whitemarsh." Now what on earth could he be doing there at this hour? Oh, sorry to interrupt, Greg. I've got to make a phone call. Tell me later, will you?

GREG: O.K. I'll take these things upstairs. (*Preparing to leave*) Dad, don't say anything about my girlfriend. I want to surprise the family.

MR. COLLINS: My lips are sealed. (GREG *exits.* MR. COLLINS *calls offstage.*) Emily! How long ago did this call come for me?

MRS. COLLINS (*Entering right*): Why, Al, you're home! I just sent Patty to meet you in the car.

MR. COLLINS: I left early and got a ride home with Tom Anderson. By the way, when did J.P. Prentice call? He was supposed to go back to Atlanta this morning.

MRS. COLLINS: Just a few minutes ago, dear. He seemed terribly anxious to talk to you. Isn't he one of the big brass from the main office?

MR. COLLINS: Yes. I'll call him right now. (MRS. COLLINS *exits. He dials phone.*) I'd like to speak to J.P. Prentice . . . . Oh, hello, J.P. What's up? I thought you'd be home by now. . . Well, no wonder. The storm's getting worse every minute. I guess all planes are grounded . . . . Say, that's tough. Marooned up here for Christmas. Well, you know where you're having Christmas dinner, don't you? . . . Sure. Right here with us. . . . No, no trouble at all. Emily would tear my hair out if I didn't ask you. Who's with you? Your daughter? . . . Well, bring her along. Always room for one more, I always say . . . . Oh, I'll bet she is disappointed . . . . (*Chuckling*) Yeah, fifteen is a bad age to be away from home at Christmas. I think I can cheer her up. The young people here always have a dance on Christmas night. Bring Sally along and I'll get her a date with my son Greg . . . . Sure, Greg's just about her age . . . Oh, he'll go for it, I know. I'm sure he doesn't have a date yet. O.K., then everything's settled . . . .We'll eat about three o'clock, but come over any time . . . . Great. And remember to tell Sally about that date. She'll be going to a dance after all. (*Laughing*) Well, that's O.K., J.P. I know you'd do the same for me . . . . Sure. Goodbye and Merry Christmas. (*Hangs up. Honk of automobile horn is heard from offstage.*)

MRS. COLLINS (*Entering right*): That's Patty tooting the horn. I'll bet she's stuck in the driveway. Al, can you go out and help her?

MR. COLLINS: Sure. I'll put the car in the garage and leave it in. What do you think, Emily? That was J.P. Prentice. His plane was grounded and he and his daughter are marooned here for Christmas. I asked them to have dinner with us.

MRS. COLLINS: Good. We'll have plenty. It must be dreadful to spend Christmas away from home. (*As* MR. COLLINS *exits,* GREG *enters. He is still in a daze.*) Hello, dear. This is the first time I've laid eyes on you since breakfast. Did you have a good day?

GREG: Super!

MRS. COLLINS: Good. Is your shopping all finished?

GREG: I think so.

MRS. COLLINS: That's a switch. You usually let things go till the last minute. Now, Greg, May Spencer was over here this afternoon finishing Kathy's evening dress. It's beautiful, all white and ruffly.

GREG: Yeah?

MRS. COLLINS: Kathy will look perfectly lovely in it. She's really very pretty. Have you ever noticed?

GREG: I guess so. Mother, did you ever know anyone could have eyes that are really and truly violet? Not blue — but real purply violet?

MRS. COLLINS: That's just what I mean, dear. Kathy's eyes are unusual. And her mother and I have a wonderful idea. We think it would be nice if you took Kathy to the dance tomorrow night.

GREG (*Shocked beyond words*): What?

MRS. COLLINS: Really, dear, it would make me very happy. I know you've never cared much for girls, but Kathy is so sweet, and her mother and I have been friends for years.

GREG: Are you asking me to take Kathy Spencer to the dance?

MRS. COLLINS: You could just go over and ask her after supper.

GREG: Ask Kathy? I'd rather eat a raw egg.

MRS. COLLINS: Why, Greg Collins, what a way to talk.

GREG: But Mother, she's awful. She's an absolute creep.

MRS. COLLINS: Now look here, Greg, you've grown up with Kathy and I'm not going to let you call her names. She's a lovely child, and besides, I promised her mother.

GREG: You what?

MRS. COLLINS: I promised May you'd take Kathy. She

is getting a lovely new dress and she's dying to go.

GREG: Then she can just die, because I'm not taking her.

MRS. COLLINS: Listen to me, Greg. I demand very little of you. In fact, I think I am entirely too easy on you. But this is one thing I am going to insist on. You're going to that dance and you're taking Kathy.

GREG: I won't, I tell you. I won't. I'll do anything else for you, Mother, but not this. You had no right to promise such a thing.

MRS. COLLINS: No right, indeed!

GREG: Absolutely no right. I'm old enough to lead my own life.

MR. COLLINS (*Entering right*): Calm down, Greg. What's going on? Who's old enough to lead his own life?

GREG: I am, and Mother has no business making promises that involve me.

MR. COLLINS: That's no way to talk to your mother, Greg.

GREG: But Dad, you don't understand. She's done something awful.

MRS. COLLINS: The awful thing I did, Al, was to ask Greg to take Kathy Spencer to the dance.

GREG: But she promised without asking me, Dad, and now she's trying to force me.

MR. COLLINS (*Clearing his throat*): Well, this is a predicament.

MRS. COLLINS: You know what a sweet girl Kathy is, Al. Why must he be so stubborn?

MR. COLLINS: Well, Emily, as a matter of fact, you did make a promise rather prematurely.

MRS. COLLINS: Al Collins, don't you dare side with him on this issue. May Spencer is a very dear friend of mine, and I'm not going to have her and her child disappointed.

MR. COLLINS: I'm afraid she'll have to be disappointed

this time, my dear. Greg simply can't take Kathy to the dance.

GREG: Good for you, Dad. Thanks.

MRS. COLLINS: But, Al, I promised.

MR. COLLINS: It so happens, Emily, that I, too, made a promise. J.P. Prentice has his fifteen-year-old daughter with him. She's brokenhearted because she's missing the Christmas dance at home, and I've promised him Greg would take her to the dance.

GREG *and* MRS. COLLINS (*Together*): What?

MR. COLLINS: I know how you feel, Greg, about not being consulted on this deal, but I had no time to ask you.

GREG: But, Dad, I can't take her.

MR. COLLINS: I'm sorry, but you must. J.P. Prentice is an important man in our company, and I'm not going to have him or his daughter disappointed.

GREG: But, Dad, this is terrible. I never heard of such a thing . . . a guy being rented out by his parents. I won't stand for it. I'll leave home first.

PATTY (*Entering right*): What's all the commotion? I could hear you shouting all the way out on the back porch. This is a fine way to spend Christmas Eve.

GREG: Christmas Eve or no Christmas Eve, I'm not going to be bullied into taking some strange girl to a dance.

MR. COLLINS: I'm not bullying you, son. I'm just telling you.

MRS. COLLINS: I must say, Al, I think you had a lot of nerve to promise Mr. Prentice without asking Greg.

MR. COLLINS: You're a fine one to talk. Didn't you do the same thing?

MRS. COLLINS: But that was different. Greg knows Kathy. After all, this Prentice girl is a total stranger.

MR. COLLINS: She's no stranger. She's my boss's daughter and Greg will have to take her to the dance.

GREG: Patty, can't you help me out of this? Can't you convince them it isn't fair to tell me whom I'm taking to the dance?

MR. COLLINS: You might as well keep out of it, Pat. My mind's made up. Greg has a date and it's Sally Prentice.

PATTY: But, Dad, this is terrible! I can't believe you did it! My life is ruined. I was counting on Greg, absolutely counting on him.

MRS. COLLINS: What on earth is wrong with you, Patty?

GREG: Wait a minute! What were you counting on me for?

MR. COLLINS: Nothing, Greg. She's just being hysterical.

PATTY: I'm not hysterical. I'm just upset. Jeff's family is making him take his cousin Millicent to the dance unless he can get somebody else, so I offered him Greg.

GREG: Did you hear that? She offered me, too! What am I, a burnt offering or something?

PATTY: But don't you see, if Greg doesn't take Cousin Milly, Jeff will have to take her and I'll be out in the cold.

MRS. COLLINS: This is too much for me.

GREG: Well, it's too much for me, too. You people ought to go into the rent-a-kid business. I'm getting out of here. When you finish fighting it out, let me know, but it just so happens I have a date of my own.

ALL (*Together*): What?

PATTY: Who?

GREG: I detect a note of surprise in your voices — more like shock, actually. Her name is Cookie — Cookie Hatfield.

MRS. COLLINS: Cookie Hatfield! I've never heard of her. Where does she live?

GREG: She's Pinky Hatfield's sister. I just met her this morning. She came home from boarding school last night.

PATTY: I never knew Pinky Hatfield had a sister.

GREG: Well, he does and she's going with me to the dance.

MR. COLLINS: Now look here, young man.

PATTY: Is Pinky home? Is he home now?

GREG: How should I know? He was home when I left his house this afternoon.

PATTY: Does he have a date for tomorrow night? Does he, Greg?

GREG: I don't know. I don't think so.

PATTY: I hope you're right. I'm going right over there now and sign him up for Milly. Wish me luck, folks. (*Exits*)

MR. COLLINS: Greg, I'm terribly sorry about this, but business is business.

GREG: And a date is a date, Dad.

MRS. COLLINS: What am I going to say to May Spencer? (*Phone rings. Picking it up*) Hello . . . . Oh, May. Yes, we were just talking about you . . . . Well, I haven't exactly asked him yet, I was just sort of leading up to it . . . . What? She doesn't want to go with him? . . . Well, for heaven's sake, why not? . . . What? Stop laughing, I can't understand you . . . . She thinks he's what? . . . Well, I must say I don't think that's very funny . . . . Oh, no, I'm not insulted, it's just that . . . Who's taking her? . . . Oh, a boy who's visiting the Emersons. Well, that's fine . . . . Oh, no, May, don't be silly, I'm not offended at all. As a matter of fact, I think Greg does have a date, two of them, if I'm not mistaken . . . . Yes, you heard me. I did say two . . . . I'll tell you about it later. Goodbye, May. (*Hangs up*)

GREG: What did Kathy Spencer call me?

MRS. COLLINS: Never mind what she called you. She has a date and that's that. If I ever get mixed up in something like this again, I'll have my head examined. (*Doorbell*) Now who could that be? (*Exits left*)

GREG: Can't you listen to reason, Dad? I really like this girl. She's the one I bought all the presents for.

MR. COLLINS (*Almost worn out*): I know, son, I know. But this Prentice guy is a big wheel.

GREG: How would you like to be shoved off to a Christmas dance with a girl you never saw?

MR. COLLINS: When you put it like that, it does seem a bit rough, but I did promise. (MRS. COLLINS *enters with a suit box.*) A special messenger just brought you this, dear. Did you order a suit?

MR. COLLINS: No. What is it? Here, let me see. (*Opens box and pulls out Santa Claus suit*) Oh, great. This is the final touch! This is all I needed.

MRS. COLLINS: A Santa Claus suit? What on earth for?

MR. COLLINS: For me. I completely forgot I promised to play Santa Claus for the Hermes Club tonight.

MRS. COLLINS: Oh, Al! Why did you ever promise such a thing? It's a terrible night. You'll be standing around in the snow for hours, and I'll bet your rheumatism will start again.

MR. COLLINS: I know, Emily, but a promise is a promise. That's why I can't give up on this Prentice deal. I'd give anything to get out of my debut as Santa, though.

GREG: Would you really give anything, Dad?

MR. COLLINS: Practically anything. What do you have in mind?

GREG: I was just thinking. I'll bet I could fill out that suit, and people say I have a nice way with kids.

MR. COLLINS: Do you mean you'd fill in for me?

GREG: Sure thing. Give me the suit. (*Pulls it on over his clothes*) You promised a Collins would play Santa Claus, and I'm a Collins.

MR. COLLINS: You're a good sport, son. Believe me, I appreciate this.

GREG: Listen, Dad. I'm not doing this for nothing. You said you'd give anything to get out of the job. Now pay up. Talk yourself out of the Prentice date and we'll call it even.

COLLINS (*Chuckling*): I guess you've got me over a barrel. Freeze to death as Santa Claus or do some fast talking to J.P. You win, Greg. I'll call him.

GREG: That's great, Dad. Go ahead, call him up right now.

MR. COLLINS: All right. I guess I can think of something. (*Phone rings*) Hello! . . . . Why, hello, J.P. I was just going to call you and you beat me to the draw. What? There's a plane going out after all? That's great . . . . Yes, the storm seems to have died down. Well, good luck, safe journey, and a Merry Christmas. (*Hangs up; mops brow with handkerchief*) Whew! That was a close one. They're going home.

GREG: Then I won't have to play Santa Claus after all.

MR. COLLINS: Oh, yes, you will. A promise is a promise.

MRS. COLLINS: And after this, let's each do our own promising.

MR. COLLINS: I second the motion. (PATTY *rushes in.*)

PATTY: I've got him. I've got him. Pinky's going to take Pilly-Milly to the dance.

MR. COLLINS: Then it looks as if we're all set for a merry Christmas after all. What do you say, Mr. Santa?

GREG: I say I'll do my best to make it a Christmas we'll never forget — and that's a promise, Dad. Shake?

MR. COLLINS: Shake. (*They shake hands as curtains close.*)

THE END

Whatever Happened to Good Old Ebenezer Scrooge?

By Bill Majeski

Ebenezer Scrooge decides that charity doesn't pay enough, and he reverts to his original nature . . .

Characters

EBENEZER SCROOGE
TV ANNOUNCER
INVESTMENT COUNSELOR
MEDIC
SMILEY
YAWNY
GROUCHY   }   *Seven Dwarfs*
SNIPPY
CUDDLY
DUMMY
SNOW WHITE
PRINCE
WITCH HAZEL
MIRROR, *offstage voice*

SCENE I

SETTING: *TV studio, with two chairs, a table and a microphone. This scene is played in front of curtain.*

BEFORE RISE: TV ANNOUNCER *is seated at table, facing microphone.*

ANNOUNCER: Once again, ladies and gentlemen, we bring you another installment in our series called, "Whatever Happened To. . . ," a nostalgic trip into the past in which we follow up on personalities of days gone by. Tonight, in our studio, we have one of the literary world's most famous characters. He's from England and was known as one of that country's most hated misers, that is, until he was visited by three apparitions — the ghosts of Christmas past, present and future. They appeared courtesy of his old business partner Marley. The ghosts so unnerved our guest that he was transformed suddenly from a penny-pinching, miserly, coin-clutching rotter to an open-handed, charitable, decent human being. Would you welcome, please, Ebenezer Scrooge. (SCROOGE *enters and shakes hands with* ANNOUNCER.) Hello, Mr. Scrooge, and welcome to our show. How are you?

SCROOGE: Getting by — barely.

ANNOUNCER: After your transition to good guy you just seemed to drop out of sight.

SCROOGE: Had to. I gave up my business, lost all my money and filed for bankruptcy. Bang. All gone. Nothing left.

ANNOUNCER: You were running a thriving concern. Where did all the money go?

SCROOGE: You know how it is — you get a little weak. You get soft. After my Christmas visit to the Cratchits, I —

ANNOUNCER (*Interrupting*): That was Bob Cratchit and his family, wasn't it?

SCROOGE: Right. He was a clerk for me. In the old days he really slaved for me, and I was putting away money hand over fist.

ANNOUNCER: Then there were those three visits.

SCROOGE: Yep. That last one — from the ghost of Christmas future — that was a kick in the head. Wiped me out emotionally. That's when I became Mr. Nice Guy. Practically gave everything away.

ANNOUNCER: You gave everything away?

SCROOGE: Uh-huh. I turned altruistic, business-wise. Somebody would come in and order something, and I'd knock twenty, maybe thirty percent off the price. I'd extend credit and make loans at no interest. Just got too flabby financially. I ended up extending myself right into the poorhouse.

ANNOUNCER: You? Mean old Scrooge, old miserly Ebenezer, in the poorhouse?

SCROOGE: No, *that* Scrooge was rich and successful. It was the new, free-spending, open-hearted Scrooge in the poorhouse.

ANNOUNCER: Very interesting. What are your plans now?

SCROOGE: Frankly, I feel I've paid my dues by being nice. I've been putting my pennies aside day after day and now I'm about ready for a comeback. I want to go into business for myself again. Be my own boss. In fact, I'm on my way to see an investment counselor right now. (*Firmly*) Don't worry about old Scrooge — I'll be back on top again.

ANNOUNCER: We applaud your determination, Mr. Scrooge. (*To audience*) Formerly rotten old Scrooge, who became good old Scrooge, is planning a trip along the comeback trail back into the hard, demanding world of business. Will he succeed? (*Standing and turning to* SCROOGE, *who also rises*) Well, Mr. Scrooge (*Shaking his hand*), we wish you luck . . . (*Turning to audience*) I think. (*They exit. Curtains open.*)

* * *

SETTING: A business office. Table and chairs have been removed. A desk and chair are at center, with another chair beside desk. Ledger, pens, etc., are on desk.

AT RISE: SCROOGE *and* INVESTMENT COUNSELOR *are seated at desk.*

COUNSELOR: Well, Mr. Scrooge, glad to see you've brought your business to us.

SCROOGE (*Gruff, all business now*): Why not? You knock off the smallest percentage of my money. I'd be crazy to go someplace where they nail you but good.

COUNSELOR: Of course. What kind of business are you interested in?

SCROOGE: A money-maker, what else? I've been on the loser route too long. I want profit, dough, bread, the long green.

COUNSELOR: I think I get the picture.

SCROOGE: You'd better believe it. I've been rich and I've been poor, and rich is better.

COUNSELOR (*Flipping through ledger*): Here's a growing agricultural concern. A guy wants to sell his place out in the hinterlands. He grows mile-high beanstalks.

SCROOGE: Beanstalks? There's no jack in beanstalks. Not interested.

COUNSELOR: O.K., let's try something else. What about women's footwear.

SCROOGE: Footwear? Well, that's a step in the right direction. Tell me about it.

COUNSELOR: The company makes glass slippers. It's run

by a sweet young thing named Cinderella. But she's getting married to a nobleman.

SCROOGE: Glass slippers? I see right through that. No glass for me. As my former partner Marley warned me long ago, glass is a pain — and it can break you.

COUNSELOR: Ah, here's a nice item. A women's hairdressing establishment. Records show you have a fifteen percent profit margin — and you take it right off the top.

SCROOGE: Fifteen percent? Not high enough.

COUNSELOR: This Rapunzel knows everything about hair.

SCROOGE: What's to know about hair? Tell Rapunzel to keep her hair to herself and to keep the fifteen percent. Look, fellow, maybe I'm not getting through to you. I want a winner. I want something that'll keep me active, forceful, driving — in a word, mean. Something with a solid bottom line. Now either find that for me or I go elsewhere.

COUNSELOR: Ah, here's just the thing. How about a small factory that makes Christmas bells?

SCROOGE: You mean those things that jingle when people come into a store?

COUNSELOR: That's right.

SCROOGE: You know, you've got some weird enterprises here. Glass slippers, mile-high beanstalks — it sounds as if you're out in never-never land. Now you give me a bell factory.

COUNSELOR: We are a little offbeat, but remember, in all these businesses they work for low wages. In the bell factory you'll have seven employees, all of them dwarfs —that means low overhead. Low overhead, get it? Dwarfs. That's a joke.

SCROOGE: I'll be the judge of that. Tell me more about these bells.

COUNSELOR: Well, as I said, they're Christmas bells. You

know, jingle bells — the kind you hang on your tree, your front door, or a one-horse open sleigh.

SCROOGE: Christmas bells, huh? How ironic. Christmas.

COUNSELOR: Cheap labor. Minimum expenses. Good profit. See? (*Shows book to* SCROOGE, *who studies it*)

SCROOGE: O.K. You said the magic word — money! I'll take it.

COUNSELOR: Fine. It's called the Best Bell Business, Inc.

SCROOGE: You're going to see old Scrooge fill the world with Christmas bells and fill his pockets with jingling coins. Goodbye. (SCROOGE *rises, shakes* COUNSELOR'*s hand and starts to exit.*)

COUNSELOR: And Merry Christmas!

SCROOGE: Bah! Humbug! (*Curtain*)

*   *   *   *   *

SCENE 2

TIME: *A few days later.*

SETTING: *The bell factory. There is a long table at left with a couple of benches around it. Scrooge's desk is at right.*

AT RISE: SCROOGE *is seated at desk. He rises, looks at watch impatiently and begins to pace.*

SCROOGE: Five minutes to seven and my workers haven't shown up yet. They should be here by now. I'll show them what it's like to work for a *real* boss. The old Ebenezer Scrooge is back. (*Seven Dwarfs enter, singing "Hi-Ho, Hi-Ho," wearing beards, funny costumes, etc.* SCROOGE *scrutinizes them as they do a short drill and an abrupt about-face and end up in a straight line across stage.* SCROOGE *shakes his head slowly.*) What did I buy, a platoon of short Marines? (MEDIC *steps forward.*)

MEDIC: Mr. Scrooge?

SCROOGE: I'm not Good-Time Charlie, the last of the big-time spenders.

MEDIC: My name is Medic, and I'm foreman of the Best Bell Business, Inc. I'd like to introduce you to the rest of your staff.

SCROOGE: Hm-m-m. I'm not sure I want to meet them. But let's get it moving. Medic, huh? Are you a real doctor?

MEDIC: No, it's just a nickname.

SCROOGE: Too bad. It would be nice to have a doctor working here. With this crew I have the feeling there are going to be a lot of little accidents.

MEDIC: Our safety record is impeccable. We haven't had so much as a hangnail in the past five years.

SCROOGE: O.K. Now get on with the introductions.

MEDIC: Here's Smiley. (SMILEY *steps forward, smiling broadly.*)

SCROOGE: What's he smiling about?

MEDIC: He's Smiley.

SCROOGE: I can see that. About what? What's there to smile about? Cost of living skyrocketing, taxes spiralling upward, Internal Revenue Service breathing down our necks. . . .

MEDIC: That's his name — Smiley. (SMILEY *bows, still grinning broadly.*)

SCROOGE: Smiley? Ought to call him Silly. (*At this,* SMILEY *bursts out into a loud roar of laughter and steps back into line.*)

MEDIC: He likes your jokes, Mr. Scrooge.

SCROOGE: He looks as if he'd laugh at a sponge cake. Go on.

MEDIC: This is Grouchy. (GROUCHY, *sour-faced and cranky, steps forward.*)

SCROOGE: What's he sore at?

MEDIC: He's mad at the world. He's cynical, cranky, cantankerous, rude and nasty.

SCROOGE: My type of guy.

MEDIC: But underneath it all, a soft-hearted man.

SCROOGE: Oh . . . well, I'll withhold judgment. (GROUCHY *steps back into line.*)

MEDIC: Next — Yawny. (YAWNY, *working on a big yawn, steps forward and stretches.*)

SCROOGE: This guy's got to go. What kind of production can he turn out?

MEDIC: He's a good worker, Mr. Scrooge. (SCROOGE *does a double take as* YAWNY *gives a huge yawn.*)

SCROOGE: Did you see that? When he yawned, his ears disappeared. Does he run around all night or something?

MEDIC: No, he sleeps twelve, fourteen hours a night.

SCROOGE: As long as he doesn't sleep during the day.

MEDIC (*Beckoning to* SNIPPY): Next we have . . . . (YAWNY *steps back as* SNIPPY *steps forward.*) He's Snippy.

SCROOGE: He won't get snippy with me. O.K., who's next in this rogues' gallery?

MEDIC: Cuddly, you're next. (*No action. No one steps forward.*) Cuddly, please step forward. (CUDDLY *tries to duck behind others. They grab him and push him forward. He reluctantly stumbles out a few paces.*)

SCROOGE: What's he ashamed of?

MEDIC: He's a little shy.

SCROOGE: A little shy? Why is his face so red?

MEDIC: He's blushing.

SCROOGE: Did I say something out of line?

MEDIC: No. He always blushes. That's why girls like him and call him Cuddly.

SCROOGE: Well, there'll be no cuddling on company time, fellow. Next.

MEDIC: Dummy!

SCROOGE (*Whirling on him*): What did you call me?

MEDIC: Dummy, sir. Not you. Dummy's our last worker. He's Dummy. (DUMMY *steps forward, thumb in mouth.*)

SCROOGE: Oh, I see. I probably could have guessed. Is he O.K. upstairs? I mean, is he playing with a full deck?

MEDIC: Dummy is perfectly normal.

Scrooge (*To* DUMMY): Hey, Dummy. How long have you been working for Best Bells? (*Silence*) I asked you a question. Answer me.

MEDIC (*Tugging* SCROOGE*'s sleeve*): He doesn't talk.

SCROOGE: He can't talk?

MEDIC: He won't talk.

SCROOGE: He refuses to talk?

MEDIC: Yes, sir.

SCROOGE: Has anyone ever heard him talk?

MEDIC: Once, sir. At breakfast, eleven years ago.

SCROOGE: What did he say?

MEDIC: He said he didn't like the cereal.

SCROOGE: Well, at least he won't spend time gossiping around the water cooler . . . or talking behind my back. O.K., now I'd like to say a few introductory words. (MEDIC *steps over with other dwarfs and they stand in a row preparing to listen.*) Now listen up. I want to say a few words before you get back into the workshop and slave your heads off for me. I believe in incentive working, but I don't believe in paying bonuses. I've checked the production figures, so I know what you can do. Not bad. But you'll improve. My name is Ebenezer Scrooge, and I came up the hard way. I was from a poor, humble family. My family was so poor my parents couldn't afford to buy me shoes. They just painted my feet black and laced up my toes. I went into business with a guy named Marley, and I was successful. A series of bad breaks, like being nice, sent me tumbling down to the bottom. But I'm back now. Old Ebenezer Scrooge is back and you boys have got him. From now on, you get a ten-minute coffee break in the morning — Wednesday morning. Cut down on your lunch hour. Take bigger bites — it'll go down faster. I demand excellent workmanship and industriousness, and I want you here working at seven o'clock every morning. Any questions? (MEDIC *raises his hand and steps forward.*) Yes?

MEDIC: Can we start now? You've kept us from working for ten minutes now. The men want to work.

SCROOGE: Oh . . . yes, by all means. Go. Dismissed. (*Dwarfs march off at fast pace.*) I think I may have bought out Weirdo City. (*Sound of bells jingling is heard offstage.* SCROOGE *cocks his head and smiles.*) But money talks . . . or jingles. (*He exits, rubbing his hands together. Curtain*)

* * * * *

SCENE 3

SETTING: *The witch's place. This scene is played before the curtain.*

BEFORE RISE: WITCH *enters left, cackling, crosses right and gazes offstage as if looking into mirror.*

WITCH:
Mirror, mirror, on the wall,
Who is the fairest one of all?

MIRROR (*From offstage*): Snow White. (WITCH *throws a mild tantrum, stamps her feet, etc.*)

WITCH (*Enraged*): Still the fairest? After my expensive ten-week mail-order beauty treatment? Well, I'll take care of little Snow White. A flavorful apple, garnished with my own special sleeping potion, should take care of that little chickie. Then *I* will be the fairest one of all. And isn't that what every woman wants? Sure, I have untold wealth and my health, but I want to be number one in beauty. When I'm number two I have to try harder and it's getting me down. (WITCH *cackles wickedly and exits. Curtains open.*)

* * *

SETTING: *Same as Scene 2.*

AT RISE: *Dwarfs march in, singing "Hi-Ho, Hi-Ho," unenthusiastically. They sit wearily on benches and on floor.*

MEDIC: Boy, that Scrooge is a harsh taskmaster.

CUDDLY (*Hesitantly*): He treats us like animals.

GROUCHY: All he needs is a whip and a chair.

SMILEY: But the factory is doing well. Christmas is coming, and we're all working and we're healthy and happy.

GROUCHY: I'll be happy some other time. Right now I'm too busy thinking bad thoughts about Scrooge. (SNOW WHITE *enters. The dwarfs rise to greet her.*)

SNOW WHITE: Hello, fellows.

DWARFS (*Ad lib*): Hello, Snow. Hi there, Miss White. Glad to see you! (*Etc.*)

SNOW WHITE: How's your new boss treating you?

MEDIC: Not bad, all things considered.

YAWNY (*Suppressing a yawn*): I must admit he's fair. He treats us all alike.

GROUCHY: Right. He treats us all like dogs.

SNOW WHITE: I never met the man.

GROUCHY: You'd be smart to keep it that way. (SCROOGE *enters, sees gathering and stops short.*)

SCROOGE: What is this? A loafers' convention?

MEDIC: We were just —

SCROOGE (*Interrupting*): You aren't "just" anything. You're standing out here gabbing with a woman.

SNOW WHITE: Mr. Scrooge? I'm Snow White.

SCROOGE: That doesn't interest me. You're distracting my men. I don't need any recreation department here. I want to hear the bells ring in the factory, not in their skulls.

GROUCHY (*To* SNOW WHITE): He's all heart.

SCROOGE: What was that?

GROUCHY: I said — she must part.

SCROOGE: Absolutely. You'll have to leave, young lady.

SMILEY (*Grinning*): We still have two minutes left on our break.

SCROOGE: Well, walk slowly back to the shop.

YAWNY (*Yawning*): Aw, let her stay for another minute.

SMILEY (*Laughing*): She's good for our morale. Look at me, I'm laughing.

SCROOGE: You'd laugh if you were caught in a blizzard without shoes and a polar bear was chasing you.

SNOW WHITE: That's all right, boys. I really must go. I'm meeting a witch.

CUDDLY (*Shyly*): Which witch?

SNOW WHITE: Hazel.

SMILEY: Hazel the rich witch?

SNOW WHITE: Yes, I think so.

MEDIC: She may be a rich witch, but she's a bad apple.

GROUCHY: Don't go, Snow. She's rotten to the core.

SNOW WHITE: Oh, she's all right, once you get to know her.

SMILEY: She's mean.

SCROOGE: I'll show you the meaning of mean if you don't get back to work.

MEDIC: Mr. Scrooge, our production is twenty percent above normal.

SCROOGE: Twenty is not thirty. It's not even twenty-five. Goodbye, Miss White.

SNOW WHITE: Goodbye, all. (*She exits.*)

DWARFS (*Ad lib*): Goodbye. Be careful. Watch that witch. (*Etc.*)

SCROOGE: All right, all right. Your two minutes are up. Back to work, on the double. (*Dwarfs march offstage. Sound of bells jingling is heard.* SCROOGE *smiles to himself and rubs his hands together. Lights dim to indicate the passage of time. They come up on* SCROOGE *poring over some papers at his desk.* MEDIC *enters.*)

MEDIC: You rang, Mr. Scrooge?

SCROOGE: Yes. I must admit, you men are showing me something. Production zooming, profits up a pile — er, a little bit — and I'm feeling great. I'll have to watch it. The other day I caught myself smiling.

MEDIC: I'm pleased, Mr. Scrooge.

SCROOGE: But we can't relax. Our busy time is coming up. That calls for hard work, overtime and double overtime. We can't let up one second.

MEDIC: Right. (*Dwarfs, frantic, usher in* SNOW WHITE, *who can barely walk, and guide her to bench, where she lies down.*) What happened?

GROUCHY: The witch got her with one of the apples.

SCROOGE: Do you mean she got conked on the head with an apple and passed out?

SMILEY: No. She ate a bad apple the witch gave her.

SCROOGE: O.K., call a doctor. Send her to the clinic.

MEDIC: You don't understand, Mr. Scrooge. Whoever eats one of the witch's apples falls into a death-like sleep.

YAWNY (*Yawning*): And stays asleep, lucky thing.

SMILEY: She stays asleep until she is awakened by a kiss from a prince.

SCROOGE: What? What are you handing me?

MEDIC: It's true, Mr. Scrooge.

SMILEY: A real, live handsome prince must kiss her into wakefulness.

SCROOGE (*Sarcastically*): I get it, I get it. Then they live happily ever after. Well, what are you waiting for? Go out and find a prince.

SNIPPY: Where are we going to find a prince? Answer me that.

SCROOGE: Don't get snippy with me, Snippy.

MEDIC: Perhaps you know where to find a prince, Mr. Scrooge.

SCROOGE: What do I know about princes? Look in the yellow pages. Only get her out of here. She can't stay here in that condition.

CUDDLY: Why . . . uh . . . why don't you . . . uh . . . kiss her, Mr. Scrooge?

SCROOGE: Me? Why, I hardly know her. Besides, I'm no handsome prince.

GROUCHY (*Aside*): That's for sure.

MEDIC: The men would like a little time off — without pay, of course — to go out and locate a prince.

SCROOGE: Impossible. It's the busiest part of the year.

SMILEY: We'll work twice as hard when we get back.

YAWNY: We'd be (*Yawning*) dynamite.

SCROOGE: I'd lose a pile of profit.

GROUCHY: But we'd have Snow White alive and well.

CUDDLY: We all like her. She's so nice to us.

SCROOGE: Can't do it.

SMILEY: Please, Mr. Scrooge . . .

YAWNY: Just till we find a prince . . .

MEDIC: Be a sport, Mr. Scrooge . . .

SCROOGE: Let me kick it around for a few minutes. (*Dwarfs watch anxiously as* SCROOGE *goes to stage right by himself.*) Let's see. Seven people looking for one prince . . . twenty minutes per person . . . lots of time away from the workbench . . . dollars down the drain . . . What would Marley have done? Would he have been tough on them? No, he's the guy who gave me bad dreams about Christmas future just because I was a little short with Cratchit and a few others . . . All right, Marley, you win. (*To dwarfs*) O.K., you can let Snow White stay here. We'll hold up production. You can go out there and find that prince with the magic lips. (*Dwarfs cheer.*)

SMILEY: Mr. Scrooge is the best boss, after all.

GROUCHY: Yeah . . . after all the rest. (*Dwarfs exit. SCROOGE looks over at SNOW WHITE, then sits down, thinking. He yawns, stretches and then leaves. Stage is now empty except for the sleeping SNOW WHITE. PRINCE enters, led into room by dwarfs. He looks around and spies SNOW WHITE. He walks over to her and kisses her gently. She stirs, awakens. She stands up. PRINCE takes her in his arms and they walk off together, as she looks lovingly up into his eyes. Dwarfs follow them off happily. WITCH enters onto empty stage. She looks at "mirror" on wall. She checks her teeth, pats her hair, and shakes head.*)

WITCH: I don't know. Maybe those beauty courses aren't doing any good. I don't know about this mail-order stuff. The beauty treatments aren't working for me, but now my mailman is prettier than I am. Oh, well . . . . Maybe I should get some beauty sleep. (*She yawns, then lies down on bench that SNOW WHITE has just vacated. SCROOGE enters. He looks at bench.*)

SCROOGE: Look at that. Still snoring away. And where are those clowns? This prince hunt is costing me a pretty penny. They'd better get back soon, because I've just stopped being Mr. Wonderful. (WITCH *stirs.*

SCROOGE *looks at her as she sits up.*) Ah, she's coming out of it. (WITCH *turns to* SCROOGE, *who does double take, blinks eyes and shakes his head.*) You've changed!

WITCH: Changed?

SCROOGE: I mean, that wasn't exactly a beauty nap you just had, Miss White.

WITCH: I'm not Miss White. I'm Hazel.

SCROOGE: The witch?

WITCH: The rich witch.

SCROOGE: Rich witch? (*Warmly*) Well, I'm really pleased to meet you. I'm Ebenezer Scrooge. I'm a prince of a fellow . . . in a manner of speaking.

WITCH: Did you kiss Snow White?

SCROOGE: Kiss her! I never even held her hand. No, that's not my line of work. I'm a manufacturer. This is my factory.

WITCH (*Glancing around*): You seem to be doing well.

SCROOGE: We're moving along. No complaints. We'll do better, too. What do you do?

WITCH: I deal with apples, potions, things like that.

SCROOGE: Hold it. Are you the one who gave Snow White that bad-news apple?

WITCH (*Nodding*): Yes . . . . I feel very bad about it now. I guess just talking about it made me feel better. You know, being a witch can be lonely — no matter how much money I have.

SCROOGE (*Eagerly*): Money . . . do you have money?

WITCH: Oodles and oodles. But still . . . I'm a witch. It seems I have to use a few tricks now and then to keep me on speaking terms with the world.

SCROOGE: I know what you mean. I've been known to resort to trickery myself once in a while.

WITCH: When you're not blessed with beauty, I guess you can get pretty nasty.

SCROOGE: True — how true.

WITCH: So I compensate with dirty tricks and money.

SCROOGE: Dirty tricks and money. What a combination!

WITCH: Do you understand me?

SCROOGE: I certainly do, young lady. You're all right in my book. (*They look at each other fondly. Dwarfs come in, leading* PRINCE *and* SNOW WHITE.)

DWARFS (*Ad lib*): We're back! We found the Prince. He kissed Snow White. She's awake, for good. (*Etc. They see* WITCH *and cringe, backing off.*)

MEDIC: What's the witch doing here?

SCROOGE: Hazel and I were just chatting a bit.

YAWNY: You know her?

SCROOGE: We are fast becoming close friends.

SMILEY: But . . . but, she's a . . .

SCROOGE: I know all about it.

WITCH: I told him everything.

GROUCHY: Which witch is she? The rich witch?

WITCH: Yes.

SCROOGE: You bet your beard she's rich.

GROUCHY: Prove it.

WITCH (*Sighing*): If I must . . . . (*She crosses right and gazes offstage, as if looking into mirror, as before.*)
Mirror, mirror, on the wall,
Who is the *richest* one of all?

MIRROR (*Offstage*): You are the richest, Witch Hazel.

SCROOGE (*Jubilantly*): That's my type of woman! Men, you can all have the weekend off. (*Dwarfs cheer. They separate and form two lines.* SCROOGE *and* WITCH *walk arm in arm between lines. Dwarfs begin jingling bells.*)
Is there a preacher in this burg?

PRINCE: Three blocks down you'll find Parson Brown.

SCROOGE (*Patting* WITCH*'s arm*): Let's go, my lovely. We'll see him and then we'll go someplace and count our money — er, blessings! Count our blessings! (*They exit with dwarfs cheering and jingling bells.* SNOW WHITE *and* PRINCE *start off behind* SCROOGE *and* WITCH. *It becomes a grand, noisy exit, as dwarfs, bells ringing, follow them merrily along offstage. Curtain*)

THE END

Red Carpet Christmas

By Helen Louise Miller

Christmas is no time for feuding! Old-fashioned Yuletide spirit and a surprising discovery bring two families together again . . .

Characters

MARCIA HITCHCOCK, *16*
ANITA PAGE, *Marcia's friend*
PAM HITCHCOCK, *14*
MRS. ETHEL HITCHCOCK
MR. HENRY HITCHCOCK
BILLY HITCHCOCK, *12*
BESSIE, *the maid*
TONY CORELLI, *18*
JIMMY HALE
MAGGIE
COUNT CORELLI
GINA CORELLI, *12*

TIME: *The afternoon of the day before Christmas.*
SETTING: *The living room of the Hitchcock family. In addition to the usual living-room furnishings, there are Christmas decorations in evidence, as well as a televi-*

sion set. A large window is right.

AT RISE: MARCIA *is kneeling on sofa, looking out of window through binoculars.* ANITA *is beside her.*

ANITA (*Excitedly*): Can you see him, Marcia? Can you see Tony?

MARCIA: I'm not quite sure, but there's somebody in the living room.

ANITA: Is it Tony?

MARCIA: I think so. Yes, I'm almost positive. I can see the back of his neck and one ear.

ANITA (*Grabbing binoculars*): Let me look! Let me look!

MARCIA: Stop shoving. You'll get him out of focus. Now he's leaning over. He seems to be moving a piece of furniture. I wish he'd come closer.

ANITA: I'll concentrate. (*Shuts her eyes tightly*) Closer, closer, closer! (*Opens eyes and leans over* MARCIA*'s shoulder*) Is he coming any nearer?

MARCIA: A little. He's stopping at the table . . . now . . . now . . . oh, Anita! He's coming toward the window. He's . . . oh, my goodness! He's looking right over here, right at our house. (*Scrambles off sofa and ducks behind curtain*) Do you think he saw me?

ANITA: Of course not. The house is too far away. (*Snatching binoculars*) I simply *must* see him! (*Pause*) Wow! He's adorable! Oops! Don't do it! Don't do it! Don't you dare do it!

MARCIA: What? What is he doing?

Anita (*With exaggerated sigh of relief*): It's all right now, but for a minute I almost had heart failure. I thought he was going to pull down the shade.

MARCIA: You've had the binoculars long enough. Let me look.

ANITA (*Holding onto binoculars*): Just a few seconds more, Marcia, please. You can look at him all afternoon after I've gone. Ummm! He has that European look — tall, blond, and romantic looking.

MARCIA: That's funny. I remember Tony as having dark hair.

ANITA: Well, his hair is blond now, and he has a marvelous tan — that real Riviera look.

MARCIA: Let me see.

ANITA: Uh-oh! Sorry! He just walked out.

MARCIA: Now I've missed him again. I've been watching for three days, and I've never once had a good look at him.

ANITA: I don't see why you don't ask him over for your Christmas party tonight. After all, you were once engaged to him.

MARCIA: Engaged to him! What are you talking about?

ANITA: You told me so yourself. He gave you a ring and everything.

MARCIA: Oh, Anita, you idiot! That was ten years ago when he was eight and I was six. The ring came out of a Crackerjack box.

ANITA: But you promised to wait for each other. And I'll bet you still have the ring.

MARCIA (*Crossly*): What if I do? It was only a silly game we played the last summer he was here visiting his grandmother Briggs. He's never been back since she died.

ANITA: But the whole family's here now. (*Digs clipping out of purse*) Did you see this write-up in the Sunday paper? (*Reads*) "Countess Corelli and family to winter in Bakersville. After a twenty-year absence in Italy, the former Margaret Briggs will re-open her family home in time for Christmas."

MARCIA: I didn't see that one. Is Tony's picture there? (*Looks at clipping*)

ANITA: No, just the Count, the Countess, and Gina. What are they like?

MARCIA: I've never seen any of them. Tony used to visit his grandmother by himself. Gina is younger — closer to Pam's and Billy's age.

ANITA: But your mother knows the Countess. Didn't they grow up together?

MARCIA: Sure. They used to be very close friends. Mother still calls her Maggie Briggs. But there was some sort of quarrel, and Mother never heard from her after she married the Count and went off to Italy. In fact, I don't think Mom's too pleased that they've come back here to live.

ANITA: I think it's great. Imagine living right next door to a Count and a Countess.

MARCIA: It's stretching a point to say we live right next door. There's a big garden between the Corelli house and ours.

ANITA: But they're still your nearest neighbors. Oh, Marcia, why don't you ask the whole family to your Open House? That would be the neighborly thing to do.

MARCIA: I told you Mother doesn't want to be that neighborly. She's already told us she doesn't want us pushing ourselves in. She's afraid people will think we were being friendly to them just because they're rich.

ANITA: But that's ridiculous! Tony is an old friend. What harm would there be in asking him? Besides, you do need an extra man.

MARCIA: But he's been here three whole days and hasn't called or dropped in. He probably doesn't even remember us.

ANITA: Well, you should certainly be able to think of some way to meet him. (*Handing binoculars to* MARCIA) Here. Take the binoculars. I promised to meet

Jimmy about four. Anything you want me to pick up downtown?

MARCIA: It would be a help if you could pick up a man to fill in for Bob Lucas. What a time for him to get tonsillitis!

ANITA: I'll see if Jimmy can think of someone. He knows everybody.

MARCIA: Thanks a lot. See you tonight. (*As* ANITA *exits left,* MARCIA *takes binoculars and resumes her lookout post*) Too bad. The room is still empty. I wonder when he'll be back. (PAM *enters right with plate of cookies, one of which she is eating.*)

PAM: At it again, are you? You'd better not let Mom catch you snooping on the new neighbors.

MARCIA: I am *not* snooping, Pamela Hitchcock.

PAM: Then I will. (*Offering cookies*) Here, have some of Bessie's hermits while I try to spot Gina. I want to see if she looks happier. When I saw her this morning after breakfast she seemed to be crying. (*Takes binoculars*)

MARCIA: Why would a girl who has everything want to cry?

PAM: Don't ask me. Hey, who's been fooling with these binoculars? I can't see a thing.

MARCIA: There's nothing to see. (*Puts cookie plate on coffee table*) Everybody's out.

PAM: I like to look at the room. Did you ever see such gorgeous decorations and such beautiful furniture?

MARCIA: I didn't notice.

PAM: That's because you're too busy looking for Tony.

MARCIA: I haven't seen him, except for one, teeny-weeny glimpse.

PAM: I sure wish Mom would invite the whole family over for Open House tonight, but I guess it's just as well. This house is so shabby!

MARCIA: What a thing to say! I like our house just the way it is.

PAM: Oh, sure, but compared to the Corelli house, it's nothing. They must have done the whole place over. They've taken up that ugly old carpeting, and they have the most gorgeous Oriental rugs.

MARCIA: Mom's been talking about getting a new rug in here.

PAM: You ought to see their draperies.

MARCIA: Now who's snooping.

PAM: *I* didn't say it was snooping. That's just what Mother calls it. To me it's just like watching a play — in fact, it's better than television. We actually know the people, and we like to see everything they're doing.

MARCIA (*Clapping her hand to her head*): Television! Oh, no! I forgot to call the repair shop! Dad told me to call right after breakfast. I hope it's not too late. (*Goes to phone and dials*)

PAM: Dad will be furious if he can't see his Christmas programs tonight. Hey, sis, come and look. Somebody's going into the Corelli house.

MARCIA: Oh, dear! The line is busy. (*Running to window*) Who? Where? Let me see. (*As girls pass binoculars back and forth,* MRS. HITCHCOCK *enters from center entrance.*)

MRS. HITCHCOCK: Marcia! Pam! Put those binoculars down this minute! I will not have you spying on the Corellis.

PAM: But, Mother, they're so fascinating, and it's so exciting, living so close to royalty.

MRS. HITCHCOCK: Royalty, my foot! In Italy everyone has a title. As far as I'm concerned, Maggie Briggs is no more royalty than we are.

MARCIA: Maggie Briggs! Oh, Mother, she's the Countess Margarita now.

MRS. HITCHCOCK: She was just plain Maggie Briggs when I knew her. Now put those binoculars down and get away from that window. Marcia, you go help Bessie with the punch and sandwiches for the party.

MARCIA: I have to call the TV repair shop first, Mother.

MRS. HITCHCOCK: Good heavens! Haven't you done that yet?

MARCIA: The line was busy. I'll try again. (*Goes to phone and dials*)

MRS. HITCHCOCK: And you, Pam, you can polish the silver tray. Bessie has so much extra work to do, making Christmas cookies besides everything else.

PAM: Oh, Mother! Do I have to?

MRS. HITCHCOCK: You most certainly do.

PAM: But she's giving them away to the whole town. She even baked a fresh batch this morning. Can't you stop her?

MRS. HITCHCOCK: That new batch was for our party. I wouldn't have the heart to stop her, even if I could. Bessie's Christmas cookies are a tradition in this town.

PAM: Maybe that's why they named it Bakersville.

MRS. HITCHCOCK: Don't try to be funny, Pam. You know how much those cookies mean to Bessie. She sends them to neighbors the way other people send Christmas cards. Now get moving.

PAM: What about Billy? What's he doing to help get ready for the party?

MRS. HITCHCOCK: Your brother did his share this morning. Now it's your turn. Get busy! (*Shoos* PAM *offstage.* PAM *exits.*)

MARCIA (*At phone*): Oh, I see. Well, I can understand that you are rushed, but couldn't you possibly? . . . That would be fine. We certainly would appreciate it. . . . Thank you. Goodbye. (*Hangs up*)

MRS. HITCHCOCK: Any luck?

MARCIA: Mr. Young said his men are working over at the Corellis, putting in two new sets.

MRS. HITCHCOCK: The Corellis! Sometimes I wish they had stayed in Europe! They've done nothing but upset this household ever since they came back.

MARCIA: But, Mother, it isn't actually their fault. They haven't really done anything. It's just that . . . well, they're so important, and glamorous . . . and it's exciting to have them as neighbors.

MRS. HITCHCOCK: We're not exactly neighbors just because there are no houses between the old Briggs mansion and 925 Hilltop Road. And, furthermore, I don't want you wasting any more time gawking at the Corelli family with those binoculars. I'm going to take them upstairs and put them under lock and key.

MARCIA: Oh, Mother, don't you understand? I'm dying to see Tony.

MRS. HITCHCOCK: If he stays here all winter and goes to public high school, you'll see him every day.

MARCIA: But I want to see him now, tonight. Oh, Mother, please, couldn't I ask him to the party to fill in for Bob Lucas?

MRS. HITCHCOCK: Forget it, Marcia. If Tony wants to see you, he knows where you live. He certainly never had any trouble finding his way over here when he was a little boy.

MARCIA: And you always liked him then. I don't see why you object to him now.

MRS. HITCHCOCK: Of course, I liked him. He was a nice child, and I have no doubt he's grown into a nice young man. But I am not going to have you falling all over anyone just because his name is Corelli. Now please hurry, dear. Bessie needs your help.

MARCIA (*With resignation*): O.K., Mom. I'll go fix the punch and sandwiches. (*Turning at door*) You can tell Dad Mr. Young said he'd send one of the men over from the Corellis to fix the TV set if they finish before five. (*Exits*)

MRS. HITCHCOCK (*To herself*): They have some nerve! We've been good customers of theirs for years, but who cares with the Corellis in town? I'll bet Maggie figures the whole town will come flocking just because she has a title and some money. I'd love to see what she's done with that old house. (*Picks up binoculars and looks around guiltily*) For two cents, I'd take a peek myself . . . (*Gets into position on sofa*) That front parlor used to be a regular mausoleum, but now I suppose . . . (*Lifts binoculars to her eyes, as* MR. HITCHCOCK *enters left with several packages.*)

MR. HITCHCOCK (*As he drops his parcels on chair*): I think I've got everything on the list. Ethel! What are you doing?

MRS. HITCHCOCK (*Startled and embarrassed*): Henry! You scared me to death! I didn't hear you come in.

MR. HITCHCOCK: Don't tell me you've succumbed to the family weakness of Corelli-watching!

MRS. HITCHCOCK: Not quite. I admit I was close. But don't you dare tell the children!

MR. HITCHCOCK: What's the big attraction? Every time I come in, somebody's glued to those binoculars.

MRS. HITCHCOCK: I know, Henry. It's terrible, simply terrible. But between you and me — and I'll be furious if you tell anyone — I'm dying to see Maggie Briggs.

MR. HITCHCOCK: It seems only yesterday I heard you swear that you never wanted to see Maggie Briggs as long as you lived.

MRS. HITCHCOCK (*Ruefully*): I know — that was the time she didn't show up at my Christmas Eve party, remember?

MR. HITCHCOCK: How could I forget? That was the night we announced our engagement. You said you'd never forgive her.

MRS. HITCHCOCK: But I did . . . or I almost did. In spite of everything I always loved Maggie. I guess I still do.

MR. HITCHCOCK: Then why don't you let bygones be bygones and invite the whole family over tonight?

MRS. HITCHCOCK: Henry! We couldn't possibly!

MR. HITCHCOCK: Why not?

MRS. HITCHCOCK: Because . . . well, in the first place, Maggie's a countess now. They have their own friends. The society pages of the papers have been full of their coming back to Bakersville and moving into the Briggs mansion. And anyhow, this house . . . this room —

MR. HITCHCOCK: What's the matter with this house and this room?

MRS. HITCHCOCK: Oh, it's fine, Henry, and I love every bit of it. But . . . well, actually, it's shabby. Look at this rug, for instance.

MR. HITCHCOCK: I'm looking at it.

MRS. HITCHCOCK: Don't you see how worn it's getting? Oh, I know this sounds snobbish and silly, but I just can't see ourselves entertaining the Corellis. . . . And besides . . .

MR. HITCHCOCK: And besides, you're still mad at Maggie.

MRS. HITCHCOCK: I guess I am. I never could figure out why she did such a nasty thing. She was my best friend!

MR. HITCHCOCK: As I remember the story, she always claimed you never invited her.

MRS. HITCHCOCK: But I *did* invite her. I even wrote her a special little note and told her what I had never told another living soul.

MR. HITCHCOCK: Not even me?

MRS. HITCHCOCK (*Shaking her head in mock exasperation*): You already knew what I wrote her.

MR. HITCHCOCK: I did?

MRS. HITCHCOCK (*Smiling affectionately*): I wrote to tell her we were engaged. Don't you remember? We were going to keep it a secret, but I always told Maggie everything. I took the note over to her house early one morning and slipped it under the door.

MR. HITCHCOCK: I still think it's about time you forgot that schoolgirl quarrel and had the Corellis over here. I understand the Count's pretty fast on the tennis court.

MRS. HITCHCOCK: You're as bad as Marcia and Pam. You seem to think we can go barging in on the Corellis as if . . . as if —

MR. HITCHCOCK: As if they were our neighbors, which is exactly what they are.

MRS. HITCHCOCK: But they're no ordinary neighbors, Henry. Besides, Tony has been ignoring Marcia. He's been here three days and hasn't come near her. And anyhow, I don't want the children getting big ideas about cars and clothes and fancy furniture and . . .

MR. HITCHCOCK: Seems to me you've been getting some of those big ideas yourself. After all, you don't seem to think our living-room rug is socially acceptable.

MRS. HITCHCOCK: But that's different, Henry. You know yourself we've been talking about replacing this rug for years. (BILLY *enters left, carrying a strip of red carpet in a roll over his shoulder.*)

BILLY: Hi, Mom. Hi, Dad. Look what I've got.

MRS. HITCHCOCK: What on earth is that?

BILLY: It's a strip of hall carpet. It'll be great for the club-house the gang's fixing up. (*Drops rug onto floor, but does not unroll it.*)

MR. HITCHCOCK: Where did you get it?

BILLY: I bought it for twenty-five cents from Eddie Murphy. Mrs. Corelli asked him to haul their trash away this morning. Want to see it?

MRS. HITCHCOCK: I most certainly do not want to see it. And you can just take it out and put it in our trash, Billy Hitchcock. I will not have any of the Corellis' castoffs in this house.

BILLY: Oh, come on, Mom. It's a perfectly good strip of carpet.

MR. HITCHCOCK: Better take it out to the garage, son. Your mother is anti-Corelli right now.

BILLY: What's the problem, Mom? I've been thinking of inviting Gina to the New Year's Eve dance.

MR. HITCHCOCK: Aren't you a little ahead of yourself? After all, we haven't met any of the family yet.

BILLY: Speak for yourself, Dad. The Countess and I are already on pretty good terms. She's nice, Mom. You'd like her.

MRS. HITCHCOCK: Oh, really! And just when and where did you meet the Countess?

BILLY: In her kitchen this morning, when I went over to borrow the sugar.

MRS. HITCHCOCK: Borrow the sugar? What did you do that for?

BILLY: Bessie. You know how she's always running out of things in the middle of her cookie-baking.

MRS. HITCHCOCK: Good heavens! What will they think of us?

BILLY: They'll think we ran out of sugar. What else?

(*Moves to television set*) Anything good on television?

MRS. HITCHCOCK: It hasn't been fixed yet. (*Acidly*) Mr. Young's men are busy installing two new color TVs for the Corellis.

BILLY: That's what we ought to have — two new sets instead of this antique. And besides, this one never works well.

MRS. HITCHCOCK: If it's not repaired soon, I'll miss my favorite Christmas programs!

BILLY: There's a little TV repair shop down on Ninth Street we could try. Maybe if we drove down there, we could bring a technician back with us.

MR. HITCHCOCK: I know the place you mean. Come on, Billy. I'll drive, and you can run in. We'll never find a place to park. (MR. HITCHCOCK *and* BILLY *exit left.*)

MRS. HITCHCOCK: This is too much! Dragging that old carpet in here, and actually running over there to borrow sugar. I certainly have a few things to say to Bessie. (*Calling*) Bessie, Bessie, where are you? I want to talk to you.

MARCIA (*Entering, right*): I can't find Bessie anywhere, Mother, and we don't have enough bread. I've used it all up. If you'll finish the punch, I'll go to the supermarket for the bread.

MRS. HITCHCOCK: No, I'll go. You might as well finish the punch, now that you've started. What do you suppose has become of Bessie?

MARCIA: Who knows? Nobody can keep track of her at Christmastime!

MRS. HITCHCOCK: I hope Bessie isn't up to something. Christmas seems to go to her head. But I suppose it's all right. She's helped us for so long, she's really part of the family. Well, I'll run along to the store. (MARCIA *and* MRS. HITCHCOCK *exit right. After a short*

pause, BESSIE *and* TONY CORELLI *enter from left.* BES-
SIE *carries a dress over her arm.*)

BESSIE: Come in, Tony, and make yourself at home.

TONY: It's wonderful to be back again, in this house, I
mean. Ours is such a complete madhouse. Mother all
upset, Gina homesick, Dad wandering around like a
lost sheep, and now Carlotta in hysterics over the new
electric stove — that was the last straw.

BESSIE: Don't worry, Tony. Everything will be all right.
I'll just run up to my room and fix this dress of Gina's.
And then, if we can't get that stove of yours to work,
I'll do your turkey over here.

TONY: I don't know what we'd do without you, Bessie.
It's so good of you to go to all this trouble.

BESSIE: Trouble? Don't be silly! I'm always glad to help
out — especially neighbors.

TONY: When we lived in Italy, Carlotta was the one who
helped everyone out.

BESSIE: Poor thing! It must be confusing when you're
working in a strange country. Maybe she never cooked
on an electric stove. But I'll have Carlotta fixed up in
no time. Just wait and see.

TONY (*Looking around room*): Gee, nothing's changed a
bit. Same furniture, same rug, even the same old television set. (*Walks over to it*) Remember how you used
to drag Marcia and me away from it when it was time
for supper?

BESSIE: I sure do. You never did know when to go home.

TONY (*Adjusting television set*): Is . . . is Marcia here?

BESSIE: Sure. She's supposed to be in the kitchen making
the refreshments for tonight. (*Calling*) Marcia, Marcia,
somebody here to see you. (*To* TONY) I'll just run upstairs and fix the dress. (BESSIE *exits center.*)

MARCIA (*Offstage*): Bessie, is that you? I've been waiting for you. I can't tell if this punch is too sweet or too sour. (*Enters left with glass of punch*) I want you to taste it. (*Sees* TONY *at TV set*) Oh, I thought Bessie was here. Did she let you in?

TONY: Yes . . . that is . . . well . . . we came in together.

MARCIA: Well, I'm glad you got here in time. I hope you can fix this stupid TV set. (*Sets down glass of punch*)

TONY (*Blankly*): Fix it?

MARCIA: Don't look at me like that! I know the set is old, but it's worth fixing. The picture jumps a lot and the sound fades out every now and then. Hey, where are your tools? Don't tell me you didn't bring them!

TONY: Well, you see . . . I —

MARCIA: Don't apologize. Just see what you can do. I'll bring you anything you need from my father's workshop. Shall I turn on the set?

TONY (*Clearing his throat*): I — I guess I should see where it's plugged in.

MARCIA: Back here. We'll have to move it out from the wall.

TONY: Let me do that. (*As they move set forward, he gets a coughing spell.*)

MARCIA: My goodness, you have a terrible cough.

TONY (*Choking and sputtering*): Yes! I know. I guess it's the climate. (MARCIA *runs to table for glass of punch.*)

MARCIA: Here, take a sip of this. (*As* TONY *drinks, his cough subsides.*) Drink all of it. The fruit juice will be good for you.

TONY: Thanks. This is delicious. Much better than cough medicine. What is it?

MARCIA: Just some fruit punch. Do you think it's sweet enough?

TONY: Perfect.

MARCIA: Maybe you'd better sit down for a few minutes till you catch your breath.

TONY: Thanks, I will. (*Sits*)

MARCIA (*Offering him plate of cookies*): Here, have some cookies.

TONY: Thanks. I didn't have much lunch.

MARCIA: I guess Mr. Young keeps you repairmen jumping this time of year. And then when people like the Corellis want two sets installed on the day before Christmas! Well, some people just have no consideration, that's all. (*As* TONY *chokes again*) Be careful of those cookies or you'll start coughing again. Let me get you some more punch.

TONY (*Rising*): No, no, thank you. I'm all right. I'll take a look at that set now and see what I can do. (*Moves set farther from wall and squats down behind it as* ANITA *and* JIMMY *enter left.*)

ANITA: Marcia! We have good news.

MARCIA: Hi, Anita. Hi, Jimmy. Help yourselves to the cookies.

JIMMY: Thanks, Marcia. Is this a sample of what we're getting tonight?

ANITA: Don't start stuffing yourself before you tell her the news.

JIMMY: I found an extra man for you, although I still don't see why you can't get that wonderful Tony Anita keeps raving about. I sure would like to see that guy.

ANITA: Maybe you can. (*Using binoculars*) Maybe he's over there now. (*Looking*) Hey, there he is. Look, Jimmy.

JIMMY: Where? Where? I don't see him.

ANITA: Right there by the window. He's moving a chair or something. Oh, Jimmy, don't you think he's the greatest-looking guy you ever saw? (TONY *raises his head above the television set and then ducks back.*)

JIMMY: I still don't see him.

ANITA: How can you miss him? He's the only person in the room.

JIMMY: But that's not Tony Corelli!

ANITA: It most certainly is! And he's a real Count!

JIMMY: That's no Count! That's Gus Flanders. He works for an interior decorator.

ANITA: It can't be!

MARCIA: Are you sure?

JIMMY: If you don't believe me, you can ask him yourself. He's the guy I invited to your party tonight.

ANITA: I can't believe it!

MARCIA: I *knew* Tony had dark hair.

ANITA: And I admired his Riviera tan!

JIMMY: Riviera? Gus has never been out of Bakersville except to the next town on holidays and weekends.

MARCIA: Then I've never seen the real Tony at all.

TONY (*Stepping forward*): I think your set will work now, miss. Shall I turn it on?

MARCIA: You startled me! I forgot you were there. This is the television repairman Mr. Young sent us. (*To* TONY) I'm sorry I don't know your name.

TONY: Just call me Mr. Fix-It!

MARCIA: These are my friends, Anita Page and Jimmy Hale.

TONY (*Beaming with mock courtesy*): Charmed, I'm sure. (*To* MARCIA) If you have any further trouble, just call Mr. Young. (BESSIE *enters, carrying dress on hanger.*)

BESSIE: I'm all set. The dress is ready to wear, and I've got some aspirin for Carlotta. We'll have her back on her feet in no time. (*To* MARCIA) Isn't it wonderful to see Tony again?

ALL: Tony!

MARCIA: Oh, no! It can't be!

ANITA: Not Tony Corelli!

JIMMY: But he's the repairman!

TONY: Not a very efficient one, I'm afraid. I didn't even bring my tool kit. But I managed to get it going.

MARCIA: Oh, Tony, I'm so embarrassed.

BESSIE: Don't tell me you didn't recognize Tony!

MARCIA: But he's changed so much, Bessie.

TONY: So have you. No braces on your teeth — no more pigtails.

BESSIE: I have to go next door. (*To* MARCIA) Their maid, Carlotta, is having hysterics over the new electric stove. Poor thing, she can't get the hang of it. I'm going over to see what I can do. Tell your mother I'll be back in plenty of time to start supper. (*Exits*)

ANITA: And we'd better go, too. I'm sure you and Tony have lots to talk about. It was good to meet you, Tony. Let's go, Jimmy.

JIMMY (*Shaking hands with* TONY): Tony, maybe I'll see you tonight after all.

ANITA: Jimmy, you're not in charge of invitations for this party.

JIMMY: I know, but something tells me Tony will be at the party tonight. See you all later! (JIMMY *and* ANITA *exit left.*)

MARCIA: Oh, Tony, I'm so ashamed. I wanted to call you, but, well . . . I guess I was waiting for you to call me.

TONY: Marcia, I'd have been over here long ago, but the doctor has had me in bed ever since we got here. The sudden change of climate gave me a bad case of bronchitis. This is the first day I've been out of the house.

MRS. HITCHCOCK (*Calling from offstage*): Marcia, where are you? Is Bessie back yet?

MARCIA: Oh, Mother, come and see who's here. (*As* MRS. HITCHCOCK *enters*) Look, Mother! It's Tony!

TONY (*Shaking hands with* MRS. HITCHCOCK): It's good to see you again, Mrs. Hitchcock.

MARCIA: Oh, Mother, he's been sick in bed, and I thought he was the television repairman, and he saw us using those binoculars, and . . . oh, Mother, the whole thing is impossible!

MRS. HITCHCOCK: I must say it's impossible for me to understand what you're talking about, but I'm certainly glad to see you, Tony. How's your family?

TONY: Terrible! We all have colds, Mother's upset, Gina is homesick, and Bessie's over at our house now trying to explain electricity to Carlotta.

MRS. HITCHCOCK: Oh, dear! I'm sorry to hear that. Is there anything we can do? (MR. HITCHCOCK *and* BILLY *enter left*)

BILLY: I'm sure I could fix it, Dad. Just let me try.

MR. HITCHCOCK: Do you want me to have to buy a whole new set?

MARCIA: Don't worry, Dad. The set has been fixed.

TONY: I think it will be O.K. now, Mr. Hitchcock.

MR. HITCHCOCK (*Beaming*): That's fine, young man. What do I owe you?

TONY: I've already been paid in punch and cookies, Mr. Hitchcock.

MARCIA: Dad, this is our neighbor, Tony Corelli.

MR. HITCHCOCK: Not that little kid who was always breaking our hedge on his way over here!

TONY: Glad to see you again, sir. (*They shake hands.*)

MRS. HITCHCOCK: And this is our son, Billy.

BILLY (*Shaking hands with* TONY): Glad to meet you, Tony. I've sure heard a lot about you.

MARCIA: Billy!

BILLY: Well, it's the truth. I'll bet if Marcia had known you were coming, she'd have spread out the red carpet for sure!

MRS. HITCHCOCK: Billy! That's enough.

MR. HITCHCOCK: Speaking of carpets reminds me. I thought your mother told you to take that (*Pointing to rolled-up carpet*) out to the garage.

BILLY: Will do. (*Shoulders roll of carpet*) Excuse me, Tony. (*As he brushes past* TONY, *he drops the carpet which unrolls at his feet.*) Oops! I didn't mean to drop it, Mom.

TONY: That looks familiar.

BILLY: It should. It came out of your house. (PAM *enters left in a dither of excitement.*)

PAM: Marcia! Mother! Guess who is coming down our walk this very minute. You'll die when I tell you.

MRS. HITCHCOCK: I hope not, dear. At least not until I've had the chance to introduce you to Tony. Tony, this is my younger daughter, Pam.

PAM: Tony? Tony Corelli?

TONY: That's right.

PAM: Why, I just looked out the window and saw your mother and father —

MRS. HITCHCOCK (*Breaking in*): Maggie? Coming here?

PAM: And she's bringing Gina.

BILLY: Gina? If she's coming, we need the red carpet for sure! (MAGGIE CORELLI *runs in, followed by* GINA *and* COUNT.)

MAGGIE: Ethel! How are you? Merry Christmas!

MRS. HITCHCOCK (*Embracing her*): Oh, Maggie! I'm so glad to see you! Why, Maggie Briggs, I believe you're crying.

MAGGIE: Look who's talking! So are you!

MRS. HITCHCOCK (*Wiping her eyes*): Come, I want you to meet my family.

MAGGIE: But I know them — every single one! Henry, of course . . . (*Shakes hands with* MR. HITCHCOCK) And this must be Marcia, and Billy, and little Pam. (*They greet each other.*)

TONY: And this is my Dad, and my sister, Gina.

BILLY: I'm certainly glad to see you, Gina.

COUNT CORELLI: This is a pleasure. Indeed, I think my wife and children would not have survived Christmas without calling on you.

GINA: I've been so lonely!

MAGGIE: Poor Gina, she's been terribly homesick. But all of us, all of us are lonely, especially because it's Christmastime. We felt as if we didn't have a friend in the world until Bessie came over and brought the cookies. Oh, Ethel, I just had to come over and tell you what it meant to me, having you send those cookies over to me! (BESSIE *enters.*)

MRS. HITCHCOCK: Oh, Maggie, it's all Bessie's doing.

MAGGIE (*Putting her arm around* BESSIE): And this blessed Bessie! She's brought Carlotta to her senses, and showed her how to work all the American gadgets, from the electric stove right down to the electric can opener.

BESSIE: Right now she's like a kid with a lot of new toys. When I left, she was opening cans right and left! Hey, where did that red carpet come from?

GINA: It looks like our old hall carpet.

BILLY: That's just what it is. I almost forgot — I was supposed to get it out of here. (*As he starts to roll it, he finds a note.*) Say, what's this thing stuck underneath? (*Stands*) It looks like an old letter. I can hardly make out the writing, but I think it's addressed to Maggie Briggs.

MAGGIE: To me? Let me see it. (*The others crowd around as* MAGGIE *opens it and reads.*) "Dear Maggie, I couldn't go to sleep without telling you my wonderful, wonderful news . . ."

MRS. HITCHCOCK: Maggie! That's the note I wrote — the invitation I slipped under your front door twenty years ago.

MAGGIE: Only you must have slipped it under the hall carpet instead, and it's been lying there all these years! Oh, Ethel, weren't we foolish to be upset over a little thing like that?

MRS. HITCHCOCK: We certainly were, Maggie. It was all a stupid mistake. But what better time than Christmas to make up our little differences? Let's forget it, and concentrate on having a good time!

BILLY: Give me a hand, Dad, and we'll get this carpet out of here.

MR. HITCHCOCK: No, Billy! I want that red carpet to stay right where it is!

BESSIE: Not right in the middle of the living room floor!

MRS. HITCHCOCK: It looks beautiful there! A red carpet's just right for Christmas and the guests of honor at our Open House tonight. (*With a curtsy*) Countess Margarita! Count Corelli, will you do us the honor?

COUNT CORELLI (*Bowing*): We will be delighted.

MAGGIE (*Throwing her arms around* MRS. HITCHCOCK): Oh, Ethel, you silly thing! We'll be thrilled to come.

TONY: Too bad you already have that extra man for tonight, Marcia.

MARCIA: Oh, Tony, please come. You too, Gina.

TONY: I wouldn't miss it.

GINA: I never thought I'd be going to a party tonight.

PAM: I guarantee you won't be lonely after tonight, Gina.

BILLY: Pam's right, Gina. There are lots of kids our age in the neighborhood, and I've invited them all to the party.

BESSIE: You know, I always did like a red carpet. There's something so warm and friendly about it. Too bad it's gone out of style.

MRS. HITCHCOCK: Gone out of style! Why, Bessie, it's the height of fashion. The Hitchcocks and the Corellis are just about to celebrate their first Red Carpet Christmas! (*Curtain*)

THE END

Star Over Bethlehem

By Graham DuBois

Long ago in Bethlehem, an innkeeper's family risked their lives so a child might be born in their stable. . . .

Characters

MICAH, *the keeper of an inn near Bethlehem*
ESTHER, *his wife*
ANN, *their daughter*
A MAID
DINAH, *an old woman*
JOSEPH
ABNER $\left.\right\}$ *shepherds*
JACOB
HEROD'S MAN
THREE WISE MEN
OTHER SHEPHERDS

TIME: *Early evening, long ago.*
SETTING: *The yard of an inn near Bethlehem. Exit right, into inn. Exit center back, into stable. Exit left, onto highway.*
AT RISE: ESTHER *is seated on a bench, facing the audience.* MICAH *enters from inn.*

MICAH: The inn is full again tonight, Esther. (*Jingling coins in his pocket*) We have never been so prosperous. In a few months we can afford to build an annex. You should be proud of your husband. (*Approaches bench*) Think of the money we will make! (*Sits*)

ESTHER (*Sighing*): That is all you ever think about, Micah.

MICAH: What else should an innkeeper think about?

ESTHER: Occasionally you might give a thought to others, like those people you turned away today just because they couldn't pay your price.

MICAH (*Indignantly*): What would you have me do, wife? I'm running an inn, not a charitable institution. (*Sound of joyous shouting is heard from offstage.*) Why are those foolish shepherds yelling so?

ESTHER: Because they are happy, I suppose.

MICAH (*Contemptuously*): Why are they happy? They earn hardly enough to keep body and soul together.

ESTHER (*Quietly*): There are other reasons for happiness.

MAID (*Entering; to* MICAH): Master, one of the guests wants to see you. He has a complaint. (*Exits right.*)

MICAH (*Rising impatiently*): Those noisy shepherds, I suppose. (*Walks toward right*) I'll go see what's wrong. (*Exits.*)

ANN (*Entering left*): I'm glad to find you alone, Mother. (*Approaching bench and looking about her*) Is Father around?

ESTHER: He went indoors just a minute ago. One of the guests was complaining about something. Why do you ask, Ann?

ANN (*Seating herself on the bench*): I have a secret to tell you, Mother.

ESTHER: Is it something you don't want your father to know?

ANN: Not right away. I'd rather have you break the news to him. He's going to be angry. Jacob and I are going to be married.

ESTHER (*Taking* ANN's *hands*): This is good news! Jacob is a good and honest man, even though he is a poor shepherd.

ANN: He is not as poor as Father thinks, either. Jacob has been saving his money. In a year he thinks he will have enough to buy his own flock, and then we will be married.

ESTHER: I hope you will be happy, daughter. I believe you will. I only wish your father would agree with me.

ANN: I know he won't. That's why I want you to tell him, Mother.

ESTHER: I will. I will tell him just as soon as I can.

ANN: You ought to see the shepherds tonight. I have been out in the fields with Jacob and the others. I have never seen them so happy. They say the greatest event in the history of Bethlehem will occur tonight.

ESTHER: Did they tell you what it would be?

ANN: Not exactly, Mother. They said that a new day was coming for all the poor and oppressed of the world. There will be only peace and justice and love on earth.

ESTHER (*Sighing*): I wish it could be true. How did the shepherds think of such a thing?

ANN: They said some wise men in Bethlehem told them. At first I doubted, just as you do now. And then suddenly — I know not how — my belief grew strong and I was as happy as the shepherds. I was singing as I started home across the fields. (*Suddenly serious*) Then something happened to spoil that happiness.

ESTHER (*Patting* ANN's *knee gently*): Tell me about it, dear.

ANN: It was that other shepherd, Abner. I met him on the way home. His face was dark and he scowled at me. I spoke to him, but he would not answer. I think he has heard I am to marry Jacob, and he's jealous.

ESTHER: I've never liked that Abner. (*Rising*) But don't worry, dear. Everything will be all right. (*Walking toward right exit*) I'll see if I can find your father. (*Exits*)

ABNER (*Entering left*): Ann, there you are! Still happy about your precious Jacob, I suppose?

ANN: Why shouldn't I be happy?

ABNER: Because something is going to happen to Jacob before very long.

ANN: What do you mean?

ABNER: You saw him out there in the fields with the other shepherds, shouting and laughing and talking about a new ruler who is coming. Well, Herod likes no ruler but himself. If his men hear what those simpletons are saying, they won't like it.

ANN: But how can they hear it? (*Rising in sudden comprehension*) Oh, Abner, you wouldn't tell the soldiers, would you?

ESTHER (*Entering right*): Why, what's wrong out here? What has disturbed you, daughter? (*To* ABNER) Is it you who upset her?

ABNER: You will be upset, too, my fine lady. There's trouble ahead for you. I'll get even with both of you. (*Exits left*)

ANN: Oh, Mother, what does he mean? A little while ago I was so happy, and now I am troubled and afraid. I am sure that Jacob is in danger.

ESTHER (*Putting her arm about* ANN's *shoulder*): Calm yourself, my child. (*Leads her to bench and sits, draw-*

ing Ann *down beside her*) Abner loves to hear himself talk. He will probably forget his words once he is out of sight of the inn.

Ann (*Rising and kissing* Esther*'s forehead*): I wish I could be as cheerful about it as you are. (*Walks toward left exit*) Abner threatened us both, you know.

Esther (*Snapping her fingers*): That for Abner's threats! Where are you going? Not following that scamp, I hope.

Ann: No, Mother. I'm going out on the highway to watch for a star.

Esther: A star? What star?

Ann: A star the shepherds said would soon rise over the horizon near Bethlehem. (*Exits*)

Esther (*Shaking her head*): Poor, credulous child! (Micah *enters right.*) She believes everything that anybody tells her.

Micah (*Walking to bench*): Who is credulous? (*Sits*)

Esther: Our daughter Ann. She was here a little while ago, telling me a wild story about a new earth.

Micah (*As if thinking aloud*): There seem to be many people credulous tonight. I have heard the same story before.

Esther: You have? Where?

Micah: Right here at the inn, from one of the guests. Do you remember that richly clad fellow who came this afternoon?

Esther: Yes. He said he was to wait here until two others arrived in Bethlehem.

Micah (*Nodding*): That's the one. They are wise men from the East. He carried a beautiful little casket with him. Remember? (Esther *nods*) Well, he showed me its contents a few minutes ago — gold, pure gold. He told me it was a gift for a king, and when I asked him

what king, he said a king who was to be born somewhere in Bethlehem tonight.

ANN (*Entering left; upset*): Father, they have nowhere to
go!

MICAH: What are you talking about, child?

ANN (*Pointing left*): A man and his wife and a donkey
out there by the roadside. They wanted to stay here tonight, but I told them there was no room at the inn.

MICAH: You did the right thing, my child. We haven't
a corner left.

ANN: But the man was so old and feeble, and his wife so
tired. I'm afraid they will not be very comfortable in
the stable. The woman is with child.

MICAH (*Astonished*): In the stable? You don't mean to
say that you —

ANN: Yes, Father, I took them into the stable. Don't be
angry with me. You would have done the same thing
if you had seen them. There is something about that
woman's face that makes me ashamed of all that is
petty and mean.

MICAH (*Shaking his head angrily*): But you know it is
against the law to shelter vagabonds. The penalty for
offenders is severe.

JOSEPH (*Entering center*): Good evening, sir. Your daughter told my wife and me that there was no room at the
inn.

MICAH: She was right. We have been full since sundown.
You had better be on your way.

JOSEPH: She was good enough to tell us that we could
use the stable. We appreciate it. How much shall we
pay you?

MICAH: I have never rented my stable before. Still, it's
not a bad idea. How much could you offer?

JOSEPH: Not much; we are very poor. (*Puts his hand into*

his pocket) But we always pay our way. What is your price?

ESTHER (*Seizing* MICAH*'s arm*): No, Micah, no!

MICAH: In order to conform to the law I must accept something. Give me a piece of silver.

JOSEPH (*Astonished*): A piece of silver! To sleep on the straw of a stable?

MICAH (*Firmly*): That is my price.

JOSEPH: It is too much. (*Hands* MICAH *a coin*) Because my wife is with child, I have no choice.

ESTHER (*Solicitously*): How is your wife?

JOSEPH: It is almost time for the baby. We were afraid that our child would have to be born by the roadside.

ESTHER: I wish we could find a better place than a stable.

ANN: Father, I have just thought of something. The baby will have no cradle. Could we use the manger instead?

MICAH (*Reluctantly*): I suppose so. But how could you fix the manger for a baby?

ANN (*Eagerly*): The men brought in fresh straw and hay just this morning. I could make it quite comfortable. (*To* JOSEPH) Come with me, sir.

JOSEPH (*To* ANN): I can never thank you enough. (*Follows* ANN. *As they exit center, a Christmas song is heard in the distance.*)

ESTHER (*Turning to* MICAH): How could you do such a thing?

MICAH: What are you talking about?

ESTHER: Charging that old man and his sick wife for a place in the stable.

MICAH (*Angrily*): It is against the law to shelter vagabonds. Besides, if I gave free lodging we'd be overrun with beggars.

ESTHER: I think the people in our stable are no ordinary vagabonds.

MICAH: Why?

ESTHER: Just now, I thought I heard distant music — so far off and faint it was that it seemed to come from the heavens. (*Looking upward and pointing*) And that star seemed to move until it came to rest over our stable. That must be the star Ann was talking about. How beautiful it is!

MICAH (*Looking upward*): It is high in the heavens. Strange that I hadn't seen it before. When did you first notice it?

ESTHER: Just about the time that old man was here. There was a sudden silence in the night, and then the music.

MICAH (*Laughing scornfully*): You did but dream. You are always hearing and seeing strange things that nobody else is aware of.

DINAH (*Entering left*): It is because your wife is in tune with the infinite when most people are blind and deaf. (*Walks toward bench*)

MICAH: Dinah, what are you doing here?

DINAH: I have come to warn you of dangers that lie ahead.

MICAH: What dangers?

DINAH: A short while ago an old man and his wife came here. You took them in.

MICAH: What if I did? There is no harm in that.

DINAH: She was riding a donkey.

MICAH: It's no crime to ride a donkey.

DINAH: Herod wants that donkey.

MICAH (*Amazed*): Herod — wants — a donkey? (*Laughs*) What a spectacle! The mighty emperor astride a jackass!

DINAH (*Quietly*): Herod doesn't want the donkey for himself; he wants him for the child of one of his favorites who took a fancy to the little beast.

ESTHER (*Puzzled*): I don't see how that concerns us.

DINAH (*Gently*): But it does, my dear. Herod's men will come here for the donkey.

MICAH: What if they do? We'll simply tell them that the donkey is not for sale.

DINAH: It is not as simple as that, my son. They will go into the stable; they will see the man and woman, and by that time the child may be born. They will recognize in him one mightier than themselves.

MICAH: What do you mean, old woman?

DINAH (*Solemnly*): The Son of God. The Prince of Peace.

ESTHER (*Awed but not convinced*): Here — in Bethlehem? In our stable?

MICAH: This is the wildest prophecy I've ever heard.

DINAH: I never make prophecies. People call me a soothsayer but I really am not; I am an interpreter.

ESTHER: What are you interpreting now?

DINAH: The words of an old prophecy, "But thou, Bethlehem, though you be little among the thousands of Judah, yet out of thee shall he come forth that is to be the ruler in Israel."

MICAH (*To* DINAH): It is a distinction, old woman, that would never be conferred upon us. Do you think that God would select a stable as the birthplace of His Son? You spoke of dangers ahead for us. What danger could there possibly be in this?

DINAH: Herod will seek to kill the child. He will leave no stone unturned to do so.

ESTHER: Are you interpreting now? Aren't you making a prophecy?

DINAH: No. I am interpreting Herod as I have learned to know him through years of his cruel rule. That wicked man —

MICAH (*Raising his hand and looking about him cau-*

tiously): Not so loud. The inn is full. There may be those here who would report to Herod anything you say against him.

DINAH: He will destroy anybody or anything that threatens his power. There have been rumors in Bethlehem all day. Many people are repeating the old prophecy. For the child will grow into a man. He may become a leader of multitudes.

MICAH: But how will Herod know that those people are in my stable?

DINAH: You have already answered that question for yourself. You said there may be people at the inn who would report them to Herod. I think someone will before very long.

MICAH (*Curiously*): Who is it? Tell me who it is and I will stop him before he gets started.

DINAH (*Rising*): It is too late. He was almost in Bethlehem when I met him.

MICAH (*Impatiently*): Give me his name, old woman.

DINAH: His name is Abner.

MICAH (*Stunned*): Abner? I trusted him!

DINAH (*Walking left*): He told me that he had seen the old man and his wife and the donkey go into your stable. (*Exits*)

MICAH (*Sinking down upon bench*): It is hard for me to believe. Why did Abner want to harm me? I trusted the rogue. I even favored him as a husband for my daughter. What reason could he have for betraying me?

ESTHER: He wants to avenge himself.

MICAH: For what? What have I done?

ESTHER: It is not you. He has done it because of Ann, our daughter, and because of Jacob.

MICAH: I can understand his resentment of Jacob, that scamp. But why Ann? She has always treated him kindly.

ESTHER: Ann has agreed to marry Jacob, and Abner is jealous.

MICAH (*Incredulously*): No! Jacob? That rascal, that good-for-nothing shepherd! Does she want to starve?

ESTHER (*Quietly*): She won't starve, Micah. Jacob is honest and thrifty. He has saved his money. Soon he will have enough to buy a flock of his own. Then he and Ann will be married.

MICAH (*Contemptuously*): Ann will die of old age before that day comes.

ANN (*Entering left*): Father, I have saved the donkey.

MICAH (*Surprised*): Saved the donkey? What are you talking about, child?

ANN: The donkey that poor woman was riding. She and her husband love him so. (*Approaches bench*) They both told me how good and patient he has been. When I met Dinah on the highway and she said Herod's men might be here any minute to take the poor little animal, I made up my mind what to do. I turned the donkey over to Jacob. He is going to hide him.

MICAH: But where?

ANN: In the cave. The one in the woods beyond the meadow. The opening is hidden by vines and rocks. Herod's whole army could never find him there.

ESTHER: But what about Abner? He may see Jacob taking the donkey into the cave.

ANN: No, Mother. Jacob was too careful. He made sure that Abner was on his way to the village before he took the donkey.

MICAH: What's to prevent the other shepherds from telling Abner? They're a talkative lot, you know.

ANN: They never will. Jacob asked them not to say anything about it, and they don't trust Abner any more than I do. (*Walks right*) I'll see if I can find something for that poor couple to eat. (*Exits right*)

MICAH: We may be in danger. (*Rises*) I know what I shall do. I'll tell that couple to get out of my stable.

ESTHER (*Laying a hand on MICAH's arm*): No, Micah, not that, I beg of you. It's too great a price to pay for our safety. I'd never forgive you. (*Points to gate, left*) It's too late now, anyway. (MICAH *sits.*)

ABNER (*Entering left, followed by HEROD'S MAN*): They are guilty, I tell you. They have broken the law. They have given shelter to two vagabonds from Nazareth.

HEROD'S MAN: From Nazareth, eh? People from that place are under suspicion. We have been warned to keep a special watch on them. (*To ABNER*) How do you know they are from Nazareth?

ABNER: I heard them talking to the daughter of this couple. She's the one that took the old man and his wife and the donkey into the stable.

HEROD'S MAN: The donkey? Are you sure they have the donkey — the one Herod wants?

ABNER: I'm positive.

HEROD'S MAN (*Reflectively*): Of course, if these people are vagabonds, we can seize the animal without any trouble; if they are not, we can offer a good price for it. (*To MICAH*) This fellow has made a charge against you, and it's my job to investigate. I must take a look into your stable.

MICAH: By all means.

ABNER (*Followed by HEROD'S MAN, exiting center*): You'll find the charge is true. I'll prove every word.

MICAH: That ungrateful scoundrel! After all we've done

for him. Just for the sake of revenge, and a few pence
thrown in, he will stoop to anything to ruin us.

ESTHER: Calm yourself, dear. He's not worth losing your
patience over. We ought to be thankful he's not the
one Ann chose.

HEROD'S MAN (*Entering center, followed by* ABNER; *to*
ABNER): You have proved a part of your case, but let
me ask these people some questions. (*To* MICAH) The
old man and his wife appear to be vagabonds, yet you
gave them lodging in your inn. (*Sternly*) You know the
law, don't you?

MICAH (*Rising*): I gave them nothing.

HEROD'S MAN: What do you mean, you gave them nothing? Are they in your stable without your consent?

MICAH: No, they had my consent.

HEROD'S MAN: What do you know about them? Where
are they from? Where are they going?

MICAH: They are from Nazareth, and they have come to
Bethlehem to pay their taxes.

HEROD'S MAN: That is all you know about them?

MICAH: That is all.

HEROD'S MAN (*Angrily*): And, with only this meager information, you gave them lodging in your stable?

MICAH: I told you, sir, I gave them nothing. The old
man had money. There was no room in the inn, and he
asked if they could sleep in the stable. I named my
price, and he paid it. (*Thrusts hand into pocket*) I
had never rented my stable before, but in these days
an enterprising innkeeper mustn't overlook any opportunity to pick up some extra money. (*Jingles money in
pocket*)

HEROD'S MAN: You have quite a reputation for being enterprising. (*To* ABNER) Well, blockhead, your vagabonds have turned out to be nothing but an old man
and his wife on their way to pay their taxes.

ABNER: There is something you don't know about them.
The woman is soon to have a child.

HEROD'S MAN: What of that?

ABNER: You have heard the story that is all over Bethlehem. They are saying that tonight, in our town, a child
will be born who will become king of Israel.

HEROD'S MAN (*Slapping his thigh and laughing*): What a
place for royalty to be born! (*Points to stable*) And
what parents for a king! (*Suddenly serious*) You are
the one we ought to arrest for giving false information.

ABNER (*Abjectly*): Please, sir, I thought it was the truth.
They looked like vagabonds. I didn't know they were
going to pay.

HEROD'S MAN: What about the donkey? You said there
was a donkey in the stable. We found none.

ABNER: There was one. I swear it. (*Points to* MICAH)
That man —

HEROD'S MAN (*To* MICAH): What do you know about
this donkey?

MICAH: I have seen no donkey on my premises.

ABNER: He's lying! A donkey was in the stable; I saw
him. They have probably hidden him in the woods.

HEROD'S MAN: If he's hidden, go find him and bring him
back here. If you don't return, it will go hard with
you. (ABNER *exits left.*) Stupid rogue! (*To* MICAH)
What he said about the rumor spreading through Bethlehem is true. We have been ordered to learn of every
woman in the vicinity who is about to become a
mother — especially those of high rank. Your inn has
always been an exclusive place. Is there any woman
here who is about to have a child? You had better hold
nothing back.

MICAH: I'm sorry, sir, but that's the kind of information
I don't get from my guests.

HEROD'S MAN (*Walking toward inn door*): Very well, I will get this information myself. (*Exits right*)

ESTHER: Oh, Micah, I'm so frightened.

MICAH (*Coming to bench*): There's no need to be frightened. (*Sits*) He will not ask the guests about the donkey.

ESTHER: But some of the rooms overlook the highway. The people there may have seen Ann leading the donkey into the stable. They may mention it.

MICAH: There will probably be no occasion for their telling Herod's man even if they did see her.

ESTHER: What if Abner should find the donkey and bring him back here? That man would say that we had deceived him, and heaven knows what he might suspect.

MICAH: Don't let us face that trouble until we have to. Abner may never find the donkey.

ANN (*Entering right with a pitcher of milk in her hands*): Who is that strange man walking about the inn asking questions?

MICAH: He is one of Herod's men. Did he question you?

ANN: He stopped me and asked me who I was, and when I told him that I was the daughter of the innkeeper, he told me to go on about my business.

ESTHER: Where are you going now?

ANN: I'm going to take those people some milk. They must be hungry. (*Exits*)

ESTHER (*Pointing to center exit*): Micah, we should not let her go in there at this time.

MICAH: Why not? She's just as safe there as she would be anywhere else.

ESTHER: But when that man comes out of the inn he may go to the stable. He will find her there, and suppose he should question her. He would have little trouble in getting the truth about the donkey from her.

MICAH: I think you are right. (*Rising*) I will go to get her.

HEROD'S MAN (*Entering right*): There is no prospective mother at your inn tonight — unless you're hiding somebody.

MICAH: I am hiding nobody.

ABNER (*Entering left; to* HEROD'S MAN): I'm sorry to keep you waiting.

HEROD'S MAN (*Angrily*): Don't stand there gibbering like an idiot! (*Approaching* ABNER) Where's the donkey? In your pocket, I suppose?

ABNER (*Frightened*): No. I couldn't find him. I asked the shepherds. They hadn't seen him.

HEROD'S MAN: Do you know why? There was no donkey to see. You are the only donkey that's been here tonight.

ABNER: Maybe he's back in the stable. (*Turns toward center exit*) I'll have a look.

HEROD'S MAN (*Clamping his hand on* ABNER'*s shoulder*): Stay where you are! None of your trickery. You're under arrest.

ABNER (*Stunned*): Under arrest? For what?

HEROD'S MAN: For giving the authorities misinformation.

ABNER: It's all true, I tell you — every word I said. Perhaps Ann, this man's daughter, brought the donkey back to the stable while you were inside the inn. She's in the stable now. I saw her as I passed.

HEROD'S MAN: I know she is. She told me where she was going. She was taking that couple a pitcher of milk.

ABNER: Ask her about the donkey! I know that she could tell you where it is.

HEROD'S MAN: Enough! I have done all the questioning I'm going to do tonight. (*To* ABNER) You've made me a laughingstock. Well, it's my turn to laugh now. I'll lock you up for a couple of months, so you can't cause any more trouble. (*To* ESTHER *and* MICAH) Sorry to have disturbed you. (*Exits left, taking* ABNER *with him.*)

ESTHER: I feel sorry for Abner. I never liked or trusted him, but I can't help feeling sorry for someone locked up in prison.

MICAH: I haven't any sympathy for him. He has what he deserves.

JACOB (*Entering left*): Good evening.

MICAH (*Angrily*): Jacob! There has been enough trouble here tonight. And now *you* appear!

ESTHER (*Quietly*): You are welcome here, Jacob.

JACOB (*To* ESTHER): Thank you. (*To* MICAH) I have come to tell you they are on their way. They will be here in a few minutes.

MICAH (*Bewildered*): Who are on their way? The inn is full. There is no room.

JACOB: They want no room at the inn, sir. I believe they will be interested only in your stable.

ESTHER (*Alarmed*): Only in the stable? You don't mean Herod's men? (*To* MICAH) They are coming for the donkey!

JACOB: No, they are not looking for the donkey. They seek a little child.

MICAH: A child? Whose child?

JACOB: The Son of God.

MICAH: Do you really believe that story?

JACOB: With all my heart and soul.

ESTHER: But we shall all be in danger. Herod will learn of this. We shall suffer.

JACOB (*Earnestly*): There are some things worth suffering for — even dying for.

MICAH: Who are these people you speak of?

JACOB: I don't really know, sir. From what I could see from the hillside, I would say they are men of importance. They are riding camels and they are attended by many servants. The shepherds rushed down from the hills to join them.

ESTHER: But how did they learn of the inn? Who brought them here?

JACOB (*Pointing upward*): They followed a star.

FIRST WISE MAN (*Entering from inn, carrying a small casket*): The time is at hand. (*Walks to left exit. The two other* WISE MEN *enter, carrying caskets. The three stand together conferring for a few moments and then walk to center stage, followed by a number of shepherds.*)

ANN (*Entering center*): A child has been born — a dear little boy.

FIRST WISE MAN: It is the Holy Child. (*Raising his hand for silence*) I have something to say of the utmost importance to all mankind. My companions tell me a rumor is spreading through Bethlehem that Herod plans to kill all new-born babies. The Child and His family are not safe here. Is there a man among you who is willing to risk his life to save the life of this Child?

JACOB (*Stepping forward*): I am. Take me.

FIRST WISE MAN: You know what it means? You must go with Him and His parents to Egypt. It means hardship and danger and perhaps even death.

JACOB (*Quietly*): I am ready.

FIRST WISE MAN: It means leaving those you love.

ANN (*Stepping forward*): He won't be leaving me. I am going with him.

FIRST WISE MAN: God bless you both. (*Leads* JACOB *and* ANN *to a position near the front of the stable*) You shall be the first to greet the King. (JACOB *throws his arm about* ANN's *shoulder and they kneel. The rest kneel slightly to the rear of them.*)

MICAH (*Holding back*): I'm not worthy even to look

upon Him. I would have turned Him away from my inn.

FIRST WISE MAN: Receive Him now into your heart. He will be happy to find a haven there. (*Leads* MICAH *to where the others are kneeling, and he and* MICAH *kneel together. A part of the stable wall is drawn aside, revealing the tableau of the manger. Lights go up, and a Christmas song is heard from offstage. As the curtain falls, all are in an attitude of adoration.*)

THE END

The Christmas Starlet

By Earl J. Dias

When a Broadway actress comes home for the holidays, her family and friends find that fame has gone to her head . . .

Characters

HENRY SAYRE
MILDRED SAYRE, *his wife*
CHRISTINE SAYRE, *their daughter, a twenty-year-old actress*
JEROME SAYRE, *Henry's brother*
OLGA KLEM, *a writer for* Trend *Magazine*
JOE MILLER, *a photographer for the magazine*
TOMMY SAYRE, *Christine's fifteen-year-old brother*
ROBERT HOLM, *a teacher of English at Lakeview High School*
LYDIA POND, *president of the Lakeview Dramatic Society*
PAULA LISS ⎫
ALICE QUIGLEY ⎭ *members of the Society*

TIME: *Morning, the day before Christmas.*
SETTING: *The attractive living room of the Sayre family in Lakeview.*

AT RISE: MR. SAYRE *is adjusting the Christmas tree decorations.* MRS. SAYRE *sits in chair, at left of table, knitting.*

MR. SAYRE (*Standing off and looking critically at tree*): There. Now, Mildred, that's what I call a Christmasy sight — even if I do say so myself.

MRS. SAYRE: Yes, it is pretty — it's a perfect setting for the holiday. (MR. SAYRE *sits near her.* MRS. SAYRE *looks at her watch.*) It's nearly ten, Henry. Christine should be back soon. Those people from *Trend* Magazine have really been monopolizing her. I won't be sorry when they leave this morning.

MR. SAYRE: It's hard to get used to having a daughter who's something of a celebrity.

MRS. SAYRE: It's nice to have her home for Christmas, of course, but the place has been wild since she arrived. Stories in the local paper, telephone ringing all the time!

MR. SAYRE: But, Mildred, having a big story in a national magazine like *Trend* can mean a lot in the career of a young actress.

MRS. SAYRE: I know. But Christine seems to have changed. I just wonder if overnight success will go to her head. Waking up one morning to find yourself hailed as the most promising young actress of the season must be an overwhelming experience.

MR. SAYRE: I suppose it is, although it's never happened to me. (*Laughing*) Small-town lawyers don't usually achieve overnight fame.

MRS. SAYRE: What I mean is that Christine has become so — well — superior. And hearing her call Lakeview a dull hick town compared to New York isn't exactly endearing to people here.

MR. SAYRE: It's hard to think of our daughter, who used

to jump at the chance to go to the local ice cream parlor, as a sophisticated New Yorker! (JEROME SAYRE *enters.*)

JEROME: Top of the morning to you, and merry day before Christmas. I've been out for a bit of a walk, and if my crystal ball is working properly, I predict we'll have snow before the day's over.

MR. SAYRE: Good to see you, Jerome. How are you?

JEROME: As the song says, "I'm dreaming of a white Christmas." It takes me back to our boyhood days, Henry. Lakeview was a good place to grow up in.

MRS. SAYRE: I wish you'd tell Christine that, Jerome.

JEROME: Why? What's my lovely niece been up to? (*Door center opens.*) Here's the lady in question now. (CHRISTINE SAYRE *enters, followed by* OLGA KLEM *and* JOE MILLER. JOE *is carrying a camera.* CHRISTINE *removes her coat, places it on table, and sinks wearily into chair.*)

CHRISTINE: Am I tired! (*With irritation*) We spent the whole morning visiting the haunts of my childhood. (*Pause; to* MR. *and* MRS. SAYRE *and* JEROME) You all remember Joe Miller and Olga Klem from *Trend* Magazine, don't you?

MR. SAYRE: Sure we do. Good to see you again. (*Greetings are exchanged.*)

MRS. SAYRE: Did you get any good pictures today, Joe?

JOE: Yes, we got some really great shots of Christine sitting in her old homeroom seat at the high school. Another down at the local ice cream parlor. And another on the high school stage where she got her start in the theater.

MRS. SAYRE: That reminds me, Christine. Somebody called again from the Lakeview Dramatic Society. They wondered if you'd change your mind and agree to present the Best Actress Award at the annual Christmas Pageant tonight.

CHRISTINE (*Impatiently*): Oh, Mother, must we go through all that again? I haven't come back to Lakeview to be put on display for the natives.

JEROME (*Quietly*): You're a native yourself, aren't you?

CHRISTINE: You know what I mean, Uncle Jerome. All they want is to get a good look at me. They don't really care anything about the theater, and they know next to nothing about it.

MRS. SAYRE: Maybe you're underestimating them, dear. You sound a little selfish, if you ask me.

OLGA: The kid's tired, that's all, and I'm ready to drop in my tracks, myself.

MR. SAYRE (*To* JOE): You must be tired, too, Joe.

JOE: All in a day's work.

OLGA: Joe has the constitution of a horse.

MRS. SAYRE: May I take your coats?

OLGA: No, we'll keep them on. We're just about finished here. The whole feature is planned — you know, the usual corn (*Dramatically*) — "Miss Christine Sayre, who was hailed by the critics for her fine performance as supporting actress in the Broadway hit, *Borrowed Beauty,* and for whom stardom is predicted, returns to Lakeview, her beloved hometown, to spend Christmas with her family. A simple, wholesome young woman, she has not been spoiled by the bright lights of the big city. Here she relaxes charmingly and gratefully amid the friends and scenes of her happy childhood." (*She shrugs.*) I wish I had five bucks for every local-girl-makes-good yarn I've had to pound out on my trusty typewriter. I could write that stuff in my sleep.

JEROME (*Ironically*): You don't sound as though you like your work, Miss Klem.

OLGA: It's a living. And *Trend*'s six million readers like their corn high on the cob.

JOE: Let's finish up here, Olga.

OLGA (*Going to* CHRISTINE *and putting a hand on her shoulder*): Just a couple more shots, Chris, and then Joe and I will be off. What we want now is a family group shot — parents, brother, uncle, whoever. Where is your kid brother — his name's Tommy, isn't it?

MRS. SAYRE: Yes, that's right. I'll get him. He's in the cellar doing some woodworking. (MRS. SAYRE *exits right.*)

JOE: I think having the family in front of the Christmas tree would make a good shot.

OLGA: You're a genius, Joe. That would be terrific! The homey touch is just right at Yuletide. Christine, will you and your dad and your uncle line up there? (CHRISTINE, MR. SAYRE, *and* JEROME *stand in front of tree.* MRS. SAYRE *returns with* TOMMY.)

JOE: Ah, here's Tommy now.

OLGA: Glad you could make it. We're going to make you immortal.

TOMMY: For Pete's sake, not another picture! You took Chris and me yesterday at the football stadium.

OLGA (*Sarcastically*): And it came out so well that eight Hollywood studios want to sign you. Come on, Tommy. Stand there (*Pointing*) between your dad and your sister. We want to get out of here as soon as we can. Joe and I want to do a little celebrating for Christmas, too.

JOE: O.K. Everybody smile, now. (*He aims camera and takes picture.*) Now, one more for good luck. (*Aims again and takes picture*)

OLGA: That does it — except for one thing. (*To* JEROME) Christine told us that you teach English at the university. Is that right?

JEROME: Right you are. (*In affected tone*) Dedicated to expounding the glories of Shakespeare and the evils of the dangling participle.

OLGA: Great. Then we ought to have a shot of you and Chris sitting here on the sofa. I have the copy all worked out in my sharp little brain: "Christine Sayre, the lovely young actress, discusses the literary merits of the script of *Borrowed Beauty* with her scholarly, college-professor uncle."

JEROME (*Sarcastically*): That's deathless prose, Miss Klem.

OLGA: I know. Why I've been passed over for the Nobel Prize, I'll never understand. O.K. Will you please sit here? (*Points to sofa.* JEROME *and* CHRISTINE *sit down on sofa.*) All right, Joe, shoot!

JOE: Right. (*Aims camera*) Here goes. (*He snaps picture.*) One more now. Ready? Good. (*He snaps another picture.*)

OLGA: That about wraps it up.

CHRISTINE (*Rising and going to* OLGA): I want to thank you, Olga, and you, too, Joe, for all your hard work.

OLGA: Think nothing of it. Just another job. The spread will appear in *Trend* in the next four to six weeks. People will look at the pictures and read my cornball copy and say, "My, isn't that Christine Sayre a sweet girl." Two weeks later, they won't be able to remember your name. So make the most of the publicity. If you get any movie offers or personal appearance bids, grab them. That's what national publicity is for. It's phony as a three-dollar bill, but what the fans don't know won't hurt them. (*Turning to* JOE) Come on, Joe. We'll go to the thriving center of beautiful downtown Lakeview. You can send your prize-winning pictures by wirephoto, and I'll phone in my story. (*She and* JOE *go to center.*)

JOE (*At door*): And Merry Christmas!

OLGA: Oh, I nearly forgot — Merry Christmas from me, too. (*They exit.*)

JEROME: Now, there's a cynical young woman.

MRS. SAYRE: I had the uncomfortable feeling that she was laughing at us all the time.

CHRISTINE: Oh, Mother, Olga is sophisticated, that's all. Besides, think what all this publicity in *Trend* will do for me. After all, just because I was a success in one small role doesn't mean that I've arrived, and this story may really pave the way to big things for me. It's the most important thing that's ever happened to me. (*Carried away*) I'll be sitting on top of the world when it's published, and I'll bet I get all kinds of wonderful offers.

TOMMY (*Sarcastically and in falsetto voice*): Oh, my, yes. It'll be just divine.

CHRISTINE: You don't have to be so fresh, Tommy.

TOMMY: I've just had a few lessons from your friend Olga.

MRS. SAYRE: Let's all get back to Christmas preparations, O.K.? Henry, will you help me bring the turkey up from the basement refrigerator? It's enormous.

MR. SAYRE: I'll be happy to help. I'm a turkey man from way back. (MR. *and* MRS. SAYRE *exit left.* JEROME *and* CHRISTINE *sit on sofa.* TOMMY *sits in chair left.*)

TOMMY (*Sighing*): I'm sure glad to see the last of Olga and Joe. They've been cutting into the work I'm doing on my model airplane.

CHRISTINE (*Laughing*): Don't let us keep you from your

artistic endeavors. (*Good-naturedly*) Back to the cellar with the rest of the termites.

TOMMY (*With sarcasm*): Very witty. You're a riot, Chris. The funniest actress in New York. But I'm going to stay up here a while. (*Stretching out in chair*) We creative artists have to relax occasionally. Besides, we're going to have another visitor.

JEROME: A visitor, Tommy?

TOMMY: Yes. Mr. Holm — my English teacher. He's a great guy.

CHRISTINE: Holm? Never heard of him.

TOMMY: He's new since your time. You're no spring chicken, you know.

CHRISTINE (*Angrily*): Is that so? Well, I didn't know teachers socialized with you tiny tots.

TOMMY: Oh, he's not coming to see me. He's coming to see *you*, Chris. I invited him.

CHRISTINE (*Annoyed*): Oh, you did, did you? Now look here, Tommy Sayre. The story in the paper was bad enough. I don't want the whole town descending on me.

TOMMY: Don't be so touchy. Mr. Holm's directing the Christmas pageant, and I thought if he could get to talk to you, he might be able to change your mind about presenting that Best Actress Award.

CHRISTINE (*Angrily*): That does it! I don't intend to spend my valuable time talking to small-town high school teachers. And I've already made it quite clear that I don't intend to be there for this provincial little pageant.

TOMMY (*Also angrily*): Wait a minute! Mr. Holm may teach in Lakeview, but he knows a lot about Broadway. He has a book on the theater coming out in the fall, and he reviews summer theater productions for the newspaper. I'll bet he knows more about the theater than you do.

CHRISTINE (*Laughing sarcastically*): Don't be silly, Tommy. Lakeview isn't exactly a citadel of culture, you know. It wasn't until I got to New York that I realized how wonderful and absorbing real theater can be.

TOMMY (*Rising*): I've changed my mind. I *will* go back to the cellar. Things are more pleasant down there. (*Goes toward right*) When Mr. Holm arrives, call me and I'll come up again.

CHRISTINE: You can come up and act as his guide right through that door. (*She points to door.* TOMMY *ignores her and exits.*) He certainly can be exasperating.

JEROME: Chris, your attitude strikes me as most peculiar. Obviously, the hometown folks are proud of you and admire you. They only want to bask in your reflected glory. That accounts for this invitation to make the award at the Christmas Pageant. I don't see why you're not cooperating.

CHRISTINE: Just what do you want me to do, Uncle Jerome? Walk through the streets of Lakeview shouting, "Look! Here I am! Christine Sayre of the cast of *Borrowed Beauty.* You may shake my hand!"

JEROME (*Smiling*): Why not? Everyone has read all about you. They'd probably get a kick out of it.

CHRISTINE (*Scornfully*): And I thought you were a sophisticated man.

JEROME: A man can be sophisticated and human, too.

CHRISTINE (*Testily*): What is that supposed to mean? You're saying I'm not human just because I don't want to be ogled by a lot of people, aren't you? There's nothing wrong with wanting privacy, Uncle Jerome.

JEROME (*Sarcastically*): I noticed you didn't exactly turn your back on the *Trend* Magazine entourage.

CHRISTINE: That's different. That *Trend* story will make my career.

JEROME: You know, Chris, you're suffering from what I like to call "big-city snobitis." I know all about it. I once had the disease myself.

CHRISTINE: Uncle Jerome, don't play psychiatrist.

JEROME: I'm not. But listen to this. After I had done my graduate work in English and acquired my Ph.D., I thought I knew everything and that only in the world's great centers of learning could I find anyone sufficiently literate to understand my profound observations. Then, while I was driving through the West, I happened to spend the night in a little mining town. I got into a long talk with an old fellow with a scraggly beard and skin tanned the color of leather. He chewed tobacco, and most of his teeth were missing.

CHRISTINE (*Sarcastically*): He sounds delightful.

JEROME: Let me finish. You know what? That old fellow knew as much about Mark Twain, one of my specialties, as I did. He'd been reading Mark Twain all his life and could quote him. What's more, he knew what he was talking about. I learned a lesson from that old man. It's not where people live that counts; it's the people themselves. Think it over, Chris.

CHRISTINE: I suppose your message is that there may be tobacco-chewing old fellows in Lakeview.

JEROME: Just think of the old fellow as a symbol, Chris. After all, this is the Christmas season. (MR. *and* MRS. SAYRE *enter at left.*)

MRS. SAYRE: A car just stopped out front.

MR. SAYRE: Looks to me like Mr. Holm.

CHRISTINE (*Smiling*): Does he chew tobacco?

MR. SAYRE: What kind of question is that? Mr. Holm is a bright, good-looking young man.

JEROME: Maybe he'll prove to be the bearded old fellow in your life, Chris.

CHRISTINE: I doubt it.

MRS. SAYRE: What is all this? Mr. Holm isn't old, and he doesn't have a beard.

JEROME: Just a little private joke between Chris and me, Mildred. (*Doorbell rings.* MRS. SAYRE *goes to door and opens it.* MR. HOLM *enters.*)

MR. HOLM: Hello, Mrs. Sayre.

MRS. SAYRE: Good morning, Mr. Holm. It's nice to see you.

MR. SAYRE: Merry Christmas. Come in, and take off your coat.

MR. HOLM: I won't be staying long. I hope I can accomplish what I want to in a short time. (*Going to sofa*) You're Christine Sayre, of course. I recognize you from your photographs. I'm Robert Holm. (*He shakes hands with her.*)

CHRISTINE: Yes, Tommy has told me about you, Mr. Holm.

MR. SAYRE: Mr. Holm, I don't think you know my brother, Professor Jerome Sayre.

MR. HOLM (*Shaking* JEROME*'s hand*): I certainly know him by reputation. (*To* JEROME) I've read your excellent book on American fiction, Professor Sayre.

JEROME (*Smiling*): Splendid. I'm glad somebody read it. It didn't exactly make the best-seller list. (TOMMY *enters.*)

TOMMY: Hi, Mr. Holm. Glad you could make it.

MR. HOLM: Hello, Tommy.

TOMMY: Mr. Holm wants to talk with Chris.

MRS. SAYRE: In that case, we'll make ourselves scarce.

I have plenty to do. Nice to have seen you, Mr. Holm. (*She exits left.*)

MR. SAYRE: I have some work to do on a brief. I'm afraid that the law marches on — even at Christmastime. (*He exits left.*)

JEROME (*Standing up*): I think I'll run along . . .

CHRISTINE (*Quickly*): I'd like you to stay, Uncle Jerome. I'm sure that you and Mr. Holm have a great deal in common. (JEROME *sits down again.* MR. HOLM *sits left of table,* TOMMY *at right.*)

TOMMY: Is the Pageant all set?

MR. HOLM: It's come along very well. You may be interested to know, Professor Sayre, that we've adapted one of Dickens' lesser-known Christmas stories for our Pageant.

JEROME: Fine. It ought to be a welcome change from "A Christmas Carol."

MR. HOLM: Anyway, it has the same message as "A Christmas Carol." The main idea is that in the Christmas season, we should overcome any selfish traits of character we have and consider the feelings and welfare of others.

JEROME (*Pointedly looking at* CHRISTINE): That's a good message for any season of the year.

MR. HOLM: Anyway, Miss Sayre, I know you're probably busy, and I don't want to take up much of your time. I suspect that Tommy has told you why I'm here.

TOMMY: I gave her a briefing.

CHRISTINE: Yes, Mr. Holm, Tommy did tell me. I don't want to seem difficult, but I'm afraid you're wasting your time. You see, I'm very tired. After completing a 35-week run in *Borrowed Beauty*, I came home to relax completely for a week or two.

MR. HOLM: That's understandable.

CHRISTINE: I vowed that when I came home, I wouldn't attend a lot of social functions. I have quite enough social life in New York.

TOMMY: Just a social butterfly — that's Chris.

CHRISTINE: Your witty comments aren't necessary, Tommy.

MR. HOLM (*Earnestly*): This pageant really wouldn't take up much of your time, Miss Sayre. You don't even have to see it if you don't want to. I suppose that as a professional actress, you look with a somewhat jaundiced eye on amateur productions. But all you'd have to do would be to make a brief appearance at the end of the pageant and to present the Lakeview Dramatic Society's award for the best actress of the year.

CHRISTINE: Really, Mr. Holm, I'd rather not.

MR. HOLM: Everyone will be disappointed. Having a Broadway actress on hand would have been a great thrill. I thought perhaps I could persuade you to reconsider, but I can see you won't.

CHRISTINE: Mr. Holm, let me be very frank with you. I suspect Lakeview's residents don't know or care much about the theater. They probably think of me as some kind of freak — a local girl who "made good" on Broadway. (*Haughtily*) I don't want my privacy invaded. If they want to see me, they can see me in *Trend* Magazine.

MR. HOLM (*Earnestly*): Miss Sayre, the members of the Society are really very proud of you.

CHRISTINE: I'm sorry. The answer is still no.

JEROME: Are you sure, Chris?

CHRISTINE (*Firmly*): Absolutely sure.

MR. HOLM: Well, you can't blame a man for trying. Tommy did warn me that he didn't think you'd agree.

CHRISTINE: For once in his life, Tommy was right.

TOMMY: Don't pay me a compliment, Chris. It might go to my head. (*Doorbell rings.* TOMMY *goes to center door and opens it.* MRS. LYDIA POND, PAULA LISS, *and* ALICE QUIGLEY *enter.* MRS. POND *is carrying a large square package wrapped in Christmas paper.*)

MR. HOLM (*Rising*): Why, Mrs. Pond, Paula, Alice . . . I'm certainly surprised to see you here!

TOMMY: Hi, Mrs. Pond.

MR. HOLM (*Uncomfortably*): Miss Sayre, I'd like you to meet some members of the Lakeview Dramatic Society — our president, Mrs. Lydia Pond, Miss Paula Liss, and Miss Alice Quigley. (*Ad lib greetings are exchanged.*)

CHRISTINE (*Curtly, almost rudely*): How do you do?

MR. HOLM: And, of course, you know Professor Sayre.

JEROME (*Trying to cover* CHRISTINE*'s rudeness*): How nice to see all of you!

MR. HOLM: What brings you here? I thought you'd all be at rehearsal.

MRS. POND: Well, Robert, when we learned that Miss Sayre could not accept our invitation to the Pageant, we just decided that we must drop by. You know why, of course.

MR. HOLM: Oh, yes. That *is* a rather important matter.

PAULA: It certainly is.

ALICE: It's something we've all looked forward to.

PAULA: Mrs. Pond will do the honors as president of the Society.

MRS. POND (*Rather importantly*): A pleasure. I'm just filled with the Christmas spirit today. We've brought over a little something for you, Miss Sayre. A sort of gift from the hometown folks because we're so delighted by your success. You know, most of us in the Society have followed your career closely. In fact, a group of us saw you in *Borrowed Beauty*.

PAULA: It was a wonderful performance.

CHRISTINE (*Surprised*): You saw me? Then why didn't you come backstage?

MRS. POND: For two good reasons. First of all, we didn't think you'd want to be bothered by a lot of chattering folks from back home.

ALICE (*Laughing*): And some of us can really chatter.

MRS. POND: Also, you looked very tired that night. We felt it would be unkind to impose on you.

CHRISTINE (*Softening*): Just when did you see the play?

PAULA: In late September.

CHRISTINE: I *was* tired then. I had just had a bout with a virus.

JEROME: I must say you folks are very thoughtful.

MRS. POND: Anyway, this is for you.

CHRISTINE: Thank you. (*She opens it.*) Why, it's a scrapbook!

MR. HOLM: Paula can tell you all about it.

PAULA: You see, when you opened in *Borrowed Beauty*, Miss Sayre, and did so well, the members of the Dramatic Society collected every newspaper and magazine review of *Borrowed Beauty* we could. (*As* CHRISTINE *leafs through book*) We thought that if we had all the reviews bound in a nice leather volume, the collection would make the right sort of Christmas present for a rising young actress.

CHRISTINE: This is beautiful. (*Genuinely touched*) I just don't know how to thank you.

MRS. POND: The whole town was in on it. Sam Craig, the printer, bound the volume. The art work on the inside cover was done by one of the high school art classes.

ALICE: And the Mayor issued a special proclamation — you'll find it reproduced on the last page — expressing the admiration and gratitude of Lakeview's citizens.

MRS. POND: Of course, we're disappointed that you won't be at the Pageant.

MR. HOLM: You see, Miss Sayre, it was the Society's intention to make this presentation to you at the Pageant.

PAULA: But we understand. We know you want to enjoy your vacation and your privacy.

TOMMY (*Ironically*): Yes, my sister needs a long rest.

JEROME (*Also ironically*): Talent must be protected. (CHRISTINE *places book beside her on sofa. She is obviously overcome emotionally.*)

CHRISTINE: I'm at a complete loss for words (*Smiling weakly*) — which is unusual for an actress. This is such a complete surprise — and it's just about the nicest Christmas present I've ever had in my entire life. (*Suddenly*) I have a wonderful idea. (*She begins to wrap the book again in its Christmas paper.*)

TOMMY: What are you going to do? Exchange it for something else? I thought you said you liked it.

CHRISTINE (*Continuing the wrapping*): I do — I love it.

PAULA (*Bewildered*): I don't understand, Miss Sayre.

CHRISTINE (*Standing up and going over to* MRS. POND): I want you to go through with your original plans — and present it to me at the Pageant. (*Smiling happily*) Suddenly, I don't feel tired at all. It must be the Christmas spirit you've all brought with you. I'll be delighted — and honored — to appear at the Pageant. (*She hands wrapped book back to* MRS. POND.)

MR. HOLM (*Excited*): Wonderful! That's the spirit, Miss Sayre.

PAULA: It will make the Pageant something really special.

MRS. POND: Everybody will be absolutely thrilled.

ALICE: We won't bother you any more this morning, Miss Sayre. And thanks for changing your mind.

CHRISTINE: Please — call me Chris. After all, I'm still one of the Lakeview natives. And it's I who should thank you.

MR. HOLM: But remember, you don't have to come by until the end of the production. About 9:30 will be fine. We don't want to impose.

CHRISTINE: Oh, no. I want to see the whole Pageant. (*Smiling at* JEROME) It's about time I became better acquainted with Charles Dickens. (MRS. POND, PAULA, *and* ALICE, *obviously happy, go upstage center.*) Merry Christmas, everybody!

MRS. POND, PAULA *and* ALICE (*At door; ad lib*): Merry Christmas! Same to you! (*Etc. They exit.*)

TOMMY: You know, Chris, there are times when I'm actually glad I'm your brother. And this is one of them.

JEROME: Ah, there's nothing so touching as brotherly love. (MR. *and* MRS. SAYRE *enter left.*)

MRS. SAYRE: I heard lots of talk out here. How did everything go?

CHRISTINE: Beautifully.

TOMMY: Chris is going to make the award at the Pageant, after all.

MRS. SAYRE: Good for you, Chris! I was hoping you'd come around.

CHRISTINE (*To* JEROME): You were right, Uncle Jerome. Old fellows do crop up in one's life.

MR. SAYRE: Do you mean Santa Claus?

JEROME (*With a satisfied smile*): I'll explain it all some time.

MRS. SAYRE (*Going left*): Well, it's back to the turkey for me. (*Turns, to* CHRIS) I'm proud of you, Chris. (*She exits.*)

MR. SAYRE: I have to drop in at the office for a little

while. Anyone want anything downtown?

CHRISTINE: No. Everything I want is right here. I'm perfectly content.

MR. SAYRE: Good. That's the way you should feel at this time of year. (*He exits.*)

MR. HOLM: I have to be going myself. (*Doorbell rings. TOMMY goes to center door and opens it. OLGA KLEM and JOE MILLER enter. Both look dejected.*)

CHRISTINE: Olga! Joe! I thought you'd left already.

OLGA (*Coming to center and speaking gloomily*): Chris, I've got bad news for you . . . . (*She breaks off and looks quizzically at MR. HOLM.*) You've got company. Shall I come back later?

JEROME: It's all right. Mr. Holm is a family friend.

CHRISTINE: What's the matter?

OLGA: Well, there isn't going to be any story in *Trend*. I phoned the story in to Ted Martin, the editor, and he had the colossal nerve to say that the story just won't do.

JOE: And after all that backbreaking work.

CHRISTINE: But why?

OLGA: Ted says the story lacks punch, that it's too pat, too ordinary, no sentiment. He says a local-girl-makes-good yarn needs some extra gimmick that your story just doesn't have. (*Sighing*) Look, I'm really sorry about this. I know what the story could have meant to you. I don't really have a heart of stone, and I have some professional pride, too. I don't like to see my stuff rejected.

JOE (*Sighing*): And those terrific photographs — all down the drain.

MR. HOLM (*To OLGA*): Your editor thinks Miss Sayre's story needs more human interest. Right?

OLGA: That's just about it.

CHRISTINE: How could we get him to change his mind?

JOE: It'd take something very special to do that.

MR. HOLM: I don't pretend to be an expert on such matters, but I think that a recent development here gives Miss Sayre's saga just that extra gimmick you're looking for.

JEROME: Of course! You're right, Mr. Holm.

OLGA: Then let's have it. I'm telling you, though, Ted Martin is a tough nut to crack.

MR. HOLM: Just listen and see what you think. We have a Dramatic Society here in Lakeview.

OLGA: Now wait a minute. Amateur theatricals are a dime a dozen.

MR. HOLM: Let me finish. This Society is giving a Christmas Pageant to which Miss Sayre has been invited so that she can present the annual Best Actress Award.

OLGA: That's no gimmick.

MR. HOLM: Miss Sayre at first refused. Then three members of the Society arrived here. They had a present for her — a leather-bound volume of all the important newspaper and magazine reviews of *Borrowed Beauty*. They've been working on the collection for a long time. It's a Christmas present to express the admiration and affection of the whole community.

JOE (*Impressed*): Say, Olga, this sounds like real human-interest stuff to me. We could stay over, and I could get some shots at the Pageant and one of the scrapbook.

OLGA (*Slapping* MR. HOLM *on the shoulder enthusiastically*): I think you've got it, pal. It's just the touch we need for a story with heart. (*Goes toward phone on table*) I'll get Ted Martin on the phone, and if I don't convince him in two minutes, then my name isn't Olga Klem.

CHRISTINE (*Pleased*): Do you really think you can?

OLGA: You've already had one Christmas present today. Take it from me — this is going to be another. From little Olga to you — with love and a Merry Christmas.

JOE: Right. (OLGA *picks up phone and dials.*)

OLGA (*Into phone*): Operator, this is a person-to-person call to *Trend* Magazine in New York. I want to talk to an idiot named Ted Martin. He's the editor . . . . O.K., but make it snappy, will you?

CHRISTINE: This is absolutely the best Christmas I've ever had. It's so wonderful to be home for Christmas.

TOMMY: It's about time you felt that way.

CHRISTINE: And, Uncle Jerome, thank heaven for old men with scraggly beards.

JEROME (*Beaming*): It's my niece who said that.

OLGA (*Into phone*): Hello, Ted? This is Olga. . . . Now hold on a minute, tough guy. Just listen. . . . I've got just the touch the Christine Sayre story needs. . . . Yes, something new *has* been added, and if you let me tell it to you, I know you'll go for it, too. . . . Ready? (OLGA *goes on talking into phone, with her back to the audience, but what she says is inaudible during the following speeches.*)

JOE: Just keep your fingers crossed. When Olga believes in something, she goes all the way with it.

MR. HOLM: This time, it's really worth her effort.

CHRISTINE: She certainly is nice to do this for me.

JOE (*Cynically, but kindly*): You know, Christine, in our business, the story, like your show, "must go on." (OLGA *turns to face other characters, smiling broadly, as she hangs up phone.*)

OLGA (*Happily*): Well, folks, we did it. Ted thinks the new angle is great, and he's starting to make up the layout and set the headings for our feature.

CHRISTINE: It's super of you to give me this kind of break. (*Goes over and hugs* OLGA)

MR. HOLM: Don't forget, Christine, it's what you did that made it possible, when you decided to come to our Christmas Pageant.

OLGA (*A bit embarrassed; gently*): That's right, Chris. You gave me just the right lead for a future leading lady!

CHRISTINE (*Dreamily*): It's more than that to me — it's made me see what Christmas really means.

JEROME: And it's going to be the merriest Christmas ever.

ALL (*Happily, joining in general merriment*): Merry Christmas, everyone! (*Curtain*)

THE END

The Trouble with Christmas

By Paul T. Nolan

"Down with Christmas," say young Santa Claus skeptics, until they find a surprise guest in their midst — wearing a red suit. . . .

Characters

TAMMY
DEBRA
HARRIETT
THOMAS
RICHARD
MISS EMILY, *a little old lady*
SANTA CLAUS

SETTING: *A conference room. Downstage center there is a long conference table with five chairs around it. Up right there is a captain's chair with a small table next to it. Upstage center, against wall, is a larger table. There is a concealed exit behind it. Up left is a pile of Christmas materials, including a small fir tree in a stand, a folding cardboard fireplace, several boxes of Christmas tree decorations including ornament for top, white tablecloth, candlesticks and five boxes wrapped with Christmas paper. A rocking chair is a little down-*

stage from these articles. There are doors downstage right and left.

AT RISE: DEBRA, HARRIETT, THOMAS, *and* RICHARD *are seated around conference table.* TAMMY, *standing at end of table, is orating.*

TAMMY: And so, fellow committee members, I say the trouble with Christmas is —

DEBRA: You should say the troubles with Christmas *are.*

HARRIETT: That's right. What's wrong with Christmas is plural.

THOMAS: Christmas is commercial and phony.

RICHARD: Hypocritical baloney.

TAMMY: Even the music is bad.

DEBRA: The decorations are sad.

HARRIETT (*Strongly*): And Santa Claus is a cad.

THOMAS (*Turning to look at* HARRIETT): Santa Claus a cad! I wouldn't go that far. (TAMMY *sits.*)

RICHARD: Neither would I. (*Nostalgically*) When I was a little boy, Santa gave me a super electric train, with two tunnels.

HARRIETT: Don't be childish, Richard. Your father gave you that train. And he probably paid too much for it because it was Christmas. There is no Santa Claus, Richard.

RICHARD: Then how come he's a cad?

HARRIETT: That's *why* he's a cad!

RICHARD (*Dreamily*): My father broke my train. It was an accident.

TAMMY: You see, Richard? Harriett's right. Shoddy merchandise.

RICHARD: It was not! My father didn't need to break shoddy things — he could break good things. He was a very strong man.

HARRIETT: I'll bet your mother was stronger. Women are stronger than men. That's a proven fact now.

RICHARD: Oh, yeah? Then how come Santa Claus is a man?

HARRIETT (*Heatedly*): There is no Santa Claus.

TAMMY: But if there were, he'd be a woman.

THOMAS: My father is stronger than my mother, but she's smarter.

HARRIETT (*Rising*): Everybody, listen to me. We're getting away from our purpose. We are here tonight for just (*Pounds table with fist*) one reason: to get rid of everything that's wrong with Christmas.

TAMMY: Christmas is just another male chauvinist institution.

DEBRA: Right on, sister!

HARRIETT: Look, Tammy, do you think Christmas would be any better if Santa Claus were a woman?

RICHARD: I don't think so. Not with his white beard.

THOMAS: The witches in *Macbeth* have beards, and they're women.

HARRIETT: Tammy, can't you see what happens when we don't stick to the subject? We're all in favor of women's lib, peace, progress, and protection of the environment. But, tonight — on the twenty-fourth of December — we have only one cause. We're going to get rid of Santa Claus.

RICHARD: If he doesn't exist, why do we have to get rid of him?

HARRIETT: It's the idea we're going to get rid of. If Santa Claus really existed, we could just expose him.

DEBRA: Yes, we could be kind and retire him.

TAMMY: Or send him to Siberia. But since he's an idea, we've got to wipe him out.

DEBRA: Without mercy.

RICHARD: I thought we were in favor of mercy.

THOMAS: Not for bad ideas.

HARRIETT: Then are we all in agreement that Santa Claus must go?

DEBRA: I agree. (*Points at fir tree.*) He's mean to trees.

THOMAS: I agree. (*Points at packages*) He's all show — like those packages there. Gift-wrapped boxes with nothing in them.

TAMMY: I agree. Santa's a fake.

RICHARD (*Slowly*): I suppose I agree. But I'm not giving back that fine train he gave me. I've kept it all these years, and when I have a child, I'm going to pass it along.

HARRIETT: You do that, Richard. But not on Christmas, and don't tell your child it's a present from Santa Claus.

TAMMY: Just look at the evidence we've collected — all the empty trinkets of Christmas. (*Stands and crosses to tree*) When we put on our exhibit, people will really see what meaningless stuff this is. (*Holds up tree*) Look at this miserable little tree. (*Sets tree down; dramatically*) For that tree alone, Santa Claus stands condemned. (HARRIETT *joins her.*)

HARRIETT (*Holding up package*): And when we open these fake packages and the public sees there's nothing inside, everyone will agree with us.

DEBRA: Santa Claus must go!

RICHARD: Are you sure all the packages are empty? I was hoping that maybe I'd get. . . .

HARRIETT: They're empty, Richard. We wrapped them ourselves.

RICHARD: I know that. But strange things happen on this night. Do you remember what happened last year? We all agreed that Santa had to go, and then before the meeting was over, we were all singing Christmas carols.

HARRIETT (*Firmly*): It will be different this year.

DEBRA (*Standing*): This is the year we get Santa Claus.

TAMMY (*Chanting*): Let's get Santa! Let's get Santa! (*Begins to march around stage, holding tree, chanting. HARRIETT, DEBRA, and THOMAS quickly get in line and follow her, chanting loudly. RICHARD shrugs, gets up and starts to follow them, walking slowly and chanting without enthusiasm. Suddenly MISS EMILY enters. She is a little old lady, in Victorian clothes, carrying a gift-wrapped package which she puts with other packages. She begins to chant happily. Others stop their chanting and look at her in surprise.*)

MISS EMILY (*Chanting alone*): We're going to get Santa. We're going to get Santa.

HARRIETT (*Angrily*): Who are you?

THOMAS: What are you doing here?

TAMMY: This is a private meeting of young people to wipe out all the evils of the world.

DEBRA: Most of which were started by people of your generation.

MISS EMILY: I know and I agree. You're going about it in the right way. (*Chants*) Let's get Santa. Let's get Santa.

HARRIETT: Now, wait a minute. Who are you?

MISS EMILY: Why, I'm Miss Emily, just a little old lady passing by. But when I heard you chanting that you wanted to get Santa Claus, I knew I'd found what I was looking for. Santa Claus always comes to young people who want him, and I must see him tonight.

DEBRA: Miss Emily, I'm afraid you don't understand.

MISS EMILY (*Happily*): Yes, I do. I was young once, and every Christmas I waited for Santa to come. I always had a glass of milk and a few cookies for him. I want Santa Claus, too.

TAMMY (*Putting down tree*): We don't want him. We want to get rid of him.

MISS EMILY: Oh, I see. Well, before you send him to his next visit, may I talk to him? It's about my little niece, Sally. I thought she wanted a pink scarf, but today she told me she wanted a blue one. But when we wrote to Santa, we asked for a pink one. Now I must tell him it should be blue.

HARRIETT: Miss Emily, you still don't understand.

TAMMY: There is no Santa Claus.

MISS EMILY (*Smiling*): You're just fooling. I remember once a little girl wrote to the Baltimore *Sun* and asked if there were a Santa Claus. And the editor said — in the paper, mind you — "Yes, Virginia, there is a Santa Claus." Why, that same editorial is still being printed today.

THOMAS: He just wrote that to get people to buy his paper.

RICHARD: I don't know about that. Editors usually tell the truth. There are laws, you know.

HARRIETT (*Angrily*): Richard, stop being an idiot.

THOMAS: Miss Emily, we don't want to hurt your feelings. But we have investigated Santa Claus thoroughly.

TAMMY: Scientifically.

DEBRA: And objectively.

HARRIETT: And we agree, democratically, there is no Santa Claus.

MISS EMILY (*Peevishly*): There is so.

HARRIETT: Miss Emily, have you ever seen Santa Claus?

MISS EMILY (*Crossing to chair and sitting*): When I was a little girl, I wanted a china tea set. And my daddy didn't have any money, so he told me to ask Santa Claus. Christmas morning, there it was. That proves there's a Santa Claus.

RICHARD (*Nodding*): Just like the time Santa gave me a train — with two tunnels.

TAMMY: Both of you know where you got those presents. Your parents gave them to you and said they were from Santa Claus.

MISS EMILY: I don't believe my parents would have done that. I've heard people blame others for things that are bad, but I've never heard anyone blame someone else for something that's good.

RICHARD: That's right. My father always took credit for my good looks, and he blames my mother's side of the family for my brains. If my father had given me that train, he'd have told me.

HARRIETT: Well . . . I'll admit it's a little strange, and not normal psychology at all. That's another thing that's wrong with Santa Claus! He makes people behave strangely.

TAMMY: Just for one day, too. Everyone is disappointed later.

DEBRA: Miss Emily, you don't think those department-store Santas are real, do you?

MISS EMILY: Of course, I don't.

RICHARD: They're just Santa's helpers.

TAMMY: They're just a bunch of actors helping themselves. I know. My Uncle Charlie works every year as a Santa Claus, and he just tries to get kids to ask their parents for the rotten toys the stores are trying to sell.

MISS EMILY: That is disgraceful. Poor Santa Claus.

HARRIETT: There is no Santa Claus!

TAMMY: There never has been a Santa Claus!

DEBRA: There never could be a Santa Claus. (SANTA CLAUS *enters. He looks worn out, his beard is thin, and his suit is patched. All look at him in disbelief.*)

SANTA CLAUS: Excuse me. I thought I heard my name mentioned.

MISS EMILY: It's Santa Claus! It really is!

TAMMY: It is not. It's probably my Uncle Charlie.

RICHARD: It could be Santa Claus.

HARRIETT: It could not. There is no Santa Claus.

THOMAS (*Going to* SANTA CLAUS): What's the matter? You look sick. (*Takes his arm*) Let me help you to this chair, so you can sit down. (*Leads him to captain's chair.* SANTA *sits.*) Maybe we'd better call a doctor.

MISS EMILY: No, that won't be necessary. I know what Santa needs. (*Exits quickly*)

HARRIETT (*Concerned*): He does look sick. (*To* SANTA) Look, old man, we don't have anything against you personally. We know that you must need a job badly to dress up like this.

DEBRA: It really is terrible that people will make a tired old man dress like Santa — for the (*Cynically*) spirit of Christmas.

TAMMY: You Santa Clauses ought to unionize. This costume they gave you is terrible. It's full of patches.

SANTA CLAUS: Thank you, children, for your concern. I *am* tired. This job gets harder every year. I don't mind the long trip, but everyone seems angry at Santa these days. Why, tonight some children threw snowballs at me.

TAMMY: That wasn't very nice of them.

THOMAS: Look, don't you think we'd better call your family or friends to take you home?

SANTA CLAUS: Oh, no. I still have work to do. (MISS EMILY *returns with a glass of milk and plate of cookies. She puts them on the table next to* SANTA. *He takes a bite from one cookie and a sip of milk, then brightens, and suddenly recovers. He stands up straight and begins to laugh loudly.*) Ho, ho, ho! (*All step back in amazement.*) All right, children, I'm your old Santa again. Come and tell me what you want for Christmas.

RICHARD: Well, Santa, there's this book about trains that I've been wanting for a long time, but I don't know the author or title. I remember seeing it when I was a child . . . it has a red cover.

MISS EMILY: Santa, I don't want anything for myself, but —

HARRIETT (*Interrupting*): Richard — Miss Emily — have you two lost your minds? This isn't Santa Claus. It's just a tired old man, a victim of the commercialization of Christmas.

RICHARD: Just because you don't want anything for Christmas, Harriett, don't try to keep me from getting what I want.

HARRIETT: I want lots of things. I need an umbrella, for example. But Santa Claus isn't going to give me one, because there isn't any Santa Claus.

MISS EMILY (*Pointing at* SANTA): There he is.

HARRIETT: He's an old man with a fake beard and a patched costume. (*Starts toward* SANTA) I'll pull off his beard and you can see for yourself.

SANTA CLAUS (*Covering his beard with his hands*): Please, young lady, not you, too! This is a real beard, but all evening people have been pulling it to prove it isn't. Soon, I won't have anything left.

HARRIETT: All right. The beard may be real, but you're not.

SANTA CLAUS: Would you believe me if I said I were Santa Claus?

MISS EMILY: I would. I do!

RICHARD: I might. I'd like to.

HARRIETT: I wouldn't, and nobody else would.

TAMMY: It would be unscientific to believe in Santa Claus.

DEBRA: And much too subjective for someone as objective as I.

THOMAS: It would be commercial, too.

HARRIETT: And definitely undemocratic. Four of us say you are not Santa Claus, and we're the majority.

RICHARD: I didn't say he was Santa Claus. I just said he might be.

MISS EMILY: Why, of course, he's Santa Claus. You can see by looking at him.

HARRIETT: I just see a man dressed like Santa Claus. It's just like this stuff here (*Indicates tree, packages*) — all pretense.

MISS EMILY: I rather like that little tree. Besides, it's real.

SANTA CLAUS: Why don't we all sit down and talk about this?

HARRIETT: There's nothing to talk about. Christmas is a big fake, and it's all because of Santa Claus.

THOMAS: That's right. If it weren't for Santa Claus, there wouldn't be all the commercialism.

DEBRA: The phoniness.

TAMMY: And the corny music.

RICHARD: I like the music — I really do. I like everything about Christmas.

HARRIETT (*Pointing to packages*): Including this commercial stuff here?

SANTA CLAUS (*Kindly, but with authority*): Now, everyone listen to me for a moment.

HARRIETT: I'm not going to listen to you any more.

SANTA CLAUS: I've listened to you and to millions like you. Don't you think it's fair to give me a chance?

THOMAS (*Going to chair at table and sitting*): That's fair. Let him speak.

DEBRA (*Sitting at table*): I guess it's only democratic.

TAMMY (*Sitting*): Maybe even objective.

RICHARD (*Sitting*): I want to hear him.

MISS EMILY (*Sitting in rocker*): He may tell us a story.

HARRIETT (*Bored*): I know it's going to be a story. (*To* SANTA) Well, go ahead. Talk.

SANTA CLAUS: Won't you please sit, too, Harriett?

HARRIETT: I don't want to sit. (*Pauses*) How do you know my name?

SANTA CLAUS (*Standing*): All right, then you can be Santa's helper. (*Waves his hand at Christmas objects*) These, I assume, are your evidence that Christmas and Santa Claus should be abolished. Is that correct?

HARRIETT: This stuff is just like you. Fake. (*Picks up tree*) Look at this tree.

SANTA CLAUS: Well, well. It does look a little puny. But let's give it a chance. Set it up on that table next to my chair, will you, please, Harriett?

HARRIETT (*Backing away, still holding tree*): I will not. I'm not going to be part of any stupid game! (RICHARD *gets up and goes over to* HARRIETT, *reaching for tree.*)

RICHARD: Here, let me take it, Harriett. (*He grabs one end of tree.* HARRIETT *does not let go.*)

HARRIETT: Stop it, Richard! (*They both tug at tree.*) You're being taken in by this old fraud.

THOMAS: Let Santa have a chance, Harriett.

DEBRA: You said you would.

HARRIETT (*Slowly letting go of tree*): I did, didn't I? Well, you win, Richard, but I'm not going to believe a word of it. (*Folds her arms and stands belligerently while* RICHARD *puts tree on table*)

RICHARD (*Stepping back to look critically at it*): It still looks terrible.

TAMMY (*Rising*): It needs some decorations. (*Gets box of decorations and joins* RICHARD) I'll trim the tree, and you can help me, Richard. (*They begin to trim tree.*)

SANTA CLAUS: I think that little tree might just surprise us.

HARRIETT (*Picking up cardboard fireplace*): I suppose this will give us a nice warm fire, too. (*Shakes her head*) I'd like to see you go up and down this fireplace.

SANTA CLAUS: Maybe I could, if it were set up.

DEBRA (*Rising*): I'd like to see that! I'll set it up. (*Takes fireplace, goes upstage and sets it up around table*)

SANTA CLAUS: Thank you, Debbie.

HARRIETT: Her name is not Debbie. It's Debra.

DEBRA: My grandfather used to call me Debbie. (*Pauses*) I liked it when he called me Debbie. You can call me Debbie, Santa.

HARRIETT: He is not Santa!

MISS EMILY (*Rising and picking up tablecloth*): I guess I'd better set the table.

THOMAS: Wait a minute! Wait a minute! What's happening here? This isn't supposed to be a Christmas party. We brought this stuff to show what's wrong with Christmas.

MISS EMILY: You can't show it unless folks can see it. Come on, Tommy, help me spread the cloth.

HARRIETT (*Indignantly*): You called him Tommy! Do you think he's a child?

THOMAS: Oh, I don't mind. (*Rising and helping* MISS EMILY *arrange cloth*) All right, we'll set the table.

HARRIETT: Thomas, not you, too!

THOMAS: Setting the table doesn't mean I believe in Santa Claus. It's just that we ought to be pleasant to each other. (THOMAS *and* MISS EMILY *place candlesticks, candles, and centerpiece on table.* DEBRA *finishes setting up fireplace and stands back to admire it.* RICHARD *and* TAMMY *put ornament on top of tree and move back. Lights dim and soften. Spotlight shines on top of tree.* HARRIETT *furiously turns her back;* SANTA *beams.*)

RICHARD: The tree looks good now, doesn't it?

TAMMY: Not bad. Not bad.

DEBRA: This fireplace looks almost real.

THOMAS: I wish we had some real food. We could have a feast.

HARRIETT (*Bitterly*): Are you all satisfied?

RICHARD: We ought to sing some Christmas songs. Come on, everybody, let's sing "Jingle Bells." (*Starts singing alone*) "Jingle bells, jingle bells —"

HARRIETT (*Striding to center*): Richard, be quiet. I'm ashamed of all of you. You're acting like children. And why? Because an old man tricks you into turning the conference room into a fake Christmas scene. I'll bet you all believe he's Santa Claus now, don't you?

RICHARD: I do.

HARRIETT: You would, Richard. But the rest of you — you have some sense. What has changed? Nothing. (*Picks up pile of packages*) These boxes are still empty, and you'll notice that our Santa Claus didn't come with a pack.

MISS EMILY (*Going to* HARRIETT *and taking boxes*): That's right. We forgot the presents. Richard, help me pass them around.

RICHARD (*Going to* MISS EMILY *and taking some packages*): I hope there's one for me. I didn't write to Santa this year.

HARRIETT: Everyone's gone crazy!

TAMMY: Oh, Harriett, we don't believe in Santa Claus. I just wanted to see if I could — well, I mean — I don't believe in Santa Claus. I'm not stupid.

HARRIETT: I should hope not.

MISS EMILY (*Reading tag on package*): The first one's for Tammy.

TAMMY: For me?

MISS EMILY: I'll put it at your place, dear. (*Puts package on table.* DEBRA, TAMMY, THOMAS, *and* RICHARD *sit at table.*)

HARRIETT: Who put name tags on those boxes?

THOMAS: I didn't . . . Well, only one, for a joke.

RICHARD (*Reading tag*): Here's one for Thomas. (*Sets package on table*)

THOMAS: I didn't make out that tag.

MISS EMILY (*Reading tag*): This one has Debra's name on it. (*Sets package on table*)

RICHARD: And one for Sally. (*Pauses*) Hey, there's no Sally here. Who's Sally?

MISS EMILY (*Taking box and putting it on table*): That's my niece. (*To* SANTA) I meant to tell you, Santa, Sally wants blue.

SANTA CLAUS: Oh, it's blue, Miss Emily.

MISS EMILY: Thank you, Santa.

RICHARD: Harriett, this one's for you. (*Puts package on table*)

HARRIETT: Just what I've always wanted — an empty box. This whole thing is making me furious!

MISS EMILY: And the last one's for Richard! (*Hands him package*)

RICHARD (*Taking package*): I'll bet it's that book on trains I've been wanting.

HARRIETT: I'll bet it's not. I wrapped that package myself, and it's just like you, Richard — full of hot air. (*To* SANTA) You're a very clever man, whoever you are. You ought to be selling patent medicine with a carnival. You really are a confidence man.

SANTA CLAUS: Thank you, my dear. I hope I am a confidence man. (*Moving to upstage center*) I hope that I can give people confidence — confidence in their goodness. Sometimes I seem old-fashioned and sometimes new-fashioned, and sometimes I may not seem to be telling the truth. There is a great deal of generosity in this world, but you have to have some confidence to see it. And you have to know how to look. Those are the real gifts I try to bring — faith in goodness, generosity, and vision. I'm sorry people use my name for things they shouldn't, but you don't throw away good money just because there are some counterfeit bills around, do you?

HARRIETT: Aha! I knew it would get to money.

RICHARD (*Unwrapping package and holding up book with red cover*): It is! It's the book on trains I've been wanting. Thank you, Santa Claus.

SANTA CLAUS: Well, Harriett, what do you say about Santa now?

HARRIETT: Not a thing. You're the big talker. You talk.

SANTA CLAUS: Do you want to tell Richard that Santa Claus did *not* give him that book?

HARRIETT (*Nervously*): I don't want to tell him anything. Besides, it's just a book.

RICHARD: How did you know I wanted this book, Santa? I didn't write you.

SANTA CLAUS: Harriett told me. (HARRIETT *looks up, startled.*)

RICHARD: Harriett! She doesn't even believe in you. How could she talk to you?

SANTA CLAUS: I guess she didn't know it was me.

RICHARD: I still don't know how Harriett knew I wanted that book.

DEBRA: There's no secret about that. You talk about that book all the time.

TAMMY: Harriett, did you give Richard that book?

HARRIETT: Why would I do a stupid thing like that? (*Points at* SANTA CLAUS) He gave it to him. He said he did.

TAMMY (*Tearing off wrapping paper and holding up framed picture*): It's the picture I've been wanting! (*Others begin to unwrap their presents.* HARRIETT, *intrigued, moves closer to table, watching.*)

MISS EMILY (*Holding up opened package to show blue scarf*): I knew it would be blue! Sally will be so happy in the morning.

THOMAS (*Opening box and holding it up to show ring*): Look at this ring, everybody! This is the one I've been telling you about. (SANTA *quietly goes to fireplace.*)

DEBRA (*Holding earrings up to ears*): These are the very earrings I wanted. (SANTA *exits through small door behind fireplace, unnoticed.*)

HARRIETT (*Bitterly*): Hooray for everyone. (*They turn to look at her.*)

TAMMY: What about your present, Harriett? (*Hands her package*)

HARRIETT (*Opening it slowly*): I know it's going to be an umbrella. But I'm not going to believe. I'm not going to believe. (*Opens package and holds up umbrella*) I don't believe it! (*Lamely*) Thanks, somebody. I sure can use this.

RICHARD: Thank Santa Claus. He's the one who gave it to you.

HARRIETT (*Dropping umbrella furiously*): I'm tired of this Santa Claus business. Somebody here was nice enough to give me a gift, and I said thank you. But it wasn't that character over there. (*Turns to point at* SANTA CLAUS) He's gone! Where did he go? (*They turn to look.*)

MISS EMILY: I'll bet he went up the fireplace. And I forgot to look.

TAMMY: He is gone. That's for sure.

DEBRA: He was here, wasn't he?

RICHARD: I saw him. At least, I think I saw him.

THOMAS: Well, Harriett, was he here? Is there a Santa Claus?

HARRIETT: There is no Santa Claus, and he wasn't here.

RICHARD: My book is here.

HARRIETT: Then somebody here gave it to you. There is no Santa Claus.

DEBRA: There couldn't be a Santa Claus.

TAMMY: And next year, we're really going to prove it.

DEBRA: Yes, just wait until next year.

THOMAS: That's what we said last year.

HARRIETT: Well, next year, we'll do it right. But since we are all here, and the place is decorated, and it is Christmas Eve, what do you say that we sing one Christmas song. There is one — just one — I almost like. (*Offstage music for a Christmas song is heard. All start singing;* MISS EMILY *goes slowly down left; music stops.*)

MISS EMILY: Merry Christmas to all, and to all a good night! (*Exits*)

ALL (*Calling after her*): Good night!

THOMAS: Next year, Harriett?

HARRIETT (*Shrugging*): Or the year after. You know, Christmas isn't so bad (*Firmly*) — as long as it only comes once a year. (*Lights fade to single spot on tree; music is heard from offstage; actors hum; and curtain falls.*)

THE END

The Christmas Visitor

By Anne Howard Bailey

The Remingtons grow fond of an orphan who arrives for the holidays, till they learn that he is not what he seems . . .

Characters

GERALD REMINGTON, *a well-to-do lawyer*
LAURA REMINGTON, *his wife*
THE BOY, *a sensitive child, about 10*
SALLY BARTLETT, *a neighbor, in her late 20's*
GRAVES, *the Remington butler*
MRS. LESTER, *a social worker*
JAMIE, *a boy, about 6*
CAROLERS

SCENE 1

TIME: *Christmas Eve.*
SETTING: *The Remington living room, a fashionably furnished room in an expensive apartment building in a large city. A large, elaborately decorated Christmas tree dominates the room. There is a stereo against a wall. A picture of Laura is on table near couch.*
AT RISE: *It is night, and the room is brilliantly lit.* GRAVES

stands on a ladder putting the finishing touches on the tree. GERALD REMINGTON *stands by the window, looking moodily out at the falling snow.* GRAVES *turns, and holds out a large tinsel star.*

GRAVES: Where do you want this, Mr. Remington?

GERALD (*Looking at* GRAVES, *then out window again*): I don't care, Graves. Hang it anyplace.

GRAVES: But sir, it's the star. (*He hesitates.*)

GERALD: Is there some special place for stars?

GRAVES: We always hang ours high, sir. To light you home by — and to wish on.

GERALD: Then let's not waste it, Graves. Even though I haven't any wish. Not a wish in the world. (*The door buzzer sounds.* GRAVES *starts down the ladder.*) That will be Mrs. Remington — beautiful, bright, wearing Christmas cheer like a tinsel halo. (GRAVES *puts down star and opens the front door at right.* LAURA REMINGTON *bursts in. She is beautiful, artificially gay, and laden with Christmas packages of all sizes and shapes.*)

LAURA: Hello, Graves. A merry, *merry* Christmas Eve!

GRAVES: Good evening, Mrs. Remington. The same to you, Mrs. Remington. (*He tries to take some of the packages, but she walks to the couch and lets them all spill out of her arms.*)

GERALD (*Sardonically*): Yes — the same to you, Mrs. Remington!

LAURA (*Surprised*): Gerald. I didn't think you'd be home.

GERALD: Even the legal business shuts down for the happy holidays.

LAURA: But I didn't plan on you for this evening. You always stop by the club.

GERALD: Oddly enough, most people rediscover home on Christmas Eve. And — this happens to be my home. Daily maid service, garbage disposal, elevators and all!

LAURA: Well, I can't help it if I have plans. The Civic Council is judging the Outdoor Christmas Tree Contest tonight —

GERALD: And of course, you, as Council president, must officiate.

LAURA: Naturally.

GERALD: Naturally.

GRAVES (*Clearing his throat*): Ah — would you like me to hang the star, Mr. Remington?

GERALD (*Picking up the star*): I think I'll reserve this last finishing touch for myself, Graves. Or better still, for Mrs. Remington. That will be all, Graves. (GRAVES *nods, takes ladder, and exits left.* GERALD *looks at the tree critically.*)

LAURA: Graves is rather artistic, isn't he? It's a lovely tree.

GERALD: By the tree's standards, or by ours? Maybe it doesn't like all this tinsel hanging in its hair. Maybe it's hungry for snow and thirsty for rain.

LAURA: Sentimentality doesn't become you, Gerald.

GERALD: No? I thought it went rather well with the season. (*He walks over to the stereo.*) Would you like to hear some Christmas music, Laura?

LAURA: Sorry. I haven't time.

GERALD: What a shame! May I comfort myself with the thought that you'll be pining for home and husband while you're out awarding blue ribbons for prize Christmas trees?

LAURA: Gerald, please. Let's not quarrel tonight.

GERALD: Is that what I'm doing? Quarreling? No, Laura, I'm asking for something that I hoped you'd be able to give me. (LAURA *holds his gaze a moment, then turns abruptly away.*) No, I guess not. Not any more.

LAURA (*Apologetically*): You *do* understand about to-night, don't you, darling? Would you care to come with me?

GERALD: No, thanks. If I get desperate, I can always listen to the carolers. (*He walks to window and opens it. From offstage, noises of the street and* CAROLERS *singing "Joy to the World" are heard.*)

LAURA (*Sharply*): Please shut that. I feel a draft. (*She starts putting on make-up at wall mirror. He shuts window.*)

GERALD: It's only fair to warn you. I haven't bought you a present because . . . well, I can't think of anything you don't have already.

LAURA: What a nice compliment, darling. To think your wife has everything! (GERALD *walks up behind her and puts his hands on her shoulders.*)

GERALD: You're very beautiful, you know.

LAURA: Thank you, but that's only my reflection. (*She spins away from his grasp.*) It's late and I'm late, and if you really want to be a darling, you'll put those packages under the tree!

GERALD (*Surveying packages on couch*): What role are you playing, *Mother* Christmas?

LAURA: Good heavens! Didn't I tell you? We're having company tomorrow. In fact, it's coming tonight.

GERALD: *It?* It — what?

LAURA: I don't know whether it's a boy or a girl.

GERALD (*Aghast*): Have you lost your mind?

LAURA: From the Orphans' Shelter, Gerald. The Welfare Committee passed a resolution last week that every member of the board should sign up for an orphan to spend Christmas Eve and Christmas Day in a home with a family. So what could I do? I'm first vice-president. The agency is delivering one sometime this evening.

GERALD (*Appalled*): Laura, haven't you any sensitivity, any feeling at all?

LAURA: Surely you wouldn't begrudge an orphan a Christmas dinner and an armful of presents?

GERALD: I wouldn't have believed it. That you could be so thoughtless and selfish and callous.

LAURA: Selfish, Gerald? Callous? I believe it was your theory that no one has any business with children who isn't able to take proper care of them.

GERALD: That was *before*, Laura. When we were just starting out.

LAURA: I know. First we were too poor. Then we were too busy and now . . . (*Her voice breaks*) You see, I'm only agreeing with you, Gerald. (*She exits quickly through front door. GERALD sighs, goes to stereo, and turns it on. A choir singing "Away in a Manger" is heard. GERALD hastily turns it off. He walks to the packages, rips the wrapping off one, revealing a child's carpenter set, with hammer, saw, etc. The buzzer rings. GERALD hurries to the door, and flings it open.*)

GERALD (*Eagerly*): Laura, I — (*SALLY BARTLETT leans against the door frame. She wears sophisticated slacks and blouse.*) Oh, Sally.

SALLY: Any room in your Christmas stocking for a next-door neighbor, Gerald?

GERALD: Any time. Come in. (*She enters and they go to center.*)

SALLY: If you're not doing anything, I thought we might slide down a few chimneys together.

GERALD: Where are all your bright young men, Sal?

SALLY (*Shrugging*): Glamour's only an eleven-month asset. Come Christmas they head for home and hearth.

I was just putting a last-minute Christmas card down the mail chute when I saw Laura leave, so I thought as long as you were alone, and I'm alone . . .

GERALD: We could keep each other company. Great! Let's go out and find some really festive place.

SALLY: You're on! Give me some time to change, and bring your own mistletoe. (*She exits, leaving door open behind her.* GERALD *shakes his head. He starts toward door, then his eye falls on a smiling picture of* LAURA, *framed, on table beside couch. He picks up picture, sits on the couch, and stares glumly at it.*)

BOY (*At doorway*): Are you sad because you've lost the lady? (GERALD *jumps, as* BOY, *bareheaded and wearing a shapeless coat, walks in at door, closing it.*)

GERALD: How did you get in here?

BOY: I'm sure I have the right apartment. 10-D?

GERALD (*Nodding*): Yes. Then you're the boy from the Orphans' Shelter?

BOY (*Putting a card on the table by the entrance*): In case you should want me again sometime — you can look for me here.

GERALD: You shouldn't be wandering around the city by yourself, at night.

BOY: Are *you* afraid?

GERALD: Well, no. But then I'm a bit older than you are.

BOY (*Looking at* LAURA*'s picture*): Are you afraid for her?

GERALD: Why do you ask that?

BOY: She's a very beautiful lady. Is she always so sad?

GERALD: Sad? Laura? She's laughing in this picture. (*He holds the picture out.* BOY *looks at it and shakes his head.* GERALD *looks at the picture again. Thoughtfully*) You know — you may be right. (BOY *wanders over and looks at tree.*) Shall I turn the tree lights on?

BOY: If you want to.

GERALD (*In disbelief*): If I want to? (*He laughs*) I'm a little old for Christmas trees, son.

BOY: Why?

GERALD: When you grow up you'll find out that unless a house is filled with kids and laughter and excitement, Christmas doesn't mean much. (*He stops.*)

BOY: Then why did you decorate the tree?

GERALD: I don't know. Habit, I guess. We've always had a tree. I remember that first Christmas tree Laura and I had. (*He breaks off again.*)

BOY: Does your wife like Christmas trees?

GERALD: She did then. We bought the biggest tree we could find, but by the time we lugged it up four flights to our room, half the branches were broken off. It looked like a picked bird. (BOY *suddenly laughs and* GERALD *laughs with him.*) Would you like to unwrap some of your presents now?

BOY: That wouldn't be quite fair.

GERALD: Why not? They're yours. Look — here's one with the paper off. (GERALD *shows* BOY *the carpenter set.* BOY *looks at it gravely. He hefts the hammer.*)

BOY: It's too small for me. I can handle a real hammer.

GERALD: Can you? Are you a good carpenter?

BOY: Not yet. But I'm learning.

GERALD: You're quite a boy. How about some cake and milk? (BOY *nods and* GERALD *puts an arm around his shoulders.*) Then come with me. The kitchen's out this way. (*They exit left. There is the sound of a key in the lock. The front door opens and* LAURA *enters. She is clearly in a temper. She rips off her coat, throws it on couch.* GERALD *reappears, alone.*) I heard your key. I thought it was Graves coming back. Have your blue ribbons been distributed so soon?

LAURA: Don't be clever, Gerald. I'm in a rush and a perfectly vile temper. The chartered bus broke down — and the Police Commissioner is getting a special car . . . (*She is prowling the room as she talks*) It's snowing up a blizzard and the streets are choked with those stupid choral groups caterwauling Yuletide music. . . . (*She starts toward door left.*)

GERALD: Wait a minute. Your guest is here.

LAURA: My what?

GERALD: Your charity case. Your orphan. It's a boy.

LAURA: That's just dandy. Have Graves put him to bed, and tomorrow morning I'll —

GERALD: Graves isn't here. He's out.

LAURA (*Eyeing* GERALD *thoughtfully*): You're not going to be difficult, are you?

GERALD: He's a pretty interesting kid. Direct. Mind of his own. Funny what having a kid in the house will do for it — on Christmas Eve.

LAURA: For heaven's sake, Gerald! I'm in a *hurry*!

GERALD: You can be a little late, can't you?

LAURA: The Commissioner's going to phone me in thirty minutes. He's coming by to pick me up. And I want to change! (*She starts out, but* GERALD *suddenly yanks her back by her arm.*)

GERALD: Don't you care about anything but yourself?

LAURA: What's the *matter* with you?

GERALD: He's a nice kid, that's all. He's lonely. You're the reason he's here, so I think you ought to see him. Will you speak to him?

LAURA: That's ridiculous. He doesn't know me from Adam, and I don't know him, so what difference does it make whether I see him or not?

GERALD: Aren't you even interested?

LAURA: If you're so interested, why don't you go talk to him?

GERALD: Because I'm not responsible for getting him here, and I've made other plans. (*He walks to closet by front door, and starts putting on hat and coat.*)

LAURA: Gerald . . . we can't leave a child alone in this apartment. (GERALD *deliberately buttons his coat. He doesn't answer.*) You told me you weren't going out. Surely you could wait till Graves gets back.

GERALD: I'm late now.

LAURA: But I'm chairman of the Tree Judging Committee. They're expecting me! The Commissioner is going to call me any minute!

GERALD: I'm sure it will make a charming anecdote for your next civic meeting. How the charitable Laura Remington rocked an orphan boy to sleep on Christmas Eve. Good night, my dear. Merry Christmas! (*He exits.* LAURA *gives a little cry of angry frustration. She chokes it back as the* BOY, *still in his shapeless coat, and holding a glass of milk, appears at door at left.*)

LAURA (*Seeing him*): Oh! I didn't hear you come in. I'm Mrs. Remington. I'll stay with you till our butler returns. Then I have to go out.

BOY: I don't mind staying by myself. I'm not afraid.

LAURA: That's out of the question.

BOY: Why? Do *you* mind being left alone?

LAURA: That's different. I'm a grownup.

BOY: Yes. But do you?

LAURA (*Suddenly*): I hate it.

BOY: Then I'll stay with *you*. Until Mr. Remington comes back.

LAURA: You might have a long wait.

BOY: I like Mr. Remington. We've been talking about Christmas trees, and he told me this was the prettiest he's seen — except for the first tree you had together.

LAURA: *That* one? (*She laughs*) Why, all the branches were broken off. (*Suddenly she sobers. Her voice is low and sincere.*) He's right. It *was* a pretty tree.

BOY: Thank you for all the presents.

LAURA: You haven't even looked at them.

BOY: My mother said you don't always have to see things to know they are there.

LAURA (*After a pause*): Suppose you knew something was there once; then it seemed to disappear and you can't find it anywhere. What would your mother say about that?

BOY: She'd say that no one sees past the wall he builds in front of his own heart.

LAURA (*Hesitantly, nervously*): I guess I'm a very silly, selfish woman.

BOY: No.

LAURA: What do *you* think of me?

BOY: I think you wish you had asked Mr. Remington to stay.

LAURA: You're a very observant boy. Talking to you, I feel . . . well, I feel as if we might be friends.

BOY: Yes.

LAURA: I'm glad you came to us for Christmas.

BOY: I wanted to come. (LAURA *smiles at him. He smiles back and crosses to her. She puts her hands on his shoulders.*)

LAURA: More milk?

BOY: Yes, please. (*She takes glass and starts out. She pauses and looks back.* BOY *has settled on couch. His eyes are heavy. She smiles and exits.* BOY *droops, finally slumping into sleep.* LAURA *re-enters with a fresh glass of milk.*)

LAURA: If you'd like it warmed, I can — (*She breaks off*

as she sees the dozing BOY. *She puts the milk down, crosses to him, and looks down at him tenderly. She bends and strokes a lock of hair back from his forehead.*) Pleasant dreams, little one. I'll try to make them come true for you. (*She glances at her watch, and pulls herself together briskly. She gently shakes the* BOY.) You can't sleep here, honey. Let's get you to bed. (BOY *half-wakens.* LAURA *helps him to his feet; he leans heavily against her. Half-supporting him, she steers him toward door at left. The phone rings.* LAURA *hesitates.* BOY *slumps more heavily against her. With a tender look, she hugs him closer. Slowly she moves on toward door, helping the* BOY. *The phone continues to ring as they exit, then finally stops. Curtain.*)

* * * * *

SCENE 2

TIME: *Later that evening.*

SETTING: *The same as Scene 1. The lights are turned low, and the Christmas tree lights are on.*

AT RISE: LAURA, *wearing a long dressing gown, is curled up on the couch, dozing. A key turns in the front door. The door opens and* GERALD *enters. He looks tired and disgusted. He slams the door violently, waking* LAURA, *who smiles with pleasure when she sees him. Then her smile dies as she sees his frowning face.*

GERALD: I'm amazed. I thought you'd be out greeting Santa Claus.

LAURA: *I'm* amazed. I never knew you to roll up the carpet so early.

GERALD: I don't like my tinsel with tarnish on it.

LAURA: What is that supposed to mean?

GERALD: It's a little silly to celebrate love and good will.

LAURA: How true. For us, anyway.

GERALD: Why beat around the bush? Can't we face it — honestly and squarely?

LAURA: Are you implying that I've failed you? All right, Gerald. Maybe I have. But it takes two, you know. (*She gets up, turns her back and walks to window. She dabs her eyes surreptitiously.*)

GERALD: Laura . . . ?

LAURA (*Harshly*): Well? (GERALD *stops, rebuffed. Suddenly two strings of tree lights go out, leaving the room very shadowed.*)

GERALD: Nothing. The lights are gone.

LAURA: Yes. They are, aren't they? (*She turns toward him.*) What do you want to do about it? (GERALD *avoids her gaze. In some confusion, he picks up the toy hammer and fingers it.*)

GERALD: Clever set. The — er — boy liked it. Funny kind of kid. Gives you the impression he's way ahead of you all the time.

LAURA: What do you want to do about *us*, Gerald?

GERALD: I'm not sure. What do you suggest?

LAURA: I've thought all this time we had *something*. Maybe just the weight of time and things shared. At least we've been together. Until tonight —

GERALD: Why drag tonight in? One Christmas Eve can't destroy everything.

LAURA: No? Somehow I think if tonight had been different, a lot that's been wonderful and good between us could have been saved.

GERALD: I don't think playing part-time mother is very admirable.

LAURA: What do you mean?

GERALD: It was a cheap trick — using a child's misfortune to feed your own vanity.

LAURA: Who walked out? *I* didn't!

GERALD: What?

LAURA: I couldn't leave. I've been here all evening. The Commissioner phoned about eight-thirty but I didn't answer the phone.

GERALD (*Quietly*): That wasn't the Commissioner. I phoned. (*Pauses, then, earnestly.*) It wasn't much fun without you, Laura. It never has been. I started thinking about you and the kid, and, well, it seemed stupid for me to be somewhere else, when I'd rather be here.

LAURA: It was really you who called?

GERALD (*Nodding*): Yes. When I didn't get an answer, I blew up. I couldn't swallow the thought that you'd go off and leave a child alone.

LAURA: I intended to, you know. But . . . there's something odd about him. Detached — sort of apart from the world. Yes, I found myself drawn to him.

GERALD: Did you feel it? Honestly?

LAURA: I've never really thought I liked children. (*She turns away.*)

GERALD (*Walking toward her*): And yet — it's funny, but always in my mind, I picture you, holding a child.

LAURA: Gerald . . . (*She turns to him and puts out her hand. He is about to take it when a key turns in the lock. The front door opens and* GRAVES *enters. Even in his sober derby and black Chesterfield, he manages to give the impression of a holiday reveler.*)

GRAVES (*Surprised*): Why, good evening, Mrs. Remington. Sir. I'm afraid I'm a little late. The crowds and — holiday spirit, you know.

GERALD: We know, Graves. I'm beginning to feel a little spirit myself.

LAURA: We have an overnight Christmas visitor, Graves. A little boy. I wonder if you would look in on him. He's sleeping in my bedroom.

GRAVES: Yes, ma'am. (*He exits, peeling off his coat as he goes. GERALD and LAURA avoid looking at each other. GERALD walks over to the tree and touches one of the branches.*)

GERALD: Do you think we ought to hang the star? (LAURA *looks at him questioningly.*) Graves said a star is to light your home by — and to wish on.

LAURA: Do you have a wish, Gerald?

GERALD: Yes. Do you? (*Slowly, she nods.*) Do you suppose they might even be the same? (GRAVES *reappears. He looks agitated.*)

GRAVES: Excuse me, Mrs. Remington, you *did* say the visitor was in your bedroom, didn't you?

LAURA: Why, yes. I put him to bed myself.

GRAVES: He doesn't seem to be there now, madam.

LAURA: But that's impossible!

GERALD: Where could he be? (LAURA *rushes out, and GERALD follows. GRAVES remains, looking puzzled. A moment later, LAURA and GERALD re-enter. Both are baffled and disturbed.*)

LAURA: Gerald, I tucked him in myself. Graves, search the apartment. He has to be somewhere! (GRAVES *nods and goes out. GERALD looks at LAURA with a frown.*)

GERALD: The bed didn't look as if anyone had slept in it, Laura.

LAURA: Gerald, I promise you. . . . I took him in, and I put him down carefully so he wouldn't wake. (*She breaks off and covers her face with her hands.*)

GERALD: Don't. We'll find him. He's around here someplace.

LAURA: No, no. I have the strangest feeling . . . (*She clings to GERALD.*) Oh, Gerald, he was such a lonely little boy. I feel as if we failed him.

GRAVES (*Reappearing in doorway*): I'm sorry, madam.

There's no one in the apartment but the three of us. (*He exits.*)

LAURA (*Half hysterically*): But where could he have gone? And *why*? Oh, Gerald, what did I do . . . or not do?

GERALD (*Soothing her*): Perhaps it was both of us. Maybe he didn't feel he belonged here.

LAURA: But he did! He did! We have everything to offer a child — security, a good home, and love.

GERALD: Love?

LAURA: We *had* love, Gerald.

GERALD: But I haven't changed, Laura. It's still the same for me. (*The door buzzer sounds.* LAURA *turns with joyful relief to the door, and hurries to open it.*)

LAURA: Gerald, maybe it's the boy. The poor baby, he must have locked himself out. (*She flings the door open. On the threshold is* MRS. LESTER, *the social worker, holding* JAMIE, *a little boy of about 6, by the hand.*) Oh!

MRS. LESTER: Mrs. Remington? (LAURA *nods.*) I'm *so* sorry to be late, but the Christmas traffic is terrible, and we've had a positive *rush* on holiday foster parents. (*She edges in, pushing* JAMIE *ahead of her.*) This is Jamie, and he'll be with you over tomorrow. Jamie, say hello to Mrs. Remington.

JAMIE: Hullo.

LAURA: There's been some kind of mistake. You see, we already have a little boy from the Shelter. He came by himself, earlier.

MRS. LESTER: Oh, no. That's impossible. We *never* permit our children out unattended. I mean, we're responsible for their welfare.

LAURA: I'm sure that's true, but just the same —

MRS. LESTER: Besides, Jamie was allotted to you the very

day you phoned in. (*She flourishes a card.*) You see, it's right here on the card. And when I realized who you *were* (*She simpers a little*), why, I wanted to bring him over personally.

LAURA: I don't understand. The other child came, and my husband and I just assumed he was the child you'd arranged for us.

MRS. LESTER: I assure you, Mrs. Remington, any other child who came here, claiming your hospitality, was unauthorized. (JAMIE *puts his fist in his eye and starts to cry.*)

GERALD: Wait, perhaps we can settle this. (*He takes* JAMIE*'s hand.*) Don't cry, son. I think perhaps we have room enough for two Christmas visitors, don't we, Laura?

LAURA (*Smiling at him*): Yes, I think we do.

MRS. LESTER: Good. I must be getting along. But if I were you I'd check this other boy's credentials, and send him right back where he came from. Merry Christmas! (*She smiles briskly, and exits.* LAURA *closes the door and looks at* GERALD.)

LAURA: But — where *is* he?

GERALD: I don't know.

LAURA: It's almost as if we dreamed he was here. (*With wonder*) But I held him in my arms!

GERALD: Whoever he is, we have a lot to thank him for.

LAURA: Yes. (*She looks down at* JAMIE *and puts a hand on his head. He clutches her skirts and leans against her.*)

GERALD: You know, my dear, you've never looked more beautiful.

LAURA: Thank you, Gerald. (JAMIE *breaks away and goes to the tree. His eye is caught by the star, still unhung.*)

JAMIE: Star . . . I want to hang the star! (LAURA *and* GERALD *do not immediately respond.*)

LAURA: I can't help feeling that somehow it was planned. Didn't he tell you his name, or where he came from?

GERALD: I never thought to ask. But (*Snaps his fingers*) — wait a minute. When he came in he said something like (*Groping for the words*) . . . "In case you want me again, you can look for me here . . ." and he put something down. (*He moves to table, picks up the card the* BOY *left.*) It says here . . . Bethlehem.

LAURA: Bethlehem, Pennsylvania?

CAROLERS (*From offstage; singing the last stanza of "O Little Town of Bethlehem"*):

O Holy Child of Bethlehem,
Descend to us we pray;
Cast out our sin and enter in,
Be born to us today.

GERALD: No. Just Bethlehem. (LAURA *and* GERALD *stare at each other, realization dawning*)

JAMIE (*From over by the tree*): I want to hang the star! (GERALD *puts out his hand to* LAURA. *She takes it and they walk to the tree.*)

GERALD: All right, son. It *is* time to hang the star. (*He lifts* JAMIE, *and* LAURA *hands him the star. He strains upward to hang it, as the curtain closes.*)

THE END

Christmas Recaptured

by Mildred Hark and Noel McQueen

When there's nothing left of Christmas but dirty dishes and torn wrapping paper, it takes a near-miracle to recreate the joyous holiday spirit. . . .

Characters

HENRY STEVENS
ETHEL STEVENS
DAVE STEVENS, *17*
JEAN STEVENS, *16*
BOBBY STEVENS, *8*
AUNT MATILDA
CHARLIE COLE
LUCILLE, *Charlie's cousin*

TIME: *Christmas afternoon.*
SETTING: *The living room of the Stevens home.*
AT RISE: DAVE STEVENS *is sitting on sofa with the wastebasket between his feet. He is picking up pieces of Christmas wrapping paper, examining them one at a time, and stuffing them into wastebasket.* JEAN STEVENS *is sprawled in chair with her legs out in front of her.*

JEAN (*Stretching and yawning*): Dave, do you know that old expression, Christmas comes but once a year? I'm thinking maybe it's a good thing.

DAVE: You said it. What do you suppose happened to all our Christmas spirit?

JEAN: I don't know. This morning everything was "Merry Christmas, Merry Christmas" — and now it's just Christmas afternoon.

DAVE: It's like these Christmas wrappings. They all looked so pretty under the tree this morning — and now they're just trash.

JEAN: Why are you digging through all that stuff?

DAVE (*Sighing*): You know I lost the necklace I bought Mom for Christmas. I thought I'd better go through all this stuff to see if I can find it.

JEAN: You don't think it's in the wastebasket, do you?

DAVE: It might have been mixed up with some of the wrappings. Jean, I feel terrible. I've been saving money all year to buy extra-special things for the family this year — like that tie for Dad, and the necklace for Mom, and now I don't have it.

JEAN: When did you have it last?

DAVE: Last night. I was just going to wrap it, when Dad asked me to help him set up Bobby's electric train in the basement. I shoved the necklace into my shirt pocket, and I haven't seen it since.

JEAN: Then it's probably down in the basement.

DAVE: That's what I thought, but I looked everywhere. (*He stuffs the last scraps of paper into the basket and bangs it on floor to pack it down.*)

JEAN (*Looking at tree*): Did you hear that? The needles are falling off the tree already.

DAVE: Yeah. (*He reaches down, picks up the last gift tag from the floor and holds it up, reading it.*) Merry

Christmas! Big deal! (JEAN *rises, goes to tree and looks at stack of boxes, as* MR. STEVENS *enters left.*)

MR. STEVENS: Kids, your mother is in the kitchen with a sinkful of dirty dishes. I've been helping her, and now it's your turn.

DAVE (*Picking up wastebasket*): O.K., Dad. I'll help her as soon as I get rid of this stuff. (*He exits, carrying basket.* MR. STEVENS *sinks into easy chair.*)

JEAN: To think that all that's left of our beautiful Christmas dinner are dirty, greasy dishes. I don't see why Mom didn't let some of the company help before they left. (*Runs fingers over stack of gift boxes, as if counting them.*)

MR. STEVENS: You know your mother. She never does. What are you doing? Counting your blessings?

JEAN: No, my handkerchiefs.

MR. STEVENS: Hm-m, sort of a blow-by-blow inventory.

JEAN: It's not funny, Dad. I got fourteen handkerchiefs! I'd have to get pneumonia to use them all.

MR. STEVENS: Handkerchiefs are useful, and you did get a lot of other lovely things.

JEAN: I don't mind it when all the cousins give me handkerchiefs — but I should think Charlie could have done better.

MR. STEVENS: Charlie who?

JEAN: You know very well, Dad. Charlie Cole. We've been going together for nine weeks! I thought he really liked me — then he gives me a handkerchief for Christmas! (*Holds up box*) When I think of the neat sweater I bought him —

MR. STEVENS: Now, Jean, you know it isn't the gift that counts. It's the thought behind it.

JEAN: That's all very well, but you wouldn't give Mother a handkerchief, would you?

MR. STEVENS: I never know what to give your mother.

JEAN: I saw you writing her a check this morning. Of course, that's not very exciting, but at least she can use it to buy what she wants. (*She slams box down onto table.*) But a handkerchief from my boyfriend!

MR. STEVENS (*Trying to be funny*): If you're so upset, perhaps you can use it to cry into.

JEAN (*Starting left*): Oh, Dad, you're no help. I might as well do dishes. (*She exits.*)

MR. STEVENS (*Sighing*): Merry Christmas. (*He notices the three long boxes on the table next to him, picks one up and opens it. He takes out a loud tie, holds it at arm's length, scowls and puts it back into box. He opens another box, takes out another loud tie, rises and goes left, holding tie in front of him as he looks into mirror. He groans and shakes his head, returns to chair, puts tie into box. He opens third box slightly, looks inside, shudders, and clamps lid back on again.*) What a hideous bunch of ties! They'll never learn what I like. (*BOBBY enters left, looking dejected.*)

BOBBY: Dad, my electric train still doesn't work. You said you'd come down to the basement and look at it after the company left.

MR. STEVENS: Bobby, it's late Christmas afternoon, and I am very tired.

BOBBY (*Disgusted*): What good is a Christmas present if it doesn't work?

MR. STEVENS: No good, son. (*Wryly*) It's something like a Christmas tie you can't wear.

BOBBY: Maybe Dave could help me fix the train.

MR. STEVENS: Your brother is helping with the dishes, and I don't think you should interrupt him.

BOBBY: All year long I've been looking forward to Christmas and thinking maybe I'd get an electric train.

MR. STEVENS: I know, Bobby. We all look forward to Christmas.

BOBBY: But now, I can't get the train to work. (MRS. STEVENS *enters left.*)

MRS. STEVENS: Henry —

MR. STEVENS (*Trying to be cheerful*): Well, Ethel, are you finished with the dishes?

MRS. STEVENS: The greasy pans still have to be done, but the children have taken over. I just thought, Henry — (*Opens flat box on table and holds up blouse*) do you think it was Margaret Burke who sent me this blouse?

MR. STEVENS: Ethel, are you still worrying about that blouse?

MRS. STEVENS: Of course. There was no card with it, it's beautiful, and it's exactly what I needed, but it's way too big.

MR. STEVENS: Can't you just exchange it?

MRS. STEVENS: I don't know where it came from, so I can't. After this, I'm not going to let the children take the outer wrappings off the parcel post packages when they arrive. And if people don't have enough sense to enclose a card —

MR. STEVENS: Maybe it came from one of the stores in town. Lots of them deliver packages. You could call a few and see if they have delivery records.

MRS. STEVENS: Henry, I'm sure it must be from out of town. Only someone who hadn't seen me in ages could have thought I'd grown this fat. (*Holding out blouse*) I can't believe it! Imagine anyone sending me a size 14!

MR. STEVENS: What size do you wear?

MRS. STEVENS: What size? Why, I wear a 12.

MR. STEVENS: Oh.

BOBBY: Dad, isn't there anything you can do about my electric train?

MR. STEVENS: No, Bobby, not until tomorrow, when we can call the store.

MRS. STEVENS: Can't you get it to work, Bobby?

BOBBY: No, Mom.

MR. STEVENS: If you want to play with the train now, all you can do is push it around the track.

BOBBY: Push it? That's no fun.

MR. STEVENS: Use your imagination. Pretend you're the engineer or something.

BOBBY (*Slowly*): Oh — all right. (*He exits.*)

MRS. STEVENS: Henry, I must say it's very strange that Bobby's train is already broken. Did you do something wrong when you put it together?

MR. STEVENS: No, when Dave and I set it up last night it ran perfectly. You saw us.

MRS. STEVENS: Yes, and my immediate reaction was that the two of you looked rather silly, sitting on the floor hypnotized by a toy train.

MR. STEVENS (*Musing*): I never had an electric train when I was a boy, and I guess I was fascinated by it, that's all.

MRS. STEVENS (*Impatiently*): I never had a bicycle, but I don't want one now. It's too bad you and Dave had to break the train before Bobby had a chance to play with it.

MR. STEVENS: I can't tell you exactly what the trouble is, but I know for sure that the train isn't really broken. There must be some mechanical defect. I'll take it back to the store in the morning.

MRS. STEVENS (*Putting blouse back into box without putting cover on*): That's more than I can do with this blouse. (*She sits down.*)

MR. STEVENS (*Pointing to tie boxes*): And more than I can do with these ties.

MRS. STEVENS: What's the matter with your ties, Henry?

MR. STEVENS (*Holding up tie*): Take this one, for instance. I can't very well return it because it's from Cousin Ezra in Nebraska. (*Shaking his head*) But I can't wear it either. (*Disgustedly*) Look at those fish!

MRS. STEVENS: It's only natural for Cousin Ezra to pick a tie with fish on it. He's quite a sportsman.

MR. STEVENS: Maybe. (*Pause, puts tie back into box*) There's a place for fish, but it's not around my neck. (*Holding up another very loud tie*) Look at this one from Dave. It's even worse! You'd think my own son would have better taste.

MRS. STEVENS (*Upset*): Henry, it's hand painted, and Dave was so excited about giving it to you. Don't you dare say a word against that tie. You'll hurt his feelings.

MR. STEVENS: I won't, but how can I ever wear it? I'd feel like the lead singer in a rock group! (*Holds up another tie*) Then there's this one.

MRS. STEVENS: Henry, that's the one I gave you!

MR. STEVENS (*Quickly changing tone*): Oh — why, yes, so it is. Well — uh — this one is very nice.

MRS. STEVENS (*Upset*): Henry, you're just saying that. You don't like it. You don't like it at all.

MR. STEVENS: All right, then. I don't. (*Sighs*) How many times have I tried to tell this family that I like conservative ties?

MRS. STEVENS: You have to change your ties with the times. Don't be such an old fogey!

MR. STEVENS (*Rising*): That's not funny.

MRS. STEVENS: I've tried and tried to get you to wear something colorful, but no! You and your drab browns and grays!

MR. STEVENS: So you choose Christmas to force every color of the rainbow on me!

MRS. STEVENS (*Annoyed*): That isn't a nice way to talk about my Christmas present.

MR. STEVENS (*Going to her and patting her shoulder*): I'm sorry, Ethel. I'm just a little irritable this afternoon.

MRS. STEVENS: I can't believe we're having a fight on Christmas day. I just don't understand what happened. I felt so wonderful last night when we were getting ready — trimming the tree, and baking Christmas cookies — and when we were singing carols I was so happy. Now, on Christmas day, I'm as cross as can be.

MR. STEVENS: You're just tired, dear. We're all tired.

MRS. STEVENS (*Sighing*): No, it's more than that. I don't have an ounce of Christmas spirit left in me.

MR. STEVENS: I feel pretty low, too. It's funny, isn't it? People are always saying how wonderful it would be if we could keep up the Christmas spirit all year round.

MRS. STEVENS: And we can't even make it last through Christmas day. All of us are even disappointed with our presents.

MR. STEVENS: I know. And I'm sure they were all chosen carefully. And they were wrapped so beautifully, too.

MRS. STEVENS (*Sighing*): Now you don't like your ties, and my blouse doesn't fit.

MR. STEVENS: Jean's in a bad mood because her boyfriend gave her only a handkerchief, and Dave's upset because he lost your necklace.

MRS. STEVENS: Bobby's train won't work.

MR. STEVENS: Then, of course, there's the present Aunt Matilda sent. (*He laughs.*) We don't even know what that is.

MRS. STEVENS: Henry, don't laugh about it. It isn't funny. I feel terrible. (DAVE *enters left, carrying empty wastebasket.*)

DAVE: That's the last straw!

MR. STEVENS: What now?

DAVE: There's no more hot water, and we still have the big roaster to do.

MRS. STEVENS: That does it. Christmas has gone down the drain with the hot water. You'll just have to let the roaster soak, Dave.

DAVE: O.K. Here's the wastebasket. I emptied it. (*He drops wastebasket upstage near tree.*)

MRS. STEVENS: The needles are falling off the tree already!

DAVE (*Trying for humor*): The Christmas tree is molting. (*He goes off left.*)

MRS. STEVENS: Henry, you said this tree was the kind that wouldn't shed.

MR. STEVENS: That's what they told me.

MRS. STEVENS: I told you to ask for balsam.

MR. STEVENS: I did ask for a balsam. The man said they were all balsams.

MRS. STEVENS: He cheated you. This must be a pine or a cedar or something.

MR. STEVENS (*Huffily*): I'm not a horticulturist.

MRS. STEVENS (*Angrily*): I thought you could at least pick out a Christmas tree that would last through Christmas day! That man saw you coming, Henry.

MR. STEVENS (*Sarcastically*): O.K., Ethel. Next year you buy the tree, and I'll stuff the turkey. (*Phone rings off left. MRS. STEVENS rises and starts left.*)

MRS. STEVENS: Oh, dear, there's the phone. Probably someone calling to wish us a Merry Christmas, and I don't feel very merry. (*JEAN enters left, sniffing.*)

MRS. STEVENS: Wasn't that the phone, dear?

JEAN: Yes, Dave's getting it.

MR. STEVENS: What are you crying about, Jean?

JEAN (*Sobbing*): Everything. Mom, do you know what Dave's done? He's invited Charlie Cole over here.

MRS. STEVENS: He has?

JEAN: Yes. He's asked Charlie Cole and his cousin Lucille to come for supper.

MRS. STEVENS: Is Lucille the girl who's staying with the Coles for the holidays?

JEAN: Yeah. And all day Dave's been saying how cute she is.

MRS. STEVENS: We certainly have enough food.

MR. STEVENS: Ethel, we've had enough company for one day.

MRS. STEVENS: We've always told the children they could invite their friends over on Christmas night. Jean, why are you so upset?

JEAN (*Almost crying*): Because I don't want to see Charlie. I'm so embarrassed! I'll have to pretend that I like his handkerchief! (DAVE *enters left.*)

DAVE: Now, we have real trouble.

MRS. STEVENS: What is it, Dave?

DAVE: Aunt Matilda just called.

MR. STEVENS: Matilda?

MRS. STEVENS (*Starting left*): My goodness, long distance? Does she want to talk to me?

DAVE: It wasn't long distance. She's here, at the bus station. She got a sudden impulse to visit us and took the bus in early this morning. She's getting a cab and coming right over.

MRS. STEVENS: I can't believe it!

MR. STEVENS: I think I'm getting ill. Ethel, you'll have to entertain her.

MRS. STEVENS (*Firmly*): No, Henry, we can't be like that.

Matilda is all alone, and she's always said she'd like to come here and enjoy a homey Christmas. We'll have to make things nice for her.

JEAN: How can we? Christmas is almost over, and all our Christmas spirit is gone.

MRS. STEVENS: Then we'll all have to try to get it back somehow.

DAVE: But, Mom, I'll have company of my own to entertain. Charlie and Lucille are coming for supper.

JEAN: You'd better call them up right now and tell them what's happened, and uninvite them.

DAVE: I can't do that.

MR. STEVENS: How did you ever happen to invite them in the first place?

DAVE: I saw them out for a walk this morning and just asked them to come over tonight. I thought it was a great idea.

JEAN: You only wanted an excuse to see Lucille.

DAVE: I couldn't invite Charlie and leave her out!

MRS. STEVENS: Now, you two, stop your squabbling. What are we going to do about Aunt Matilda? We can't let her know how we feel about Christmas. She always writes that she pictures us all so happy and merry at Christmastime. Maybe we should all practice saying Merry Christmas again. (*Weakly*) Merry Christmas, Henry.

MR. STEVENS: No, Ethel, it won't work. You can't warm over Christmas spirit like leftover turkey.

JEAN (*Sinking onto sofa*): I feel about as Christmasy as a toad.

MRS. STEVENS (*Looking around*): We *look* Christmasy enough — if only the tree doesn't shed much more.

DAVE: Where's the present she sent us? We still don't even know what it is.

MRS. STEVENS: I forgot about that. Get it out quickly, Dave. It's under the tree. We'll have to figure out what it is before Aunt Matilda gets here.

MR. STEVENS: How can we, Ethel? We all tried to guess this morning. (DAVE *goes to tree and takes gadget from under it. It is a cube-shaped box about six inches high and wide, with a small crank sticking out of one side. This can be made from a cardboard carton painted any bright color.* DAVE *places gadget on small table near easy chair.*)

DAVE: Here it is. (*He peers into gadget and turns crank.*) I said maybe a coffee grinder, but I could be wrong. (*Shrugs*) It beats me. (BOBBY *enters left.*)

BOBBY: Hey, Dave, could you try to fix my train?

DAVE: Don't bother me now, Bobby.

MR. STEVENS: Aunt Matilda is coming, Bobby, and we have to find out what her present is.

BOBBY: That's easy. I already told you — it's an egg beater.

MRS. STEVENS: I don't think so, Bobby.

BOBBY: Well, it's as good a guess as anybody's. (*He goes off left.*)

MRS. STEVENS: Maybe it's just meant to be ornamental.

JEAN (*Rising and coming to look at gadget*): No, Mom, there's nothing ornamental about it. Why the crank and all those funny wheels inside?

MRS. STEVENS: I just don't know. What'll we say? What'll we do?

MR. STEVENS: Nothing. We'll just have to leave it here on the table in a prominent place and thank her for it. Maybe she'll say something that'll give us a clue. (*Doorbell rings off right.*)

MRS. STEVENS: Here she is. (BOBBY *runs in left with an egg in each hand.*)

BOBBY: Mom, I know it's an egg beater. I'll show you. (*He runs upstage to table, and is about to crack eggs together into gadget.*)

MRS. STEVENS: Bobby, for heaven's sake, don't put those eggs in there! (MR. STEVENS *reaches over and grabs both of* BOBBY*'s wrists.*) Take those eggs back to the kitchen, right now! (BOBBY *goes out left with eggs.*) Now let's all try to look happy. I'll go to the door. (MRS. STEVENS *exits right.*)

MR. STEVENS (*Sinking back into easy chair*): Happy!

JEAN (*Going to sofa*): Merry, Merry Christmas!

DAVE: This is going to be some ordeal!

MR. STEVENS: Dave, when your friends come, take them into the den. And you go with them, Jean. We'll have enough here with Aunt Matilda.

DAVE: Sure thing, Dad.

JEAN: Dave can entertain them all he wants. I don't want anything to do with Charlie Cole.

DAVE: That's news.

MR. STEVENS: Come on, now. We're all in this together. We need teamwork, and your bickering isn't helping any. (MRS. STEVENS *enters right with* AUNT MATILDA, *who wears old-fashioned clothes.* MRS. STEVENS *carries* AUNT MATILDA*'s small bag, which she sets down near door.* MR. STEVENS *rises and goes toward them.* JEAN *rises and walks toward* DAVE.)

MATILDA (*Beaming*): Merry, Merry Christmas all! Henry, I hope you don't mind my coming in on you unexpectedly like this.

MR. STEVENS (*Heartily*): Of course not, Aunt Matilda. It's delightful, just delightful.

MATILDA: Here you are looking just as homey and happy as I always imagined. Family Christmases are wonderful! (*Going to* JEAN *and* DAVE) Jean and Dave — how you've grown!

JEAN *and* DAVE (*Together*): Merry Christmas, Aunt Matilda.

MATILDA: Where's the little fellow?

MRS. STEVENS: Bobby? Oh, he's down in the basement with his electric train, I guess.

MATILDA: A boy and his train. That's part of Christmas, isn't it? I may spend most of my Christmases alone, but I know there's nothing like a real family Christmas. This year I just made up my mind I'd have a share in one.

MRS. STEVENS: Let me take your things, Aunt Matilda. (MRS. STEVENS *takes* MATILDA's *hat and coat and puts them on chair.*)

MATILDA: Thank you, Ethel.

MR. STEVENS: Do sit down, Aunt Matilda.

MATILDA: Not just yet, Henry. I want to look around, and take in everything. (*Walking slowly around room*) My, what a beautiful tree. (*She starts toward it.*)

DAVE (*Taking her arm*): I wouldn't get too close, Aunt Matilda.

MATILDA: Why not?

DAVE: It's just that — well — it looks better at a distance.

JEAN (*Trying to help out*): The effect, Aunt Matilda. You get the effect of the lights better.

MATILDA: A Christmas tree looks good at any distance. (*Looking about*) Isn't that right, Henry?

MR. STEVENS: Oh, yes, indeed, Aunt Matilda.

MATILDA: My, so many presents. I can just picture you all sitting here this morning opening them — such excitement! (*Spotting the gadget*) There's the gadget I gave you. Did you like it?

MR. STEVENS: Of course. Thank you very much, Aunt Matilda.

MRS. STEVENS: Thank you very much indeed.

MATILDA: Have you tried it out yet?

DAVE (*Hastily*): Not yet.

JEAN: We've been so busy all day.

MATILDA: Then let's try it out now. (*She sits down in easy chair, takes gadget in her lap and smiles at all of them.*)

MR. STEVENS: Yes, let's. (*All stand around* AUNT MATILDA, *looking blank.*)

MATILDA (*Taking deck of cards from purse*): I forgot to put in part of the present and had to bring them in my purse. A nice new deck of cards. (*She places deck into the box and turns the crank.*) See, it's so easy and it shuffles them beautifully.

DAVE: An automatic card shuffler!

MRS. STEVENS (*Looking into box*): Well, so it is. I mean, isn't that ingenious?

MATILDA: I thought you'd like it. I knew you all enjoyed playing cards. Maybe we can play something later on.

MRS. STEVENS: Yes, of course. In fact, as soon as I saw your present I thought — by all means, yes. We'll play later. (*Places card shuffler on table*)

MATILDA (*Rising*): Do show me some of your other presents. What did you get, Henry?

MR. STEVENS: Er . . . mostly ties.

DAVE: Show her the one I gave you, Dad.

MR. STEVENS (*Holding up tie*): Here it is. Quite something, don't you think?

MATILDA: Yes, indeed.

DAVE: Why don't you let me try it on, Dad? Then you can really see what it looks like.

MR. STEVENS: Good idea, Dave. (*He hands tie to* DAVE.)

DAVE: Thanks. (*He steps in front of mirror and quickly ties tie, then turns.*) How's that?

MR. STEVENS: Remarkable.

DAVE: Dad, you wouldn't let me wear it tonight, would you?

MR. STEVENS: I don't see why not, son. As a matter of fact, feel free to wear any of my ties whenever you want. Family ties, we'll call them.

DAVE (*Very pleased*): Thanks a lot, Dad. I wanted to look special tonight.

JEAN: He wants to wear your new tie just to impress Lucille.

DAVE: That's not true!

MR. STEVENS (*To* MATILDA): Jean and Dave have invited some of their friends here for the evening.

MRS. STEVENS: I hope you don't mind more young people, Aunt Matilda.

MATILDA: Mind? I should say not. (*Walking toward left, looking at everything*) I'd love to see the rest of the presents. (*Picks up blouse from table.*) This is a pretty blouse. Is it yours, Ethel?

MRS. STEVENS: Yes, that's mine.

MATILDA (*Holding it up*): Isn't it too large for you?

MRS. STEVENS: As a matter of fact, it is.

JEAN: It's such a shame. Mother can't exchange it. There was no card — she doesn't know who sent it.

MATILDA: You can find out somehow, Ethel. (*Looking inside collar*) No one who knows you would send such a large size.

MRS. STEVENS: That's what I thought.

MATILDA: Unless, of course, a man bought it. You know, they never can understand women's sizes.

DAVE (*With a grin*): Ah-ha! So there's a man in the case!

MR. STEVENS: That's right.

MRS. STEVENS: How do you know, Henry? Besides, what man would give me a blouse?

MR. STEVENS (*Sheepishly*): This one. I bought the blouse, Ethel.

MRS. STEVENS: You!

MR. STEVENS: Yes. I asked for a size 10, but the store delivered a 14 instead. Then when you carried on about who could think you were so fat, I was afraid to admit that I'd bought it, so I gave you a check instead.

MRS. STEVENS: Henry, you old darling!

MR. STEVENS: You mean you aren't angry?

MRS. STEVENS: Angry? To think that you really asked for a size 10. That makes me feel wonderful! I haven't been a 10 in years! (BOBBY *rushes in left.*)

BOBBY: Listen, Dad!

MR. STEVENS: Slow down, Bobby. Aunt Matilda's here.

BOBBY: Hello, Aunt Matilda. Merry Christmas.

MATILDA: Merry Christmas, Bobby. (*Walking around him*) How you've grown! I hear you have an electric train. I suppose you've been running it all day.

MR. STEVENS: He hasn't exactly been running it, Aunt Matilda.

MATILDA: Why not?

BOBBY (*Excitedly*): But I have been running it, Dad. That's what I came upstairs to tell you. It's all fixed.

MR. STEVENS: Really?

MRS. STEVENS: That's wonderful, Bobby. What did you do?

BOBBY: Nothing much. I was pushing the train around the tracks, when I saw a little spark between the rails. Then I fished out this thing that was stuck and right away my train started running again!

MR. STEVENS (*Nodding*): A short circuit. What was stuck in the rails, Bobby?

BOBBY: This thing. It's a chain or something. (*Hands necklace to* MR. STEVENS)

MR. STEVENS (*Holding it up*): A silver necklace.

DAVE (*Grabbing it*): That's mine. I mean, it's Mom's. It's Mom's necklace!

BOBBY: Isn't it super? My train is running!

DAVE (*Going to* MRS. STEVENS): Mom, it's your Christmas present. (*Handing necklace to her*) Here — Merry Christmas, Mother.

MRS. STEVENS (*Taking it*): Why, Dave, it's beautiful!

DAVE: It must have fallen out of my pocket and into the train tracks. I never even thought of looking there.

MRS. STEVENS: I just love it, dear. Thank you. (AUNT MATILDA *sits in easy chair, right.*)

MATILDA (*Smiling*): I'm really getting in on some of your Christmas, anyway. Families are wonderful. Christmas is wonderful!

MRS. STEVENS (*Smiling, too*): It is, isn't it? (*She sits in chair left, and* MR. STEVENS *sits right, near* AUNT MATILDA. *Doorbell rings.*)

DAVE: That must be Charlie and Lucille. (*He goes off right, happily.*)

BOBBY (*Starting left*): I think I'll play with my train.

JEAN (*Starting left*): I'll come down and watch, Bobby.

BOBBIE: O.K. (*Exits*)

MR. STEVENS (*Stopping* JEAN): Jean, what about Charlie?

JEAN: I don't want to see him.

MRS. STEVENS (*In low voice*): Now, Jean, please. Everything's going so nicely.

JEAN: But, Mom! (DAVE *enters with* CHARLIE *and* LUCILLE.)

CHARLIE *and* LUCILLE (*Together*): Merry Christmas, everyone!

MR. *and* MRS. STEVENS (*Together*): Merry Christmas!

DAVE: I guess you know everyone but Aunt Matilda. Aunt Matilda, Lucille and Charlie.

MATILDA: How do you do? (CHARLIE *and* LUCILLE *ad lib greetings.*)

MRS. STEVENS: I'm glad both of you could come.

CHARLIE: It's certainly nice to be here. (CHARLIE *goes toward* JEAN.) I've been so anxious to see you, Jean — and thank you for this sweater. I love it.

LUCILLE (*Looking at* DAVE *and smiling*): Somebody got a new Christmas tie.

DAVE (*Looking at his father*): As a matter of fact, it isn't really mine.

MR. STEVENS: That's all right, son.

CHARLIE: I've been kind of worried about what I gave you, Jean.

JEAN (*Sarcastically*): Worried?

CHARLIE: Yes. Is it all right about next Saturday?

JEAN: What does a handkerchief have to do with next Saturday?

CHARLIE: Nothing, except to cry in, maybe.

JEAN (*Angrily*): That's what Dad said.

CHARLIE: They say everyone cries. It's so sad.

JEAN (*Puzzled*): What's so sad?

CHARLIE: That new play you've been wanting to see. Didn't you look underneath the handkerchief? (JEAN *runs to table upstage, opens box, takes out handkerchief and looks into box.*)

JEAN: Wow!

MRS. STEVENS: What is it, Jean? A surprise?

JEAN: I'll say. Theater tickets! (*All smiles*) Oh, Charlie, this is the greatest! (*Holding up two tickets*) Look, Mom, fourth-row-center seats for *Romance and Roses!*

CHARLIE: I thought maybe we could have dinner first at the Tower House.

JEAN: Dinner? This is the most wonderful Christmas present I've ever had!

DAVE: Now everybody's happy. Hey, why don't we go into the den and listen to some records?

LUCILLE: Terrific!

JEAN (*Taking* CHARLIE's *hand*): Come on, Charlie. (DAVE, JEAN, CHARLIE *and* LUCILLE *exit happily.*)

MATILDA: My, my, it does me good just to see the young folks so full of high spirits.

MR. STEVENS: Yes, they are, but I'd better warn you, Aunt Matilda. When they start that record player, you can expect almost anything. We don't always agree with their choice. Hard rock is hard on my ears.

MRS. STEVENS (*Happily*): Let them have their fun, Henry. If it gets too loud, we'll ask them to turn it down. We can sit here and enjoy our Christmas.

MR. STEVENS: Sounds good to me. (*He settles back.*)

MATILDA (*Sighing happily*): I'm so glad I came. Everything is — well, just the way I imagined it would be. (*Looking toward tree*) And that beautiful tree. I can't get over it. There's nothing as beautiful as a balsam.

MRS. STEVENS: A balsam?

MR. STEVENS: We're not sure it is a balsam, Aunt Matilda.

MATILDA (*Going to tree*): It must be, it's so fresh and green. (*Touches branch, and "snowflakes" fall from tree.*) But this snow is more like hailstones. (*More snowflakes fall in shower.*)

MR. STEVENS (*Rising and going to tree*): The children made the snow out of soapflakes.

MRS. STEVENS (*Rising and joining them*): They must have mixed them too dry, and the snowflakes keep falling off. (*To* MR. STEVENS) I guess you did get a balsam after all, Henry. (MR. STEVENS *grins broadly.*)

MATILDA (*Touching branch*): Look, every time you touch it, the snow falls.

MRS. STEVENS: Isn't that pretty? Just like a miniature snowstorm. And look under the tree — like a Christmas card scene. (*Music starts off left, a familiar Christmas carol.*)

MR. STEVENS: Ethel, listen — music.

MRS. STEVENS: It's the children. They're playing Christmas carols.

MATILDA: Isn't that lovely? I tell you, this house is just full of the Christmas spirit.

MRS. STEVENS (*Happily*): Yes, I don't know what happened, but I've never felt so full of Christmas spirit in all my life. I wish we could keep it all year.

MATILDA: You know, my dear, I think some things are too precious to hang onto every moment. At times like this we glimpse the true meaning of Christmas, and that gives us strength to carry on all year. I'll remember this Christmas as long as I live!

MRS. STEVENS (*Going to* MATILDA): You'll just have to remember it until next Christmas. You have no idea how much you've helped us to enjoy this one. We want you to join us every year from now on.

MATILDA (*Beaming*): Do you really mean that?

MR. STEVENS (*Rising*): Of course, she does. We've had a truly Merry Christmas this year, and we'll have another one next year. (*Putting an arm around each of them.*) And in between, a Happy New Year for us all! (*Music up. Curtain*)

THE END

Christmas Coast to Coast

By Lewy Olfson

John Lannon comes home on Christmas Eve to find a pear tree and seven swans in his apartment. . .

Characters

JOHN LANNON, *25*
PEGGY LANNON, *his wife*
MILKMAN
MRS. SCHULTZ, *pompous, matronly dancing instructor*
MISS GEORGE, *her middle-aged pupil*
TWO DELIVERY BOYS
MR. HENRIES, *Boy Scout leader*
JEFFREY LORD, *acrobat*
DULCIE BAKER, *television emcee*
THREE TV TECHNICIANS
EXTRAS, *as many as possible*

TIME: *The present. The day before Christmas, 10:30 in the morning.*
SETTING: *The Lannon living room, in their New York City apartment. There is a huge potted tree standing in the middle of the room.*

183

AT RISE: *The stage is empty. After a moment,* JOHN *enters through door, right, without seeming to notice tree. He is dressed in a warm overcoat and scarf, carries a briefcase.*

JOHN (*Calling out*): Hello, I'm home! Peggy? Anybody home? (*To himself*) " 'Twas the day before Christmas, and all through the house, not a creature was stirring, not even my wife." (*He starts toward the closet with his coat when opposite door opens and* PEGGY *enters. She is in her work clothes. She carries a pitcher of water. She seems surprised to see* JOHN, *and not particularly pleased.*)

PEGGY: What are you doing here?

JOHN (*Taken aback*): What do you mean? Don't you remember me? I'm your husband. John Lannon. I live here.

PEGGY: Don't be silly, John, of course I know who you are. But what are you doing home so early? You're supposed to be down at the newspaper, working.

JOHN: I know, honey, but I got the day off.

PEGGY: The day off! No, John, that's tomorrow. Tomorrow's Christmas, and tomorrow's the day you get off!

JOHN: But you don't understand, Peggy. I'm getting today *and* tomorrow off.

PEGGY: Really?

JOHN: Really. Tomorrow I get off because it's Christmas. Right?

PEGGY: Right. And today?

JOHN: And the boss gave me today off because I'm going to be on television.

PEGGY: But we're not supposed to be on television until this evening!

JOHN: Well, the boss thought I could use a few hours to rest. And then we'll be having a rehearsal, won't we?

You know, they say it's tough being on television. I'll bet this "Americans at Home" program isn't as easy as it looks.

PEGGY: You don't have to tell *me* that! I've never been so nervous in my life.

JOHN: I must admit I'm a little nervous myself.

PEGGY: You, nervous? That's ridiculous! After all those terrible stories you've covered for the newspaper? That awful murder case, and the series about juvenile delinquency! You have nerves of iron.

JOHN: Maybe that's why I got to be such a good reporter. Maybe that's why we've been selected to appear on the "Americans at Home" television show. But Peggy, what's wrong with you? You don't seem very happy to see me home.

PEGGY: I'm *not* happy to see you home.

JOHN: You're *not*! Well, *why* not?

PEGGY: Look, John, not only are *you* going to be on television, but *I'm* going to be on television, and this apartment of ours is going to be on television, too. Do you know how much work I have to do between now and the broadcast to get this living room fixed up like a typical Christmas living room?

JOHN: That's O.K., honey. Now that I'm home, I can help.

PEGGY: No, John. You'll only be in the way.

JOHN: I've never been in the way before when we've decorated for Christmas. *I* string the lights, *I* string the mistletoe, *I* string the popcorn . . .

PEGGY: Yes, but that's for ordinary Christmases. This one is different.

JOHN: What do you mean by "different"? Every Christmas is the same.

PEGGY: That's just the trouble. Christmas is always the

same, everywhere, all over the country. What fun will it be for people to tune in their TV sets and see the same old things they have themselves? Like lights, and mistletoe, and popcorn . . .

JOHN: But people *like* those things.

PEGGY: Maybe they do. But our Christmas — our television Christmas — is going to be different. No lights, no . . .

JOHN: *No lights!*

PEGGY: Right! And no popcorn and no mistletoe! Our Christmas is going to be unusual, and original, and different, and glamorous, and exciting!

JOHN (*Skeptically*): Just what did you have in mind?

PEGGY: Well . . . John, I want it to be a surprise.

JOHN: But I'm your husband! You can tell me!

PEGGY (*Considering*): No, I don't think so. You'll say I'm foolish, and you won't let me do it. And I have all the arrangements made. So you'll just have to leave the apartment until it's time for the telecast, and leave the rest to me.

JOHN: Leave the apartment! But, Peggy, it's below zero out there. I'll freeze!

PEGGY: Then sit in the subway. Or go to the library.

JOHN: Look, dear, I'm a patient man, but I won't be driven out of my house on the coldest day of the year! May I stay if I promise not to interfere with anything you've planned?

PEGGY: Do you promise not to ask any questions?

JOHN: I solemnly promise not to ask any questions.

PEGGY: All right, then. You can stay.

JOHN (*Seeing the tree for the first time and pointing to it*): Good grief! What's that?

PEGGY (*Going to the tree protectively, watering it from the pitcher*): Now, John, you promised you wouldn't ask any questions.

JOHN (*Trying to control his temper*): All right, I won't ask a question. I'll make a declarative statement — an order, in fact. Tell me what that thing is!

PEGGY: Well, dear, it's a tree.

JOHN: I can see that for myself! But what's it doing here?

PEGGY: That's part of the surprise, John. Now don't go back on your word!

JOHN: Peggy, do you mean to say that *that* is for our Christmas?

PEGGY: That's it, dear. It's sort of a Christmas tree!

JOHN: I've seen pine Christmas trees and spruce Christmas trees and juniper Christmas trees, and even *plastic* Christmas trees. But a fruit tree for Christmas? Never!

PEGGY: Dear, I know it's hard to understand, but just be patient and everything will become clear in a little while. Just have faith in me, dear.

JOHN (*Smiling*): O.K. I'm sorry I blew up at you, honey. I'm sure whatever you're doing is very clever, and will be just right for the television show.

PEGGY: Thank you for trusting me, John. When you see what I've planned, you'll be so proud of me! I know you will.

JOHN: Hey, what's that tag tied to the tree?

PEGGY: I don't know. I haven't had a chance to look. Probably tells what kind of tree it is.

JOHN: Oh. Would it spoil the surprise if I looked at it?

PEGGY (*On her way out the door*): Not at all, dear. Go right ahead. (*Exits*)

JOHN (*Going to the tree*): It's pretty, whatever it is. (*Looks at the tag and lets out a yelp*) Peggy! Come in here at once!

PEGGY (*Entering in alarm*): What is it, dear? You sound as though you've been shot!

JOHN: I just read the tag.

PEGGY: Oh, dear. You mean it's a . . . a poisonous tree?

JOHN: No, but it might as well be. The tag says this tree costs three hundred dollars!

PEGGY (*Alarmed*): Three hundred dollars! Oh, there must be some mistake!

JOHN: There certainly must be, and I think the mistake was in ordering it. It's a good thing you haven't paid for it! (*Pauses, looking at her*) You haven't paid for it, have you?

PEGGY (*Hesitating*): No, not exactly. I . . . I charged it.

JOHN: Then call up the store right now and tell them to take it back!

PEGGY: I'd like to, dear, but I can't. It seems there's some kind of state law that won't allow it. Something about tropical diseases. You know, the kind trees get. The man was very nice; he explained it all to me.

JOHN: For three hundred dollars, I'll *bet* he was nice!

PEGGY: Now don't get yourself all upset, dear. We can take it out of the housekeeping budget.

JOHN: Three hundred dollars? At what rate?

PEGGY (*Meekly*): Fifty cents a week?

JOHN (*Calmly, wonderingly*): Peggy, sometimes I wonder how I ever married you.

PEGGY: It was very simple, dear. You just said "I do."

JOHN: I see. I guess we're stuck with the tree. I hope there aren't going to be any more little surprises like that.

PEGGY (*Smiling winningly*): No, dear. Now be a darling and hang your coat in the closet. I have a million things to do.

JOHN: O.K. But remember; no more surprises!

PEGGY: Yes, John. (*She starts to exit.* JOHN *goes to the closet, opens the door, is about to hang up his coat, does a "double-take," slams the door, and leans against it as though he has seen a ghost.*)

JOHN (*Shakily*): Peggy . . .

PEGGY: Yes, dear?

JOHN (*Slowly, deliberately*): There are two birds in the closet. (*She hesitates, seeming to think. Actually she is stalling for time.*) Peggy, I said there are two birds in the closet.

PEGGY: Oh. Yes. I meant to tell you about them.

JOHN: How much did these two birds cost?

PEGGY (*Smiling brightly*): Nothing, dear. I borrowed them from Mr. Johnson across the hall. He was very sweet about it. He's going to watch them on television this evening.

JOHN: You mean the birds are going to be on the program with us?

PEGGY: That's right.

JOHN (*Sarcastically*): Wonderful! I've always wanted to do an animal act on television!

PEGGY: Now, John, there's really nothing to be upset about. I have everything under control. Why don't you go inside and take a nice, hot shower? That'll relax you.

JOHN: You know, that's the first good idea you've had today. I think I'll do just that. A nice, hot shower! (*He goes out through the door, left.* PEGGY *faces front, smiling blissfully. Suddenly, a look of horror and alarm crosses her face.*)

PEGGY: John! Wait! Don't go into the bathroom, John! John! (JOHN *reappears, looking resigned.*)

JOHN (*Calmly*): What, may I ask, is a flock of geese doing in our bathroom?

PEGGY: They aren't geese, John. They're swans.

JOHN: Oh, of course. I couldn't understand why we had a bathroom full of geese, but now that I know they're swans, that's a different matter. (*Pauses*) Peggy! What on earth are swans doing in our bathroom?

PEGGY: Don't get excited, John, that's part of the surprise. And they didn't cost anything, either. I borrowed them from the Bronx Zoo. They wanted the publicity!

JOHN: Wait a minute. Wait just a minute. Light is beginning to break.

PEGGY: That's fine, dear.

JOHN: Would there, by any chance, be *seven* swans in our bathtub?

PEGGY: That's exactly right, seven. I didn't think you were in there long enough to count them.

JOHN: And would the birds in the closet be partridges?

PEGGY: That's right, dear, from Mr. Johnson. I told you about them.

JOHN: And this tree. This wouldn't be a *pear* tree, by any chance, would it?

PEGGY: I should have known you'd recognize a pear tree! Didn't you get a merit badge in nature study when you were a Boy Scout?

JOHN: "The Twelve Days of Christmas!" Of course!

PEGGY (*Hurt*): Oh, John. You've guessed it! Now the surprise isn't a surprise any more.

JOHN: That's all right, Peggy. We've only covered three days so far. It seems I have nine more surprises left, don't I? (*The doorbell rings.*) Well, what do you know? Surprise number four just popped up.

PEGGY: Now, you sit right down, dear, and relax. I'll see who's at the door. (*She opens the door.* MILKMAN *in white coveralls stands there.*)

PEGGY: Oh, hello.

MILKMAN: Are you the lady that wrote this letter to the milk company? (*Looking at the letter he holds in his hand*) Mrs. Lannon?

PEGGY: Yes, that's right. Won't you come in? This is my husband, Mr. Lannon.

MILKMAN (*Shaking hands with* JOHN): How do you do? I'm the milkman.

JOHN (*Dully*): Pleased to know you.

MILKMAN: Now about this letter . . .

PEGGY: Oh, it's very simple. I just want to borrow eight of your milkmaids for a few hours today. You see, we're doing a television broadcast of the old Christmas carol, "The Twelve Days of Christmas," and we need eight milkmaids. Of course, we'd give the milk company credit. It would be wonderful publicity!

MILKMAN: I'm sure it would, Mrs. Lannon. The only trouble is, we don't have any milkmaids.

PEGGY: You don't? But that's ridiculous! How do you get the milk from the cows?

MILKMAN: We use electric milking machines.

PEGGY: I never thought of that.

MILKMAN: You don't suppose you could change the line of the song to "Eight milking machines a-milking," do you?

PEGGY: No, no, I don't think so. No, we've got to have real milkmaids.

JOHN (*Sarcastically*): Why don't you just get eight milkmen, dear, and put wigs and dresses on them?

PEGGY: Why, John, that's a wonderful idea!

MILKMAN: Lady, I think your husband was only joking.

PEGGY: Even if he was, it's a brilliant idea. Do you think we could find eight milkmen who are free tonight, who'd like to appear on national television?

MILKMAN: I don't know, Mrs. Lannon. I guess I could try.

PEGGY: Would you? Oh, that would be just wonderful!

MILKMAN: Of course you'd have to pay them the union rate. That's six dollars and seventy cents an hour.

PEGGY: Apiece?

MILKMAN: Yes, ma'am. That's a union rule.

PEGGY: Oh, dear! John . . .

JOHN: Now, Peggy —

PEGGY: Oh, please, John, say yes. I know it's costing you a lot of money, but even if we wanted to fix up a regular Christmas now with trees and lights and things, we wouldn't have time before the broadcast. And we've got to have *something* Christmasy when we go on the air.

JOHN: O.K. I guess you win. If you can round up eight milkmen, get them over here as soon as possible, and I'll pay them all.

PEGGY: Oh, thank you, John, dear. (*To* MILKMAN) And would you tell each of them to bring one of his wife's dresses and old hats? That way, at least, we'll save on the costume expenses.

MILKMAN (*Skeptically*): Each one should dress up like a woman, huh? O.K., I'll tell them.

PEGGY: I don't suppose *you'd* be interested in being one of my milkmaids, would you?

MILKMAN (*Hastily beating a retreat through the door*): No, ma'am! I have a sick grandmother at home I have to take care of.

PEGGY (*Calling after him*): Oh, I'm sorry. But thank you so much. And Merry Christmas! (*Closing the door*) Wasn't he a nice man?

JOHN: Yes, he was. Considering that he didn't call the mental health unit and ask them to come lock you up, I thought he was very nice, indeed.

PEGGY: Now, John. (*The telephone rings.*) You sit right there, dear, and relax. I'll get it. (*Into phone*) Hello? Oh, yes. Yes, of course. Send them right up. (*Hangs up*) That was the doorman. He called to tell me that the nine ladies dancing are here. They're on their way up.

JOHN: All of them?

PEGGY: Now don't be silly, John. Only two of them. It's the head of the dancing school that I called, and her star pupil.

JOHN: Well, if they come from a dancing school, they're probably pretty good. That's *one* thing in our favor.

PEGGY: I certainly hope so! (*The doorbell rings.*) Here they are now. (*She opens the door and admits* MRS. SCHULTZ, *a pompous lady, and* MISS GEORGE, *nervous.*)

MRS. SCHULTZ: Mrs. Lannon?

PEGGY: That's right. Won't you come in? You must be Mrs. Schultz.

MRS. SCHULTZ: That's right, Gladys Schultz, director of the "Chic Schultz Salon." So very nice to meet you. And this is my star pupil, Miss Minnie George.

PEGGY: How do you do, Miss George?

MISS GEORGE: Charmed, I'm sure.

PEGGY: Mrs. Schultz, Miss George, this is my husband, Mr. Lannon.

JOHN (*Rising*): How do you do?

MISS GEORGE: Please don't get up. I like to see a man comfortable!

JOHN: Then I'm afraid you're looking at the wrong man.

MRS. SCHULTZ: Let's not chat, shall we, but let's get right down to business. Now, Mrs. Lannon, you said when you called that you want to put nine of my best pupils on television.

PEGGY: That's right. This evening, on the "Americans at Home" show. We'll give you credit, of course.

MRS. SCHULTZ: And there's no charge for this opportunity?

PEGGY: Why, no, not at all.

MRS. SCHULTZ: Well, then, it sounds ideal!

MISS GEORGE: Just think: one of us ladies might be discovered by some important talent scout, and go to Hollywood and have a big career!

PEGGY: Yes! Wouldn't that be wonderful? (MISS GEORGE *begins circling* JOHN's *chair, her eyes closed, her body swaying in an exotic dance.)*

MRS. SCHULTZ (*To* PEGGY): Now what sort of dance did you have in mind? (*The doorbell rings.*)

PEGGY: Will you excuse me for a moment? There's someone at the door.

MRS. SCHULTZ: Certainly. (*She crosses to* MISS GEORGE.) That's it, Minnie, keep your chin up. *One,* two, three. *One*, two, three. (PEGGY *opens the door to admit* 1ST DELIVERY BOY, *carrying a covered bird cage in one hand and a large crate in the other.*)

1ST DELIVERY BOY: Mrs. Peggy Lannon?

PEGGY: Yes.

1ST DELIVERY BOY: Sign for these, please.

JOHN: Just a moment. Where are you from?

1ST DELIVERY BOY: The prop department at the network. These are for the broadcast this afternoon.

JOHN: Peggy, do you mean to say you've let the *network* in on this foolishness?

PEGGY: Of course, dear. I wouldn't want to get into any trouble without getting authorization for it first!

JOHN: All right, I'll sign for this stuff. At least there won't be any charge. (*He signs the slip.*)

1ST DELIVERY BOY: You mean I hauled all this stuff over here through the wind and snow, and I'm not even going to get a tip?

JOHN (*Giving him some change*): I take it back about there being no charge.

1ST DELIVERY BOY: Thank you, sir.

JOHN: Say, what's in these packages, anyway?

1ST DELIVERY BOY: Four live calling birds in the cage, and

six stuffed geese in the crate. Don't uncover the cage until you're ready to go on the air. Those birds make quite a racket!

JOHN: Nothing, I'm sure, to what my wife can do.

1ST DELIVERY BOY: How's that again, sir?

JOHN: Nothing. Merry Christmas!

1ST DELIVERY BOY (*Going*): Same to you, sir!

PEGGY: Now, ladies, where were we?

MRS. SCHULTZ: I had just asked you what kind of dances you wanted my girls to do on your program.

PEGGY: I thought a minuet would be nice.

MRS. SCHULTZ (*Horrified*): A minuet!

PEGGY: Or maybe a schottische! No, I think a minuet would be better.

MRS. SCHULTZ: But nobody dances the minuet these days! My students don't know how!

PEGGY: Then what would you suggest?

MISS GEORGE: Well, *I'm* an expert at the hustle! (*Does a few steps.*)

JOHN (*Aghast*): The hustle? For "The Twelve Days of Christmas"?

MRS. SCHULTZ: Perhaps you'd prefer the Latin hustle. (MISS GEORGE *goes into an active dance.*)

PEGGY: Ladies, it's too late to worry about it. Just have nine of your best dancers here as soon as possible for the dress rehearsal, and we'll take it from there!

MRS. SCHULTZ: Fine, Mrs. Lannon! I'm sure everything will work out perfectly!

PEGGY: I hope so. See you later! (*She shows them out. MISS GEORGE has continued to do the hustle. She does a kick just as she goes outside the door. Telephone rings. JOHN goes to answer it.*) And Merry Christmas!

(MISS GEORGE *sticks her head back into the room, just as* PEGGY *is about to shut the door.*)

MISS GEORGE: If I don't see you again, Mr. Lannon, have a nice holiday!

JOHN (*From telephone, into which he is talking*): Thank you! The same to you!

MISS GEORGE: I'll see you later, Mrs. Lannon!

PEGGY: Goodbye, now. (*She shuts the door.*)

JOHN (*Into telephone*): I see. I see. Yes, I'll tell her. Goodbye (*Tired*) — and a Merry Christmas.

PEGGY: Oh dear, John, I'm afraid to ask you who that was. From the look on your face I just know I've done something else wrong.

JOHN (*Almost too calmly*): No, dear. It was just one of your guests calling to check on the time his group was supposed to be here.

PEGGY: Oh, good. I'm glad at least *one* thing is all right. Which group was it, dear?

JOHN: It was the eleven pipers. You know: "Eleven pipers piping."

PEGGY: Good! Since that's one of the biggest groups, it was one of my biggest worries. I'm glad to know they'll all be here.

JOHN (*Patiently*): Tell me, Peggy, what made you decide to call the plumbers' union?

PEGGY: The plumbers' union? Oh, I just looked in the yellow pages under "Pipes," and that was the number they listed.

JOHN: Of course! How obvious! It must have sounded stupid for me to ask such a simple question. Did you know that union plumbers get fourteen thirty an hour?

PEGGY (*After a pause*): Oh. (*Smiling*) Well, dear, after the housekeeping budget has paid for the pear tree, you can collect for the plumbers. (*The doorbell rings.*)

JOHN: Now who could that be? Ten lords a-leaping, or three French hens?

PEGGY: Well, we'll know in a moment. (*She opens the door to admit* MR. HENRIES, *a middle-aged Scout leader in full Boy Scout regalia — short pants and all.*)

MR. HENRIES: Mrs. Lannon? (*He salutes smartly.*) Westborough Boy Scout Fife and Drum Corps reporting for duty.

PEGGY (*Saluting*): You must be Mr. Henries. How nice of you to come! But you didn't have to wear your short pants — especially in this below-freezing weather!

MR. HENRIES (*Heartily*): My good deed for the day!

JOHN: Hello, Mr. Henries. So you're the twelve drummers drumming!

MR. HENRIES: I beg your pardon?

PEGGY: Don't mind my husband, Mr. Henries. He's a bit nervous. We're going to be on television, you know.

MR. HENRIES: Well, all the boys are downstairs in the lobby rehearsing their drums. Whenever you want us, you just let us know.

PEGGY: I will, Mr. Henries, and thank you so much for your cooperation.

MR. HENRIES: The pleasure's all ours.

PEGGY: I'm sure you're just saying that!

MR. HENRIES (*Saluting*): Nope! Scout's honor! (*The doorbell rings.*)

PEGGY: Excuse me a moment, I'll get it. Just relax, John, dear. Relax!

JOHN (*Clenching his fists and pacing the floor*): Relax!

PEGGY (*At the door*): Yes?

JEFFREY LORD: Mrs. Lannon? I'm Jeffrey Lord.

PEGGY: Oh yes, of course. Come in, Mr. Lord!

JEFFREY (*Giving her a large box*): This package was in the lobby for you. I took the liberty of bringing it up.

There was a troop of Boy Scouts there, and I didn't think it would be too safe.

MR. HENRIES (*Indignantly*): Sir!

PEGGY (*Smoothly*): How kind of you! Do sit down while I open it, won't you?

JOHN: How do you do, Mr. Lord. I'm Mr. Lannon.

JEFFREY: It's a pleasure to meet you, sir. You're the man to whom I give my bill, aren't you?

JOHN (*Weakly*): Your bill?

JEFFREY: Yes. Didn't your wife explain?

JOHN: No, I'm afraid not.

JEFFREY: It's quite simple. I'm the leader of a vaudeville act. All my family are acrobats — perhaps you've heard of us. The Lively Lords and their Terrific Trampoline.

JOHN: Don't tell me how many there are in the act; let me guess. Would it be — ten?

JEFFREY: Why, yes. How clever of you!

JOHN: Ten lords a-leaping!

JEFFREY: Ordinarily, our television performance fee is a thousand dollars. But since this is not a sponsored show, I'll give you a break and make it seven hundred. Quite reasonable, eh?

JOHN: Oh, quite!

PEGGY (*Who has opened the box and now holds up an egg*): Look, John! The three French hens have arrived! Aren't they cute?

JOHN (*Smiling bravely*): Just darling, darling! (*Door opens and* DULCIE BAKER *enters. She is very brisk and efficient. She wears a mink coat over her shoulders; she whips this off and tosses it on the floor.*)

DULCIE (*Aggressively*): How do you do, Mr. and Mrs. Lannon? I'm Dulcie Baker, the emcee of "Americans at Home." I'm afraid the snowstorm has delayed things miserably, and all of our live remote pickup gear is stuck in Manhattan. I do wish the weatherman would check with the network before he decides to send us a blizzard. It causes *such* inconvenience. However, we *did* manage to get one of our video-tape trucks through, so we're going to do the actual broadcast right away and put it on tape. I figure we should be able to begin the show (*Looks at her watch*) — in about fifteen minutes.

PEGGY *and* JOHN (*Gasping simultaneously*): Fifteen minutes!

DULCIE: That's right. But don't worry or get nervous; everything will be ready on time. Our crew is very efficient. (*Calls off*) O.K., fellows, bring in the stuff. (TV TECHNICIANS *begin to bring in miles of cable, microphones, a camera and other such paraphernalia.*)

DULCIE (*To* JEFFREY *and* MR. HENRIES): Would you two men move that easy chair out of the way? You'd better put it in the kitchen.

JOHN: But that's my chair!

PEGGY (*To* DULCIE): Are we really going on the air in fifteen minutes?

DULCIE (*Checking her watch*): Thirteen minutes, dear, but there's nothing to worry about. You're in safe hands when you're in the hands of Dulcie Baker. (*To the crew*) That's right, fellows, just move the camera in here.

MR. HENRIES: Mind if I use the phone, Mr. Lannon?

JOHN (*Dazed*): No, go right ahead.

MR. HENRIES: I'm going to have the Boy Scouts sent right up. I wouldn't want them to miss one minute of this excitement.

JOHN (*Numb*): Fine, fine.

PEGGY: Gosh! My hair isn't combed! My face isn't washed! I haven't dressed! I'm not ready!

DULCIE (*Efficiently*): Sorry, dear, but time, tide and the networks wait for no man. (*The doorbell rings.*)

PEGGY: Come in!

2ND DELIVERY BOY (*Appearing in the door*): Package for Mrs. Lannon from Cartier's.

JOHN: Cartier's! Cartier's the jeweler?

2ND DELIVERY BOY: That's right, sir.

PEGGY: Oh, of course. The five golden rings!

JOHN (*Putting his foot down*): I'm sorry, Peggy, that's going too far. I cannot afford to buy five twenty-four-carat gold rings from Cartier's!

PEGGY: They're only eighteen carats!

JOHN: No! Sorry, young man, you'll have to take them back.

2ND DELIVERY BOY (*Scratching his head*): You're the boss!

PEGGY: But, John! What can we use for rings? According to the song we have to have five golden rings!

JOHN (*Looking around the room desperately*): I don't know. We'll find something!

DULCIE: Quiet, everybody! I'm going to start testing mike levels!

JOHN (*Excited*): The curtains! (JOHN *and* PEGGY *rush to the windows and start pulling down the draperies, which are hung on large curtain rings. The front door flies open, and in come as many extras as possible: milkmen dressed as women, plumbers with lead pipes, Boy Scouts with drums, acrobats doing cartwheels, matrons doing the hustle.*)

DULCIE (*Standing calmly down center, full front, reading from a script*): Good evening, ladies and gentlemen of the viewing audience. This is Dulcie Baker, with another program in my "Americans at Home" television series. Tonight, we are visiting the home of news-paperman John Lannon and his charming wife, Peggy, who are busy preparing for a peaceful, leisurely, quiet, old-fashioned Christmas. (*The stage is utter pandemonium and chaos, with people doing all the things called for in the song "The Twelve Days of Christmas," and* JOHN *and* PEGGY *pulling the rings off the draperies, as the curtain falls.*)

THE END

The Villain and the Toy Shop

By Barbara Winther

On Christmas Eve, the evil Mr. Glowerpuss threatens to foreclose the toy shop mortgage unless Carolyn agrees to be his bride . . .

Characters

THE TOWN WATCHMAN
CHINA DOLL
TIN SOLDIER
CALICO CAT
CLOWN ⎬ *toys*
RAGGEDY ANN
HUMPTY DUMPTY
JACK-IN-THE-BOX
JOE, *the toy shop clerk*
CAROLYN, *the heroine*
JEREMY TOYMAKER, *her father*
SARAH TOYMAKER, *her mother*
GLOWERPUSS, *the villain*
JOHN, *the hero*
BANKER
ASSISTANT BANKER
FAIRY GODMOTHER
THREE CITIZENS

SCENE 1

TIME: *Morning of December 24th.*

SETTING: *The toy shop. A street scene can be seen through a large window upstage. Beneath the window is a shelf for the toys. Up left is the box for Jack. There is a table up right.*

AT RISE: *Cut-outs or stuffed toys are on the shelf.* JACK *is inside his box with the lid closed.* JOE *is dusting the toys with a feather duster.*

TOWN WATCHMAN (*Passing by window outside shop, ringing his bell and shouting*): Eight A.M. December 24th. Last shopping day before Christmas! (*Exits*)

JOE: Dust, dust. I shoo you away every morning, and the next morning the sun brings you back again.

CAROLYN (*Entering right*): Dusting already, Joe? How are the toys? (*Goes to shelves*) China Doll, Tin Soldier, Calico Cat, Clown, Raggedy Ann, Humpty Dumpty, and Jumping Jack. (*Lifts lid and* JACK *springs up*)

JOE: Christmas is almost here. Do you think we'll sell some of your father's toys today, Miss Carolyn?

CAROLYN (*Sadly*): I hope so. There are hardly any children here anymore, and we haven't sold any toys for a very long time. We haven't been able to pay your salary for months, Joe. (*Closes lid on* JACK*'s box.*)

JOE: Now don't you worry your pretty head about me.

CAROLYN: Bless you, Joe. You are such a darling.

JOE (*Embarrassed*): Aw, Miss Carolyn.

JEREMY (*Entering right with gusto*): Good morning, everybody. (*Stands in doorway left, breathes in deeply, and does a few knee bends*)

JOE: I see you are in good form, Mr. Toymaker.

JEREMY: Always, Joe, always. Carolyn, run along and

help your mother find the forks for breakfast. They seem to be lost again.

CAROLYN: Yes, Father. (*Exits right.*)

JEREMY (*Sitting in chair with a sigh*): Joe, today is the day the rent is due. And our landlord, Mr. Glowerpuss, will take over the toy shop and turn us out into the cold and snowy street if we don't pay him by midnight tonight!

JOE: Do you have the rent money, sir?

JEREMY: Alas, no. I have an appointment with the town bankers this morning, to ask for a loan.

JOE: But, sir, you have already borrowed money from the bankers.

JEREMY: Well, Joe, we'll just have to try to borrow some more. We have no choice, if we want to save the toy shop.

SARAH (*Calling from off*): Breakfast is ready. Jeremy! Joe!

JEREMY (*Rising*): Not a word about this to my wife, now. I don't want her to worry. (*Exits right.*)

JOE: Yes, sir. (*Exits right*)

GLOWERPUSS (*Peering in window, then entering left with an evil laugh, wearing a dark suit, black cape, tall black hat, and large moustache, rubbing his hands together*): This little toy shop will soon be mine!

CAROLYN (*Entering right, singing to tune of "Happy Birthday"*): "Good morning, dear toys, good morning, dear toys." (*Sees* GLOWERPUSS *and gasps*) Mr. Glowerpuss, what are you doing here?

GLOWERPUSS: I came to look over my new possessions.

CAROLYN: You shall *never* have our toys!

GLOWERPUSS: This shop and all the toys in it will be mine if the rent is not paid by midnight tonight!

CAROLYN: We need a little more time.

GLOWERPUSS: You have had enough time. (*Grasps her arm*)

CAROLYN (*Squealing*): Go away! You frighten me.

GLOWERPUSS (*Twirling moustache*): You know you can't pay the rent. You haven't sold a toy in years!

CAROLYN: Unhand me, you villain!

GLOWERPUSS: Listen, my proud beauty. I have a little deal for you.

CAROLYN: A deal?

GLOWERPUSS: Your mother and father can keep the toy shop — if —

CAROLYN: If what?

GLOWERPUSS: If you will be my wife.

CAROLYN (*Pulling away and running to opposite side of stage*): No! Never! Leave me alone, you nasty old man!

GLOWERPUSS: I am *not* old!

CAROLYN: I shall never consent to marry you.

GLOWERPUSS: You'd better reconsider. It's the only way you can save your mother and father from bankruptcy.

CAROLYN: But I am engaged to marry John.

GLOWERPUSS: Bah! I can't stand John.

CAROLYN: John is a fine, honest, upstanding young man.

GLOWERPUSS: That's why I can't stand him. Remember, if the rent is not paid by midnight, then it's either the toy shop or *you*. You'd better forget John. (*Slinks off left, laughing and twirling moustache.* CAROLYN *sinks into chair and sobs.* JOHN *enters left, unwraps muffler, runs to* CAROLYN *and kneels beside her.*)

JOHN: My dear Carolyn, what is the matter?

CAROLYN (*Looking up*): John, it's you! (*Sadly*) You had better go away. I can't see you anymore.

JOHN (*Rising*): What? (*Strides to window and looks out*) There goes old Glowerpuss. Does he have something to do with this? (CAROLYN *cries louder.* JOHN *takes out large red handkerchief and gives it to her.* CAROLYN *blows her nose loudly.*) Alas, when you cry, Carolyn, my heart pounds like a pile driver. You must tell me your troubles. I will carry your burdens upon my shoulders.

CAROLYN: Mr. Glowerpuss wants his rent for the toy shop. He will turn us out into the cold if we do not pay him by midnight tonight!

JOHN: What a dastardly deed!

CAROLYN: And we have no money to pay him.

JOHN: Your poor parents. What are you going to do?

CAROLYN (*Rising and staring straight ahead*): I am going to marry Mr. Glowerpuss. (*Bursts into tears*) So I cannot marry you, John! (*Exits right, crying*)

JOHN: That dastardly man! My dear Carolyn shall not be his! (*Paces*) I must think of a way to save the toy shop.

SARAH (*Entering right, squinting*): Oh, my gracious, a customer. May I help you, sir?

JOHN: It's John, Mrs. Toymaker.

SARAH (*Going closer*): So it is. The light is a bit bad in here.

JOHN: The light is fine, Mrs. Toymaker. You need glasses. (*Continues pacing*)

SARAH: Oh, my gracious, no! We're too poor for such luxuries as eyeglasses! What is the matter, John? Why are you pacing like that?

JOHN: I am thinking, Mrs. Toymaker. I think better when I walk.

SARAH (*Pacing with him*): I'll help you think, John. (*He stops suddenly and she bumps into him.*)

JOHN: Pardon me.

SARAH: That's all right. Maybe we bumped out a thought.

JOHN (*Snapping his fingers*): I have an idea! (*Starts left*)

SARAH: Where are you going, John?

JOHN: Mrs. Toymaker, tell Carolyn to sit tight. (*Puts on muffler*) I'll be back before midnight. (*Exits left*)

SARAH (*Calling after him*): That's rather late, John.

JEREMY (*Entering right*): Who was that, Sarah?

SARAH: It was John. He's acting mighty peculiar. Where is Carolyn?

JEREMY: In her room. Said she wasn't feeling well.

SARAH: Poor dear. I'll brew her a cup of sassafras tea. (*Moves toward left exit*)

JEREMY: No, no, Sarah. That's the door to the street.

SARAH: Oh, my goodness. I do believe you're right. (*Exits right. There is a knock on the door and* JEREMY *opens door.* BANKER *and* ASSISTANT BANKER *march in.* ASSISTANT BANKER *carries briefcase.*)

BANKER: Mr. Jeremy Toymaker?

JEREMY: Yes, gentlemen. Do come in. (BANKER *and* ASSISTANT BANKER *move downstage with precise steps, following each other closely. They execute a military turn at center, then face front.*)

BANKER: I am the President of the Rosemont Bank.

ASSISTANT: I am the Vice-President of the Rosemont Bank.

BANKERS (*Together*): Our motto is (*Chanting, with broad gestures*):

> Oh-h-h, if your funds are getting low,
> Just sign your name on the line below.
> And when it's money that you need,
> We'll gladly use your property deed.
> Security! Security!
> Think how poor we bankers would be
> Without loans on security.
> All hail to security! Whee!

(*They resume military stances.*)

JEREMY (*Clearing throat*): Gentlemen, I'd like to take out a little loan.

BANKER (*To* ASSISTANT): Check his record. (ASSISTANT *opens briefcase, fumbles through a pile of papers, finds correct one.*)

ASSISTANT (*Reading*): "On January 21st, Mr. Jeremy Toymaker and his wife, Sarah, took out a loan with the Rosemont Bank in the amount of $500,00."

BANKER: Payments?

ASSISTANT: None. (*Reads*) "On August 15th, the Rosemont Bank was forced to take over the Toymaker car, which was security for the loan."

BANKER (*To* JEREMY): Your record with us is not exactly spotless, is it, Mr. Toymaker?

JEREMY: Business has been bad.

BANKER: Naturally. (*To* ASSISTANT) Read the report of the census. (ASSISTANT *fumbles through papers again, finds correct one.*)

ASSISTANT (*Reading*): Report on the last town census. I quote from page three, paragraph two, line five. "Rosemont has a population of 2,321 people. There are 2,000 people over the age of fifty, 300 people between twenty-five and fifty, 20 people between fifteen and twenty-five, and 1 child, named George. Most young people have moved to the nearby town of Barnesville, in order to enjoy bigger supermarkets, larger business opportunities, and more smog. Rosemont has become a little town for the aged." (*Closes briefcase with difficulty*)

BANKER: Business, my dear Mr. Toymaker, has gone. You might as well close your door, pack up your toys, and steal away into the night.

JEREMY: Do you mean no loan?

BANKERS (*Together*): No loan!

BANKER: Now, please excuse us. We have an important

board meeting to attend. Good day, sir. (BANKER *and*
ASSISTANT *march out.*)

JEREMY (*Sadly*): Good day, gentlemen. (*Sighs, and
touches each toy fondly*) Where am I going to get the
money to pay Mr. Glowerpuss? This looks like the end
of the toy shop. It will be a bleak Christmas for us.
(*Slow curtain*)

* * * * *

SCENE 2

TIME: *Evening, the same day.*

SETTING: *Same as Scene 1.*

AT RISE: CHINA DOLL, TIN SOLDIER, CALICO CAT,
CLOWN, RAGGEDY ANN, HUMPTY DUMPTY *are sitting
on shelf, in place of stuffed toys.* JACK *is in his box.
Light shines through window. Stage is dim.*

WATCHMAN (*Passing by window outside shop, ringing
bell and shouting*): Nine o'clock and all's well!
(WATCHMAN *exits.* FAIRY GODMOTHER *enters left and
stands in light from window.*)

FAIRY: Someone sent for the Fairy Godmother, and here
I am. (*Looks about*) Something seems to be wrong
here. I feel all sorts of problems in the air. I think I'll
bring the toys to life and see if they can tell me. (*Waves
magic wand*) Iddily, widdily, diddily, strife, all the toys
may come to life. (*Full stage lights. Toys jabber, come
off shelf, mill around.* FAIRY *stands on shelf and
shouts*) Order! Order! Let's have a little order. (*All
quiet down and sit around stage.*) That's better, Now,
what seems to be the difficulty here? (*Toys all speak
at once*)

CLOWN: Well, you see, it's this way —

CHINA: Ching-a-ling-choy!

CAT: Meow!

FAIRY: Not all at once, please. Let me see. Clown, come forward and tell me what's happened.

CLOWN (*Jumping up*): Mr. Toymaker can't pay the rent for the toy shop.

JACK: Tell about the boys and girls.

CLOWN: They've all grown up and moved away. (*Turns a cartwheel*)

SOLDIER: Nobody to buy us anymore.

RAGGEDY: We've been sitting on that shelf for years!

SOLDIER: It's almost Christmas, and Glowerpuss wants to turn the Toymakers out into the cold.

RAGGEDY: Poor Miss Carolyn has to marry Glowerpuss.

HUMPTY: But she really loves John.

RAGGEDY: Mrs. Toymaker needs glasses.

HUMPTY: No money for those either.

CHINA: Ching-a-ling-choy!

SOLDIER: You're always saying that, China Doll.

CLOWN (*Doing acrobatics*): Say, who's telling this story, anyway?

FAIRY: You, Clown. Now, stand on your feet and get on with it.

CLOWN (*Standing*): It all comes to this. If the rent isn't paid by midnight, either the toy shop or Miss Carolyn becomes the property of that cruel old villain, Glowerpuss.

FAIRY: My, my, that is a problem.

CLOWN: John has gone for help, but we don't know where he went.

RAGGEDY: Isn't there something we can do to help?

FAIRY: Hm-m-m. Let me see. There must be some way we can help the Toymaker family. I can't print any money to pay the rent, or I might get in trouble with

the government. I can't send Glowerpuss to the moon
or we might all get in trouble with lots of governments.
Ah! I have it! (*Motions toys around her and whispers.*)

ALL (*Ad lib*): Great! Good idea! Wonderful! We'll do it!
(*Etc.*)

CHINA: Ching-a-ling-choy!

CAT: Meow!

FAIRY: All right, now, back on the shelf. (*The toys return
to places on shelf.* JACK *returns to his box.*) Remember, at the stroke of twelve, you must go back to being
toys again. Don't forget what I told you.

ALL (*Together*): We won't!

FAIRY: I must go now. I have eighteen more distress calls
to make before Christmas! Good luck, toys.

ALL (*Together*): Thank you, Fairy Godmother.

FAIRY (*Smiling*): You are all quite welcome. Goodbye.
(*Exits left*)

ALL (*Together*): Goodbye! (CHINA, TIN SOLDIER, CAT,
CLOWN, RAGGEDY ANN, HUMPTY DUMPTY *take still
poses;* JACK *closes the lid to his box. Curtain*)

*   *   *   *   *

SCENE 3

BEFORE RISE: 1ST *and* 2ND CITIZENS, *wearing winter
clothes, are sitting on a bench near a street lamp.*

1ST CITIZEN (*Leaping up*): It's getting late in Rosemont.
(*Exits right*)

2ND CITIZEN (*Leaping up*): The Watchman rings his bell.
(*Exits left*)

3RD CITIZEN (*Poking head around left curtain*): And cries
into the quiet night — (*Pulls head back*)

WATCHMAN (*Entering left, ringing bell and yelling*): Ten
o'clock, and all is well. (*Exits right*)

BANKER (*Entering right*): That was a long board meeting.

BANKER'S ASSISTANT: Terribly, terribly long.

BANKERS (*Together*): Long. (*Sing or chant*) No loans without security (*They move left*), security, security. (*Exit left*)

JOE (*Entering left, wearing muffler and crossing to street lamp*): This night air feels mighty cold. (*Looks off right*) Uh-oh! Here comes old Glowerpuss. That man's so mean that flowers wither when he looks at them, trees shudder, and the moon tries to hide. Only two more hours and Glowerpuss takes over the toy shop. (*Sadly*) I'm really going to miss my job. (*Exits left*)

GLOWERPUSS (*Entering right, laughing evilly*): I just saw Miss Carolyn leave the toy shop. She is coming to find me, no doubt. (*Rubs hands gleefully*) Tonight I shall whisk her away on my Honda-Built-for-Two. We shall zoom across the border, and there we shall be married. (*Laughs and peers off left*) Ah, here she comes.

CAROLYN (*Entering left, nervously*): Is that you, Mr. Glowerpuss?

GLOWERPUSS: Yes, Miss Carolyn. Have you reached a decision?

CAROLYN (*Sitting on bench*): I shall become your wife, Mr. Glowerpuss. But first you must draw up and sign an agreement giving my mother and father the toy shop.

GLOWERPUSS: Gladly, my dear. (*Sits beside her*)

CAROLYN (*Rising quickly*): I shall return to the toy shop and pack my things.

GLOWERPUSS (*Standing*): When shall I call for you?

CAROLYN: You may come at ten minutes before twelve. Knock twice, and I will let you in, but I beg of you, be quiet. (*Tearfully*) My mother and father must not wake up and discover what I am about to do. (*Exits left*)

GLOWERPUSS (*Aside to audience*): The little wench is

mine. She doesn't know it, but I will have *two* agreements drawn up. One will say the toy shop is theirs. I won't sign that one. The other will say that the rent is *double*. I *will* sign that one. Then, when Miss Carolyn isn't looking, I'll just switch the papers. (*Laughs*) She'll make an excellent wife. Mornings she can scrub the floors of my ten mansions; afternoons, she can wash and iron the clothes of my eighteen relatives; evenings, she can cook, sew, wash dishes, chop wood, and polish my Honda-Built-for-Two. What a wonderful life, for a little wife! (*Exits right, laughing evilly and twirling moustache*)

WATCHMAN (*Entering right, ringing bell and yelling*): Half past the hour, and all is turning sour! (*Exits left as curtains open*)

* * *

TIME: *Almost midnight, the same evening.*

SETTING: *Same as Scene 1.*

AT RISE: *Dim lights. Toys are in their places on the shelf. JACK is in his box with the lid down. GLOWERPUSS crosses by the window and knocks twice. Lights go up as CAROLYN enters right, crosses to left doorway, and admits GLOWERPUSS, who is carrying a sheet of paper.*

CAROLYN: Please be quiet. Do you have the agreement?

GLOWERPUSS: Of course!

CAROLYN: Let me see it.

GLOWERPUSS (*Handing her paper*): There. Your parents will own the toy shop forever. Are you satisfied?

CAROLYN (*Nodding*): Yes. Leave the agreement on the table, please.

GLOWERPUSS: Of course! (*Puts paper on table.*)

CAROLYN (*Trying to be brave*): My dear family is safe at last. (*Turns away*) I must get my coat and suitcase. (*Exits right*)

GLOWERPUSS (*Laughing gleefully and twirling moustache; aside*): Everything is going just as I planned! (*Takes another piece of paper from his pocket, puts it on the table, and takes back first paper, putting it in pocket.*) Little does Miss Carolyn know that the real agreement for her parents doubles the rent! (*Chuckles and twirls moustache*) What a beautifully evil deed!

JACK (*Popping up*): Boo!

GLOWERPUSS (*Startled*): There must be something wrong with the spring on that Jack-in-the-Box. It gave me quite a scare. (*Goes over to box.* JACK *bites* GLOWERPUSS'*s sleeve.*) Ouch! Let go of me. (*Pulls away.*)

JACK: All right, everybody! Remember our plan! We only have a few minutes!

CLOWN (*Grabbing* GLOWERPUSS'*s cloak and dancing away*): Look at me! Whee!

CHINA (*Going to* GLOWERPUSS): Ching-a-ling-choy!

CAT (*Hitting* GLOWERPUSS'*s legs*): Meow! Hiss! Hiss!

GLOWERPUSS: Help! The toys are alive! (*Rushes about*)

HUMPTY (*Grabbing* GLOWERPUSS'*s hat and putting it on*): I've always wanted a hat.

RAGGEDY (*Flapping her arms at* GLOWERPUSS): Whoo-oo!

GLOWERPUSS: I think I am going mad!

SOLDIER (*Marching up and putting toy sword to* GLOWERPUSS'*s back*): Halt!

GLOWERPUSS (*Raising hands*): I give up. (*Sinks to knees beside table*) I'll be good. I promise.

SOLDIER: We saw you switch the agreements. Quickly, sign the *other* agreement, the one that gives the toy shop to Mr. and Mrs. Toymaker.

GLOWERPUSS: Yes, yes, anything you say. (*Pulls out pen and other agreement and signs.* SOLDIER *takes it from him.*)

CLOWN (*Tearing up agreement on table and throwing it*

down on floor): There we are. (*Sound of clock striking twelve is heard.*)

SOLDIER (*Putting paper on table*): Glowerpuss, leave the town of Oldenhurst and never come back.

ALL (*Chanting together*): Go, go, go, go!

HUMPTY: Never come back or we'll get you.

ALL (*Chanting together*): Get, get, get, get.

GLOWERPUSS (*Frightened*): Curses, foiled again. I think I will go away and live in a rest home. I must be losing my mind. (*Exits left, leaving hat and coat on floor. Toys return to places on shelf, and* JACK *returns to box. At stroke of twelve, they freeze.*)

CAROLYN (*Rushing in right with coat on and carrying suitcase*): What was all that noise? (*Looking around*) Mr. Glowerpuss?

JEREMY (*Entering right in flannel nightgown and cap*): What is all this?

SARAH (*Entering right, also in flannel nightgown and cap*): It sounds like a burglar. (*Looking at* CAROLYN) Oh, my goodness, a customer!

JEREMY: No, no, Sarah. It's Carolyn. What are you doing with that suitcase, Carolyn?

CAROLYN: I was going to marry Mr. Glowerpuss, but he disappeared. (*Puts down suitcase*)

JEREMY: Marry him? Why?

CAROLYN: So you could keep the toy shop, Father.

JEREMY (*Sinking into chair, shocked*): Oh, no!

SARAH (*Running to* CAROLYN *and hugging her*): My poor little Carolyn. (*Sound from off left of motorcycle starting up and roaring off*)

JEREMY: What was that?

CAROLYN: Sounds like a Honda to me.

JEREMY (*Picking up agreement*): What's this? (*He reads it.*)

CAROLYN (*Picking up cloak, hat, and torn papers*): Mr.

Glowerpuss must have left in quite a hurry. Look at all of this he left behind. (*Picking up torn paper, and reading it*) Why, that horrible man! He had two agreements. He was planning to cheat me.

JEREMY (*Leaping up excitedly*): Listen to this! (*Reads*) "Mr. and Mrs. Toymaker may have the toy shop, and it shall be theirs for the rest of their lives." It is signed "Mr. Glowerpuss."

SARAH *and* CAROLYN (*Hugging excitedly; ad lib*): Isn't that wonderful? I'm so happy! (*Etc.*)

JOHN (*Striding in left, waving papers*): I have the solution!

CAROLYN: John!

JEREMY: What do you have there, John?

JOHN: Contracts, Mr. Toymaker. I have contracts from all the toy shops in Barnesville. They want you to make enough toys to supply the entire town of Barnesville, and they will pay you thousands and thousands of dollars!

CAROLYN: Oh, John, you're so noble! (*Goes to him*)

JOHN (*To* CAROLYN): For you, my dear, I'd do anything! (*To* JEREMY) And I'll deliver the toys for you, Mr. Toymaker.

SARAH: What a wonderful Christmas we'll have this year!

JOE (*Dashing in left*): Guess what, everybody? I just saw old Glowerpuss zooming out of town at ninety miles per hour, on his Honda-Built-for-Two, with seven suitcases tied onto it. And his relatives were running behind him! (*Everyone cheers.*)

TOWN WATCHMAN (*Peeking in window and shouting*): Twelve-fifteen —

ALL (*Shouting to audience*): And all is peachy keen! (*Curtain*)

THE END

Santa Goes Mod

By Elbert M. Hoppenstedt

Santa wants to get rid of his traditional red suit, reindeer and sleigh. But he's in for a big surprise when he makes his announcement . . .

Characters

MS. BETTY TAYLOR, *Channel 7 newscaster*
STEVE, *TV cameraman*
SANTA CLAUS
MRS. CLAUS
SIX REPORTERS, *3 male; 3 female*
JOE }
BILL } *letter carriers*
FIVE ELVES, *male and female*
OTHER ELVES, *extras*

TIME: *The day before Christmas.*
SETTING: *Santa's workshop. Long tables are set up across rear of stage, covered with packages in Christmas wrappings, toy trains and cars, etc. A large sack, partially filled with wrapped packages, is on floor beside table. A decorated tree stands in one corner of the*

stage and on rear wall is sign reading SANTA'S WORK-
SHOP.

AT RISE: *Some* ELVES *are busy wrapping packages, as-
sembling toys, putting bows on dolls, etc. at tables;
others bustle on and off stage, holding clipboards,
half-finished toys, boxes, etc. One arranges packages
in sack, periodically making check marks on large pad.*
ELVES *continue in this fashion throughout play.* REPORT-
ERS, *holding pads and pencils, are talking together in
pantomime, downstage.* STEVE *is downstage left, holding portable TV camera with sign on it reading,*
CHANNEL 7 NEWS. BETTY TAYLOR *enters and stands
up right. She has a microphone around her neck, and
holds a clipboard and pencil. There is a general feeling
of bustling activity on the stage.*

TAYLOR (*Calling* STEVE *as she enters*): Steve! Hey, Steve!

STEVE (*Turning to look*): Betty! (*Trying to spot her
through crowd of* REPORTERS) Where are you?

TAYLOR (*Waving arms over her head*): Over here! (TAYLOR
goes to STEVE.) Say, this is pretty exciting! Just think
— our TV news show on Christmas Eve will be live
from Santa's workshop! It should do wonders for our
ratings. Steve, let's get a shot of those reporters so the
viewers can get a feel for the excitement and tension
here tonight. Do you think you can manage that?

STEVE: Are you kidding? How do you expect me to get
a shot in this madhouse?

TAYLOR: Come on, Steve. You're a good cameraman —
show a little initiative. Get your camera on top of that
table. (*Pointing*) From there you can pan the whole
room.

STEVE: That table where the elves are working?

TAYLOR: Of course. What other table is there?

STEVE: But I'll be right on top of them.

TAYLOR: So what? (*Indicating* ELVES) Those little peanuts won't be needed anymore, anyway. Not if Santa goes through with the plans he announced yesterday. Now get going.

STEVE: O.K. You're the boss. (STEVE *pushes his way past* REPORTERS, *clears away a portion of the table, and climbs up, facing audience and* MS. TAYLOR.) O.K. Now what?

TAYLOR: Pan for five seconds for an establishing shot. Then zoom in on me over there. (*Points to right*) When I finish, follow me over to the elves. When I finish with them, dissolve the shot and hold for Santa's and Mrs. Claus's entrance. (STEVE *does as instructed, as* BETTY *goes to right.*)

TAYLOR (*Into microphone*): Good evening. This is Betty Taylor, RBC News, Channel 7, live from Santa's workshop at the North Pole. As you can see, there's an atmosphere of tension and expectation here as members of the press wait for Santa Claus to appear. It's been just twenty-four hours since Santa made his startling announcement to the world that he plans to modernize Christmas, and he should be here any minute now to tell the world exactly what he has in mind. Rumor has it that Santa wants to do away with all the Christmas traditions that everyone knows and loves, and, of course, it's expected that people all over the world will react quite strongly to the news. Now, while we're waiting for Santa, let's go over and get a reaction from some of Santa's elves. (*Moves over beside* ELVES; *to* 1ST ELF) Pardon me. You're one of Santa's elves, aren't you? (1ST ELF *nods.*) Would you give us your reaction to Santa's plan to modernize Christmas?

1ST ELF (*Without looking up*): It won't work.

TAYLOR (*To camera audience*): There! You heard it from

one of Santa's helpers. It won't work! (*To* 1ST ELF)
Will you explain that?

1ST ELF: It's simple. You can't change Christmas. Nobody can change Christmas, not even Santa.

2ND ELF: Right! The world won't stand for it. You'll
see. It just won't succeed.

TAYLOR (*As she sees* SANTA *entering*): Here comes Santa
now! And that looks like Mrs. Claus with him. But
wait until you see what they're wearing! You won't believe it! My goodness, this *is* a moment the world
won't soon forget. (SANTA *and* MRS. CLAUS *enter.*
SANTA *has long, white beard and wears sunglasses, red
pants and T shirt with* SANTA *in big red letters on the
front.* MRS. CLAUS *wears matching outfit.* REPORTERS
move forward. TAYLOR *crosses to meet* SANTA *and*
MRS. CLAUS; *into microphone*) Here he is, boys and
girls! Here's Santa Claus! If it weren't for his white
beard you'd never recognize him! (*To* SANTA) Santa,
are these outfits you're wearing part of your plan to
modernize Christmas? (*Holds mike for* SANTA*'s answer*)

SANTA: Yes, they are. That suit I used to wear is out-
dated. They're wearing more sophisticated clothes
nowadays. I'm going to slim down, too. No more
round and jolly elf.

TAYLOR: How do you feel about this, Mrs. Claus?

MRS. CLAUS: I have my doubts, but Santa's usually right
when it comes to Christmas.

1ST REPORTER (*With pad and pencil*): What about your
reindeer, Santa? Are you getting rid of them, too?

SANTA: Of course. I'm using a helicopter tonight. It's
much more efficient.

2ND REPORTER: Would you explain that, Santa?

SANTA: Explain it? Isn't it obvious? Today everything is

scientific. Children don't believe in reindeer flying through the sky.

3RD REPORTER: What about the elves, Santa? I see they're still busy making toys.

SANTA: Next year we'll have an ultra-modern toy factory in operation here at the North Pole. Everything will be manufactured on an assembly line. Each child's Christmas wish will be programmed into a computer and the present will be automatically manufactured, wrapped and labeled.

REPORTERS (*Shouting out at once, ad lib, and waving hands*): Santa! Mr. Claus! I have a question! (*Etc.* SANTA *points to* 4TH REPORTER.)

4th Reporter: Santa, what will happen to your elves?

SANTA: They'll be moved into managerial positions. Next question? (*Pointing*) The reporter over there.

5TH REPORTER: I suppose, then, that you'll farm out your reindeer.

SANTA: Yes. They deserve a rest, don't you think?

5TH REPORTER: Santa, you've told us all about your plans to modernize Christmas, but have you consulted the children? Is this what they want?

SANTA: Of course, it's what they want!

5TH REPORTER: Have you asked them?

SANTA: I don't have to ask them. I know what the children want. After all, I *am* Santa Claus.

TAYLOR: The elves don't agree with you, Santa. They don't think it will work.

SANTA: They'll come around to my way of thinking. They don't know children the way I do. They've been at the North Pole for so many years they don't realize how things have changed.

TAYLOR: Do you mean that the children have changed?

SANTA: Of course. Children today keep up with all the

latest scientific advances. They will be delighted that I've modernized Christmas.

TAYLOR (*To* MRS. CLAUS): Mrs. Claus, how do you feel about all this?

MRS. CLAUS: I have faith in Santa. He knows what the children want. (*There is loud knocking at door, left stage.* MRS. CLAUS *opens door.* JOE *enters, wearing postal uniform and carrying large mail sack.*)

JOE (*To* MRS. CLAUS): Post office delivery for Santa Claus!

MRS. CLAUS: Goodness! I thought all the children's letters had arrived.

JOE: These letters just came today.

MRS. CLAUS: A whole bag of them?

BILL (*Entering, in uniform*): Not just one bag. There are at least fifty more outside.

MRS. CLAUS: Oh, dear! Santa, what shall we do with all of this mail?

SANTA (*To* JOE *and* BILL): Please bring some of it in here and leave the rest outside.

BILL: O.K., sir. (*Turns to leave, then speaks to* 1ST REPORTER) Who's that dude, anyway?

1ST REPORTER: That's the *new* Santa Claus.

BILL: That guy? You're kidding. He doesn't look any more like Santa than I do. (JOE *and* BILL *exit; during following dialogue, they come in and out with additional mail sacks.* MRS. CLAUS *starts to open and read mail.*)

MRS. CLAUS: These are all from children, but they're not asking for presents. They're about Santa's plans.

SANTA: Good, good.

1ST REPORTER: Looks as if you're getting a reaction from the public, Santa.

SANTA: Yes. This is wonderful. It's heartwarming to know that people approve of what I'm doing.

MRS. SANTA (*Reading letter and frowning*): I'm not so sure, Santa. Maybe you'd better look at these yourself.

6TH REPORTER: Read some of them out loud, Santa!

REPORTERS (*Ad lib*): Yes, read what they have to say. Let's hear how they like your plan. (*Etc.*)

SANTA: All right. (*To* MRS. CLAUS) Pick one at random, dear. (MRS. CLAUS *hands him a letter, and he reads it*) "Dear Santa, please *don't* change Christmas. I like it just the way it is." (MRS. CLAUS *hands him another, and he reads*) "Dear Santa, please don't change. I love your red and white suit, and your little round belly." (SANTA *pats stomach uneasily.*) These two letters are both against my plan! I just don't understand it.

MRS. CLAUS (*Handing letter to* SANTA): Maybe this letter will be more positive.

SANTA (*Taking letter*): I hope so. (*Reading*) "Dear Santa, I cried all night when I heard you wanted to change Christmas. Even Mom and Dad were sad. Dad said, 'Why does everything have to be modern?' Please stay just the way you are, Santa." (SANTA *puts letter down, scratches head.*) Dear me! (*Picking up another letter*)

TAYLOR (*While* SANTA *is opening letter; to* STEVE): Steve, pan in on me, then zoom in on Santa. (*Facing camera; into mike*) Something new has entered the picture here at the North Pole. Santa has received an avalanche of letters and cards from children all over the world. So far, every one he's read has been an anguished cry not to change the Christmas that children the world over have come to love and cherish.

SANTA (*Reading*): "Dear Santa Claus. I love your cute little elves. When I go to bed on Christmas Eve, I think of that beautiful poem, 'A Visit from St. Nicholas,' and I can almost hear the reindeer on the roof. So please, Santa, don't change a thing. I like Christmas just the way it is." (*Looks up*) I can't believe this! Everyone wants Christmas to stay the way it's been. I'll read one more. (*Picking up another letter, and reading*) "I look forward to Christmas all year long. I know every one of your reindeer by name. It won't be magic anymore if you come in a helicopter." (*Pause*) Dear me, I don't want to make the children unhappy!

1ST REPORTER: Let's see some of those letters, Santa.

2ND REPORTER: Yes, Santa. Give us a chance to read some. (SANTA *reaches into carton and tosses letters out to* REPORTERS. *They open letters and read them over.*)

3RD REPORTER: Another one against your plan, Santa.

4TH REPORTER: Same here.

2ND REPORTER: This one would break your heart, Santa.

5TH REPORTER (*Sadly*): This one, too.

6TH REPORTER: I never realized how much children love you, Santa. Not to mention your reindeer and sleigh, and the elves.

TAYLOR (*Into mike*): These letters are one hundred percent in favor of keeping Christmas just as it's always been. Surely, they must have touched Santa. (*To* SANTA) Santa, have these letters changed your mind about modernizing Christmas?

SANTA (*Musing*): I'm not sure. I have to do what's best for the children.

TAYLOR: But you've read their letters. You know that they want you to keep your red and white suit, the sleigh and reindeer — even your little round belly.

SANTA: Yes, but children don't always know what's best for them. I still think a modern Christmas may be best.

4TH ELF (*Entering in a rush*): Santa! Santa!

SANTA: What's the matter?

4TH ELF: Donder and Blitzen are sick. Dancer doesn't look at all well, either. In fact, all the reindeer are upset. They know you're not taking them tonight. They've seen the helicopter, and they don't feel needed anymore.

SANTA: Oh, dear. Still, progress is progress.

MRS. CLAUS (*Crossing to* SANTA): Santa, your idea is all wrong. I've felt it all along. These letters prove it. And now the reindeer are sick!

SANTA: There, there, my dear. Everything will be all right — I hope. It takes time, you know. Everyone has to get used to changes.

MRS. CLAUS: No, Santa. Deep down inside, I know this is all a mistake. I've thought so from the first moment you made up your mind to modernize Christmas. When I think of those poor little reindeer, I could cry!

SANTA: Come, come, my dear. They'll adjust.

MRS. CLAUS: And just look at your elves, working away at the toys. Inside, they must be miserable. (*Sound of loud crash is heard from offstage.*)

ALL (*Ad lib*): What was that? Goodness! It sounds as if the roof caved in! (*Etc.*)

5TH ELF (*Rushing in*): Santa! Santa! Your helicopter!

SANTA: What about it?

5TH ELF: It's wrecked!

SANTA: Wrecked? How can that be? I haven't even used it yet.

5TH ELF: I'm not sure exactly what happened, but the wind is very strong tonight, and I think it just picked up the helicopter and slammed it against an icecap. (*Shaking head*) It's completely wrecked, Santa.

SANTA: Good heavens! What shall I do? How can I deliver my presents?

MRS. CLAUS: Santa, have you forgotten so soon? Your reindeer will take you! They haven't failed you in a thousand years.

SANTA: You're absolutely right, dear. I guess I've been too hasty in thinking a modernized Christmas was best for everyone. There's no reason why we should get rid of things that have worked for a thousand years, and have also brought so much love to so many people!

MRS. CLAUS: That's right, Santa. (*Happily*) I'll go tell the elves to harness the reindeer. They'll all be so happy! (*She exits.*)

SANTA (*To* REPORTERS): And you can tell the world that Santa has finally been convinced that he has made a mistake. No one, not even I, can change Christmas. Christmas just wouldn't be Christmas without my sleigh and reindeer and my pack loaded with toys. (RE-PORTERS *cheer.* ELVES *wave toys, cheering.*)

REPORTERS (*Making quick exit, shouting ad libs*): Where's the telephone? What a story! Wait till the world hears about this! (*Etc.* Ms. TAYLOR, SANTA, STEVE *and* ELVES *remain on stage.*)

TAYLOR (*To* STEVE): Pan in for a close-up, Steve. (*To camera; into mike*) It's official, boys and girls! Santa has changed his mind. Christmas won't be modern after all! (MRS. CLAUS *enters, carrying* SANTA's *red and white jacket and wearing an old-fashioned dress and apron.*) And here's Mrs. Claus, back in her tradi-tional costume!

MRS. CLAUS (*Handing jacket to* SANTA): You bet I am! But it won't seem like Christmas to me until Santa gets into his costume, too. Santa, change — this instant!

SANTA: You bet I will! (*As he slips into jacket*) I'm be-ginning to feel like my old self again! (*To audience*) Merry Christmas to one and all! And I mean a good, old-fashioned Christmas! Ho! Ho! Ho! (*Quick curtain*)

THE END

The Greatest Christmas Gift

By John Murray

Three kind-hearted but poor Irish lasses risk the evil spells of a wicked witch to search for the real meaning of Christmas . . .

Characters

MAUREEN
FLOSSIE } *the Finnegan sisters*
SUSAN

ANNE
KATHLEEN } *their friends*
PAT
DORIS

MOLLY } *their parents*
SEAN

WILLY WISP
THREE LEPRECHAUNS
HERALD
KING OF TARA
PRINCE KEVIN
WIG-O'-THE-WAG, *a witch*
WIDOW O'SHEA
TOWNSPEOPLE, *extras*

SCENE 1

TIME: *Morning, three days before Christmas.*

SETTING: *The village square in Killybog Town, an old country village in Ireland, decorated for Christmas.*

AT RISE: *In the village square,* MAUREEN, FLOSSIE *and* SUSAN *stand center, unhappily watching the festive events going on around them.* TOWNSPEOPLE *enter and exit, talking and laughing.* ANNE, KATHLEEN, *with shawl,* PAT, *with pipe, and* DORIS, *with tea kettle, at right, excitedly show each other the various items, Christmas gifts, talking in pantomime.* TOWNSPEOPLE *grow quiet.* MAUREEN *speaks sadly to her sisters.*

MAUREEN: Two days before Christmas Eve, and it seems we're the only sisters in Killybog Town without a present for our parents. 'Tis hard to be so poor!

FLOSSIE: I tried to earn the money for a gift, Maureen. I went to the castle to help set the table for the Christmas celebration. But since Prince Kevin disappeared three months ago, there is only sadness in the castle, and the King has decreed that there will be no Christmas celebration.

SUSAN: I tried too, Flossie. I thought I could sell my artificial flowers at the market. They are so lovely! Marigolds, pansies, and mountain pinks. (*Mournfully*) Alas, the good people of Killybog Town are as poor as we are! No one bought my flowers.

MAUREEN: What are we to do, Susan? Even though you are the youngest, you have always seemed wise beyond your years — and your ideas have often helped the family.

SUSAN (*Dreamily*): If only I could find a gift for our parents — not just any gift, but the greatest gift in the world!

FLOSSIE: You're daft, girl!

MAUREEN: Pure fancy!

ANNE (*Proudly*): Good day to you, Finnegan sisters. Is this not the most beautiful shawl in Killybog Town?

KATHLEEN: Anne and I saved for many months to buy it. 'Tis a Christmas gift for our mother.

MAUREEN: Sure and the shawl is beautiful, Kathleen. (PAT *shows pipe proudly*.)

PAT: And I worked extra hours, plowing for the neighbors, to get the money for this fine briar pipe I'm giving Father. (*He puts pipe into mouth and struts about.*)

FLOSSIE: 'Tis a wonderful gift for your father, Pat!

DORIS (*Showing them tea kettle*): Think of the fine tea my kettle will brew for the family!

SUSAN: They will be proud of the kettle, I'm sure, Doris. (*All continue to examine gifts and talk quietly.* WILLY WISP, *an old man clutching a cane, enters left, followed by* THREE LEPRECHAUNS, *who wear long beards. Finnegan sisters and their friends cast nervous glances at them.*)

WILLY (*Looking back*): Is she gone, my friendly leprechauns?

1ST LEPRECHAUN: I do not see her, Willy Wisp.

2ND LEPRECHAUN: That Widow O'Shea is a cagey one.

WILLY (*Unhappily*): For ten years, Widow O'Shea has tried to make me her husband. (*Smiles*) But thanks to your help, faithful leprechauns, I have escaped her wiles. I will reward you one day.

WIDOW O'SHEA (*From offstage*): Yoo-hoo! Willy Wisp! Wait for me!

WILLY: 'Tis the Widow O'Shea once more!

1ST LEPRECHAUN: She's found us again! (WILLY *frantically looks around, sees Finnegan sisters and their friends, and brightens.*)

WILLY (*Brightly*): All is not lost. (*He points to children.*) Perhaps those children will hide us.

WIDOW (*From offstage*): Willy Wisp! Where are you? (WILLY *and* LEPRECHAUNS *rush over to children.*)

WILLY (*To children*): Quick! We must hide. Will you help us?

2ND LEPRECHAUN: The Widow O'Shea is after Willy again.

ANNE: The widow? (*Nervously*) Oh, if she sees the shawl, she'll tell my mother and ruin the Christmas surprise! (*Backs away*)

PAT (*Cringing*): She always pinches my cheek and wants to kiss me. What a terrible fate! No, no, I must avoid her. (*Starts off*)

DORIS: I must be going home. It's very late. (ANNE, KATHLEEN, PAT *and* DORIS *rush off, right.*)

WILLY (*Desperately, to* MAUREEN): Please help us!

MAUREEN: But how?

FLOSSIE: We're no match for Widow O'Shea.

SUSAN (*Brightly*): I know how we can help! (*She spreads wide her skirt.*) Quick — hide behind our skirts. (MAUREEN *and* FLOSSIE *stand beside* SUSAN *and spread their skirts.* WILLY *and* LEPRECHAUNS *quickly hide behind girls.* WIDOW O'SHEA *enters left, carrying a large covered dish. She glances around with mounting disappointment.*)

WIDOW (*Calling*): Willy Wisp! (*To herself*) That awful man! He's disappeared again. (*To sisters*) Girls, have you seen Willy Wisp anywhere?

MAUREEN: No, Widow O'Shea. (*Nervously*) He's not in sight.

WIDOW (*Sighing*): Oh, dear, and I prepared a fine Irish stew for him. I've taken a fancy to that man.

SUSAN: Perhaps he's in the forest.

WIDOW: That's a good idea! I'll look for him there. (*Moving right, gaily*) Girls, if you see Willy Wisp, tell him he can have the hand of Widow O'Shea in marriage as his Christmas gift. (*She exits right.* WILLY WISP *and* LEPRECHAUNS *peek out from behind sisters, then come out.* WILLY *wipes his brow.*)

WILLY: A Christmas present? That's one gift I'd like to exchange.

1ST LEPRECHAUN: You are safe now, Willy, at least for a time.

WILLY (*Beaming*): I owe it all to the wonderful Finnegan sisters.

SUSAN: We're always willing to help. (*Sadly*) Besides, it made us forget about our troubles.

WILLY: Troubles?

SUSAN (*Nodding*): Yes. We have no Christmas gift for our parents.

MAUREEN: And Christmas is only three days away.

WILLY (*Nodding*): I see. (*To* LEPRECHAUNS) Come here, my friends. (WILLY *and* LEPRECHAUNS *huddle together, talking quietly, then face sisters, smiling.*)

3RD LEPRECHAUN: 'Tis all agreed.

WILLY (*Nodding*): We will tell you where you can find a wonderful gift. In fact, three gifts!

SUSAN (*Excitedly*): Three gifts! Please — lead us to them!

WILLY (*Waving hand*): It is not so simple as that.

1ST LEPRECHAUN: You must choose only one gift — and it must be the greatest gift of all.

2ND LEPRECHAUN (*Ominously*): If you do not choose the greatest gift, a dire fate will befall you.

MAUREEN: I do not understand.

SUSAN: How will we know which one is the greatest gift?

WILLY: That is for you to decide.

1ST LEPRECHAUN: There is a gift of diamonds, diamonds of fiery beauty, diamonds that rival the stars!

MAUREEN: Diamonds? Surely they must be the greatest gift!

2ND LEPRECHAUN: And there is a gift of gold — enough gold for a king's ransom.

FLOSSIE (*Excitedly*): Gold! Yes, that is the greatest gift, indeed!

SUSAN: Patience, my sisters. (*To* WILLY) And what is the third gift?

3RD LEPRECHAUN: The third gift must remain unnamed. But we can tell you this — it is as great as the heart of the one who bestows it.

WILLY (*Cautiously*): Now you must choose carefully.

1ST LEPRECHAUN: If you choose a gift which does not prove to be the greatest one, you will be turned to stone! (*Sisters look at each other, frightened.*)

MAUREEN: Where will we find these gifts?

WILLY: They are hidden in a castle in the forest. Doomsday Castle! Do you know it?

FLOSSIE: Not Doomsday Castle — that evil place is guarded by a witch!

SUSAN: Yes — the Wig-o'-the-Wag!

WILLY: 'Tis true. I told you where to look for the gifts. That is all my powers allow. You must find them for yourself, and choose the greatest.

FLOSSIE: But which of us is brave enough to go? The Wig-o'-the-Wag is evil, indeed. She casts spells, makes a devil's brew, and captures the children of Killybog Town.

SUSAN: They say that children who venture into Doomsday Castle are never seen again. (*Determined*) But, sisters, we must find the greatest gift for our parents, in spite of the danger.

MAUREEN (*Bravely*): It must be my task, for I am the oldest. I will set out for Doomsday Castle this very day to seek employment with the Wig-o'-the-Wag, and search for the greatest gift. I will return on Christmas Eve.

WILLY (*Shaking finger*): Beware, girl! Remember, you must choose the greatest gift, or you will be turned to stone!

MAUREEN: I am not afraid. I must hasten to Doomsday Castle. There is little time! (*She starts to exit and others wave as curtains close.*)

* * * * *

SCENE 2

TIME: *One day later.*

SETTING: *The main room in Doomsday Castle. Fireplace with artificial flames is down right. There is screen beside door up right.*

AT RISE: MAUREEN *is on her knees scrubbing floor. She rinses rag in bucket, brushes wisp of hair from her forehead, then stands, rubbing her back.*

MAUREEN (*To herself*): I have been in the castle for twenty-four hours, and yet I have not seen a trace of the three great gifts. (*Glances around*) Where can they be hidden? I have searched hard and long, but I cannot find them. And which is the greatest gift? Is it diamonds? Is it gold? Or perhaps it is the third, unnamed gift. (*Distressed*) I wish someone could help me! (WIG-O'-THE-WAG *enters left, carrying broom, which she points accusingly at* MAUREEN.)

WIG-O'-THE-WAG: Are you dreaming on the job, girl? Remember, there's much work to be done.

MAUREEN: Forgive me, Wig-o'-the-Wag. I was resting.

WIG-O'-THE-WAG (*Scornfully*): Resting, indeed! Remember . . . (*Chants*)

> You must finish your work,
> Attend to the chores,
> Polish the silver,
> Scrub the floors,
> Watch the fire,
> And never lag,
> Or you'll feel the wrath
> Of old Wig-o'-the-Wag!

(*She chuckles wickedly and does a little dance as MAUREEN cringes.*)

MAUREEN: I will obey!

WIG-O'-THE-WAG (*Menacing*): That's good. You don't want to join my little friends in the dungeon, do you? (*Points to door left*)

MAUREEN (*Frightened*): Oh, no, please! (*She takes out handkerchief and wipes tears.*)

WIG-O'-THE-WAG: Very well, girl. But I shall watch to see that you do your work. Now I must leave for Killybog Town. The people are filled with the spirit of Christmas. The Wig-o'-the-Wag will spoil their fun! (*To MAUREEN*) One thing you must remember. (*She points to fireplace at right; ominously*) You must never look into the fireplace. If you do, you will regret it for the rest of your life.

MAUREEN (*Drying her tears*): No, no! I will never look into the fireplace. I swear it!

WIG-O'-THE-WAG: Heed me well. The fireplace will be your undoing. (*She walks to right exit, turns, waves her broom.*) I'll return at dusk! (WIG-O'-THE-WAG *exits.* MAUREEN *looks after her a moment, twisting handkerchief in hands.*)

MAUREEN (*Hopefully*): The fireplace! Perhaps the greatest Christmas gift is hidden there. (MAUREEN *crosses to fireplace. She does not notice as* WIG-O'-THE-WAG *reenters at right, slips behind screen next to door and peers out, watching* MAUREEN.) I'm going to look for it while old Wig-o'-the-Wag is gone. If I can find the gift, I can return to my sisters. (MAUREEN *kneels beside fireplace.* WILLY WISP *and* THREE LEPRECHAUNS *enter right.*)

WILLY (*Waving hands*): Stop, Maureen! (MAUREEN *turns and rises.*)

MAUREEN: Why, Willy Wisp! What a surprise! Come help me. I think the greatest gift is hidden in the fireplace.

1ST LEPRECHAUN (*Quickly*): No, Maureen. Don't take another step. We came to warn you about the Wig-o'-the-Wag. She will try to trick you.

2ND LEPRECHAUN (*Nodding*): If you do not find the greatest gift, you will be turned to stone!

3RD LEPRECHAUN: The Wig-o'-the-Wag may be watching you this very minute.

MAUREEN (*Shaking head*): No, she has gone to Killybog Town. She will not return until nightfall.

WILLY (*As if in trance*): My magic senses tell me that the witch is here in the castle this very minute. (WIG-O'-THE-WAG *exits right, unnoticed.*)

1ST LEPRECHAUN: We will search for her. (MAUREEN *watches as others search room.* WILLY *looks under table,* 1ST LEPRECHAUN *peers through left door which leads to dungeon.* 2ND LEPRECHAUN *looks into cauldron near fireplace.* 3RD LEPRECHAUN *looks behind chairs and screen. Finally all meet center.*)

2ND LEPRECHAUN: There is no witch here.

WILLY: Then it is safe for us to leave now — and may

the Christmas spirit protect you this day! (WILLY *and* THREE LEPRECHAUNS *exit right.*)

MAUREEN: What strange little men! (*Suddenly*) Now I can get back to the fireplace! (*She kneels at fireplace, looks into flames. A bag containing diamonds suddenly falls from fireplace. Note: Bags of diamonds and gold are thrown from offstage through fireplace by a member of stage crew.*) The gift! (*In her excitement,* MAUREEN *drops handkerchief in front of fireplace. She picks up bag, walks to table, opens bag and takes out some diamonds.* WIG-O'-THE-WAG *enters right, again hides behind screen and watches.*) Diamonds! How lovely! Yes — I'm sure this is the greatest gift! (WIG-O'-THE-WAG *leaves her hiding place, rushes downstage, grabs diamonds and bag.* MAUREEN *screams.*) Wig-o'-the-Wag!

WIG-O'-THE-WAG: Faithless girl! You tried to steal my treasure.

MAUREEN (*Terrified*): I meant no harm! Here, I will return the diamonds to the fireplace!

WIG-O'-THE-WAG (*Cruelly*): It is too late. Your fate is sealed. Foolish one, do you think that diamonds are the greatest gift? Diamonds have brought misery and despair to men throughout the ages. Diamonds are *not* the greatest gift! (*She gestures dramatically.*)

MAUREEN (*Crying*): Please, don't harm me!

WIG-O'-THE-WAG (*Chanting*):
Wig-o'-the-Wag, and Wig-o'-the-West,
Wig-o'-the-East, the worst and the best.
Stone you shall be, and stone you shall stay,
'Til the greatest gift is given away.

(WIG-O'-THE-WAG *gestures again. Crash of cymbals is heard offstage.* MAUREEN *freezes, as if turned to stone.* WIG-O'-THE-WAG *cackles wickedly.*) It's off to the dungeon with this fair prize! I'll keep her there with the other children I've turned to stone! (*Cackles again and advances on* MAUREEN *as curtains close*)

* * * * *

SCENE 3

TIME: *Late that evening.*

SETTING: *The Finnegan cottage. This scene may be played before curtain if desired.*

A:T RISE: SEAN FINNEGAN *and his wife,* MOLLY, *sit at table at left.* SEAN *shakes his head, rises.*

SEAN: There'll be no Christmas gifts for our daughters, I fear.

MOLLY: Please, Sean, don't carry on so. We may not be rich, but at least we'll have our daughters when Christmas dawns in two days. They mean more to us than any gifts and feasting would.

SEAN (*Concerned*): I wonder why they are so late returning from Killybog Town. (FLOSSIE *and* SUSAN *enter right.*)

MOLLY (*Relieved*): Girls, we were beginning to fret! Where were you?

SEAN: And where is Maureen?

SUSAN: She'll be here shortly. (*Gives* FLOSSIE *a guilty look*) She might have a surprise, too.

MOLLY: I'd better prepare the evening meal. Please set the table, girls. (*Sadly*) There'll be little enough food to share. (MOLLY *exits left.*)

SEAN: And I must fetch the cows from the high pasture. Poor creatures! The grain is almost gone. I shall be forced to sell them in the market place. (*Exits right*)

SUSAN (*Reproachfully*): Flossie, you didn't tell our parents about Maureen.

FLOSSIE: How could I tell them she left for Doomsday

Castle yesterday? They don't realize she didn't sleep in her room last night.

SUSAN: You were a clever one, stuffing her bed with straw. But what are we to do now?

FLOSSIE (*Abruptly*): Please, Susan, I can't think about it.

SUSAN: Perhaps she cannot return.

FLOSSIE (*Upset*): Then we must go find her! We must go to Doomsday Castle this very night! (*Fanfare of trumpets is heard from offstage.*)

SUSAN (*Startled*): Someone is coming!

FLOSSIE (*Rushing right*): It must be someone important, to be announced by trumpets! (*Looks out, gasps*) Susan, 'tis the King! (HERALD *enters.*)

HERALD: His Royal Majesty, the King of Tara. (KING *enters.* SUSAN *and* FLOSSIE *curtsy.*)

KING: Arise, daughters of Finnegan, and hear me well.

FLOSSIE: Your Majesty, we are at your command.

SUSAN: Our humble cottage is honored, indeed.

KING: It is a sad plight which brings me here tonight. My son, Prince Kevin, has been missing for three months.

FLOSSIE: All Killybog Town knows this sad tale, Your Majesty.

SUSAN: 'Tis a tragedy!

KING: One evening at the rise of the summer moon he rode off into the forest, and he has not returned to the kingdom since that night.

FLOSSIE: But what can we do to help?

KING: I have been told that Willy Wisp and his three faithful leprechauns have befriended you.

SUSAN: Yes. They have told us many wondrous things.

KING: I hoped they might be here. I beg of you to entreat them to help me. Half my kingdom will go to the person who returns my son to his rightful place.

FLOSSIE: We do not know how to find Willy and the leprechauns. They appear by magic, it seems.

SUSAN: We will help search for the Prince Kevin ourselves. Alas, our sister Maureen has disappeared, too. She set off for Doomsday Castle yesterday and promised to return tonight, but she has not come back.

FLOSSIE (*Decisively*): We must find her. Perhaps we will find Prince Kevin, too. (WILLY *and* THREE LEPRECHAUNS *rush in right. They bow before* KING.)

WILLY: Your Majesty, we heard you call us. We are at your service.

KING: We must search for my son, the Prince, and the Finnegans' dear daughter, Maureen.

WILLY (*To* SUSAN): Where is Maureen? Has she not returned?

SUSAN (*Sighing*): Alas, no.

1ST LEPRECHAUN: We saw her at Doomsday Castle yesterday.

2ND LEPRECHAUN: She said the Wig-o'-the-Wag had left for Killybog Town, but no one there has seen her evil face.

3RD LEPRECHAUN (*Nodding*): The witch must have returned to the castle.

FLOSSIE (*Frightened*): Oh, dear, do you think she has harmed our sister?

WILLY (*Sadly*): It is likely, I am afraid.

SUSAN: I fear that Maureen has been turned to stone.

KING (*Waving arms*): Stop! Enough! If there is evil in Doomsday Castle, my soldiers will storm the walls at once.

WILLY: It will be to no avail.

1ST LEPRECHAUN: No mortal can stand up against the magic spell of old Wig-o'-the-Wag.

SUSAN (*Despairingly*): What can we do?

FLOSSIE: I am the eldest sister now, so I will go to Dooms-day Castle. Perhaps I will be able to help Maureen.

SUSAN: How will you enter the castle?

FLOSSIE (*Faltering*): Why, I'll tell the Wig-o'-the-Wag that I'm a poor serving maid.

SUSAN: No, no! The witch will be suspicious.

WILLY (*Suddenly*): The spirits have sent Willy Wisp a brilliant thought. (*To* FLOSSIE) You will pretend to be lost in the dark forest with your three hungry babes. You will seek shelter from the Wig-o'-the-Wag. Such a sad tale will warm even a witch's heart!

SUSAN: Splendid! But where will Flossie find three babes?

WILLY (*Smiling*): They are right at hand. (*He looks meaningfully at* LEPRECHAUNS.) You, my worthy leprechauns, will be the three babes.

1ST LEPRECHAUN (*Quickly*): But I am too old —

2ND LEPRECHAUN: And I am too fat —

3RD LEPRECHAUN: Besides, we have long, white beards. (*Triumphantly*) What about that?

WILLY: That can be changed with a razor! (*To* KING) Your Majesty, will you help me?

KING: Willingly! (*He grabs* 1ST LEPRECHAUN. WILLY *grabs* 2ND *and* 3RD LEPRECHAUNS. *They all exit left, followed by* HERALD.)

FLOSSIE: What gallant little men!

SUSAN (*Sadly*): I'm sure they treasured their beards. (SEAN *and* MOLLY *enter left.*)

SEAN: Our good King and Willy Wisp are shaving the beards off some leprechauns! What is going on?

FLOSSIE: Have patience, Father. Everything will be explained in good time. (KING, WILLY *and* THREE LEPRECHAUNS *enter left.* LEPRECHAUNS *no longer wear beards.*)

1ST LEPRECHAUN (*Rubbing his chin*): I'm naked!

2ND LEPRECHAUN (*Distressed*): How will I ever be able to strain my soup?

3RD LEPRECHAUN: I shall have nothing to keep my chest warm on those cold, wintery nights!

WILLY: It's for a good cause, my friends. Now be off with Flossie. We will await your safe return at this cottage. (FLOSSIE *and* THREE LEPRECHAUNS *exit right. Others wave farewell. Curtains close.*)

* * * * *

SCENE 4

TIME: *Later that night.*

AT RISE: WIG-O'-THE-WAG *sits before fireplace, staring into flames.*

WIG-O'-THE-WAG (*Chanting*):
Flames rise high,
Fire burn bright,
Strengthen my powers
This very night.

(*She cackles wickedly, rises, walks left to dungeon door. She opens door, calls.*) My little friends — my works of stone — are you happy tonight? (*Loud rapping on door at right is heard. She closes dungeon door quickly, crosses right and opens door.* FLOSSIE *enters with* THREE LEPRECHAUNS. WIG-O'-THE-WAG *points finger at* FLOSSIE *accusingly.*) What are you doing in my castle?

FLOSSIE (*Innocently*): Kind woman, have pity on me. Give me refuge from the dark, menacing forest! My children and I are lost and friendless. We have had no food for two days.

1ST LEPRECHAUN: Make that three days!

FLOSSIE: We wish to seek shelter. You have a warm, kindly face. (2ND LEPRECHAUN *nudges* 3RD LEPRECHAUN.*)

2ND LEPRECHAUN: She needs glasses.

WIG-O'-THE-WAG (*Coldly*): This is not a tavern or an inn. Begone — and take those hateful children with you!

FLOSSIE (*Protestingly*): They are wonderful children! Please look at their innocent, pleading faces. (WIG-O'-THE-WAG *stares at* 1ST LEPRECHAUN. *He sticks out his tongue. She looks at* 2ND LEPRECHAUN, *who makes a wry face.* 3RD LEPRECHAUN *dances crazily around room.*)

WIG-O'-THE-WAG: These are the strangest children old Wig-o'-the-Wag has ever seen. (*She picks up broom.*) Begone, I say, or you will feel the wrath of this old woman! (3RD LEPRECHAUN *kicks her in the shin. She hops on one foot in pain. He starts to clap in rhythm to her jumping. She stops, turns on him angrily.*) You scalawag! I'll fix you, all right. (3RD LEPRECHAUN *runs out right.* WIG-O'-THE-WAG *follows.*)

FLOSSIE: All is not well, I'm afraid.

1ST LEPRECHAUN: At least our friend got rid of the Wig-o'-the-Wag. Now we can search for the greatest Christmas gift!

FLOSSIE (*Determined*): We must find my sister Maureen first. (*Suddenly sober*) But where will we start? Dooms-day Castle is such a large place. (*She walks near fire-place, sees and picks up* MAUREEN'*s handkerchief; excitedly*) This is my sister's handkerchief, I'm sure! She must have been here — in this very room!

1ST LEPRECHAUN: And near the fireplace, too. Do you suppose the gift is hidden there?

FLOSSIE: Perhaps it is. Maureen probably dropped her handkerchief while searching for the gift. But where is she now? What has old Wig-o'-the-Wag done to my sister? I have a feeling she's very near.

MAUREEN (*From offstage in filtered voice*): Flossie! Here I am, dear sister!

FLOSSIE: Yes, I can hear her voice! Maureen, where are you?

MAUREEN (*Offstage*): I can't come to you now, Flossie, but I must warn you. Beware — beware of the fireplace!

FLOSSIE: I hear you, Maureen, but I am not afraid. I *must* search the fireplace. (FLOSSIE *drops to her knees, stares into fire. Bag of gold is flung from fireplace, as before. She picks up bag, crosses to table.* LEPRECHAUNS *follow eagerly. She opens bag of gold. Coins spill onto table.*)

FLOSSIE (*Joyfully*): Gold! The bag is filled with gold! (LEPRECHAUNS *clap excitedly.*)

1ST LEPRECHAUN: It's more gold than I've ever seen!

2ND LEPRECHAUN: A king's ransom, indeed!

FLOSSIE: This must be the greatest gift! (*Quickly, she returns coins to bag. A commotion is heard offstage.*) Oh, no! Old Wig-o'-the-Wag is coming back! (*She hides gold under her apron as* WIG-O'-THE-WAG *enters right, pulling* 3RD LEPRECHAUN *after her. He rubs seat of his trousers.* WIG-O'-THE-WAG *shakes her broom.*)

WIG-O'-THE-WAG: That is how I handle a spoiled child! A good spanking taught him a lesson. (*To* FLOSSIE) Now, be off with these incorrigible children — and never enter Doomsday Castle again!

FLOSSIE (*Meekly*): Yes, old woman, I will seek shelter elsewhere. (*She turns. Bag of gold falls to floor.* WIG-O'-THE-WAG *shrieks in rage.*)

WIG-O'-THE-WAG: My gold! My bag of gold!

1ST LEPRECHAUN (*Boldly*): It is *not* your gold, old woman! You stole it from the villagers in Killybog Town.

2ND LEPRECHAUN: We will return it to the villagers.

FLOSSIE: It is the greatest gift.

WIG-O'-THE-WAG: The greatest gift? (*She laughs nastily.*) I see it all now! You weren't lost in the forest. You came here looking for the greatest gift. Well, you have chosen the wrong one. Gold is *not* the greatest gift. Have not the greatest crimes been committed for the love of gold? No, gold is not the greatest gift. (*She chants, gesturing.*)

Wig-o'-the-Wag, and Wig-o'-the-West,
Wig-o'-the-East, the worst and the best.
Stone you shall be, and stone you shall stay,
'Til the greatest gift is given away.

(*Crashing of cymbals is heard from offstage as* WIG-O'-THE-WAG *laughs. Suddenly* FLOSSIE *and* THREE LEPRECHAUNS *freeze into position.* WIG-O'-THE-WAG *cackles again. Curtains close.*)

* * * * *

SCENE 5

TIME: *Early morning, day before Christmas.*

SETTING: *Same as Scene 3.*

AT RISE: MOLLY *and* SEAN *sit at table.* SEAN*'s head is buried in his hands.* KING *paces nervously.* SUSAN *stands near entrance, right, looking offstage.* KING *stops pacing, pounds fist on table.*

KING (*Impatiently*): Where are they? What has happened to Flossie and the leprechauns? (SUSAN *joins others.*)

SUSAN: The day breaks. It is Christmas Eve, and there is no sign of Flossie and the leprechauns.

MOLLY: My poor daughters!

SEAN: Who knows what evil has befallen them in Doomsday Castle!

KING (*Determined*): I will lead my army against the castle this very day, magic powers or not!

SUSAN (*Coaxingly*): That would not be wise, Your Majesty. We must be as clever and cunning as the Wig-o'-the-Wag.

KING: What do you mean?

SUSAN: I have a plan. I will leave for Doomsday Castle now.

SEAN (*Standing*): No! I forbid it. I have lost two daughters already. You must not go to the witch's castle.

SUSAN (*Gently*): I must go, Father. I do not fear Wig-o'-the-Wag. (*She reaches under table, takes out covered basket.*) I have something more powerful than her evil magic.

KING: You are a brave girl, and you may go with my blessing.

SUSAN: Thank you, sire. Sweet thoughts of Christmas will cheer me on my way. (*She exits right.* KING, SEAN *and* MOLLY *wave farewell. Curtains close.*)

* * * * *

SCENE 6

TIME: *Later that day.*

SETTING: *Same as Scene 2.*

AT RISE: WIG-O'-THE-WAG *stands before stone-like figures of* FLOSSIE, MAUREEN, THREE LEPRECHAUNS *and* PRINCE KEVIN.

WIG-O'-THE-WAG: 'Tis Christmas Eve! A fitting day to release you from the dungeon, my friends of stone. Yes, we will have a happy day together, but you will return to the dungeon while I wreak havoc on the villagers of Killybog Town tonight. It will be a dismal Christmas for them, I assure you! (*She laughs wickedly. There is a knock on door, right. Hastily* WIG-O'-THE-WAG *covers "statues" with sheets.*) Again, some intruder comes to my door. I am ready! Who knows? Perhaps the intruder will join my friends in the dungeon this very day. (*She opens door.* SUSAN *enters, carrying basket.*)

SUSAN (*As she enters*): I bring you Christmas greetings, Wig-o'-the-Wag! (*She displays basket.*) Here is a small offering to show my good intentions.

WIG-O'-THE-WAG: You seem familiar, girl. (*Stares at* SUSAN *carefully*) Yes, you resemble two of my friends.

SUSAN: I'm certain we have never met before, but I feel that I must give you my gift.

WIG-O'-THE-WAG: How kind, my child. But first, I will perform my own kind deed. I have a little gift for *you*. (*She gestures toward fireplace.*) If you will step to the fireplace and gaze into the flames, you will be changed for the better, indeed! (*Cackles*)

SUSAN (*To herself*): That is a strange request, but perhaps I will find a gift for my parents. (*She walks to fireplace.* WIG-O'-THE-WAG *rubs her hands in glee.*)

MAUREEN *and* FLOSSIE (*Together, from under sheets*): Do not look into the fireplace, sister!

SUSAN (*Confused*): Do I hear voices?

WIG-O'-THE-WAG: It is only the wind moaning through the trees in Doomsday Forest.

SUSAN (*Thoughtfully*): Yes, the wind — (*She kneels before fireplace.*)

WIG-O'-THE-WAG: Look into the fire now, my child. (WIG-O'-THE-WAG *walks over to* SUSAN *and bends over her. Quickly,* SUSAN *opens basket, takes out handful of hand-made flowers, rises and turns.*)

SUSAN (*Sweetly*): You are so kind, Wig-o'-the-Wag, to offer me a gift. But please, accept my gift first. (*She displays flowers.*)

WIG-O'-THE-WAG (*Frightened*): Get away from me. (*She retreats. covering her eyes.*)

SUSAN (*Advancing towards* WIG-O'-THE-WAG; *innocently*): Don't you like my flowers? I made them myself. Aren't they beautiful? See, there are marigolds, pansies, and mountain pinks.

WIG-O'-THE-WAG (*Still retreating*): No! No! Take them away!

SUSAN (*Following*): But they are my special gift to you. The flowers are beautiful — and beauty cannot be destroyed by your evil, wicked ways. (*Triumphantly*) You cannot withstand the power of beauty, grace and love, and these flowers represent all of those things. Begone, witch! (*She flings flowers at* WIG-O'-THE-WAG, *who shrieks in terror.*)

WIG-O'-THE-WAG (*Enraged*): You have found the greatest gift! (*Crash of cymbals is heard offstage.* WIG-O'-THE-WAG *freezes. Slowly,* FLOSSIE, MAUREEN, *and* THREE LEPRECHAUNS *stretch, then remove their covers. They rub their eyes, shake their heads.* SUSAN *rushes over to them.*)

SUSAN (*Ecstatic*): My sisters! Kind leprechauns! You are alive! You are free!

MAUREEN (*Dazed*): It seems we have slept forever.

FLOSSIE: What a strange experience! (THREE LEPRECHAUNS *do a little dance, click their heels.* SUSAN *notices that one figure remains covered.*)

SUSAN: Who is this? (*She goes to remaining "statue" and removes cover, revealing* PRINCE KEVIN.)

FLOSSIE: It is Kevin, the missing prince!

MAUREEN: The king's son!

SUSAN (*Bewildered*): But why is he not free of the wicked spell? (*Points to* WIG-O'-THE-WAG) She is turned to stone, but Kevin is still under her evil spell.

MAUREEN: What are we going to do?

FLOSSIE (*Downcast*): We have failed our good King.

SUSAN (*Brightly*): Don't worry. The greatest gift will free Kevin. (*She takes a flower from her basket and pushes it into his hand.*)
>Oh, worthy prince,
>Please take this flower.
>Its beauty and love,
>Will free you this hour!

(KEVIN *stirs slowly, shakes his head, looks at flower, then stares at* SUSAN *and smiles.*)

KEVIN: Fair maiden! With this great magic — this flower and your love — you have spared me an evil fate. (*He drops to one knee.*) This day, if you are willing, I will make you my bride, and you will be proclaimed princess of all the land. (SUSAN *smiles, nods, and extends her hand to him. He rises to clasp it.*) We will share your magic flowers forever. Truly, they are fashioned with love!

MAUREEN (*Wistfully*): What miracles love can perform!

FLOSSIE: Our dear little Susan, a princess! What a wonderful Christmas we will have!

MAUREEN: Sisters, Christmas Day is drawing near.

KEVIN: Then we must hasten to Killybog Town to show the villagers they will have a joyous Christmas, after all. (*Suddenly bags containing diamonds and gold are flung from fireplace.* THREE LEPRECHAUNS *open bags, scoop up contents.*)

1ST LEPRECHAUN: Diamonds!

2ND LEPRECHAUN: Gold!

3RD LEPRECHAUN: The house of Finnegan is blessed this day!

SUSAN: And I have found the greatest gift of all. (*She smiles at* KEVIN *and sisters as curtains close.*)

*   *   *   *   *

SCENE 7

TIME: *Later that day.*

SETTING: *Same as Scene 1.*

AT RISE: KING, HERALD, SEAN, MOLLY, PAT, DORIS, ANNE, KATHLEEN, WILLY WISP, THREE LEPRECHAUNS, MAUREEN, FLOSSIE, SUSAN, PRINCE KEVIN *and* TOWNSPEOPLE *are assembled onstage, talking excitedly.* MAUREEN *and* FLOSSIE *hold bags.*)

KING: What a joyous day this is! Prince Kevin has returned to us, and everyone is safe from the Wig-o'-the-Wag, thanks to the Finnegan sisters. In gratitude, I hereby proclaim that Flossie, Susan and Maureen Finnegan shall have half of my kingdom!

ALL (*Ad lib*): Hurrah! Three cheers for the brave Finnegan sisters! (*Etc.*)

WILLY: What *is* the greatest Christmas gift? Everyone is talking about it.

SUSAN: Please be patient! You will find out all in good time. (MAUREEN *steps forward, hands bag of diamonds to* MOLLY.)

MAUREEN (*Proudly*): Here is our Christmas present to you, dear Mother — diamonds so shining and bright that they rival the stars at night! (FLOSSIE *hands bag of gold to* SEAN.)

FLOSSIE: And for you, Father, a shower of gold to bring riches and contentment to our home!

SEAN: These are wonderful gifts, indeed, but gifts we cannot keep for ourselves. They were stolen from our good neighbors by the evil Wig-o'-the-Wag, and so we will share them with all of Killybog Town.

ALL (*Ad lib*): Hurrah for Sean Finnegan! What a kind, honest man! (*Etc.*)

WILLY (*To* SUSAN): We owe everything to you, Susan, because you destroyed the Wig-o'-the-Wag with your wonderful flowers.

1ST LEPRECHAUN: They must possess some magic power!

3RD LEPRECHAUN (*To* SUSAN): Please explain to us this magical power — the greatest Christmas gift. (SUSAN *takes* KEVIN's *hand.*)

SUSAN (*Reciting*):
> Upon this earth,
> Or Heaven above,
> The greatest gift
> Of all is — Love!

(TOWNSPEOPLE *cheer, then begin to sing and dance.* WIDOW O'SHEA *rushes in with covered dish, grabs* WILLY *by arm.*)

WIDOW: I have a little magic of my own, Willy Wisp. 'Tis my famous Irish stew! It will make you a changed man, my husband-to-be!

WILLY (*Sadly*): Woe is me! I can hear the ringing of the wedding bells! (*Suddenly he grins broadly.*) But you *are* the greatest cook in Killybog Town, and I am a lonesome man! (*He puts his arm around* WIDOW, *who laughs with delight. All form tableau with* KEVIN, SUSAN, MAUREEN, *and* FLOSSIE *at center.*)

ALL (*Together, to audience*):
> Now, may the joy of Christmas Day
> Bring cheer to speed you on your way.
> The greatest gift we're speaking of —
> Our Christmas gift to you — is Love!

(*All sing familiar Christmas carol.* WIG-O'-THE-WAG *enters, riding broomstick. She waves flowers, blows kisses to audience, as curtains close.*)

THE END

Silent Night

By Madge Crichton

On a snowy night in an Austrian village, the most beloved Christmas carol was first sung. . .

Characters

FATHER NOSTLER, *parish priest*
FATHER JOSEPH MOHR, *assistant priest*
FRAU SCHMIDT, *parish housekeeper*
FRANZ GRUBER, *church organist*
FRAU GRUBER, *his wife*
WILLY ⎫
INGE ⎭ *his children*

SCENE 1

TIME: *1818. Noon on Christmas Eve.*

SETTING: *The living room of the parish house in Oberndorf, Austria. It is simply furnished with desk, chairs, tables.*

AT RISE: *The stage is empty. Then* FATHER NOSTLER*'s voice is heard offstage, calling angrily.*

FATHER NOSTLER (*Offstage*): Father Mohr! Father Mohr!

(*He enters right, stamps angrily across to left and turns.*) Father Mohr!

FATHER MOHR (*Hurrying in right, looking worried*): Yes, Father Nostler? Were you calling me?

NOSTLER: No, I was just exercising my tonsils. Of course, I was calling you. Have you been to the church?

MOHR: Yes.

NOSTLER (*Folding his arms*): Well, what happened to the organ?

MOHR (*Nervously*): I'm afraid it was mice, Father.

NOSTLER (*Roaring*): Mice!

MOHR: Mice have eaten the bellows. It's winter, you know, and I guess they were hungry.

NOSTLER (*Interrupting sarcastically*): You guess they were hungry! (*Mockingly*) It's winter, you know. (*Shouting*) Of course, I know it's winter. (*More angrily*) And I'll tell you another thing I know. I know it's Christmas Eve, and I know we'll have no organ music for the services tonight!

MOHR (*Defensively*): But, Father, Franz Gruber told you last summer to have new bellows put into the organ. The ones we have are so old that they just ripped completely between the mouse bites.

NOSTLER: Don't be clever with me, young man. (*Shakes his head*) Anyway, what does Gruber know about anything?

MOHR: He is the church organist.

NOSTLER (*Interrupting*): What are you going to do about the Christmas service?

MOHR (*Looking at him in amazement*): What am *I* going to do?

NOSTLER: Oh, yes, you were the one who said, oh, please let me plan the service for Christmas Eve. Now look what's happened!

MOHR: Well, don't blame me. I didn't chew holes in the bellows.

NOSTLER: You think it's funny, don't you? This is Christmas Eve. The people will be expecting to have music for the midnight service. See that there is some. (*He starts to exit left.*)

MOHR: But, how? The organ doesn't work at all. (NOSTLER *turns.*)

NOSTLER: That's your problem. (*Exits left.* FATHER MOHR *sits dejected, holding his head in his hands.*)

FRAU SCHMIDT (*Entering left*): Father Nostler? Oh, it's you, Father Mohr. I thought I heard Father Nostler.

MOHR (*Raising head*): You certainly did. (*Sadly*) I'm in trouble again.

FRAU SCHMIDT (*Coming over to him and patting him on shoulder*): I heard about the organ. Is that the trouble?

MOHR (*Nodding*): Yes, and the way Father Nostler carries on you'd think I'd done it on purpose. Why am I always in trouble with that man? I try to get along with him.

FRAU SCHMIDT (*Sympathetically*): It's just that . . .

MOHR: I know, he thinks I spend too much time playing music and writing poetry.

FRAU SCHMIDT: And he does think you are too soft on the parishioners. It's just that you are young — and, and — well, he's older, and you look at things in a different way.

MOHR (*Throwing his hands up in despair*): It seems there's nothing we agree about. Except maybe one thing. Father Nostler thinks I should never have become a priest, and I'm beginning to think he's right.

FRAU SCHMIDT (*Horrified*): You mustn't say that! The people love you.

MOHR (*Smiling*): Thank you, Frau Schmidt. (*Knock at door is heard.*)

FRAU SCHMIDT: I'll get the door, Father. (*She goes out as* FATHER MOHR *stands looking down pensively.* GRUBER *enters.*)

GRUBER: Mohr, my old friend. A good day to you.

MOHR (*Shaking hands with* GRUBER): And to you, Franz. I hope it's a better day for you than for me.

GRUBER (*Shaking his head*): I've just been to the church.

MOHR: Did you see the organ?

GRUBER: What's left of it. I told Father Nostler this would happen if he didn't get those bellows fixed. Wilhelm, the organ repairman, won't be back up the mountain until the spring thaw. Well, at least this is one thing Father Nostler can't blame you for.

MOHR: Oh, no? He acts as if it's all my fault.

GRUBER (*In disbelief*): Surely not!

MOHR: Oh, yes. What's more, he told me to arrange to have music for the service tonight.

GRUBER: But that's impossible! You can't get one wheeze out of that old organ. It's completely ruined.

MOHR (*Sitting at desk*): Sit down, Franz. (GRUBER *sits with hands on knees.*) You know all there is to know about organs. Couldn't you fix the organ somehow? Just so that it will play tonight?

GRUBER: I'm sorry, Joseph. (*He shakes his head sorrowfully.*) If it were a small patching job, perhaps I could. But the leather is too rotten to patch, and I don't know how to make a set of bellows.

MOHR: Yes, of course you're right. (*He looks up hopefully again*) Franz, you're the schoolmaster at Arnsdorf — and choirmaster. Can't you think of any way we could improvise music?

GRUBER (*Shaking his head again*): Joseph, if I could, I

would. But the organ music is one of the most important parts of the Christmas service.

MOHR (*Getting up and pacing about*): I know, I know. There are times I think I would have gone crazy here, if you hadn't come and played the organ with me.

GRUBER (*Smiling*): Yes, we've had some good times on that old organ. I think our four-handed Bach sounds pretty good.

MOHR: It's been such a long, hard year for the people here. How can they celebrate Christmas if they have no music to help them lift their hearts and spirits? (*Turns to* GRUBER) We must think of something!

GRUBER (*Stroking chin thoughtfully*): I'll tell you what I'll do, Joseph. There is a chance (*Rising*) — just a chance, mind you, that Wilhelm, the organ man, is at his sister's for Christmas.

MOHR (*Eagerly*): What? Here in the village? Do you think he might be?

GRUBER: Now, don't get excited. It's only a very small chance. He doesn't like our mountain winters. But I'll go over there now and see. (*Starts right*) I'll be back as soon as I can.

MOHR (*As* GRUBER *exits*): Oh, thank you, Franz. I'll wait for you here. (*He walks slowly back to desk as curtains close.*)

* * * * *

SCENE 2

TIME: *Later that day.*

SETTING: *The same as Scene 1.*

AT RISE: FATHER MOHR *is sitting at desk, writing.* FRAU SCHMIDT *enters.*

FRAU SCHMIDT (*Nervously twisting her hands, concerned*): Oh, Father Mohr, could I not get you something to eat? You've not had a bit of lunch.

MOHR (*Looking up*): No, thank you, Frau Schmidt. I'm not hungry.

FRAU SCHMIDT: But it's not good for you, going on this way.

MOHR (*Shaking his head and smiling*): Thank you for your concern, dear Frau Schmidt. (*Knock is heard offstage.*) Please see who that is.

FRAU SCHMIDT (*Going off right*): Yes, Father. (*Returns in a minute with* FRAU GRUBER) Frau Gruber is here. (FRAU SCHMIDT *exits.*)

MOHR (*Getting up and shaking hands with* FRAU GRUBER): Good day to you. Please come in and sit down.

FRAU GRUBER (*Sitting*): Thank you, Father Mohr. I hope you don't mind, but Franz suggested that I come here to meet him. I was just doing some shopping to prepare for Christmas, you know. And Inge and Willy are coming, too — they've gone to get Franz's guitar. He was having it repaired.

MOHR (*Sitting again at desk*): I'm delighted to see you. It's a pleasure I don't often have.

FRAU GRUBER (*Laughing*): Well, taking care of twelve children keeps me pretty busy. (*Looking around*) Where is Franz?

MOHR: He's off on an errand of mercy. You see, mice have ruined the organ —

FRAU GRUBER: No!

MOHR:Yes, they've eaten the bellows. Franz has gone off to see if Wilhelm is at his sister's. Perhaps he can repair it.

FRAU GRUBER: Oh, I am so sorry. (*Glances at desk*) And now I've come along and interrupted you at your work.

MOHR (*Going to desk*): I was just reading over a little

poem I wrote the other night. I was coming home after a late call. It was so peaceful, with the snow falling quietly all around . . . (*He stops, as if thinking*)

FRAU GRUBER: Would you let me read it? I do like to read poetry.

MOHR (*Handing her poem*): Here it is. (*As she reads, he walks back to desk.*)

FRAU GRUBER: I think this is just beautiful! (*Looks up*) You should do something with it. (*Suddenly*) Why not teach it to the children and have them sing it tonight?

MOHR (*Astounded*): In church?

FRAU GRUBER (*Getting more excited*): Yes. It would be something new. Since you can't have the usual service, why not have something really different?

Mohr (*Getting excited in his turn*): Do you think it might work?

FRAU GRUBER: Of course!

MOHR: But what about music? How could the children sing this without music? (*Knocking is heard.* GRUBER *enters.*)

FRAU GRUBER: I think we may have solved that problem, too.

GRUBER: What's this? (*To* FRAU GRUBER) Hello, my dear. (*Kisses her on cheek*)

FRAU GRUBER: Father Mohr and I have been having such a nice talk.

GRUBER (*Turning to* FATHER MOHR): I'm sorry, old friend. Wilhelm is not there. I've been racking my brains to think of some other way we can have music for tonight. But not one idea have I had. (FATHER MOHR *and* FRAU GRUBER *smile at each other.*)

FRAU GRUBER: We have the most wonderful idea, Franz. (*Turns to* MOHR) Tell him, Father.

MOHR (*Shyly*): Well, Franz, you know I write a little

poetry (GRUBER *looks at him skeptically.*), and I've written this poem. (*He holds out paper to* GRUBER.)

GRUBER (*Holding hands up in the air*): Oh, Joseph, Joseph. Not another poem.

MOHR: Yes. If you'd just read it . . . .

GRUBER: Joseph, you are my friend. I've read some of your poetry, and to be honest. . . .

FRAU GRUBER (*Commandingly*): Franz, sit down and read that poem. (*Both men look startled, then* GRUBER *smiles, takes poem and sits.*)

GRUBER: Yes, my dear. (*He reads, as both* FATHER MOHR *and* FRAU GRUBER *watch him intently.*) Joseph, this is good. It's really very good. Still, I don't see how it can help us tonight.

FRAU GRUBER (*Getting up*): Franz, you are going to write a melody for it, and the children will learn it and sing it at Mass tonight.

GRUBER (*Amazed*): What! But, my dear, I couldn't possibly! It's out of the question.

FRAU GRUBER (*Folding arms*): Then not another strudel do I make for you.

GRUBER (*Throwing up hands in despair*): That's not fair, my dear. It takes time to write music.

FRAU GRUBER (*Firmly*): Then you'd better get started.

GRUBER (*Looking at* MOHR, *who is grinning broadly*): You can certainly see who is the boss in our family. (*He walks toward desk, just as knocking is heard.*) But I have no instrument.

FRAU GRUBER: Yes, you do. That will be the children. I sent Inge and Willy to pick up your guitar. They will have it with them.

MOHR (*As* INGE *and* WILLY *enter with guitar*): And so they do. (*He takes guitar from* WILLY *and hands it to* GRUBER) Good day to you, children.

WILLY *and* INGE (*Together*): Good day to you, Father. Merry Christmas.

MOHR: And a Merry Christmas to you, too.

FRAU GRUBER: Now, children, come and sit quietly. (*They sit next to her.*) Your father has a little work to do. (GRUBER *takes guitar from case, tunes it and strums a little, then sets it down and, sitting at desk, studies poem. Children start to fidget, then poke at each other.*)

INGE: Owwww!

FRAU GRUBER: Willy, stop it!

WILLY: She poked me first!

GRUBER: Stop that, children. How can I concentrate? (*Children settle down again for a second.*)

INGE (*In loud stage whisper*): Father Mohr?

MOHR (*Leaning over her*): Yes, Inge?

INGE: I'm asking Kris Kringle for a new sled for Christmas.

WILLY: No, I am. (*He pokes* INGE *again, who promptly pokes back.*)

GRUBER: Silence! How can I work with these ragamuffins starting wars every two seconds?

FRAU SCHMIDT (*Entering from right*): Come, children. I have a nice hot gingerbread in the oven. Why don't you come out to the kitchen with me, and we'll see if it's ready to sample.

WILLY *and* INGE (*Together*): Oh, yes. (*They turn to their mother.*) May we? (*She nods and the children rush off.*)

FRAU SCHMIDT: And what would you say to a nice hot cup of coffee, Frau Gruber?

FRAU GRUBER (*Getting up and following* FRAU SCHMIDT *off*): That sounds delicious. (*They exit.*)

GRUBER (*Sitting back and taking up guitar*): That's better. Now maybe I can get something done here. (FATHER MOHR, *sitting quietly, watches* GRUBER, *who strums guitar, murmurs to himself, then shakes his head and puts guitar down.*) But, Joseph, how will we be able to keep the children on key if there's no accompaniment?

MOHR: There will be.

GRUBER: But, how?

MOHR: Your guitar, of course.

GRUBER (*Horrified*): A guitar! In church! On Christmas Eve! What will Father Nostler say?

MOHR: He can't get any more angry with me than he is already.

GRUBER: Then, let's have another go. (*He bends his head again over guitar, tries a few chords, then stops and shakes his head.*) No, this poem is a lullaby. Yes, that's it, a lullaby. Sleep in peace. . . .It is Mary singing to her baby. . . . It is every mother singing to her baby. Yes, a lullaby. (*Softly, he sings the first lines of "Silent Night," playing guitar accompaniment.*)

MOHR: That's it, Franz! That is beautiful! Let me get the others so they can hear it, too! (*He rushes right and calls.*) Frau Schmidt, Frau Gruber, come quickly!

FRAU GRUBER (*Rushing in with* FRAU SCHMIDT *and children*): What is it? What has gone wrong?

MOHR (*Exuberantly*): Nothing is wrong! Everything is right! Just listen to what Franz has composed! (*All listen, as* GRUBER *plays and sings "Silent Night."*)

FRAU GRUBER (*As the music ends*): Oh, yes, Franz, that is exactly right! It will be beautiful tonight in the church, with the church full of candles, all shining down on us. Oh, let's hear it again! (*As* GRUBER *plays again,* MOHR *holds up paper so that all can see, and they sing "Silent Night." If desired, an offstage chorus may join in. As they sing the last line, the curtains slowly close.)*

THE END

A New Angle on Christmas

By Rollin' Albert

Ace reporter Joe Know must file a holiday story before the deadline or lose his job, and the competition is gaining on him. . . .

Characters

JOE KNOW, *star reporter of "The Star"*
EDITOR
ORVIL, *the office boy*

WOMAN C		GIRL C	
MAN H		BOY H	
MAN R		GIRL R	
WOMAN I		BOY I	
MAN S	*crowd*	GIRL S	*children*
WOMAN T		BOY T	
MAN M		GIRL M	
MAN A		BOY A	
WOMAN S		GIRL S	

SANTA CLAUS

SCENE 1

TIME: *A few days before Christmas.*

SETTING: *A newspaper office. Sign reading* THE STAR, *is painted on the backdrop over a graph which shows a rising line, representing the newspaper's rising circulation. Sign reading,* JOE KNOW, STAR REPORTER, *is on desk at center. Desk is piled with papers and newspapers. A typewriter is on the desk and an overflowing wastebasket is next to desk.*

AT RISE: JOE *sits at desk, types a few words, frets, crumples paper, and practices pitching paper into wastebasket. After a few shots he flings down pencil, rises, knocks over chair, and kicks wastebasket.*

JOE: No, no, no! I can't do it! But I've got to do it! (*Sits down at desk and tries again*) Joe, force yourself. You're the star reporter here at "The Star." If you don't do it, who will? (*Shakes head*) This assignment has made me so crazy, I'm even talking to myself! (EDITOR *enters.*)

EDITOR: Is the copy ready yet, Joe?

JOE (*Looking into wastebasket*): It's not quite finished yet.

EDITOR: Just give it to me. I'll put it together.

JOE: What?

EDITOR: Give it to me.

JOE (*Handing him wastebasket*): Here. I'm a failure.

EDITOR: That bad, eh? (*He sets down basket.*) There, there, no need to cry — yet. (ORVIL *enters, slouching, as* EDITOR *is speaking. He eyes the placard on* JOE'*s desk.*) Of course, I might have to look for another star reporter.

ORVIL (*Dropping to knees and crawling over to* EDITOR): Is there something you need, sir? As long as I'm on my knees, may I shine your shoes?

EDITOR (*Ignoring* ORVIL): I'll bet anyone could handle this assignment, even someone simple, someone slow, someone sloppy — any idiot at all!

ORVIL (*Jumping up*): That's me! I'll do it! I'm ready! Whatever it is you want done, sir, I'm the idiot who'll gladly do it!

JOE (*Aghast*): No! Not Orvil! I'll do it! Just give me a little more time.

EDITOR: We go to press in an hour.

JOE: I'll be ready. (*He opens desk drawer, takes out hat and puts it on as he talks.*) I'll write you the best story on Christmas you ever had!

EDITOR: But from a new angle this time!

JOE: New, new! (*He opens another drawer, takes out a coat, and puts it on. This procedure is repeated with his scarf, boots and gloves, muffler, etc., according to number of drawers in desk.*) How about trying —

EDITOR: Nah, we did that last year!

JOE: Well, what about —

EDITOR: That old stuff again?

JOE: Then how about —

EDITOR: New! I said new! All you ever come up with is the same old Christmas story. Now go out and get me a brand-new view of Christmas — or else. (*He holds up placard and starts bending off* STAR REPORTER *as* ORVIL *watches expectantly.*)

JOE: Oh, no! Yes, yes! I will! (*Exits*)

ORVIL: Is there anything I can do for you, boss?

EDITOR: Yes. Clean up this mess! (*Exits*)

ORVIL: Drat! (*He starts to clean up, sees wastebasket is full, tries to push down paper with foot, gets foot jammed in wastebasket, can't get foot out, and so hobbles off with one foot in basket.*) Help! Hey! Help! (*Exits. Curtain*)

*　*　*　*　*

SCENE 2

TIME: *A short time later.*

SETTING: *Street scene. A chair or bench to right.* NOTE: *This scene may be played before curtain.*

AT RISE: JOE *enters, talking to himself.*

JOE: New, new, always new! How can I write something new about something two thousand years old? (JOE *walks toward center stage as* FIVE MEN *and* FOUR WOMEN, *each wearing letter on chest, enter. They form a line in front of curtain, facing away from audience.*)

JOE (*Approaching* WOMAN C *at end of line*): Excuse me, miss. (*He taps* WOMAN C *on shoulder. She turns around to reveal "C" on her chest. All actors react similarly when* JOE *approaches them, revealing letters on chest.*) I'm a reporter for "The Star." I'm writing an article on Christmas, and I would like to ask you what that holiday means to you.

WOMAN C (*Surprised and flattered*): You mean I'm going to be in the newspaper?

JOE: Yes, ma'am.

WOMAN C: You want to know what Christmas means to me, right?

JOE: Yes, ma'am.

WOMAN C: Aren't you going to write it down?

JOE: Yes, ma'am. (*He takes out pad and pencil.*)

WOMAN C: Well, um, crowds! Yes, sir, crowds! Crowds of men, women and children, pushing and shoving and — (MAN H, *next to her, pushes into her.*) Ouch! Watch it! You're on my toes! (*Turns to curtain*)

MAN H (*To* WOMAN C): Sorry.

JOE (*To* WOMAN C): Thank you. (*To* MAN H) What does Christmas mean to you?

MAN H: To me? Hurry! Hurry, hurry, hurry. Buy a hat for Hannah, a hobby horse for Harry, a hymn book for Helen, and a box of handkerchiefs for Horace. And always, hurry, before it's too late. All I can say is, help! (*He turns back.*)

JOE: Thank you. (*To* MAN R) What about you, sir, what does Christmas mean to you?

MAN R: Rushing and rushing. I race here and there to get the right things for the relatives. Christmas shopping runs me ragged! (*Turns to face curtain*)

JOE (*To* WOMAN I): Now, ma'am, if I can just ask you what Christmas means to you.

WOMAN I (*Nastily*): Br-r-r! I'll tell you what Christmas means to me. Christmas means icy winter weather, icicles overhead, and inconvenience. (*Angrily*) I hate winter and I hate Christmas!

JOE (*Surprised at the vehemence of her answer*): Uh — thank you. (*To audience*) These answers are terrible! I can't go back to the Editor with the same old batch of complaints and gripes about Christmas. Is that what people think Christmas means? Trouble? One thing's certain — it's sure causing me a lot of trouble today! I'll lose my job if this keeps up. Maybe others in the crowd have something to say. (*To next in line*) You, sir, what does Christmas mean to you?

MAN S: Spending! Spending every last penny I have. Why, I —

JOE (*Interrupting him and going to next person*): Thank you. And you, madam? (MAN S *turns back.*)

WOMAN T: Toys! Toys that are broken to tiny, teeny itsy-bitsy pieces by the day after Christmas. And let me tell you —

JOE: O.K. O.K. And you, sir? (WOMAN T *turns back.*)

MAN M (*Turning*): Money! Money, money, money, money! Buy me this! Buy me that! Do I look like Santa Claus?

JOE: No, sir. Thank you. (MAN M *turns back.*) I'll try just two more before I give up. (*To next character*) What does Christmas mean to you? (MAN A *and* WOMAN S *turn to answer* JOE.)

MAN A: Well, I can't speak for my wife, here, but to me, it means advertisements. All those ads, urging us to buy things we really can't afford or won't use.

WOMAN S: No, it's snow. Shoveling snow off the sidewalk. He takes a nap while I have to go out and shovel and shovel and shovel. And another thing —

JOE (*Impatiently*): Thanks a lot. (*He walks to center stage, making notes on his pad and shaking his head sadly. Crowd edges off stage, excited and making lots of noise.*) Crowds, hurry, rushing, ice, spending, toys, money, ads, snow. It all spells Christmas. (*Raising his voice, agitated*) But this is not at all what I want! (ORVIL *enters stealthily and sneaks up behind* JOE.) Hm-m-m. I have to think. (*Absently waves his pad from side to side as he ponders, unaware that* ORVIL *is behind him.*) A new angle — a new angle — a new angle.

ORVIL (*Grabbing pad*): That's all I wanted to know!

JOE (*Startled*): What?

ORVIL (*Running off right*): Bye-bye!

JOE: Give me back my note pad! I'll get you! (*Exits right, chasing* ORVIL)

ORVIL (*Re-entering from left, out of breath*): No, he won't. (*Exits swiftly right again*)

JOE (*Entering from left*): Where is he? Come back here, you thief! (*Exits*)

ORVIL (*Re-entering*): Hah! I'll just rip out this page of notes with the new angle. (*He does so, putting it into his pocket, and flips note pad onto stage.*) And when I'm the star reporter, Joe can clean out *my* wastebasket. (*Exits.* JOE *enters from opposite side.*)

JOE: Darn! Lost him again. (*Sees pad*) He dropped my pad! (*Picks up pad and slips it into pocket*) Not that there was anything worthwhile on it, anyway. (*Children edge on stage, their backs to audience.*) Look at this line of children waiting to see Santa Claus. Maybe I ought to stand in line, too, and ask Santa Claus for a story, a new angle on Christmas.

GIRL C (*Turning so audience can see "C" on her chest*): Are you waiting to see Santa Claus too, mister?

JOE: No, I was hoping for a new story on the meaning of Christmas.

GIRL C: I think Christmas means children, and the young-at-heart who grow more cheerful as Christmas comes closer.

JOE: That's it! The children! I'll ask the children! Maybe that will give me the new angle I want. (*He taps the shoulder of the next child in line,* BOY H. *Children respond to* JOE*'s question in succession, turning as they speak and continuing to face forward while the remaining actors deliver their lines.*) What does Christmas mean to you?

BOY H (*Turning*): Help — for those who have few toys and little food or clothing; help — given with our hands, and with love in our hearts. (JOE *makes notes.*)

GIRL R: Respect for the rights of each religion to celebrate the holidays in its own way.

BOY I: It's our imagination, which helps us relive a story that took place so many years ago.

GIRL S: Sharing with family and friends — and even with strangers, just as the three Wise Men did, as they followed the star in the East.

BOY T: Travel — as we gather our families together around the tree.

GIRL M: Merry, because that's how I feel when I remember that we get a vacation from school!

BOY A: Appreciation! — for all the time and trouble people take to do special things for us.

GIRL S: Singing the songs that sound especially sweet at this time of year. (SANTA *enters as* GIRL S *finishes speaking. He stands, listening, as* JOE *refers to his pad.*)

JOE (*Becoming increasingly excited*): I knew it! I knew it! That's the Christmas story I wanted from these kids! Instead of grumbling and complaining like the adults, they're happy and excited that Christmas is here. They speak about cheerfulness, helpfulness, the right to religious freedom. They recognize the importance of imagination, and sharing, and the significance of the Christmas tree. They sing of merriment, and take time to be grateful and appreciative of all that others do for them. (*Looks up and notices* SANTA) Santa, maybe you can tell me more of what Christmas is all about.

SANTA CLAUS: Ho, ho, ho! A Merry Christmas to you, young man. And would you like to tell me what you want for Christmas? You're rather big for a little boy, aren't you?

JOE (*Impatiently*): I don't want anything. I already have what I want. I have my Christmas story — I have a new angle!

SANTA (*Chagrined*): Well, these days I suppose everyone has an angle. (*Sits down on chair*) All right, now, sit down on my lap and tell me what you want. I *know* you want something. (*Pulls* JOE *onto his lap*)

JOE (*Struggling out of* SANTA*'s grasp*): No, no! You don't understand, Santa. (EDITOR *enters, dragging* ORVIL *along by his shirt sleeve. During following dialogue, children take turns sitting on* SANTA*'s lap.*)

EDITOR: Come on now, Orvil. When I tell you to move, move!

ORVIL: Stop! Stop! You'll ruin this fine shirt.

JOE (*Noticing* EDITOR *and* ORVIL): Ruin his shirt! That guy almost ruined my career.

EDITOR (*Noticing* JOE): Aha! Joe, I've been looking all over for you. It's nearly press time, and this ninny has been driving me up a wall with some drivel about rushing and hurrying and shoveling snow. Have you got your story?

JOE (*Squaring off to hit* ORVIL): I sure have, but first I have a score to settle with little Orvil, here, for trying to steal my story.

ORVIL: Please, Joe, don't. I'm no match for you.

EDITOR: Now wait a minute, Joe. What are you two fighting about, anyway? Why don't you just give me your story, Joe? (EDITOR *finally releases* ORVIL's *shirt sleeve.*)

JOE: I was working on my Christmas assignment when this skunk came along and stole all my notes. I managed to finish the interviewing anyway and now I have a terrific scoop from these kids. Just the sort of Christmas article you wanted for the paper, sir.

EDITOR: Let's take this one at a time. (*To* ORVIL) Orvil, did you steal Joe's notes?

ORVIL (*Embarrassed*): Oh, no, Mr. Editor, sir. Not me. No, sir. Why, I was only playing a little joke on my good friend Joe. Wasn't I, Joe? All in the spirit of Christmas.

JOE (*Angrily*): That was no joke, Orvil, and you know it. Stealing my notes was a dirty trick.

EDITOR: Orvil, you've done your last bit of mischief. So get packing, fellow, and don't show your face around here again. You're fired!

ORVIL: Oh, please sir. Just give me one more chance. I'll do better, really I will.

EDITOR: What do you say, Joe? Shall we give him another chance?

JOE: No real harm was done. As it worked out, I got a better story because he took my notes.

EDITOR (*Reconsidering*): Well, since it's Christmas, we might just put you on six months' probation instead of firing you.

ORVIL: Thanks a lot, Mr. Editor.

EDITOR: But you'd better shape up fast, Orvil, and do your job. Now, Joe, where is that great new story of yours?

JOE: Right here, sir. (*Holding up notebook*) I've got a story about the real meaning of Christmas that our readers are going to love. You'll love it too, boss. Thanks to these kids, here, I have a terrific story about the *good* things Christmas means — about the happiness, the helpfulness, the cheerfulness, the caring. It's just the story you wanted. (*Flips through the pages of his note pad*) If only I could remember what that last "S" stood for.

SANTA (*Crossing to center*): Songs, young fellow. Christmas songs. Here, we'll help you remember. (*All join hands and start to sing "We Wish You a Merry Christmas" or any Christmas song. Entire cast re-enters, singing, and encourages audience to join in. At conclusion of song, curtain closes.*)

THE END

What, No Santa Claus?

By Mildred Hark and Noel McQueen

The toys are packed, the reindeer are ready, but where's Santa? Huddled in a blanket, sneezing and sniffling, too sick to make the trip . . .

Characters

SANTA CLAUS
MRS. SANTA CLAUS
JINGLE
DINGLE
WINKY
BLINKY   *Santa's elves*
HOLLY
JOLLY
MISTLETOE
1ST RADIO ANNOUNCER   *offstage voices*
2ND RADIO ANNOUNCER

SETTING: *The living room of Santa Claus's house at the North Pole.*

AT RISE: SANTA CLAUS *is sitting in a big chair in front of the fireplace. He is wearing his traditional costume but his shoes and socks are off and his feet are in a basin of hot water. He is huddled in chair, with red blanket thrown around his shoulders. On a table at the side of his chair are a box of tissues, a spoon, and three bottles of medicine, with labels reading* COUGH MEDICINE, SNEEZE MEDICINE, *and* PILLS FOR CHILLS. SANTA *begins to sneeze.*

SANTA CLAUS: Ker-chew — ker-chew! (MRS. SANTA *rushes in from left, carrying a big white blanket. She is wearing a red dress.*)

MRS. SANTA: Santa Claus, you're sneezing again. You're worse! You ought to be in bed.

SANTA CLAUS: Bed? How can you talk about bed when it's Christmas Eve? I ought to be getting ready for my trip.

MRS. SANTA: Here, put this blanket around you.

SANTA CLAUS: Mrs. Santa, I will not be coddled! (*Starting to raise himself up*) I'm going to get up out of this chair.

MRS. SANTA: You certainly are not.

SANTA CLAUS: Who's the boss around here? Who wears the pants in this household?

MRS. SANTA: Oh, dear, it's not like you to be so cross — but I don't mind. You're usually such a merry old soul. Now, please sit still.

SANTA CLAUS: Mrs. Santa, I will not be ordered about! (*He starts to sneeze again.*)

MRS. SANTA: There, see what happens when you get excited? You'd better take some more of your sneeze medicine. (*She pours a spoonful from bottle and* SANTA *takes it. He makes a face.*)

SANTA CLAUS: Awful stuff. After this, I'm not going to consider children bad if they don't like to take medicine. I don't blame them.

MRS. SANTA (*Feeling his hands*): Your hands are like ice. You'd better have some chill pills too. (*She gives him some from the bottle, and he sneezes again.*)

SANTA CLAUS: Can't you see? All this medicine is making me worse. How much longer do I have to sit here dangling my feet in this water? I ought to be down in the workshop. The elves are good workers, but without me to direct them, they're bound to get into mischief. Why don't they come up here and report? (*Turns left and shouts*) Jingle! Dingle! Winky! Blinky!

MRS. SANTA: Stop shouting, dear.

SANTA CLAUS (*Raising one foot out of the pan as if to get up*): Holly! Jolly! Mistletoe!

MRS. SANTA: Stop that before you lose your voice. And don't take your feet out of the hot water.

SANTA CLAUS: It isn't hot any more. It's getting cold.

MRS. SANTA: Relax, dear. The elves are bringing more.

SANTA CLAUS: Oh, they are! Just as I thought! They ought to be down in the workshop, getting things ready and packing the sleigh!

MRS. SANTA: Now, now, Jingle and Dingle are the only ones who aren't busy packing the sleigh. But I don't see much sense to it, if you can't go on your trip.

SANTA CLAUS: Can't go? Mrs. Santa, what are you talking about? Don't you realize it's Christmas Eve? What would Christmas be without Santa Claus? I've got millions and millions of presents to deliver!

MRS. SANTA: Nonsense. You can't go climbing down chimneys tonight, not in your condition. Think of the ashes and soot. Why, you'd sneeze all the dust up your nose.

SANTA CLAUS (*Sneezing again*): Ker-chew!

MRS. SANTA: Besides, you'd wake up all the children, with your sneezing and sniffling.

SANTA CLAUS: Well, so what? Maybe some of the boys and girls would like to wake up and see Santa Claus in person.

MRS. SANTA: They'd never recognize you. Where are your twinkling eyes and those dimples they always talk about? You're in an awful mood, and your nose is red.

SANTA CLAUS: My nose is always red. It's supposed to be.

MRS. SANTA: But a cheerful red — not a fiery red. (*Hands tissue to* SANTA) Here, you'd better blow it.

SANTA CLAUS: Oh, very well.

MRS. SANTA: Don't look like such a martyr. I'm only trying to make you feel better. (JINGLE *and* DINGLE *enter left.* JINGLE *carries a kettle of hot water and* DINGLE *a big box labeled* MUSTARD. *They look at* SANTA CLAUS *and shake their heads.*)

JINGLE *and* DINGLE (*Together*): Oh, dear!

JINGLE:

> Oh, Santa has the sniffles,
>
> And it's very sad to see;

DINGLE:

> If Santa has the sniffles,
>
> What Christmas will there be?

SANTA CLAUS (*Sneezing*): Ker-chew!

MRS. SANTA (*Clapping her hands*): Jingle, Dingle! Come now, there's no time to waste. Prepare the hot water and the mustard! (*The elves run to* SANTA. JINGLE *pours some hot water into pan and* DINGLE *sprinkles some mustard into it from his can.*)

SANTA CLAUS (*Holding his feet up*): Ouch! It's hot! Get out of here, both of you.

JINGLE: But Santa Claus!

DINGLE: We're only trying to make you well.

SANTA CLAUS: You ought to be down in the workshop, both of you — packing dolls, packing drums, packing candy and bicycles and baseballs!

JINGLE: Yes, sir, we'll go at once, sir.

SANTA: And send Winky and Blinky up here. I want a

report on how things are going. It's getting late. I'll have to start soon.

DINGLE: Yes, sir. (JINGLE *and* DINGLE *run out.*)

MRS. SANTA: You won't stir an inch out of this house until you're better. It's snowing harder, it's colder than ever. I stuck my head out of the door once and got icicles in my hair.

SANTA CLAUS: What's new about that? It's always cold at the North Pole.

MRS. SANTA: But it's worse than ever tonight.

SANTA CLAUS: All the more reason to let me go. I could soon be in a warmer climate.

MRS. SANTA: And catch double pneumonia. Sudden changes like that are bad for people with the sniffles.

SANTA CLAUS: Oh, stop fussing. Why did I have to catch this cold, anyhow?

MRS. SANTA: It's your own fault. I told you not to go out last night in the sleigh.

SANTA CLAUS: But I had to exercise the reindeer. Dancer and Prancer are getting fat and Comet and Cupid and the rest of them are getting lazy. They had to be in good shape for tonight.

MRS. SANTA: I could have exercised the reindeer.

SANTA CLAUS: You? Mrs. Santa? A woman? Don't be silly. That's a man's job.

MRS. SANTA: Women are doing lots of things these days, Santa. All kinds of jobs. (*Shaking head*) It beats me. You go out into the world every year and I still know more about what's going on than you do.

SANTA CLAUS: That's because you're always watching the news and reading the paper while I'm making toys.

MRS. SANTA: That's right, dear. I listen to the radio, too, and I think I'll turn it on now. It'll help take your mind off things. (*She goes to the radio and turns the knob. Music of "Jingle Bells" is heard.*)

SANTA CLAUS (*Crossly*): Take my mind off things, hah!

1ST RADIO ANNOUNCER (*Offstage*):
> 'Twas the night before Christmas,
>> when all through the house
> Not a creature was stirring,
>> not even a mouse;
> The stockings were hung by the
>> chimney with care,
> In hopes that St. Nicholas soon
>> would be there.

SANTA CLAUS: What did I tell you? All the children are expecting me, waiting for Christmas to begin. Turn that thing off. It makes me nervous.

MRS. SANTA: I'll try another station. (*She turns knob and voice of* 2ND RADIO ANNOUNCER *is heard.*)

2ND RADIO ANNOUNCER (*Offstage*): "Yes, Virginia, there is a Santa Claus. He exists as certainly as love and generosity and devotion exist and you know that they abound and give to your life its highest beauty and joy."

MRS. SANTA: That's what the New York *Sun* wrote to that little girl so long ago.

2ND RADIO ANNOUNCER: "Alas. How dreary would be the world if there were no Santa Claus."

SANTA CLAUS: Certainly it would be dreary. Of course it would be dreary!

MRS. SANTA: Oh dear, I'd better turn it off. (*She turns radio off.*) I'd like to have listened. It's so beautiful. But it's making you nervous.

SANTA CLAUS: Naturally, at a time like this! Don't you see? If I don't get started on my trip soon, people won't believe in me any more. They'll think there isn't any Santa Claus.

MRS. SANTA: Perhaps if you didn't go this year they'd appreciate you more than ever. After all, you've never missed a Christmas before.

SANTA CLAUS: And I'm not going to miss this one! Where are those elves? I thought I told them to come right up. (WINKY *and* BLINKY *run in.*)

WINKY *and* BLINKY (*Together*): Here we are, Santa Claus!

WINKY: I'm Winky.

BLINKY: I'm Blinky.

SANTA CLAUS: Never mind. What difference does it make which is which? How are things in the workshop? All finished? What about dolls, drums, candy canes, sleds?

WINKY: There are millions of sleds and millions of drums —

BLINKY: And millions of dolls and sugar plums.

SANTA CLAUS: Have you got some redheaded dolls?

WINKY: Oh, yes, Santa Claus.

SANTA CLAUS: Some of the children like redheads.

BLINKY: Holly and Jolly have given permanents to all the dolls this year.

WINKY: Then if the children take them out in the rain, the dolls won't lose their curly hair.

SANTA CLAUS: Good, good! What about ponies?

BLINKY: The ponies have already been sent on ahead. They're waiting in neighbors' barns all over the country.

SANTA CLAUS: Then I'll need some long ribbons — yards and yards long.

WINKY: What for?

SANTA CLAUS: Well, you can't put a live pony under a Christmas tree, so I'll loop a ribbon around its neck and then run the ribbon through a window and tie it on the tree with a note.

BLINKY: Wonderful!

MRS. SANTA: Excuse me, but it's very foolish making all these plans, Santa Claus, when you know as well as I do that you're not going. (HOLLY *and* JOLLY *run in.*)

HOLLY: I'm Holly.

JOLLY: I'm Jolly.

HOLLY: And we have come to say —

JOLLY: That we've finished packing all the toys —

HOLLY: You can soon be on your way.

MRS. SANTA: Santa Claus, I tell you there's no use. (JINGLE *and* DINGLE *run in right, covered with snowflakes.*)

JINGLE: I'm Jingle.

DINGLE: I'm Dingle.

JINGLE:

We're hitching up the reindeer —
Dasher and Dancer and Vixen;

DINGLE:

And Comet and Cupid and Prancer —
And also Donder and Blitzen!

(*Elves run right to window and look out. Sound of sleigh bells is heard from offstage.* MISTLETOE *enters from right, also covered with snow.*)

MISTLETOE:

I'm Mistletoe.
I've been putting on the sleigh bells.
Did you hear them ring?
Oh, the sound makes me so happy
I could start to sing!

(*All elves begin dancing around the room.*)

JINGLE: I'm Jingle —

DINGLE: I'm Dingle —

HOLLY: I'm Holly —

JOLLY: I'm Jolly —

WINKY: I'm Winky —

BLINKY: I'm Blinky —

MISTLETOE: And I'm Mistletoe.

ELVES (*Together*):

Oh, we've made toys the whole year through
For every girl and boy;
And now it's time for Christmas —
For happiness and joy!

(SANTA CLAUS, *growing excited, tries to get up from the chair.*)

SANTA CLAUS: Yes, yes, of course it is! It's time for me to be off! It's getting late.

MRS. SANTA (*Trying to push him back into his chair*): Santa Claus, you know that you can't go anywhere tonight. It's impossible.

SANTA CLAUS: Nonsense. I've got to go. (*All the elves gather around him.*)

ELVES:

Come on, come on, oh, Santa dear,
O'er all the world you'll fly;
We'll help you get onto the sleigh —
You'll be off in the wink of an eye!

SANTA CLAUS: Yes — yes! (*He stops and puts his hand to his head.*) No — no — I don't know. I feel dizzy. My head's stuffed up and my nose — (*He begins to sneeze again.*) Ker-chew — ker-chew — ker-chew!

MRS. SANTA: There, you see? You're sneezing again. You sit right down in that chair and don't try to get up again. (*She pushes SANTA CLAUS back into the chair.*)

JINGLE: But Mrs. Santa Claus, the presents!

DINGLE: What about Christmas?

WINKY: It's time for Santa Claus to go!

MRS. SANTA: It's no use — he can't go. He knows that as well as I do. (*She tucks the blanket around him again.*)

BLINKY: Do you mean there won't be any Christmas this year?

MRS. SANTA: Of course there'll be a Christmas, but he won't have any part in it. (*She starts left.*) Don't you try to get up again, Santa Claus.

SANTA CLAUS: Mrs. Santa, where are you going?

MRS. SANTA (*As she goes out left*): Never you mind!

HOLLY: Oh, dear! No Christmas, Jolly!

JOLLY: I can't believe it, Holly.

BLINKY: Oh, Winky, I'm going to cry.

WINKY: I know, Blinky, so am I.

JINGLE: Oh, Dingle, what can we do?

DINGLE: Jingle, I wish I knew.

MISTLETOE: I feel so blue! (SANTA CLAUS *begins to sneeze again and the elves run to him.*)

ELVES (*Ad lib*): Oh, poor Santa Claus. Can we help? (*Etc.*)

SANTA CLAUS: No, no. I just feel miserable — utterly miserable! No Christmas. Imagine it! No Christmas this year.

JINGLE (*Wailing loudly*): No Christmas!

DINGLE (*Not quite so loud*): No Christmas at all.

WINKY (*Fainter voice*): No Christmas anywhere.

BLINKY (*Still fainter*): No Christmas for the children.

HOLLY (*Fainter still*): No filled socks.

JOLLY (*Practically a whisper*): No trimmed trees.

MISTLETOE (*Tiniest voice of all*): No Santa Claus.

JINGLE: There must be some way. What can we do, Mister Santa? You ought to be able to figure something out.

SANTA CLAUS: I'm sorry. There just doesn't seem to be any hope.

DINGLE: But didn't Mrs. Santa Claus say there'd be a Christmas?

WINKY: How can there be a Christmas without Santa Claus?

BLINKY: What did she mean?

HOLLY: Maybe she's going to *send* all the presents to the children.

JOLLY: Why, yes, through the mail.

MISTLETOE: Special delivery.

SANTA CLAUS: No, no. That wouldn't do at all. The children get presents through the mail from their aunts and cousins and grandparents. They're used to that kind of present. It wouldn't be the same as a visit from Santa Claus. (MRS. SANTA *enters left, wearing one of* SANTA*'s suits and a cap. She has a big pack full of toys over her shoulder.*)

JINGLE: Why, it's Mrs. Santa.

DINGLE (*Astonished*): And she's wearing Santa's suit!

MRS. SANTA (*Briskly*): Certainly. I'm going to deliver the presents!

SANTA CLAUS: Mrs. Santa, I won't have it. You can't wear my other suit!

MRS. SANTA: Certainly I can. If I'm going to work, I need the right clothes.

SANTA CLAUS: I won't have it! Such a thing has never happened at the North Pole.

MRS. SANTA: Now, now, don't get so excited. Lots of women work nowadays in the world. I'm going to do your job tonight.

SANTA CLAUS: But it's unheard of!

MRS. SANTA: While I'm gone you and the elves can get Christmas ready here the way I usually do. Here's a list. (*She hands him a sheet of paper and he looks at it.*)

SANTA CLAUS: But I can't do these things!

MRS. SANTA: Now, now, no buts. Roast the turkey, fill the socks, mash the potatoes, don't burn the gravy — well, it's all there. Just follow directions. I know it's more work than you and the elves are used to, but at least you'll be here in the warm house. I'll be back in time for Christmas dinner.

SANTA CLAUS: I won't allow it! I won't allow you to go!

MRS. SANTA: Would you rather cancel Christmas and have all the children disappointed? (*There is a pause.*) No, I didn't think so.

SANTA CLAUS: But Mrs. Santa, this is impossible!

MRS. SANTA: Santa, there's no time to argue. I must get moving!

SANTA CLAUS: Do you have the addresses? Will you know what to do?

MRS. SANTA: Of course I'll know. I'll just stop at every house.

SANTA CLAUS: But certain things go certain places.

MRS. SANTA: I won't mix them up and if I do, someone might like a surprise.

WINKY: Yes, yes!

BLINKY: A surprise!

MRS. SANTA (*Starting for door right*): Well, I'm off! And if any child peeks there'll be no harm done. I think I can pass for Santa Claus, in this suit. Merry Christmas. (*She goes out right. The elves all run to the window and relay information to* SANTA CLAUS, *who is leaning forward anxiously.*)

JINGLE: She's climbing into the sleigh.

DINGLE: The reindeer are pawing and prancing.

WINKY: She's getting all wrapped up in the big blanket.

BLINKY: She looks as merry as can be.

HOLLY: Her eyes are twinkling.

MISTLETOE: She's off! There they go! Listen! (*Sound of sleigh bells from offstage, then* MRS. SANTA*'s voice, getting fainter and fainter.*)

MRS. SANTA (*Offstage*): Now, Dasher! Now, Dancer!

Now, Prancer and Vixen! On, Comet, on, Cupid! On, Donder and Blitzen!

JOLLY: There's going to be a Christmas after all.

SANTA CLAUS: Yes, yes. But, I don't know what to think! Of course I'm glad the children are going to have Christmas, but it's not right for Mrs. Santa to take my place.

DINGLE: Yes, it is, Santa.

JINGLE: Just this once.

MISTLETOE: Just for this year.

SANTA CLAUS: Hm-m-m, you never can tell. Now she may want to do it every year. You'd be surprised. She's getting more and more publicity all the time. Last year some stores featured Mrs. Santa in their Christmas window displays.

WINKY: They showed you too, I'll bet, Santa Claus.

BLINKY: Of course.

HOLLY: There'll always be a Santa Claus.

ELVES (*Together*): And there'll always be a Christmas! Merry Christmas! Merry Christmas!

SANTA CLAUS (*Smiling now and waving his hand with a flourish*): Merry Christmas to all! (*Quick curtain*)

THE END

We Interrupt This Program . . .

By Claire Boiko

An unidentified flying object is heading for the North Pole, and scientists predict it will arrive on Christmas Eve!

Characters

MASTER OF CEREMONIES
SUSAN JAMISON, *pianist*
J. HOLLY BARBERRY, *anchorman*
MESSENGER
TWO CAMERAMEN
IVY GREEN, *commentator*
GENERAL REVEL
THREE SCIENTISTS
ROBBIE SMITH
TWO AIDES
TWO GRENADIERS
COMPUTER TECHNICIAN
ASSISTANT
TWO ELVES
SANTA CLAUS
MRS. SANTA CLAUS
CAROLERS
CHILDREN OF THE WORLD

SCENE 1

BEFORE RISE: MASTER OF CEREMONIES *enters through curtain, as if to begin Christmas assembly program.*

MASTER OF CEREMONIES: Good afternoon! A happy holiday season to you all. We will now present a special program of Christmas music, and to begin, we'll hear a medley of favorite carols played by Susan Jamison on the piano. (MASTER OF CEREMONIES *exits right, as* SUSAN JAMISON *enters, takes place at piano and begins to play a Christmas song. After several bars are played,* MASTER OF CEREMONIES *rushes onstage from right, a sheet of paper in hand, crosses to* SUSAN *and whispers into her ear.*)

SUSAN (*Excited*): What! Unidentified? Over the *North Pole?* Oh, my goodness! (SUSAN *picks up music and exits right, shaking head.*)

MASTER OF CEREMONIES (*To audience*): Boys and girls, I've just been handed a news bulletin from television station N-O-E-L. (*Reads*) "An unidentified flying object has been sighted above the Earth flying toward the North Pole." This is all the information we have at present, but we are going to switch you directly to the studios of station N-O-E-L. (*He exits through curtains. A broadcast news desk, decorated with small Christmas tree, is rolled out. Front of desk has banner in red and green which reads,* YOUR HOLIDAY STATION — N-O-E-L. J. HOLLY BARBERRY, *wearing a neck microphone, enters and sits at desk.* 1ST CAMERAMAN *enters with television camera and follows action onstage. Sound of newsroom ticker is heard.*)

J. HOLLY BARBERRY: Greetings, boys and girls, this is your television anchorman, J. Holly Barberry, with a fast-breaking story about an unidentified flying object headed directly for our North Pole. Where has it come from? We don't know. What is its mission? That, too, is a mystery, but we will keep you informed as bulletins sizzle off the news wires. . . . (MESSENGER *runs in from down left, carrying sheet of paper.*)

MESSENGER: Here's some hot copy, chief! (MESSENGER *runs to* BARBERRY, *gives him bulletin, then races offstage.*)

J. HOLLY BARBERRY (*Reading bulletin*): Boys and girls, the skywatchers at the space laboratories on Christmas Island have issued this bulletin: the object in the sky is definitely a rocket. I repeat, a rocket. But why is a rocket streaking across the heavens toward the North Pole?

MESSENGER (*Running back onstage with paper*): Another scorcher, chief! (*Drops paper on desk, then runs off.*)

J. HOLLY BARBERRY: The mystery deepens, folks! (*Reads, looks up*) Now we can tell you where the rocket came from. Listen to this — the tracking stations say that the rocket was launched from a small backyard in a middle-sized town somewhere in the center of the United States. How about that, folks! Stand by as we switch you to the center of these new developments. Take it away, Ivy Green, at the space laboratories on Christmas Island. (*Recording of Christmas music played on electronic instruments is heard as desk and camera are rolled offstage.* 1ST CAMERAMAN *and* J. HOLLY BARBERRY *exit right as curtains open.*)

*   *   *

SETTING: *Interior of a space laboratory with astronomical charts on walls, and large computer console upstage, with a music stand beside it. Up left is a door marked* PRIVATE, TOP SECRET. *Down left is a table with three red and green telephones, labeled* OPERATION YULE-

WATCH. *At right is another table with lab equipment.*

AT RISE: GENERAL REVEL *and* 1ST AIDE *sit at table at left, consulting large maps.* TWO GRENADIERS *stand guard at door.* THREE SCIENTISTS *sit working intently at table at right.* 1ST SCIENTIST *pours liquid from test tube into beaker.* 2ND SCIENTIST *listens through pair of earphones.* 3RD SCIENTIST *peers through microscope.* COMPUTER TECHNICIAN *works at console.* IVY GREEN, *wearing neck microphone and carrying a hand microphone, stands at center.* 2ND CAMERAMAN, *with portable television camera, stands down right, following action.*

IVY GREEN: Boys and girls, this is Ivy Green, your on-the-spot reporter, here in the main laboratories of the space research station on Christmas Island. To your left, you will see the special guardian of the holiday season, General Revel, and his staff, preparing to defend Santa's Workshop at the North Pole from the mysterious rocket. Over here, at the other table, are three world-famous scientists now about to compute the results of their research on the rocket. (ASSISTANT *enters right.* THREE SCIENTISTS *hold out data sheets.*)

THREE SCIENTISTS (*Together*): Compute, please! (ASSISTANT *collects sheets, handing them with a bow to* COMPUTER TECHNICIAN, *who places them on music rack, rubs his hands, then plays on computer keys like an organist.* ASSISTANT *turns pages. Recording of Christmas carol performed on electronic instruments is heard, followed by excited computer chatter, then loud cymbal clash.* ASSISTANT *removes from computer three punch-out cards, handing them with flourish to* THREE SCIENTISTS.)

1ST SCIENTIST (*Shocked*): Unbelievable!

2ND SCIENTIST: Inconceivable!

3RD SCIENTIST (*Mystified*): Absolutely incomprehensible!

1ST SCIENTIST: The rocket is made of tin whistles!

2ND SCIENTIST: The rocket is propelled by fizzy soda.

3RD SCIENTIST (*Amazed*): The rocket is guided by a compass — a little, itsy-bitsy pocket compass!

IVY GREEN (*Impatiently*): But the cargo — the freight. What is *inside* the rocket?

1ST SCIENTIST: Odds and ends . . .

2ND SCIENTIST: This and that . . .

3RD SCIENTIST: Trifles and trinkets . . . (*Music to "The Twelve Days of Christmas" is heard, and* THREE SCIENTISTS *sing following lines to that tune.*)

1ST SCIENTIST (*Singing*):

Down in the rocket

The strangest things you'll see —

2ND SCIENTIST (*Singing*):

Twelve ginger cupcakes,

3RD SCIENTIST (*Singing*):

Eleven candy kisses,

1ST SCIENTIST (*Singing*):

Ten braided bookmarks,

2ND SCIENTIST (*Singing*):

Nine fancy pillows,

3RD SCIENTIST (*Singing*):

Eight homemade bookends,

1ST SCIENTIST (*Singing*):

Seven lacy doilies,

2ND SCIENTIST (*Singing*):

Six scarves of cashmere,

3RD SCIENTIST (*Singing*):

Five . . . Spanish . . . shawls,

1ST SCIENTIST (*Singing*):

Four calling cards,

2ND SCIENTIST (*Singing*):

Three French pens,

3RD SCIENTIST (*Singing*):
>   Two furry gloves,

1ST SCIENTIST (*Singing*):
>   And a nightcap on a shoe tree.

2ND SCIENTIST (*Sitting abruptly down at table, shaking head in bafflement*): Unbelievable!

1ST SCIENTIST (*Also sitting down*): Inconceivable!

3RD SCIENTIST: Absolutely incomprehensible! (*Several telephones ring at once.* GENERAL REVEL *speaks into each phone in rapid succession.*)

GENERAL REVEL (*Into first phone*): Hello . . . General Revel here. . . . What? You've found the fellow who built the rocket? Splendid. Fly him here by double-swift high-speed jet. (*He hangs up. Into second phone*) General Revel here. . . . What? He's here? The fellow who built the rocket has landed at Christmas Island? . . . Splendid. Rush him here by special-delivery helicopter. (*He hangs up, answers third phone*) Hello? . . . The fellow who built the rocket is here at the space laboratory? . . . (*Looks at watch*) Well, what kept him? (*To* 1ST AIDE) Aide, bring in the fellow who built the rocket! I have a lot of important questions to ask him.

1ST AIDE: Yes, sir. (*As* 1ST AIDE *crosses to door and exits,* IVY GREEN *continues her narration.*)

IVY GREEN: Boys and girls, things are really popping now! In one moment we will see and hear the genius who built the rocket which is now streaking toward the North Pole. (1ST AIDE *re-enters, followed by* 2ND AIDE *and* ROBBIE SMITH. *They take a step into the room but are stopped by* GRENADIERS, *who cross swords and hold them in front of* 2ND AIDE *and* ROBBIE.)

1ST AIDE: Advance and be recognized. What is the pass word?

2ND AIDE: Marzipan!

1ST AIDE: Correct. (GRENADIERS *lower swords.* ROBBIE *and* 2ND AIDE *advance to* GENERAL REVEL.)

GENERAL REVEL (*Bewildered*): Here now! Who is this? (*Points to* ROBBIE) Where is the fellow who built the rocket?

ROBBIE (*Embarrassed*): I think you mean me. I'm Robbie Smith. (*Proudly*) I built the rocket. I launched it too, from my own backyard!

GENERAL REVEL (*Astonished*): *You* — a tadpole like you — built and launched a rocket? (*All ad lib surprise.*)

ROBBIE (*Modestly*): I had help. Lots of help and technical advice.

GENERAL REVEL (*Knowingly*): Aha. I suspected as much. Now, don't be afraid, my boy. Who helped you?

ROBBIE: I'm not afraid to tell you. (*He fishes in his pocket, and brings out a bubble gum wrapper.*) Here's a list of my technical assistants. Sorry that it's written on a bubble gum wrapper, but it was the handiest paper I had.

GENERAL REVEL (*Snatching paper and reading it aloud*): Taro Watanabe — Tokyo, Japan. Sven Pedersen — Oslo, Norway. Juan Sanchez — Lima, Peru. (*Triumphantly*) Aha, secret agents, eh, Robbie?

ROBBIE (*Surprised*): Oh, no, sir. They're *children.* Children from all over the world. That list is only part of them. The rocket was their idea as much as mine.

GENERAL REVEL (*Mystified*): But why? Why in the name of all the happy holidays did you build a rocket? What is in it — and why is it headed for the North Pole?

ROBBIE (*Apologetically*): I can't tell you. Not until midnight tonight — Christmas Eve! That's when the rocket lands. Then you'll know everything.

GENERAL REVEL (*Sternly*): But you must tell me now,

Robbie. The safety of Christmas and all other holidays is in my hands. I must know what is in that rocket and why it is going to the North Pole.

ROBBIE (*Bravely*): But I promised the other children I wouldn't tell.

GENERAL REVEL (*Wheedling*): Not even for a triple-dip banana split?

ROBBIE (*Wavering*): A triple-dip banana split! Mm-m-m.

GENERAL REVEL: With nuts!

ROBBIE: With nuts? (*He shakes his head stubbornly.*) No, sir. My lips are sealed.

IVY GREEN (*To camera and audience*): What a dramatic development! Robbie Smith, builder of the rocket, refuses to tell General Revel the mission of the rocket. What will the General do now, I wonder?

GENERAL REVEL (*Into phone*): Get me the jet patrol. . . . General Revel, here. (*Importantly*) Send me a high-speed jet. . . . When? Immediately, of course! (*Gives bubble gum wrapper to* 1ST AIDE) Here — have jets sent to every city on this list. Pick up each and every one of these children.

1ST AIDE: Yes, sir. But, sir — where shall I dispatch the jets? What is their destination?

GENERAL REVEL (*Airily*): Why — the North Pole, of course. (*With a sweeping gesture*) That's where we're going — where we're *all* going. To the North Pole! (*Determined*) I'll find out the secret of that rocket if it's the last thing I do!

IVY GREEN: Boys and girls, keep your television sets tuned to this station. Stand by for a remote transmission from the North Pole. (*Curtains begin to close.*) Meanwhile, we invite you to enjoy a program of seasonal music as we switch you now to our regularly scheduled broadcast. (*Curtain closes.* CAROLERS *enter before curtain and sing a medley of Christmas carols. At conclusion of music,* CAROLERS *exit, and curtains open.*)

* * * * *

SCENE 2

TIME: *Immediately following.*

SETTING: *North Pole. Backdrop shows northern lights and Santa's workshop.*

AT RISE: GENERAL REVEL, ROBBIE, TWO AIDES, THREE SCIENTISTS, COMPUTER TECHNICIAN, *and* ASSISTANT *are seated on benches at left.* TWO GRENADIERS *stand behind them. At right are more benches.* IVY GREEN *stands center.* 2ND CAMERAMAN *is down right, following action with camera.*

IVY GREEN (*To camera and audience*): Here we are at the actual North Pole, boys and girls. There is a beautiful display of northern lights over Santa's workshop in the distance. (CHILDREN *are heard offstage singing "Here We Come A-Wassailing."*) Listen! I hear children's voices. . . . The jet planes have landed, bringing boys and girls from all over the world to the North Pole. (CHILDREN *enter, carrying flags.*) What a sight! There are children from North America, South America, Europe, Asia, Africa and Australia. I think they have a song to sing. (CHILDREN *stand center. They sing "Here We Come A-Wassailing" or other song. After ending song, they sit on benches. Jingle bells are heard offstage.*)

IVY GREEN: Did you hear that? Jingle bells — coming from Santa's workshop! Boys and girls, we're going to have a television first. A visit from Santa Claus before Christmas! (*Bells ring louder.* TWO ELVES, *doing cartwheels or somersaults, enter right.* IVY GREEN *crosses left and sits with* GENERAL REVEL's *party.* TWO ELVES *cross to center.*)

TWO ELVES (*Together*): Make way! Make way for their royal jollinesses, Mr. and Mrs. Santa Claus! (*All applaud and cheer.* SANTA CLAUS *and* MRS. CLAUS, *very bewildered, enter right, crossing to center.* TWO ELVES *sit cross-legged in front of benches where* CHILDREN *are seated.*)

SANTA CLAUS (*Mystified*): What in the name of aurora borealis is *this?*

MRS. SANTA CLAUS (*Startled*): Oh, my goodness, gracious me. Visitors! I didn't invite any visitors. Did you, Santa?

SANTA CLAUS: Certainly not. We never invite visitors during our busy season.

MRS. SANTA CLAUS: Look, Santa. There are children here. (*Distressed*) Oh, my goodness, gracious me. There shouldn't be children at the North Pole on Christmas Eve!

SANTA CLAUS (*To* CHILDREN): Now, children, I want you all to go home. (CHILDREN *giggle.*) It's the middle of the night! A very special night. . . . Go home now, little ones. Shoo! Scat! Go home to bed before — (*Chimes sounding twelve are heard from offstage.*)

MRS. SANTA CLAUS: Oh, my goodness, gracious me! It's midnight! (*Loud whistling sound is heard from offstage.*)

ALL (*Ad lib; shading eyes and looking up*): Look, the rocket! The rocket is here! (*Etc.*)

SANTA CLAUS (*Bewildered*): Rocket? What rocket? I didn't order a rocket — did you, my dear?

MRS. SANTA CLAUS (*Shaking head*): Oh, no, my dear. *I* didn't order a rocket. Did you order a rocket, elves?

1ST ELF: I ordered a locket and a socket, but not a rocket.

2ND ELF: I ordered a sprocket and a pocket, but not a rocket.

SANTA CLAUS: Well, my dear, if you didn't and I didn't and the elves didn't — who *did* order that rocket?

ROBBIE (*Proudly*): *We* did!

CHILDREN (*Together*): We ordered the rocket.

SANTA CLAUS (*Confused*): You did? But, why? (*Sound of a loud bump is heard at back of auditorium, and there is a flash of light. All onstage point toward source of noise.*)

ROBBIE (*Excitedly*): Look! The rocket has landed. (CHILDREN *applaud and cheer.*) Now we can finally tell you why we built the rocket.

GENERAL REVEL (*Impatiently*): Wait! I want to know what is in that rocket. Guards — bring the cargo here. (TWO GRENADIERS *run offstage and return carrying a large sack of wrapped Christmas gifts which they bring to center and open.*)

1ST GRENADIER (*In surprise*): Well, well, well!

1ST *and* 2ND GRENADIERS (*Together*): Christmas presents! (*They begin taking wrapped packages from sack.*)

CHILDREN (*Together*): Surprise! Surprise!

ROBBIE (*Gratefully*): Mr. and Mrs. Santa Claus, for years and years you have filled our stockings and our shoes, and left us gifts beside our fireplaces or beneath our Christmas trees. You've never asked us for anything — not even so much as a thank you. (*Proudly*) This year, things are different. This year it's *our* turn. This year, *we* want to wish *you* a Merry Christmas! (*Music to "Jolly Old St. Nicholas" is heard.* CHILDREN *sing following lines to that tune, as* TWO GRENADIERS *carry presents to* SANTA CLAUS *and* MRS. SANTA CLAUS.)

CHILDREN (*Singing*):
>   Jolly old St. Nicholas, lean your ear this way,
>   Here is what we've brought to you,
>   On this Christmas day.

GERMAN SOLO:
>   Gingerbread from Dusseldorf,
>   Kisses from Dundee,

DUTCH SOLO:
>   Bookmarks made in Rotterdam,
>   Near the Zuider Zee.

MOROCCAN SOLO:
>   Pillows stitched in Marrakesh,

PERUVIAN SOLO:
>   Bookends from Peru,

IRISH SOLO:
>   Doilies made of Dublin lace,

NEPAL SOLO:
>   Scarves from Katmandu.

JAPANESE SOLO:
>   Calling cards from Tokyo,

FRENCH SOLO:
>   Pens from gay Paree,

ESKIMO SOLO:
>   Furry gloves from Anchorage,

WELSH SOLO:
>   And a Welsh shoe tree. (CHILDREN *all bow.* SANTA CLAUS *begins opening packages.*)

MRS. SANTA CLAUS (*Amazed*): Oh, goodness, gracious me. It's our very finest Christmas!

SANTA CLAUS (*Pleased; holding up nightcap and shoe tree*): Bless my soul! A nightcap and a shoe tree. Just what I always wanted! Thank you, thank you, my dear little children. (*Chime sounding one is heard offstage.*)

MRS. SANTA CLAUS (*Dismayed*): Santa — it's one o'clock. We're late.

SANTA CLAUS (*Quickly*): Elves — hitch up the reindeer. (TWO ELVES *rush off right.*) Come, now, children. You really must go home to your beds now. (CHILDREN *nod. To* MRS. SANTA CLAUS) Come, my dear. We have work to do. (*He puts finger beside his nose and winks at* CHILDREN.) Important work. Ho, ho, ho! (SANTA CLAUS *and* MRS. SANTA CLAUS *cross up right, turn and wave to* CHILDREN.)

ROBBIE: Three cheers for Mr. and Mrs. Santa Claus!

ALL (*Together*): Hip, hip, hooray! Hip, hip, hooray! Hip, hip, hooray! (*All sing "We Wish You a Merry Christmas" as* SANTA CLAUS *and* MRS. CLAUS *exit.*)

IVY GREEN (*Crossing center*): This concludes our broadcast from the North Pole. But before we go, perhaps we can catch a final farewell from Santa Claus. Listen . . . (*She holds up hand mike.*)

SANTA CLAUS (*Offstage, trailing off as jingle bells ring*): Merry Christmas to all, and to all a good . . . night. . . .

IVY GREEN: We now return you to your school assembly. (*Curtain.* CAROLERS *return and sing "Up on the Housetop" or a familiar carol.*)

THE END

Nine Times Christmas

By Maurus Jokai
Adapted by Lewy Olfson
based on "Which of the Nine?"

On Christmas Eve, a poor cobbler and his nine children believe they are richer than the wealthiest man in the world. . . .

Characters

JOHN THE COBBLER
ALEX *(18)*
MARIA *(17)*
FERENC *(16)*
JOHNNY *(15)*
JOSEPH *(14)*   } *his children*
MONIQUE *(13)*
PAUL *(12)*
MAGDA *(11)*
LISA *(10)*
MR. HARD-HEART, *their upstairs neighbor*

TIME: *Some years ago, Christmas Eve.*
SETTING: *The sparsely furnished combination sitting*

room-dining room-workshop of John the Cobbler and his family.

AT RISE: *The nine* CHILDREN *of* JOHN THE COBBLER, *dressed in shabby clothes, are busily preparing the poor room for Christmas. Girls wear caps and aprons over dresses. All dust the furniture, polish the mirror, fluff up the pillows on the big chair, etc.*

MARIA (*Proudly surveying the room*): Wonderful! The room looks so much better already!

JOHNNY: Why shouldn't it? We've been scrubbing and polishing and dusting for over an hour. I'm tired!

PAUL: Yes, Maria. We're all tired!

MARIA: Why, shame on you, Paul! For shame, Johnny! What right have you to grumble and complain? And on Christmas Eve of all nights! Don't you want the house to look bright and clean for Papa when he comes home?

ALEX: Of course they do, Maria. But you have to admit —

MARIA: What must I admit?

ALEX: Well, it *is* a little bit disappointing. To do all this cleaning for Christmas, I mean, and then not have anything to celebrate Christmas with! No tree —

JOSEPH: No candy.

MAGDA: No stockings.

JOSEPH: No candy.

LISA: No presents.

MONIQUE: No pudding.

JOSEPH: No candy.

FERENC: Nothing! For all the celebrating *we'll* be doing, it might as well be the first day of school!

MARIA: That's nonsense! We have each other . . . and we have Father! That's more than some people have. We ought to be grateful.

ALEX: That's true. Think of Mr. Hard-Heart upstairs. He has nobody at all!

MONIQUE: It must be terrible to be all alone on Christmas Eve.

MARIA: That's true. You see, in spite of the fact that Mr. Hard-Heart is the richest man in the whole city — in the whole world, perhaps — and can afford the biggest tree with the brightest stars, the finest roast goose and the sweetest plum pudding — in spite of all those things, we're much luckier than he is, although we don't have four coppers among the nine of us.

FERENC: But Mr. Hard-Heart is such an old grouch! Nobody would want to spend Christmas with him!

MARIA: That's why he's alone! We have each other — and Mr. Hard-Heart has no one at all.

ALEX: I guess you're right, Maria.

MARIA: Of course I'm right, Alex! Now let's stop chattering and start working again. It's getting late and Papa will be home soon. We wouldn't want him to find the room in this condition, would we? (MAGDA *goes to window. Others begin working again.*)

JOSEPH: Poor Papa! His coat is so thin, and the night is getting so cold!

JOHNNY: We shouldn't have let him make the deliveries himself. We should have gone for him!

MARIA: Papa would never let you do that. It's part of a cobbler's job to make sure that the shoes and boots he has made are a perfect fit before he accepts payment. And since one can hardly expect rich folk to come to the cobbler shop on Christmas Eve, Papa must go to them.

JOHNNY: All the same, it doesn't seem fair. He's the best cobbler in the whole city!

MAGDA (*At the window*): Look! It's Papa, it's Papa!

LISA (*Running to the window*): He's home! He's home!

MARIA: Quick, everybody! Away with the brooms and dusters! Off with your caps and aprons! We don't want Papa to find us working! (*There is a mad scramble as* CHILDREN *put away the cleaning clothes and equipment and line up according to height in front of the door with broad smiles on their faces.* MARIA *does not join the line but stands behind her father's easy chair. Door opens and* JOHN THE COBBLER *enters.*)

JOHN (*Smiling happily*): Hello, children! (CHILDREN *swarm round him.*)

CHILDREN (*Ad lib*): Papa! Hooray! Merry Christmas! We're so glad you're home! Give me your coat. (*Etc.*)

JOHN: Well, my lovely children, hello, hello! Are you all here? No, someone seems to be missing. One, two, three, four, five, six, seven, eight . . . why, where's Maria? Maria's missing!

MARIA (*Coming from behind the chair, laughing*): Here I am, Papa. I was hiding behind your chair!

JOHN: Ah yes, so you were. All here and accounted for, then. Good! (*Glances around approvingly, as he sits down in chair*) How bright the room looks tonight. It seems to me that nine pairs of hands have been very busy while I've been out!

MONIQUE: Of course, Papa. It's for the holiday.

JOHN: Ah, so you know it's a holiday, do you? A very gay holiday!

CHILDREN (*Shouting happily*): Yes, Papa!

JOHN: And do you know what holiday it is?

CHILDREN (*Exuberantly*): It's Christmas!

JOHN (*Laughing*): That's right! What smart children I have! Christmas it is indeed. Tonight we do not work; we rejoice.

LISA: What does "rejoice" mean, Papa?

JOHN: It means to sing and to dance and to have a good time all day long.

JOHNNY *and* JOSEPH (*Together*): Hooray! Hooray!

JOHN: Now, I have a surprise for you!

ALEX: A surprise, Papa?

PAUL: What kind of a surprise?

JOHN: It's a Christmas surprise. Do you think you can guess it?

LISA: Perhaps it is a pudding!

JOHN: Did you ever see *one* pudding big enough to feed as many healthy children as I have in my family?

MAGDA: Is it a shining star, then?

JOHN: Of what use would a star be, when we have no Christmas tree?

FERENC: Tell us, Papa, tell us!

JOHN: First you must all sit down. That's it! Johnny, there by the fire. Lisa, up on Papa's lap. (CHILDREN *all sit on the floor or the workbench.* LISA *sits on* JOHN*'s lap.*) There you go. Now then, all settled?

MONIQUE: Yes, Papa.

ALEX: Tell us about the surprise.

JOHN: The surprise is a song.

MARIA: A song, Papa?

JOHN: Yes, yes, my children, a song. Not just an ordinary song: this is a very beautiful song. I have saved it all year to give to all my nine wonderful children as a Christmas present.

PAUL: Oh, sing it for us, Papa!

CHILDREN (*Ad lib*): Yes, Papa. Sing it for us! Let us hear the song. Please! A Christmas song. (*Etc.*)

JOHN: Wait now. Hush! You cannot hear it if all of you are going to yammer and clammer and jammer like that. Hush, hush.

MARIA: Quiet, children.

JOHN: Let's see if I can teach you the beautiful song I know. (CHILDREN *sit very quietly and* JOHN THE COB-BLER *sings first verse of "Hark, the Herald Angels Sing."*)

"Hark, the Herald Angels sing,

Glory to the new-born King." (*Etc.*)

MARIA: How beautiful that was, Papa!

PAUL: Oh, teach it to us, Papa, please!

MAGDA: Yes, yes, I want to learn it, too!

JOHN: What did I tell you? Is it not a beautiful song? Now I will try to teach it to you. But remember, we must sing softly. It wouldn't do to disturb our neighbor, Mr. Hard-Heart.

ALEX (*Indignantly*): Hard-Heart! That old skinflint! Why should we consider him? He never considers us!

JOHN: My son! Where is your Christmas spirit?

ALEX: Christmas spirit indeed! Where is *his* Christmas spirit? Always sulking, always complaining.

MARIA: None of us likes him, Alex, but you must forgive him for his coldness just this once — for all our sakes, as well as for the day's.

ALEX (*Glumly*): Very well. I'll forgive him — but I won't like doing it.

MONIQUE: Now, Papa, teach us the song!

CHILDREN: The song! The song!

JOHN: Yes, the Christmas song. Line up nicely; that's it. (CHILDREN *line up according to height in front of the fireplace.*) Maria, you there, and the younger children there and there. Now then. Silence! I'll begin, and when you think you know the rest, you join in with me. All ready?

CHILDREN: All ready!

JOHN: Good. Let's begin. (JOHN *begins singing the song, and one by one* CHILDREN *join in, until the song is being sung by all in harmony. Just as the song is finished, pounding is heard at door.*) Who could that be, calling on us on Christmas Eve — especially at this late hour?

MARIA: Shall I open the door, Papa?

JOHN: Yes, child, do. It would be wrong to keep someone waiting out in the cold, and unforgivable on this night of all nights. (MARIA *opens door, revealing* MR. HARD-HEART.)

ALEX: It's Mr. Hard-Heart, from upstairs!

MARIA (*A bit nervously*): A merry Christmas to you, Mr. Hard-Heart.

HARD-HEART (*Uncomfortably*): Humph! Yes! Well!

FERENC: Please don't stand outside in the cold, sir. Come in!

HARD-HEART (*Entering the room*): All right, I'm in!

JOHN (*Going over and extending his hand*): Welcome to my shop on this happy night, neighbor. (HARD-HEART *does not take the proffered hand.*) What can I do for you?

HARD-HEART (*Sternly*): You are John the Cobbler, aren't you?

JOHN: That I am, and at your service, Your Excellency. Do you wish to order a pair of patent leather boots?

HARD-HEART: No, no. Not boots — nor shoes, either, for that matter. I came for something else.

MARIA: What could that be?

HARD-HEART (*Sternly*): Do you have any idea, Cobbler John, of the time?

JOHN (*Meekly*): Yes, sir. It's Christmas-time!

HARD-HEART: It is also nine o'clock at night! Do you have any idea how much noise your children can make at nine o'clock at night?

JOHN: Yes, sir.

HARD-HEART: And when those nine children are *singing,* I hardly need tell you that the sound they make is enough to wake up all the statues in the park!

MARIA: Oh, sir! Did our singing disturb you?

HARD-HEART (*With sarcasm*): Did your singing disturb me? *Did your singing disturb me?*

ALEX: Indeed we are sorry, sir, if our singing has upset you.

JOHN: The next time we sing, Excellency, we shall try to sing more sweetly.

HARD-HEART (*Firmly*): There will be no next time! There must be no more singing!

MARIA (*Indignantly*): Why should we not sing? We are poor people, sir, and poor people must sing if they are to enjoy themselves.

HARD-HEART: Let me tell you something, young lady. There is no point in trying to enjoy yourself. There is no point in trying to be happy. I am rich, and I am not happy. Am I? (*Thundering*) *Am I?*

MARIA (*Meekly*): I suppose not, sir.

HARD-HEART (*Firmly*): Nobody is happy in this world! So why should you try to be?

JOHN: Allow me to disagree with you, Excellency. Everyone *can* be happy. If you had someone you cared for, and that person cared for you, then you would be happy, too. That is all it takes! And that is why our family is always happy: because there are so many hearts here, each one busy loving somebody else, and being loved in return.

HARD-HEART (*Somewhat taken aback*): And you say you are always happy, eh?

MONIQUE: We're so happy that we sing all the time!

HARD-HEART: You need hardly remind me of that, young lady! (*Considering the idea*) You can be happy when you have somebody to care for, and when that some-body cares for you. An interesting idea. A very in-teresting idea. A very interesting proposition! (*In a changed tone*) I notice, Cobbler, that you have many children. If I am not mistaken, there are nine of them!

JOHN (*Proudly*): Yes, Excellency, there are nine of them. Alex, Maria, Ferenc —

HARD-HEART (*Interrupting*): Never mind about their names! It is the size of the family that interests me.

JOHN: It is a good size for a family, Excellency. Quite a few mouths to feed.

HARD-HEART: It seems like even more mouths when they sing! (*Abruptly*) But look here, Master Cobbler John, I'd like to do you a favor.

JOHN: That is indeed good of you, Your Excellency. What is it you wish to do?

HARD-HEART: I want to take one of your children!

JOHN (*Incredulous*): What? I don't think I understand you.

HARD-HEART (*Gruffly*): You understand me all right, Master Cobbler! I want to take one of your children. Give me one of them. The lucky one will be adopted and educated as my own child, will travel all over Europe and the Americas, be dressed in the finest clothes, eat the finest of foods, and become a fine member of society. Then one day that child will be in a position to help the rest of you!

JOHN: But why should Your Excellency make such an offer?

HARD-HEART: You just said the way to make yourself happy is to do something for someone else. So I want to do something for your family!

ALEX: Just think, Papa! It would be the chance of a lifetime for one of us!

JOHNNY: I could go to school, Papa, instead of having to learn a trade.

MAGDA: I could live in a big house, and you could all come to visit me.

JOSEPH: If I were to be the one, I'd send you all presents every week!

JOHN: A cobbler's child — to become a gentleman! Oh, it would be a great stroke of good fortune for one of them. How can I refuse?

HARD-HEART: Good! I'm glad to see that you're a sensible man.

JOHN: But, Your Excellency, think of all the trouble and expense. What good will this do *you?*

HARD-HEART (*Blustering*): Me? Heh-heh. Well, as a matter of fact . . .

MARIA: Perhaps, Papa, in spite of all his money, Mr. Hard-Heart is lonely. Perhaps he envies us, that we have each other!

HARD-HEART (*Angrily*): What difference does it make *why* I make this offer? All that matters is that the offer is made.

JOHN: Which of the children will you take?

HARD-HEART: That doesn't matter to me! Pick one of them yourself, but be quick about it. The sooner this is over with, the better I'll like it.

JOHN: Very well, Your Excellency! Come, children, line up and let me look at you! (CHILDREN *line up again.*) I'll begin at this end, if it's all right with Your Excellency.

HARD-HEART (*Impatiently*): Certainly, certainly. Whatever you like.

JOHN (*Considering*): The oldest boy, he's Alex. No, I couldn't let him go. He is a wonderful student, and just between the two of us, he is going to become a priest. The next one? Maria has the most beautiful singing voice, and it brings us all so much joy. No, I could never let her go. (*Each child smiles with relief after being "rejected."*) Ferenc? He's already quite a help to me in the trade. Almost as good a cobbler as I am! No, I couldn't get along without him! Johnny? (*He pauses, thinking seriously.*)

HARD-HEART: Yes, yes?

JOHN (*Shaking his head*): No, he is named after me. I couldn't give him away. (JOHNNY *smiles in relief.*) Joseph, here, is the image of his mother — it's as if I see her every time I look at him. Oh, I couldn't sacrifice him! The next is Monique — she loves this little town, and would hate to leave it. Little Paul, here, was his mother's favorite. I cannot be unfaithful to my wife's wishes by giving him to you. The last two are so small, they'd be too much trouble for Your Excellency. And that is the end of the line. No, no, I cannot decide.

HARD-HEART: Well, then, let the children themselves decide.

JOHN (*Happily*): Yes! That is the best idea! Come, my children — you do the choosing. Which one of you wants to go away to become educated and live in style? Which of the nine shall it be? Who wants Mr. Hard-Heart to be his new Papa?

HARD-HEART (*Advancing on* CHILDREN, *who retreat uncomfortably before him*): Come now, speak up! Don't be bashful! Who wants to be the lucky one?

ALEX (*Timidly*): I've been thinking, Papa. It would be better for me to learn a trade than to go to school. Then I could give you money for the smaller children.

MAGDA: I guess it wouldn't be any fun living in a big house if I could only see the rest of you once in a while.

JOSEPH: And what good would sending all of you presents do? You'd soon forget all about me if I were gone. I couldn't bear that!

HARD-HEART (*Gruffly*): What about you, little Paul?

PAUL: No, no, no! (*He runs to* JOHN *and throws his arms around him in fear.*)

JOHN (*Laughing*): It's no use. You see, Excellency? It can't be done! They just cling to their poor old Papa. Ask of me anything in the world, but I can't give you a single one of my children so long as the good Lord has given them to me.

HARD-HEART: Well, I am sorry enough for that. But there is one thing you *shall* do for me.

JOHN: What is that, Excellency?

HARD-HEART: You shall do no more singing this evening.

MONIQUE (*Unhappily*): No more singing?

MAGDA: But it's Christmas!

HARD-HEART: Wait! I have not finished speaking. You will do no more singing tonight; but in exchange, I will give you one thousand florins! (*He holds up black moneybag.*)

MARIA: One thousand florins!

ALEX: Oh, Papa!

JOHN (*Taken aback*): Your Excellency!

HARD-HEART: Is it a bargain?

JOHN: Yes, it is a bargain. A thousand florins!

HARD-HEART (*Giving him the moneybag*): Just remember. *No more singing!* And now, good night! (*He strides to the door and goes out.*)

JOHNNY (*Dully*): Good night, Mr. Hard-Heart.

MAGDA (*Listlessly*): And a merry Christmas.

MARIA (*Dully*): One thousand florins.

JOHN (*Amazed*): Why such long faces, children? Think of what a merry Christmas we shall have with all this money!

MONIQUE: But it won't *be* Christmas any more. Not if we can't sing.

JOHN: Tomorrow will be another day. We will be able to sing tomorrow! What a happy day tomorrow will be. You'll see!

LISA (*After a pause*): Papa . . .

JOHN: Yes, Lisa?

LISA: Teach us the song again, the pretty song. Teach it to us again, Papa. I have already forgotten how it goes.

JOHN (*A bit crossly*): No, Lisa. Enough singing. Mr. Hard-Heart does not wish it.

FERENC (*Glumly*): To think that our upstairs neighbor should tell us how to celebrate the holiday!

JOSEPH: If we can't sing, Papa, what can we do instead?

MARIA (*Resignedly*): There is nothing else to do. We might as well all go to bed. Perhaps tomorrow will come more quickly if we are asleep.

ALEX: Come, children. Maria and I will help you get ready. (ALEX *and* MARIA *take all* CHILDREN *except* FERENC *into the next room.*)

JOHN (*Trying to be lively*): Well, Ferenc, it's too early for a big boy like you to go to bed, isn't it?

FERENC (*Dully*): Yes, Papa.

JOHN: Why don't we work on this pair of boots, then? (*Taking him to the cobbler's bench*) If we work on them together, the time will go more quickly!

FERENC: Very well, Papa.

JOHN: That's the boy! Remember, busy hands make happy hearts. (*They begin hammering on the boots.* ALEX *and* MARIA *enter.*)

MARIA: The little ones are ready for bed now.

JOHN (*Looking up*): Fine, fine. I shall go in and wish them sweet dreams in a few minutes.

ALEX: What kind of sweet dreams can they have on such a Christmas Eve?

JOHN: Enough of this grumbling, children. It is not the end of the world, simply because we cannot sing a song for one night in our lives!

MARIA: Yes, Papa. (MARIA *and* ALEX *sit down quietly at the table.* JOHN *and* FERENC *go back to their work in silence. After a moment,* JOHN *unconsciously whistles the first bars of the carol, then begins to sing.*)

JOHN (*Singing*): "Glory to the new-born King."

FERENC: Papa!

JOHN (*Blankly, looking up*): Yes?

ALEX: You're singing!

JOHN (*Surprised*): What? I am? (*Crossly*) Well, what if I am? Why should we *not* sing? The devil take old Mr. Hard-Heart!

MARIA (*Happily*): Oh, Papa, do you really mean it?

JOHN: Of course I mean it! We do not need his money. We have gotten along very nicely until now without his thousand florins, and I dare say God will help us to continue to get along without his thousand florins!

FERENC: Good for you, Papa!

JOHN: Alex, go upstairs and knock on Mr. Hard-Heart's door. Tell him I want to see him at once. At once!

ALEX (*Springing to his feet*): Yes, Papa. At once! (*He dashes out the door, calling as he goes.*) Mr. Hard-Heart! Mr. Hard-Heart!

JOHN: Ferenc, put away the cobbler tools. It's Christmas Eve! We should not be working on such a night as this!

FERENC (*Obeying with speed*): Yes, Papa!

JOHN: And you, Maria, get the other children up! Tell them to come in here at once!

MARIA (*Happily*): Yes, Papa! How happy they will be!

JOHN: I won't let that old grouch of a neighbor spoil

my children's holiday, I won't! (MARIA *enters with the other* CHILDREN, *all of whom are in long white night-gowns and tasseled sleeping caps.*)

JOHN: Ah, here you are, my angels!

PAUL: What is it, Papa?

LISA: Why are we getting up? Is it morning so soon?

MONIQUE: What is happening?

JOHN (*Gleefully*): Just a moment, children, and you'll see! (ALEX *dashes in, a broad smile on his face.*)

MARIA: Well, Alex? Is he coming?

ALEX: He didn't want to, but I pounded on his door and shouted and made such a racket that he just *had* to come!

MONIQUE, PAUL *and* JOSEPH (*In unison*): Who? (*At this moment,* MR. HARD-HEART *appears in the doorway, wearing a long white nightgown, a tasseled nightcap and a bathrobe.*)

CHILDREN (*In unison*): Mr. Hard-Heart!

HARD-HEART (*Fuming*): Master Cobbler, what is the meaning of this noise?

JOHN (*Timidly*): Mr. Hard-Heart, I have decided . . .

HARD-HEART (*Eagerly*): Have you decided to give me one of the children after all?

JOHN: No!

HARD-HEART: No?

JOHN: No! Good, kind Excellency, I am your most humble servant. Please, do me a favor. Take back your money.

HARD-HEART: What?

JOHN (*Pushing the moneybag into his hands*): Here it is. Take it. Let it not be mine, but let us sing whenever we want. Please let us sing, because to me and my children, that is worth more than a thousand florins.

HARD-HEART (*Angrily*): Well, you are surely a fool, Master Cobbler. To a man in your position, nothing should be worth more than a thousand florins!

JOHN: Excuse me, good Mr. Hard-Heart, if I do not share your opinion.

HARD-HEART: But why *don't* you share it? See what it's done for me? I am rich! And what has your foolishness done for you? You are poor — and stupid as well.

JOHN: That may be true, Excellency, for, as you say, you are rich and I am poor. But princes have been poor, and rich kings have knelt before them.

HARD-HEART (*Bewildered*): What are you talking about? You are speaking in riddles, Cobbler!

MARIA: Excuse me, Mr. Hard-Heart. Do you know what night this is?

HARD-HEART: Why, yes. It is December twenty-fourth!

ALEX: It is the night that a great star burst forth in the heavens with radiant glory!

HARD-HEART: A star?

FERENC: A glorious star, that heralded the coming of the Prince of Peace.

HARD-HEART (*Thoughtfully*): The Prince of Peace.

JOHN: Yes, it is He — the Prince of Peace — that I spoke of; the Prince who was so poor He was born in a stable and wrapped in rags.

JOHNNY: Yet kings — rich and wise, like yourself, Mr. Hard-Heart — came from miles away, bringing gifts, to kneel before Him and pay homage to Him.

HARD-HEART: The Christmas story. I had forgotten it. It has been many years.

JOHN: So you see, Mr. Hard-Heart, when my children and I sing our little song, it is not because we are fools wanting to make noise. It is because we are happy, and our hearts are filled with the wonderful memory of what happened two thousand years ago. Mr. Hard-Heart, would you — would you care to join us in our Christmas meal? I know it won't be a fine feast, such as the ones to which you are accustomed, but . . .

HARD-HEART (*Dazed*): Because . . . your hearts . . . are happy. Because . . . you remember. But what did you say? Would I care to join you at dinner?

JOHN: Yes, yes — at our Christmas meal. Would you?

HARD-HEART: Master Cobbler, you are very kind to a lonely old man. I *want* you and your children to sing your Christmas song, over and over, all night long. I, too, must learn to remember. Yes, yes. Sing your song. And keep the thousand florins as a Christmas gift to your children, from me.

CHILDREN (*In awe*): Your Excellency!

HARD-HEART: No, I will do better than that. I will make it *two* thousand florins. To help me remember! Two thousand, for the number of years.

JOHN: Will you join my family and me tonight, Excellency? Say that you will! You must share our Christmas with us. And you must join in the singing of our song. Will you?

HARD-HEART: I don't know what to say. I haven't — why, I haven't sung a song in years. My throat is full of cobwebs.

MARIA: It doesn't matter what's in your throat, Mr. Hard-Heart. What matters is what is in your heart.

JOSEPH: Say you will come!

HARD-HEART: Yes, I will come. Thank you, Cobbler John. Thank you, children! This is the happiest Christmas of my life! (CHILDREN *start to sing their song in full, triumphant tones. On the words "Joyful all ye nations rise,"* JOHN *and* HARD-HEART *join in, their hands clasped in friendship. All are smiling and gathered in a warm family grouping as the curtain falls.*)

THE END

He Won't Be Home for Christmas

By William Moessinger

When Jimmy Benson doesn't get his wish, he angrily exclaims that there is no Santa Claus. . . .

Characters

JIMMY BENSON
TOMMY, *his friend*
BOY
GIRL
OTHER CHILDREN
DEPARTMENT STORE SANTA
SANTA CLAUS
ENGLEBERT ELF
EVELYN ELF
INGRID ELF
AMY ELF
OTHER ELVES, *extras*
MRS. BENSON, *Jimmy's mother*
WILLARD, *Jimmy's brother*
JANICE, *Jimmy's sister*
WESTERN UNION MESSENGER
MR. BENSON, *Jimmy's father*

SCENE 1

TIME: *A few days before Christmas.*

SETTING: *Grommel's Department Store. There is an armchair for Department Store Santa at right. This scene may be played before curtain.*

AT RISE: DEPARTMENT STORE SANTA *is seated in armchair, talking to* BOY. GIRL *and* OTHER CHILDREN *are lined up to see him.* JIMMY *and* TOMMY *are in middle of line.*

JIMMY (*To* TOMMY): He'll never be able to do it. Not even a real Santa Claus could get me what I want for Christmas.

TOMMY: What makes you think he's not the real Santa Claus? He sure looks like it.

JIMMY: I don't believe there *is* a Santa Claus. And even if there were, Grommel's Department Store is the last place he would go.

STORE SANTA (*To* BOY): Now, what would you like for Christmas, young man?

BOY: I'd like a two-wheeler, a model airplane, and a different teacher in school.

STORE SANTA: A different teacher? Why? Don't you like your teacher?

BOY: I like her, but I want a teacher who'll play baseball with us.

STORE SANTA: Why, I'll bet your teacher would play baseball if you asked her. I'll work on getting the airplane for you, and you work on getting your teacher to play ball.

BOY: Thanks, Santa! (*Exits right.* GIRL *sits on* STORE SANTA*'s lap.*)

STORE SANTA: Now, young lady, tell me what you would like for Christmas. (GIRL *whispers into* STORE SANTA*'s ear, and* STORE SANTA *nods, as* TOMMY *and* JIMMY *continue conversation.*)

TOMMY (*To* JIMMY): What do you want for Christmas that's so special, anyway?

JIMMY: I want my father to come home from Alaska. He's been working there for three months, and we never get to see him. He's supposed to come back for good in the spring, but I want him here for Christmas.

TOMMY: Are you going to ask Santa Claus to bring him home?

JIMMY: Yes. I already sent a letter to the North Pole. I don't think there really is a Santa Claus, but I'm not taking any chances.

STORE SANTA (*To* GIRL): Is there anything else you want to ask me, little girl?

GIRL: Yes. May I pull your beard, Santa?

STORE SANTA: I'd rather you didn't. Santa Claus has to stay neat, you know! (SANTA *pats* GIRL *on head.* GIRL *exits right.* 1ST CHILD *whispers into* STORE SANTA*'s ear.*)

JIMMY (*Excitedly*): Did you hear that? Did you hear that? I'll bet it's a fake beard, Tommy. If I pulled it, it would come right off.

TOMMY: You'd be afraid to pull it.

JIMMY: Oh, yeah? You'll see.

STORE SANTA: Children, it's been a long day. Santa needs to stand up and stretch. (*He stands, stretches and yawns.* OTHER CHILDREN *also yawn.*) Let's all stretch a little and sing. (*All except* JIMMY *stretch.* JIMMY *turns and does not sing.*)

STORE SANTA, TOMMY, OTHER CHILDREN (*Singing to tune of "We Wish You a Merry Christmas"*):

Let's stand up and stretch our legs now.
Let's stand up and stretch our legs now.
Let's stand up and stretch our legs now.
It's a good time to try!

Let's stand up and stretch our arms now,
Let's stand up and stretch our arms now,
Let's stand up and stretch our arms now,
And reach for the sky.

We wish you a Merry Christmas,
We wish you a Merry Christmas,
We wish you a Merry Christmas,
And a Happy New Year!

STORE SANTA (*Sitting down*): Now, children, come and tell me what you want for Christmas. (CHILDREN *go up to* STORE SANTA *one at a time. Each whispers into his ear, then exits right.* STORE SANTA *speaks ad lib.*) Yes, of course . . . What a wonderful idea! Ho, ho, ho! (*Etc.* JIMMY *comes up to* STORE SANTA.) Hello, young man. What's your name?

JIMMY: Jimmy Benson.

STORE SANTA: Have you been a good little boy, Jimmy?

JIMMY: I'm not a *little* boy.

STORE SANTA: Well, have you been a good *big* boy?

JIMMY: I guess so.

STORE SANTA: What do you want for Christmas?

JIMMY: If you were the real Santa Claus, you'd know. I sent you a letter telling you what I want.

STORE SANTA: I get so many letters. . . . If you'll give me a hint I might be able to remember yours.

JIMMY (*Angrily*): I think you're a fake — a great big fake. I'll bet even your beard's not real. (*Reaches for* STORE SANTA*'s beard*)

STORE SANTA (*Nervously*): Now, wait a minute, sonny. (JIMMY *pulls off* SANTA*'s beard and holds it over his head.*)

OTHER CHILDREN (*Shocked, ad lib*): Ooooh! Look! He pulled off Santa's beard! It wasn't real! (*Etc.*)

JIMMY (*Angrily, to* SANTA): You *are* a fake! Why did I ever think that Santa Claus could bring my father home? You're just a big fake, and this (*Shakes beard*) proves it! (STORE SANTA *turns head away and covers eyes with arm.* JIMMY *holds beard high with one hand and points to* STORE SANTA *with other. Others freeze in shocked positions. Curtain.*)

*   *   *   *   *

SCENE 2

SETTING: *Santa's workshop at North Pole. There are two worktables downstage. Each holds toys, tools, wrapping paper, ribbon, etc. Empty gift boxes are piled on floor beside tables. There is a file cabinet at right. Telephone on small stand is at left.*

AT RISE: ENGLEBERT, EVELYN, INGRID, AMY *and* OTHER ELVES *are standing at worktables, making toys, packing toys into boxes, and wrapping boxes.* SANTA CLAUS *is going from table to table, inspecting work.*

ELVES (*Singing to tune of "Frère Jacques"*):

Working, working,
Working, working,
All day long,
All day long,

Making Christmas toys now,
For good girls and boys now,
We must work,
While you play.

(*Repeat as round if desired. One group of* ELVES *may sing while others dance or keep time by hammering.*)

SANTA CLAUS: Ho, ho, ho! How are you elves doing? Are the toys almost ready for Christmas?

ELVES (*Together*): Yes, Santa. (ENGLEBERT ELF *goes to file cabinet and pulls out sheaf of papers.*)

ENGLEBERT ELF: We've had some complaints, Santa.

SANTA: Complaints! How many complaints?

ENGLEBERT: Two hundred and seventeen.

SANTA (*Shocked*): Two hundred and seventeen?

ENGLEBERT: I know that sounds like a lot, but there are 117,286 Department Store Santas working for us.

SANTA: I guess 217 complaints out of 117,286 isn't bad. What are they complaining about?

ENGLEBERT: You see, Santa, there just aren't many people in the world who look like you. So some Santa's helpers don't look the part.

EVELYN ELF: Right. Some have to wear false beards.

INGRID ELF: I heard about a baldheaded Santa Claus who had to wear a wig.

AMY ELF: And a few Santa Clauses are even skinny.

INGRID: They stuff pillows into their coats, but sometimes that doesn't make them look jolly and fat.

EVELYN: Just lumpy.

ENGLEBERT: But even Santa Claus can't be everywhere at once. So we do the best we can, and Santa's helpers keep in touch by mail.

SANTA: Yes, and in case of emergencies we do have the magic telephone (*Points to telephone at left*) — the direct line to the North Pole. We call it the cold line. Ho, ho! (*More seriously*) Speaking of emergencies, elves, we'll have quite a few emergency calls if we don't get back to work. Christmas isn't far away. (ELVES *continue with work.*)

ELVES (*Singing to tune of "Frère Jacques"*):
Working, working,
Working, working,
All day long,
All day long,

Making Christmas toys now,
For good girls and boys now,
We must work,
While you play.

(*Telephone rings.* ELVES *stop singing and working, and turn to stare at telephone.* SANTA *crosses slowly to phone as it rings and picks up receiver.*)

SANTA (*Into phone*): I'm sorry to hear that. Very sorry. (*To* ELVES) It's the Santa from Grommel's Department Store.

ENGLEBERT: What does he want?

SANTA (*To* ENGLEBERT): Shush! (*Into phone*) Yes! . . . (*To* ENGLEBERT) Get out Jimmy Benson's file. (ENGLEBERT *rushes to file cabinet, gets out folder and rushes back to* SANTA, *waving it.*)

ENGLEBERT: Here it is, Santa!

SANTA (*Into phone*): I'm sorry to hear that (*To* ELVES) Jimmy Benson pulled off my helper's beard. Now he doesn't believe in Santa Claus anymore.

ELVES (*In dismay; ad lib*): Oh, no! Too bad. That's awful! (*Etc.*)

SANTA (*Into phone*): What did he want for Christmas? . . . He said that Santa would know, did he? Well, Santa will know in one minute. Don't you worry. You go back to work now, and I'll take care of everything. . . . Goodbye. (*He hangs up phone and turns to* ENGLEBERT.) What do you see in Jimmy Benson's file, Englebert? (ENGLEBERT *opens folder, takes out letter.*)

ENGLEBERT: Here's the letter he wrote you this year, Santa. (SANTA *takes letter, then pats pockets, looking for glasses.*)

SANTA: I can't find my reading glasses. Ingrid, will you please read the letter to us? (*He hands letter to* INGRID.)

INGRID (*Reading*): "Dear Santa, I don't want any toys this year — I just want you to bring my father home for Christmas. He's working far away, in Alaska, and in his last letter he said it's so cold there that polar bears wear long underwear, and the snow is so deep that no one can find the roads. I know it's a lot to ask, but I'd give anything if my father could come home for Christmas."

SANTA: Elves, put on your thinking caps. We are going to find a solution to Jimmy's problem, or my name isn't Santa Claus. (*All* ELVES *and* SANTA *pace back and forth, scratching their heads. Then* INGRID *runs in to* ENGLEBERT *and whispers into his ear;* ENGLEBERT *goes to* EVELYN *and whispers into her ear;* EVELYN *goes to* AMY *and whispers into her ear;* AMY *goes to* SANTA *and whispers into his ear.*) Why, yes, that would do it. Of course, of course. We can solve this problem and bring a Merry Christmas to the whole Benson family.

ELVES (*Singing to tune of "Frère Jacques" as curtain begins to close*):
Working, working,
Working, working,
All the day,
All the day,

Making Christmas toys now,
For good girls and boys now.
We must work,
While you play.
(*Curtain.*)

*   *   *   *   *

SCENE 3

TIME: *Christmas Eve.*

SETTING: *Benson living room. There is a sofa down left. Bare Christmas tree is at right, with boxes of decorations under it. Tree lights are turned off.*

AT RISE: MRS. BENSON *is standing near tree, admiring it.* WILLARD *is gazing out over audience, as if looking out window.* JIMMY *and* JANICE *are sitting on sofa.*

MRS. BENSON: Why don't you help me trim the tree, Jimmy? It'll help get you into the Christmas spirit.

JIMMY: I really don't feel like it, Mom.

MRS. BENSON: I'm sorry. We have such a pretty tree this year.

WILLARD (*Pointing over audience*): Look at the snow coming down. It's going to be a white Christmas.

JANICE: I wish I could stay up and watch Santa Claus come down the chimney.

JIMMY: I wish someone would come down our chimney, but not Santa Claus.

JANICE: Who is it?

JIMMY: You know who I wish it were. I wish it more than anything — more than anything in the world.

ALL (*Singing to tune of "Alouette"*):
> Home for Christmas,
> Please come home for Christmas,
> While the snow is
> Falling 'neath the moon.
> You're away and
> Working night and day,
> Yet we want you
> Home for Christmas soon.

JIMMY (*Singing*):
> Everybody ought to be —

OTHERS (*Singing*):
>   Everybody ought to be —

JIMMY (*Singing*):
>   At home with his family —

OTHERS (*Singing*):
>   At home with his family.

JIMMY (*Singing*):
>   Ought to be —

OTHERS (*Singing*):
>   Ought to be —

JIMMY (*Pointing to himself, singing*):
>   Here with me —

OTHERS (*Pointing to themselves, singing*):
>   Here with me.

ALL (*Singing*):
>   Oh-h-h-h-h,
>   Home for Christmas,
>   Please come home for Christmas,
>   While the snow is
>   Falling 'neath the moon.
>   You're away and
>   Working night and day,
>   Yet we want you
>   Home for Christmas soon.

MRS. BENSON: Jimmy, you know that your father would come for Christmas if he could, but he's snowed in. The airport is over 200 miles from where he works, and there's no way for him to get to it in time for a Christmas flight.

JANICE: I miss Daddy.

WILLARD: Me, too.

MRS. BENSON (*Sighing*): I know. So do I. But tomorrow's Christmas, and you know Santa Claus can't come while you're still awake. So get to bed now, and don't wake up until Christmas morning.

JIMMY, JANICE *and* WILLARD (*Together*): Aww-w! (*They leave reluctantly as* MRS. BENSON *shoos them off right. Stage lights dim; spotlight illuminates tree.*)

MRS. BENSON (*Singing to tune of "Alouette"*):
>   Home for Christmas —
>   Please come home for Christmas,
>   While the snow is
>   Falling 'neath the moon.
>   You're away and
>   Working night and day,
>   Yet we want you —
>   (*Spoken*) Home for Christmas.

(*She puts tinsel on tree, and Christmas lights come on. She gives tree appraising look, yawns, and exits right. All stage lights go off except for those on tree. Slow curtain.*)

*   *   *   *   *

SCENE 4

TIME: *Christmas Day.*

SETTING: *Same as Scene 3, but boxes for decorations have been removed and there are presents under tree.*

AT RISE: *Stage is empty.*

JANICE (*Running in, right*): Look at all the presents. Mom! Mom! Come see what Santa Claus has brought! (MRS. BENSON *enters right, followed by* WILLARD *and* JIMMY.)

MRS. BENSON: Oh, my! So many presents! They all have names on them, too! I know — let's each pick a present and open it. (WILLARD *and* JANICE *excitedly take presents and open them.* JIMMY *sits sadly in chair.*)

WILLARD *and* JANICE (*Ad lib*): Wow! What a present! Isn't this neat? It's just what I wanted. Boy, are you lucky! (*Etc.*)

MRS. BENSON: Go on, Jimmy. Open one of your presents.

JIMMY: I don't want to.

MRS. BENSON (*Concerned*): What's wrong, Jimmy?

JIMMY: The only present I want isn't here. I wrote Santa Claus a letter and asked for it, but he didn't bring it to me. Now I know for sure that there is no Santa Claus. (*Doorbell rings. All freeze for a few seconds.*)

MRS. BENSON (*Incredulous*): It *couldn't* be. . . .

JANICE: Mom, do you think that Santa Claus sent Jimmy's present, after all?

JIMMY: Maybe I was wrong. . . .

MRS. BENSON (*Hurriedly*): Well, don't just stand there. Willard, go answer the door. (WILLARD *exits left, then re-enters with* WESTERN UNION MESSENGER.)

MESSENGER: Western Union. I have a telegram for Mrs. Benson.

MRS. BENSON: That's me. (*He hands her telegram and receipt with pen.*)

MESSENGER (*Indicating line on receipt*): Sign here. (*She signs, and returns receipt and pen to him.*) Merry Christmas! (*Exits left.*)

MRS. BENSON (*Calling after him*): Merry Christmas to you, too. (*She opens telegram.*) It says — (*Reading*) "Dear Martha, Jimmy, Janice, and Willard: I wanted to surprise you by being home today. Stop. Roads impassable — helicopter stalled — no way to get to airport. Stop. See you in the spring, I guess. Stop. Miss you all. Stop. Merry Christmas. Love, Dad."

JANICE (*Disappointed*): Oh.

JIMMY: I should have known. For a second I thought —

well, you know what I thought. But I was wrong. There's no Santa Claus at the North Pole. All those letters to Santa Claus probably end up in the post office wastebasket. Santa Claus is a fake!

MRS. BENSON: Now, Jimmy.

JIMMY (*Starting to sniff*): I wanted Daddy to come home today.

JANICE *and* WILLARD (*Together*): Me, too.

JIMMY (*Dejectedly*): But he won't be home for Christmas. He won't be home. . . . (*Doorbell rings.*) That's probably the Western Union messenger again. I'll get it. (*He exits left. From offstage*) DAD! (*He re-enters with* MR. BENSON *by his side.*) Mom! Mom! Dad is home!

MRS. BENSON (*Hugging* MR. BENSON): George, it's so good to have you home! (*He hugs* WILLARD *and* JANICE.) How on earth did you get here?

MR. BENSON: It was a miracle.

JIMMY: A miracle?

MRS. BENSON: Tell us about it, George.

MR. BENSON: I was just coming out of the telegraph office when a fat old man walked over to me and started talking about how terrible the weather was. I agreed with him and said that it was so bad that I wouldn't be able to get home for Christmas. He scratched his beard and said that he might be able to get me to the airport on his sled. I thanked him for his offer but told him that no sled could get me to the airport on time. Then I walked back to my hotel.

MRS. BENSON: But that doesn't explain how you got to the airport.

MR. BENSON: I'll get to that. When I got back to my hotel there he was again — waiting in the lobby, all bright-eyed and red-cheeked. This time he asked me when I had to be at the airport to catch the Christmas flight. I told him, "In three hours, but no one can drive through 200 miles of snow in three hours." And he answered, "Maybe no one else can, but I know a short cut, and my sled goes very fast — so fast you might say it flies." Before I could say another word, he had taken me by the arm to the front of the hotel, where he pointed to his sled. It was snowing so hard, I could barely see it, but I knew I had never seen anything so strange ·before. We got inside, the old man took up the reins, and off we went into the blizzard. The towns, rivers and hills passed by in a blur, we were going so fast, and before I could sing "Jingle Bells" we were at the airport. And here I am.

JIMMY: Santa Claus *did* read my letter!

MR. BENSON: Now, I didn't say that he was Santa Claus.

JIMMY: You didn't have to. I know it now. I know it.

MRS. BENSON: George, we're so happy to have you home for Christmas.

MR. BENSON: I'm so happy to be home. And Jimmy, I told the old man with the sled that I felt my oldest son especially needed his father home for Christmas — and guess what he did!

JIMMY (*Excitedly*): What did Santa Claus do?

MR. BENSON: Jimmy, I didn't say that the man was Santa Claus.

JIMMY: What did he do?

MR. BENSON: He wrote you a letter and asked me to give it to you. (*He hands* JIMMY *envelope.* JIMMY *tears it open and goes to front of stage to read letter aloud.*)

JIMMY: "Dear Jimmy: Getting your father home for Christmas wasn't easy, but I know you'll agree it was worth it." (*He looks up.*) I do. (*Reading from letter*) "I hope that after today you will always believe in the true meaning of Christmas." (*Looks up*) Oh, I will,

I will. (*Reading from letter*) "And please share this Christmas greeting with your family."

WILLARD: What is the Christmas greeting?

JANICE: What does it say? (*They all move to front of stage around* JIMMY *to look at letter.*)

MRS. BENSON: Oh, isn't it nice?

JANICE: It says —

ALL (*Singing*):

> We wish you a Merry Christmas,
> We wish you a Merry Christmas,
> We wish you a Merry Christmas,
> And a Happy New Year!

JIMMY: And the same to you, Santa Claus. Wherever you are! (*Curtain*)

THE END

Santa Claus Is Twins

By Anne Coulter Martens

---

*Only one Santa was expected, but two show up
— and one of them may be in trouble . . .*

Characters

DONNA, *14*
BETSY ⎫
MACK ⎬ *her friends*
FREDDY ⎭
MRS. SHELDON
WOODROW, *her son, 6*
OFFICER PERKINS
MRS. AVERY
SHARON, *her daughter*
PARENTS ⎫
CHILDREN ⎬ *extras*

TIME: *Saturday morning, a few days before Christmas.*
SETTING: *The recreation room in Donna's home.*
AT RISE: DONNA *and* BETSY *are putting Christmas decorations on a highbacked chair.* FREDDY *stands on a
small stepladder behind sofa, attaching to the wall a*

sign that reads: TOYS FOR TOTS. *Above it is another sign reading,* OUR CLUB PROJECT, *and beside this is a sign reading* HAVE YOUR CHILD'S PICTURE TAKEN WITH SANTA CLAUS. *An open costume box is on the coffee table with a Santa Claus suit and some jingle bells hanging over side.*

FREDDY: What time is it?

DONNA (*Looking at her watch*): Ten of ten.

FREDDY: I thought Mack was supposed to be here to help.

DONNA: Mack's late, as usual. He has no sense of time at all.

BETSY: And he knows we want to make as much money as we can for the Gifts-for-Children project.

DONNA: If the Fire Department can make time for this, I should think Mack might make some effort to get here.

FREDDY: How much do you think we'll make on this picture-taking?

DONNA: A lot, I hope. The more we make, the more the Fire Department will have to buy toys for needy kids. (*Goes to costume box.*) Mack was going to borrow a new Santa suit for you, but if he doesn't get here soon, you'll just have to wear this old ratty one. (*Holds up a red jacket with white trim*)

FREDDY (*Sitting on top of ladder*): Playing Santa Claus really isn't my thing.

DONNA: Now, Freddy. Where's your Christmas spirit? (*Telephone rings.*) I'll get it. (*Into phone*) Hello . . . Certainly Mrs. Sheldon, we'll be ready to take a Polaroid picture of your little boy at ten o'clock sharp. (*Picks up appointment book*) Yes, I know you're very busy, but there won't be any delay. . . . Of course, Mrs. Sheldon. Ten o'clock, on the dot. (*Hangs up*) Oh, dear!

BETSY: What's the problem?

DONNA: Mrs. Sheldon. You know what a grouch she can be. She practically chewed my ear off! What if she gives us a hard time?

BETSY: Our schedule would go haywire! Let's hope she doesn't. (*Checking camera on desk*) The camera's loaded and ready. I'm glad we could get the film at cost.

DONNA: I guess everybody likes to help out as much as possible at Christmas.

FREDDY (*Getting down from ladder*): The more I think about it, the more I realize I'm just not the Santa type. You should have asked Mack. (*Takes ladder behind screen*)

DONNA (*Sarcastically*): We did. He said he'd rather supervise.

BETSY: Then why isn't he here?

FREDDY (*Coming from behind screen*): Should we call his house to see if he's left yet?

DONNA: Good idea. (*Picks up phone, dials*)

FREDDY: You did a great job decorating this chair. And those lollipops look terrific. (*Reaches toward box on coffee table*)

BETSY (*Stopping him*): Oh, no, you don't! These are for the kids who have their pictures taken.

DONNA (*Into phone*): Hello . . . Mrs. Barnett? . . . This is Donna. Has Mack left yet? . . . Half an hour ago? He must have been sidetracked somewhere. We're waiting for him to bring the Santa suit . . . Thanks anyway. (*Hangs up*)

BETSY: I guess Freddy will have to wear this old suit after all!

DONNA (*Holding up the red jacket*): You'll need a couple of pillows to fatten you up.

FREDDY (*Unhappily*): Can't we wait a few more minutes for Mack?

DONNA (*Shaking her head*): Time's running out.

BETSY: Come on, Freddy, let's hear you give us a "Ho, ho, ho!"

FREDDY: I'm too nervous. (*Clears his throat and speaks in a flat unconvincing voice*) Ho, ho, ho. (*Sighs*) See? I told you I'm no good as Santa.

BETSY: Don't worry, Freddy. You'll be great. (*Pauses*) Anyway, you're elected.

DONNA (*Matter-of-factly*): Here, put this jacket on. (*Hands it to him*)

BETSY: All you have to do is ask each child if he's been good and what he wants for Christmas.

DONNA: And don't forget that you are supposed to be jolly!

FREDDY (*Resigned*): How do I get myself into these situations? (DONNA *takes red pants out of box and hands them to* FREDDY.)

DONNA: Here are the pants. (*Reaches into box again*) Your hat and boots are in here, too. (*Takes them from box and gives them to* FREDDY)

FREDDY (*Putting on costume*): I'll be quite a sight, all right! (DONNA *takes beard and bells from box.*)

DONNA (*Handing beard and bells to* FREDDY): There, that does it! You're all set now. (FREDDY *adjusts beard, puts on hat and boots, and rings bells.*)

BETSY: You're dynamite as old Saint Nick. (*Pats him lightly on the back*) We really appreciate the way you've volunteered to do this, Freddy.

FREDDY (*Ringing bells again; then in unenthusiastic voice*): Ho, ho, ho.

DONNA: Try putting a little more pep into your ho-ho-ho. You're supposed to be jolly, remember?

FREDDY (*Not doing much better*): Ho, ho, ho. (FREDDY *holds out his arms, the bells in one hand, and* DONNA *places box on extended arms.*)

BETSY: Take these cushions, too. (*She piles two sofa cushions on top of the box.*)

FREDDY: This isn't exactly the kind of "pack" Santa's supposed to carry.

DONNA: Very funny. (*Points left*) You wait out there, and we'll signal when you're to come in. (*He starts toward left.*)

FREDDY: What's the signal?

DONNA: We'll sing "Jingle Bells." O.K.?

FREDDY: I should have stayed in bed. (*Sighs and exits*)

BETSY: Poor Freddy.

DONNA: At least he's reliable. That's more than we can say about Mack.

BETSY: If only his voice didn't squeak!

DONNA: And the suit is sort of ratty. That Mack has no sense of time or responsibility! (*Telephone rings.*)

BETSY (*Into phone*): Hello. . . . Just a moment, Mrs. Avery, and I'll check. (*Looks in appointment book*) Yes, we can take your daughter's picture with Santa at ten-fifteen. Thank you for calling. (*Hangs up*)

DONNA: We're booked solid from ten to twelve. Not bad, Betsy.

BETSY: And with all the posters I've put up, there are sure to be some drop-ins. (*Pauses*) I do wish we had a better Santa suit, though.

DONNA: Once the children are sitting on Santa's lap, it will be all right. They'll never notice. (*Annoyed*) That Mack makes me so angry! (*There is a quick knock, and* MACK *enters, carrying a costume box and a small Christmas tree on a stand. He wears a heavy turtleneck sweater in a bright pattern.*)

MACK (*Jauntily*): Are you talking about me? (*Puts costume box on coffee table*)

DONNA: Mack! What do you mean by getting here so late? We've been waiting for you for half an hour. You look like a clown in that ridiculous sweater.

MACK: So I'll be Santa's clown. What are you two so upset about?

BETSY: Freddy had to put on the old Santa suit because you were so late. Our first customer will be here at ten sharp (*Looks at watch*) — in about two minutes!

DONNA: Where were you, anyway?

MACK: I stopped to buy you a bargain tree. (*Holds up tree*) Cute, huh? I bought it from a kid on the corner down the street and paid for it out of my own pocket.

DONNA: Sure, it's a nice tree, and thanks. (MACK *puts tree on desk.*) There are some miniature lights in the garage. They'd look pretty on it.

BETSY: I'll go get them. (*Exits left*)

DONNA (*Looking at costume box* MACK *brought*): I don't know what we'll do with this costume now. We don't need two Santas.

MACK: Sorry. I must have lost track of the time. (*Takes a white beard from box and holds it to his face. Speaks in a deep voice*) Ho, ho, ho!

DONNA: It's not funny.

MACK: Are you mad at me?

DONNA: Yes, I am! I'm furious.

MACK: Oh, come on, it's no big deal.

DONNA: Not to you, maybe, but it is to us. When you promise to be somewhere at a certain time, you should be there.

MACK (*Mocking*): Are you going to tell Santa I was a bad boy?

DONNA (*Still angry*): I just wish I could.

MACK: Maybe there's still time to put this suit on Freddy. (*There is a knock on door.*)

DONNA: It's too late. That must be Mrs. Sheldon. She's our first customer, and she may be touchy! Mack, put this extra suit out of sight, behind the screen. (*Puts box in his arms*) Hurry! (*He takes box and goes behind screen.* DONNA *calls*) Come in, please! (MRS. SHELDON *and* WOODROW *enter right.* BETSY *enters left with a string of small lights and begins putting them on tree.*)

MRS. SHELDON: Hello, girls.

WOODROW: Where's Santa Claus?

BETSY: He'll be here in a minute.

MRS. SHELDON: This has been such an upsetting morning for me. Sit down, Woodrow, and be very quiet. (*Points to a chair, where* WOODROW *sits.*) He's such a good little boy. (*Looking around*) I'm looking for a nasty young man in a loud turtleneck sweater. (MACK *peers over top of screen, then ducks down.*) Did he come in here?

DONNA (*Uneasily*): Why would he come here?

WOODROW: Wow! Look, lollipops! (*He dashes over to box of lollipops, grabs one, rips the wrapper off and puts it into his mouth.*)

MRS. SHELDON: Woodrow, that's a no-no! (*Reaches for lollipop, but* WOODROW *backs away.*) I never allow sugar because it's bad for him.

BETSY: I'm sorry. We didn't know. (*As she reaches to take lollipop from him,* WOODROW *runs to other side of room.*)

MRS. SHELDON: Wait till Santa hears about this!

WOODROW: I'll bet Santa likes candy.

MRS. SHELDON: Never mind that. Now, look at you.

Your face and hands are all sticky. (*To* DONNA) Does
he have time to wash up before you take the picture?

DONNA: Sure. (*Pointing*) Right there — first door to the
left.

MRS. SHELDON: March, Woodrow. (WOODROW *goes out
left, still sucking the lollipop.*) He's usually so obedient.
But after what happened this morning, I'm just too
jittery myself to keep a close eye on him.

BETSY (*Putting lights on tree*): What happened, Mrs.
Sheldon?

MRS. SHELDON (*Pacing about*): I could *cry*. You know
that beautiful evergreen tree on my front lawn? Some
vandal sawed the top off it!

DONNA: Who would do such a thing? (MACK *again peeks
over the screen, unseen by* MRS. SHELDON.)

MRS. SHELDON: The boy in the turtleneck sweater, that's
who! The police station is sending an officer over here,
to investigate the vandalism.

BETSY: Did you call the police?

DONNA (*Breaking in excitedly*): And did you tell them to
come *here?*

MRS. SHELDON: Yes! I want that boy punished, and
there's no time to lose. Not half an hour ago I saw
him walk right past my house.

DONNA: Do you know him?

MRS. SHELDON: Not by name. But I'd recognize that
sweater anywhere. (MACK *looks over top of screen,
puts his hand to his neck, then ducks down.*)

DONNA: But why would he do such a thing?

MRS. SHELDON: That boy is out for revenge, because I
complained about him in the supermarket yesterday.

BETSY: What did he do?

MRS. SHELDON (*Self-righteously*): He rammed his shopping cart into me just as I was picking up a carton
of eggs!

DONNA: It must have been an accident!

MRS. SHELDON: No! I'm sure he did it on purpose. (*Pompously*) The manager made him pay for the eggs.

BETSY: Couldn't it have been an accident?

MRS. SHELDON: I'm sure it wasn't.

DONNA: Maybe you stopped short, and he couldn't stop in time.

MRS. SHELDON: Since when does a person have to give a signal to stop at the egg counter? No, he did it deliberately. (*Getting worked up*) He probably followed me home and then came back this morning to ruin my tree. This time I'll have him arrested! (MACK *pops his head up, then down.*)

DONNA: Isn't that a little drastic?

MRS. SHELDON: After what he did to my tree? It had a perfect shape, and now this much is sawed right off the top. (*Indicates about twelve inches*) Just about the size of that little tree you have.

DONNA: Really? (*Looks uneasily at tree.*)

MRS. SHELDON: There were a few brown needles near the top and I was considering spraying. (*Goes to look at their tree closely*) Brown needles! This looks just like it!

DONNA (*Nervously*): That's not possible, Mrs. Sheldon.

MRS. SHELDON (*Imperiously*): Where did you get this little tree?

BETSY (*Indignantly*): You don't think one of *us* . . .?

MRS. SHELDON: No, no, it was that boy. But where did you get it?

BETSY (*Quickly*): It was a gift from a friend.

MRS. SHELDON: What is your friend's name?

BETSY: I forgot. Do you remember the name, Donna?

DONNA: It just escapes my mind.

MRS. SHELDON: I'd certainly like to know! While you're thinking (*Goes left*), I'll see what's keeping Woodrow.

I do hope he's not running water in your bathtub, because that's a no-no. (*She exits left.* MACK *dashes out from behind screen, tugging at the zipper at the neck of his sweater.*)

MACK: The zipper's stuck!

DONNA: Mack, was it you?

MACK: Never mind. Just help me. (BETSY *tries to release zipper.*) I've got to get out of this sweater or I'll spend Christmas in jail!

BETSY (*Trying to work zipper*): It won't budge.

DONNA: Tell us, Mack. Did you saw off the tree?

MACK: No. I told you the truth about where I got that tree. But the eggs in the supermarket — that *was* an accident, and I paid for them!

BETSY: She'll never believe you.

MACK (*Anxiously*): But you do, don't you?

DONNA: Well . . . I guess so. (BETSY *struggles with zipper*)

MACK: Come on, hurry up with that zipper!

BETSY: I think the zipper's broken. (*There is a knock on door right.*)

DONNA (*Tugging at zipper*): Betsy, go peek and see who it is. (BETSY *hurries out right.*)

MRS. SHELDON (*From off left*): Come on, Woodrow, dear.

MACK (*Frantically*): I can't go that way. She'll see me!

BETSY (*Looking in from doorway*): The policeman! Beat it, Mack! (*Goes out right, as knock on door is repeated*)

MRS. SHELDON (*Offstage*): Don't dawdle, Woodrow. (MACK *dashes behind the screen just as* MRS. SHELDON *enters left with* WOODROW, *and* OFFICER PERKINS *comes in right with* BETSY.)

BETSY: Officer Perkins is here to see you, Mrs. Sheldon.

MRS. SHELDON: It was good of you to come so promptly, officer.

PERKINS: Are you the woman who phoned about some vandalism?

MRS. SHELDON: Yes, in my yard down the street. I have an appointment here, but I'll be ready in a minute. (WOODROW *stands up on chair*) That's a no-no, Woodrow. (*He ignores her.*) Santa Claus will be here in a few minutes.

PERKINS (*Taking out small notebook and pencil*): Just what was the nature of this vandalism?

MRS. SHELDON: The top of my prettiest evergreen was sawed off. (*Points to little tree*) See? I'm sure this is it!

PERKINS (*Going to it*): Do you really think this is it?

MRS. SHELDON: I'm positive. (MACK *sneezes from behind screen. As* MRS. SHELDON *and* PERKINS *turn,* DONNA *sneezes quickly.*)

DONNA: Excuse me, please.

PERKINS: May I ask where you girls got this little tree?

MRS. SHELDON: *They* say it was a gift. *I* think they're covering for somebody.

PERKINS (*To girls*): Is that true?

DONNA: Officer, I give you my word we don't want to obstruct justice.

BETSY: If we knew who sawed off the tree, we'd tell you. (MACK *sneezes again and so does* DONNA.)

DONNA: I hope I'm not catching a cold.

PERKINS (*To* MRS. SHELDON): Can you give me a description of the vandal?

MRS. SHELDON: He was a very ordinary looking boy. (*There is a noise behind screen;* DONNA *quickly pushes a book off the desk.*) What was that noise?

DONNA: I dropped this book. (*Picks it up*)

MRS. SHELDON: As I was saying, he was ordinary looking. But I remember one thing — he was wearing a very loud turtleneck sweater. It was so loud, nobody could forget it!

BETSY: Lots of boys wear turtlenecks.

MRS. SHELDON: Not like this one. (WOODROW *jumps up and down on sofa.*) That's another no-no, Woodrow! (*He keeps on jumping, as she turns to others.*) I believe in reasoning with children. Woodrow is always such a good little boy. (*Another noise is heard from behind the screen.*)

WOODROW: I heard a noise.

PERKINS: Where? (WOODROW *points to screen.*)

MRS. SHELDON: That screen. Hm-m-m. Someone could be hiding back there.

DONNA (*Quickly*): It's just an ornamental screen, Mrs. Sheldon.

BETSY: There's nothing but a stepladder back there.

PERKINS: Is that all? Maybe I'd better take a look.

DONNA: I'll check. (*Goes behind screen, calling*) Yes, I'm happy to report that the stepladder's still here. (*She remains behind screen.*)

PERKINS: A stepladder didn't make that noise we heard. Let me take a look.

DONNA (*Coming out from behind screen*): Surprise! (*She brings* MACK *out from behind screen; he is dressed in Santa suit, carries jingle bells.*)

MACK (*Heartily, ringing bells*): Ho, ho, ho!

MRS. SHELDON: Why, it's Santa Claus! (WOODROW *hides behind her.*) Don't be afraid, darling. Santa likes good little boys. Don't you, Santa?

MACK: Ho, ho, ho! (DONNA *guides* MACK *to high-backed chair, and he sits down.*)

DONNA: Any time he's ready, I'll take the picture.

WOODROW (*Turning to his mother*): I want to sit on Santa's lap.

MRS. SHELDON: Why, of course, dear. Go sit on Santa's lap. Isn't that sweet?

BETSY: Santa will be delighted.

MACK (*Half-heartedly*): Ho, ho, ho.

MRS. SHELDON (*Setting* WOODROW *on* MACK*'s lap*): Before you get your picture taken, tell Santa what you want for Christmas. (*To others*) He's so good that I'm sure he'll get all he wants.

PERKINS: This is a great idea. It puts me right in the Christmas spirit. (*He begins to sing "Jingle Bells."* MRS. SHELDON *joins in. They are looking at* MACK, *their backs to the door left, as* FREDDY, *also dressed as Santa Claus, comes in left and crosses to sofa, ringing his bells.* MACK *sees him and quickly rings his own bells.* DONNA *signals* FREDDY *to go back.* BETSY *hurries over to him and pushes him down behind sofa.*)

MACK: Speak up, sonny. What would you like for Christmas? (WOODROW *whispers in his ear.*) A bike, eh?

MRS. SHELDON: Well, maybe. (BETSY *walks toward screen, covering* FREDDY *as he creeps to screen.*)

MACK: What else? (WOODROW *whispers again.*) A walkie-talkie set? Well, I'll think about it.

MRS. SHELDON: I never have to punish him, Santa.

MACK: Fine! Anything else? (WOODROW *whispers to him.*) A new tool set? I guess that means you already have an old one. (WOODROW *whispers to him.*) I see. You broke the little saw.

MRS. SHELDON: This morning, yes. His saw is absolutely destroyed. The poor darling was so distressed about it.

DONNA: I can imagine. (*Picks up camera*) Ready for the picture?

MRS. SHELDON: Smile, Woodrow.

DONNA: A nice big smile. (*All look toward camera as she takes picture. At the same time,* BETSY *shoves* FREDDY *behind the screen.*) Very good. All done!

BETSY (*Coming from screen*): It won't take long for the picture to develop.

MRS. SHELDON: Good. I don't like to keep the officer waiting.

DONNA (*To* MRS. SHELDON): Would you please pay Betsy? She's the treasurer of our club. (*To* OFFICER PERKINS) We're giving the money to the Fire Department to buy toys for needy kids.

PERKINS: Very enterprising of you. (MRS. SHELDON *gives* BETSY *some money, and* BETSY *puts it into desk drawer.*)

BETSY: Thank you. I know it'll be a great picture. (FREDDY *peeks over screen, then ducks down again. Screen wobbles.*)

MACK (*As* WOODROW *whispers again*): Oh, you want a model plane, too? (WOODROW *whispers*) And a cowboy suit and a wagon and an electric train? Slow down there, young fellow.

BETSY: Santa has to save some things for other little boys.

MACK (*As* WOODROW *whispers*): And finger paints? And balloons? And a big box of candy?

MRS. SHELDON: Candy's a no-no, Woodrow, dear.

DONNA: O.K. The picture's ready.

MRS. SHELDON: Let me see. (*Goes to look at it.* DONNA *holds it up for her to see.*)

DONNA: It's still a little damp, so be careful.

MRS. SHELDON: Adorable. Woodrow is such a photogenic child. (*As* DONNA *mounts the picture,* FREDDY *peeks over the screen again and* WOODROW *sees him.*)

WOODROW (*Pointing*): Look! Look!

MRS. SHELDON: Quiet, darling. We'll be on our way as soon as the picture's ready. (*Beckons to him*) Come to Mother, Woodrow. (*He stays on* MACK*'s lap.*) How sweet. He wants to stay with Santa! (*A sound is heard from behind the screen, which wobbles again.*)

WOODROW (*Pointing to screen*): That thing's moving!

BETSY (*Quickly*): Woodrow, you mustn't keep your mother and the officer waiting. (*Takes his hand, but he pulls it away.* DONNA *gives the picture to* MRS. SHELDON.)

DONNA: Here you are, Mrs. Sheldon. Thanks for coming.

MRS. SHELDON: Glad to help a good cause. (*Screen wobbles.*) That screen *did* move!

BETSY: How could it? (*Suddenly,* FREDDY *loses his balance and knocks screen over.*)

PERKINS (*Startled*): Santa Claus is twins! (*Helps* FREDDY *to his feet*)

FREDDY (*Weakly*): Ho, ho, ho!

WOODROW (*Looking from* FREDDY *to* MACK): Another Santa!

MRS. SHELDON: I don't understand. (WOODROW *runs to* MACK, *yanks his white beard, pulling it off. Startled,* MACK *stands up. Without beard, they can see his sweater.*) Look at that sweater! He's the one who broke my eggs! He's the vandal!

MACK: I am not!

MRS. SHELDON: Do you deny that you brought that little tree in here?

MACK: No, but —

PERKINS: Mrs. Sheldon, are you sure you want to lodge a complaint?

MRS. SHELDON: I certainly am.

PERKINS: All right, young man, you'll have to come along with me.

DONNA: He's innocent, officer! Teli him who sold you that tree, Mack. I think you know now who cut it.

MACK: I can't, Donna. I hate to be a squealer.

DONNA: Maybe there's another way. (*Bends down beside* WOODROW) You broke your little saw this morning, didn't you, Woodrow? (*He nods*) How did you break it? Tell me.

WOODROW: I was sawing something.

DONNA: *What* were you sawing, Woodrow? (WOODROW *pulls away, frightened.*) Come now, Woodrow, you must tell me. What did you saw?

WOODROW: My mommy's tree.

DONNA: Your mommy's tree? (*He nods.*)

MRS. SHELDON (*Shocked*): I can't believe it!

DONNA: Tell me why, Woodrow. (*He whispers.*) I see. (*To the others*) He wanted the money he'd get for the tree to buy some candy.

MRS. SHELDON: But he knows that sugar is bad for him. I've told him so many times.

DONNA: At his age, that's hard to believe. And not having any candy may make him want it all the more.

MRS. SHELDON: You may be right.

PERKINS (*Pointing to* MACK): It wasn't this other fellow at all, then.

MACK: I bought the tree from Woodrow, but I didn't know where it came from.

MRS. SHELDON (*Pointing to* FREDDY): What is Santa going to think? (WOODROW *hangs his head, ashamed.*)

MACK: May I say something? (*Takes* WOODROW *by the hand*) This other fellow and I . . . (*Indicating* FREDDY) we're just Santa's helpers. But I think the real Santa will say, "Woody was bad, but he told the truth about it." (*To* MRS. SHELDON) That's important, isn't it?

PERKINS: I'll say it is!

MRS. SHELDON: Why . . . why, yes, I guess you're right. And I'm sorry about all this. (*To* PERKINS) I hope you'll excuse the fuss I made.

PERKINS (*Smiling*): I will.

MRS. SHELDON: Come now, Woodrow. (*Takes him by the hand, and they exit right, as* WOODROW *waves.*)

PERKINS: Listen, kids, when I get off duty, I'll bring my

niece to see Santa. I hope there'll be one this time —
not two! (*Waves and exits*)

DONNA: Wow! That was a close call. Mack, you're quite
a guy, to take the blame for what that little boy did.

MACK: It was nothing.

BETSY: Front and center, everyone! Our schedule is
jammed with kids, and they all want to have their pictures taken with Santa. Which of you is it going to be?

FREDDY: Not me! I'll blow it again.

DONNA: O.K. Mack, you're elected. (*Sound of knock on
door is heard*) That's our next appointment! Let's get
going. (BETSY *pushes* FREDDY *off left.* MACK *sits in
Santa's chair.* DONNA *admits* MRS. AVERY, SHARON,
PARENTS *and* CHILDREN.)

SHARON: Hello, Santa Claus!

MRS. AVERY: I hope we're not too early.

DONNA: Not at all. You're right on time. (*She guides*
SHARON *to sit on* MACK*'s lap.*)

MACK: Ho, ho, ho! Tell old Santa what you want for
Christmas!

MRS. AVERY: Isn't that cute? Let's sing a Christmas
carol. (*She starts to sing "Jingle Bells," joined by
other* PARENTS *and* CHILDREN.)

DONNA *and* BETSY (*Ad lib*): Stop! Wait! Don't sing
that song! (*Etc.*)

FREDDY (*Bursting in, left*): You rang? (*He rings bells.*
MRS. AVERY *and others look from* FREDDY *to* MACK *in
confusion.*)

BETSY (*Pushing* FREDDY *out left*): Freddy, that's a no-no!

DONNA (*Shrugging*): This year, you get twice as much for
your money. Santa Claus is twins! (*Quick curtain*)

THE END

The Year Santa Forgot Christmas

By Sheila L. Marshall

Santa loses his memory on the most important night of the year. . . . Will the children get their gifts on Christmas Eve?

Characters

SANTA CLAUS
MRS. SANTA CLAUS
WILLY, *an awkward elf*
JOLLY JINGLE, *Santa's head elf*
HAPPY
HOLLY   } *Santa's elves*
TWINKLE
SMILEY
JEAN
BILLY   } *three children*
JOEY
GERMAN CHILDREN } *extras*
ENGLISH CHILDREN

TIME: *Christmas Eve.*
SETTING: *Santa's workshop. Two tables are at center, with toys and tools, a sprig of mistletoe and a poin-*

settia plant on them. A door and window are at right, and a large, throne-like chair is at the head of the table, left. Santa's pack of toys is on the floor near one of the tables.

AT RISE: HAPPY, HOLLY, *and* TWINKLE *are at tables, busy making toys and putting them into* SANTA*'s pack.* JOLLY JINGLE, *carrying a clipboard, walks back and forth inspecting their work and checking off items on his list.* SANTA *enters left.*

SANTA: Ho! Ho! Ho! How is your work going, my good elves? Are the toys almost ready?

JOLLY JINGLE: Yes, Santa! We've finished all the toys. I'll have these wrapped and packed in your sleigh by dinnertime.

SANTA: Good for you, Jolly Jingle. Your elves have worked extra hard this year. It's going to be a good Christmas. I'm sure I'll be able to give all the good children everything they have asked for.

HAPPY, HOLLY *and* TWINKLE (*Together*): Thank you, Santa.

SANTA: When you finish, bring my pack of toys to the front door. I have my sleigh and reindeer tied up there, ready to go. Dasher and Dancer were too excited to stay in the stable a second longer.

JOLLY JINGLE: I'll do that, Santa. (MRS. SANTA *hurries in, carrying a plate of cookies.*)

MRS. SANTA (*Calling*): Willy — Willy! Where is that elf? You can never find him when you need him. (*She places the plate on one of the tables and turns to* SANTA.) Oh, Santa, have you seen Willy? I've looked all over. Do you know where he is?

SANTA: I sent him into the forest a little while ago to look for a Christmas tree for our living room. I've been so busy that I didn't have time to get one myself.

MRS. SANTA: Into the forest? Santa, do you think that was wise? You know how clumsy he is. What if he gets hurt?

SANTA (*Patting her on the shoulder*): He'll be fine! (*Turning to window, right, and gesturing*) Look! Here he comes now, and he has a fine tree. (WILLY *enters right, carrying a small fir tree.*)

WILLY: I found a beautiful tree! And I cut it down all by myself! Look, Santa, look! (*As* WILLY *crosses to* SANTA, *he trips, lose his balance, and bumps into* SANTA *with the tree.* SANTA *falls.*)

ALL (*Ad lib*): Oh! Look out! Be careful! (*Etc.*)

WILLY: Are you hurt, Santa? Let me help you up.

MRS. SANTA: Santa, Santa! Are you hurt? Here now, be careful getting up. (*She takes* SANTA*'s arm and assists* WILLY *in getting him to his feet.*) Jolly, please get a chair for Santa, quickly. (*She turns to* WILLY *angrily.*) Willy, you are very clumsy. You must be more careful. (WILLY *hangs his head, ashamed.*)

JOLLY JINGLE (*Bringing chair*): Sit here, Santa. (SANTA *sits. He has a puzzled expression and he rubs his head.*)

SANTA: What happened?

MRS. SANTA: Willy bumped into you, Santa. Are you all right?

SANTA (*Feeling his head and arms gingerly*): I think so. My head felt funny for a minute, but it's better now. Nothing else hurts.

MRS. SANTA: That's a relief!

JOLLY JINGLE: I'll say! We can't have Santa getting hurt on the day before Christmas.

SANTA (*Puzzled*): Christmas?

MRS. SANTA *and* JOLLY JINGLE (*Exchanging glances; together*): Yes, Christmas.

SANTA: What's Christmas?

MRS. SANTA: Santa, don't be silly! Of course you know what Christmas is! Are you trying to fool us?

SANTA (*In hurt voice*): I'm not trying to be silly. I don't know anything about Christmas. Won't you please tell me what it is?

MRS. SANTA: You mean you don't remember Christmas?

SANTA: I don't! I seem to have heard of it before — but I just can't remember! (*He puts his head down in his hands for a minute.* MRS. SANTA *and* JOLLY JINGLE *move down right.*)

MRS. SANTA: What are we going to do? Santa has lost his memory.

JOLLY JINGLE: If he doesn't remember about Christmas, there won't be any holiday. The children will wake up tomorrow morning and their stockings will be empty.

WILLY (*Suddenly crossing to them*): It's all my fault. I made Santa lose his memory. Christmas will be ruined. (*He exits right, slamming the door behind him.*)

MRS. SANTA (*Starting to follow* WILLY): Come back, Willy!

JOLLY JINGLE (*Catching her arm*): Wait, Mrs. Claus. Let him go. I'm sure he'll be all right in a little while. But we have to do something about Santa — quickly!

MRS. SANTA (*Turning back to him*): You're right, Jolly Jingle. It's Christmas Eve, after all.

JOLLY JINGLE: We must make him remember Christmas somehow.

MRS. SANTA: We'll tell him all about Christmas and show him the presents and decorations. Surely he'll remember them!

JOLLY JINGLE: It's worth a try. My elves and I will help. Let's get started. (MRS. SANTA *goes over to stand behind* SANTA*'s chair.* JOLLY JINGLE *picks up* SANTA*'s pack and* HAPPY *and* HOLLY *help him carry it over to* SANTA.) Look, Santa. Do you remember this?

SANTA: No. What is it?

HAPPY: Why, Santa, it's your pack, and it's full of toys. Every Christmas Eve, you go all over the world in your sleigh, pulled by eight faithful reindeer. You visit good children everywhere and leave toys for Christmas morning.

HOLLY (*Reaching into bag, and taking out a large, filled Christmas stocking*): In England and the United States, you leave the children's gifts in stockings, like this one, that they hang by the fire. But in France and Holland, the children put out their shoes to be filled with goodies.

JOLLY JINGLE: The children all love you very much. The American children know you by the same name we call you, Santa Claus. But in other parts of the world, you are known as St. Nicholas, or Father Christmas.

MRS. SANTA (*Hopefully*): Do you remember now, Santa? Did we help you to remember what Christmas is all about?

SANTA (*Sadly shaking his head*): No. I still don't remember. Why would I want to do all these things for strange children? What's so special about Christmas, anyway?

JOLLY JINGLE: Christmas is the day on which Christians celebrate the birthday of the Christ child. The Three Wise Men visited Him in Bethlehem and brought Him gifts. The custom of exchanging gifts at Christmas arose in memory of this.

HAPPY: Santa, you are the most joyous symbol of gift-giving in the world. Your "ho, ho, ho" brightens everyone's holiday and makes us all feel merry.

SANTA: I don't feel much like laughing today. I still can't remember anything about Christmas.

MRS. SANTA (*To* JOLLY JINGLE): What are we going to do?

JOLLY JINGLE: We'll just have to keep trying. (*Turning, he picks up the tree that* WILLY *brought in.*) Look, Santa. You must remember this. It's a Christmas tree!

SANTA: A Christmas tree? It looks like an ordinary fir tree to me. What are we going to do with it?

TWINKLE (*Stepping forward from his place at the table*): We're going to put it in the house and decorate it for Christmas, as people do in many parts of the world. The custom originated in Germany, and here are some German children to sing a traditional Christmas song. Listen. (GERMAN CHILDREN *enter, singing "O Christmas Tree" and exit.*)

HOLLY: People have been decorating homes with trees since ancient times. It's supposed to bring good luck. In England, people bring a huge log into the house to burn at Christmas. (ENGLISH CHILDREN *enter.*) They keep an unburnt piece of this Yule log to light the next year's log. (CHILDREN *sing "Deck the Halls" and exit.*)

TWINKLE (*Taking mistletoe from table*): In Scandinavia, mistletoe was considered a plant of peace. If enemies met under it, they declared a truce for the day. That is the reason we kiss under the mistletoe.

HAPPY: In Mexico, where Christmas comes in the warm season, people use the poinsettia plant for decoration. (*Shows poinsettia to* SANTA)

SANTA: It sounds lovely. I wish I could remember it all.

MRS. SANTA: Wait a minute! I just thought of something! (*Turning to table, she picks up plate and shows* SANTA *that it holds cookies.*) Look, Santa! Here are your favorite Christmas cookies. They are called Lebkuchen, and they come from Germany. The German people are famous for their Christmas cookies.

SANTA (*Sampling cookies*): Hmmm — they are good!

(*Reaching for another cookie*) No wonder my stomach is so plump. I love your cookies, but I still can't remember any of the things you're talking about.

MRS. SANTA (*Shaking her head sadly*): I'm afraid we'll have to give up. There will be no Christmas this year. (SMILEY *rushes in.*)

JOLLY JINGLE: Smiley! What are you doing here?

SMILEY: The reindeer are gone! I searched the whole yard and they're nowhere to be seen. Santa's sleigh is missing, too!

JOLLY JINGLE: That's impossible! Nobody drives them but Santa, and he's right here. Where could they be?

MRS. SANTA (*Taking a handkerchief from her pocket and beginning to weep*): Oh, dear! This is terrible! Santa has lost his memory, and now the reindeer are missing!

SANTA: Listen! I hear bells!

MRS. SANTA: Bells! That's even worse.

JOLLY JINGLE: No, wait a minute! I hear them, too! (*Sleighbells are heard offstage. They grow louder and then stop.* JOLLY *goes to window.*)

JOLLY JINGLE: It's your sleigh, Santa! Willy is driving it.

SANTA (*Astonished*): Willy?

JOLLY JINGLE: Yes, here he comes now. There's someone with him. (WILLY *enters with* JEAN, BILLY *and* JOEY.)

WILLY: Santa, I borrowed your sleigh to get three friends of yours. I hope that they will help you remember Christmas.

JEAN (*To* SANTA): I'm Jean. You come to my house every year. I always leave cookies and milk for you under my Christmas tree.

BILLY: And I'm Billy, Santa. We moved last year, but you found my house anyway. It's the white one with the red door, remember? I tried to be good this year.

JOEY: I'm Joey, Santa. Remember me? You brought me

a new bike last year and it's great! I have a new baby brother this year and he needs a playpen. So when I wrote my letter to you last week, I asked for that instead of a present for myself. Do you remember?

WILLY (*Lifting* SANTA*'s pack*): You see, Santa? Here is your pack of toys. This is how you carry the gifts from house to house. (*He swings pack over his shoulder, accidentally striking* SANTA *with it.* SANTA *falls. All exclaim.*)

MRS. SANTA: Willy! You've done it again! (SANTA *stands, rubs his forehead, hesitates for a minute, and then smiles.*)

SANTA: Now I remember Christmas! Who could forget it? I remember it all now! The sleigh, the toys, the stockings — everything.

JOLLY JINGLE: Willy, you're a hero! Santa got his memory back when you hit him with your pack.

MRS. SANTA: Thank you, Willy, for helping Santa remember Christmas.

JEAN, BILLY *and* JOEY (*Together*): Hooray!

SANTA (*Pulling out his watch and looking at it in alarm*): Look at the time! It's late and I must be setting off soon in my sleigh. Jolly Jingle, you and your elves get that sleigh packed quickly. Mother Claus, please pack some of those delicious cookies for me to take along. Children, hurry out to the sleigh and I'll drop you off in your beds on my way. Willy! Come here!

WILLY: Yes, Santa?

SANTA (*Patting him on the shoulder*): Willy, you saved the day. Would you like to come along on my sleigh tonight and help me?

WILLY: Wow! I'd love to! Thank you, Santa. Merry Christmas, everyone!

ALL: Hooray for Willy! Merry Christmas! (GERMAN

CHILDREN *and* ENGLISH CHILDREN *enter, singing, "Up on the House-top," or other Christmas song. Others hurry to carry out* SANTA*'s orders as curtains close.*)

THE END

A Visit from St. Nicholas

By Clement C. Moore
Adapted by Sylvia Chermak

A dramatization of the popular Christmas poem, with recitations by solo readers, and pantomimes and dances for any number of actors . . .

Characters

FOUR SOLOS (*More if desired*)
THREE CHILDREN
DANCERS, *extras*
PAPA
MAMMA
ST. NICHOLAS
EIGHT REINDEER

SETTING: *Living room, with fireplace and mantel in rear wall. Next to fireplace there is a window with colored shutters. At the back of the fireplace, there should be a cloth backdrop which can be pushed aside like a curtain to allow St. Nicholas to enter. Three cots stand right, each with large, long stocking at end. A loveseat with a cushion and a couch with a pillow stand left.*

AT RISE: *Room is dimly lighted.* SOLOS *stand downstage right and left.* CHILDREN *are asleep in cots.*

1ST SOLO (*Stepping forward, speaking in a hushed voice*):
> 'Twas the night before Christmas, when all through the house
>
> Not a creature was stirring (*Puts fingers to lips*), not even a mouse. (*Steps back*)

2ND SOLO (*Stepping forward*):
> The stockings were hung by the chimney with care,
> In hopes that St. Nicholas soon would be there.

(*As he speaks,* CHILDREN *rise from cots, take stockings, run to mantel and attach them to top, then run back to cots and scramble under covers.*)

3RD SOLO (*Stepping forward*):
> The children were nestled all snug in their beds,

(*Points to* CHILDREN, *now back in cots*)

> While visions of sugar-plums danced in their heads;

(*If desired, at this point a lively Christmas air may be played with recorders or other instruments, as three or four* DANCERS *enter and do acrobatic dance, somersaults or cartwheels across stage. They exit on opposite side.* 3RD SOLO *steps back.* 1ST SOLO *steps forward.*)

1ST SOLO:
> And mamma in her kerchief, and I in my cap,

(PAPA *and* MAMMA *enter from opposite sides of stage.*)

> Had just settled down for a long winter's nap —

(MAMMA *goes to loveseat, plumps up pillow and prepares to lie down and* PAPA *goes to couch and sits on it.* MAMMA *lies down on loveseat, pulls up blanket;* PAPA *lies down on couch, sighs loudly, and goes off to sleep.*)

> When out on the lawn there arose such a clatter

(*Puts hands to ears as sound of sleigh bells and calls of "whoa" are heard from offstage.*)

I sprang from my bed to see what was the matter.

(PAPA *jumps out of bed and rushes over to window.*)

    Away to the window I flew like a flash,

    Tore open the shutter, and threw up the sash.

(PAPA *opens shutters, then opens window wide. Sound of sleigh bells continues.* 1ST SOLO *steps back, as* 2ND SOLO *steps forward.*)

2ND SOLO (*In astonishment*):

    The moon on the breast of the new-fallen snow

    Gave a lustre of midday to objects below;

(PAPA *leans out window.*)

    When what to my wondering eyes should appear

    But a miniature sleigh and eight tiny reindeer,

(PAPA *draws back and shakes his head in amazement.*)

    With a little old driver so lively and quick,

    I knew in a moment, it must be St. Nick!

(PAPA *taps forehead with finger and nods.* 2ND SOLO *steps back.*)

3RD SOLO (*Stepping forward; dramatically*):

    More rapid than eagles his coursers they came,

    And he whistled and shouted and called them by
        name.

(*Sounds of whistling are heard.* 3RD SOLO *steps back.*)

ST. NICHOLAS (*From offstage*):

    "Now, Dasher! now, Dancer! now, Prancer
      and Vixen!

    On, Comet! on, Cupid! on, Donder and Blitzen.

    To the top of the porch, to the top of the wall,

    Now, dash away, dash away, dash away all!"

(EIGHT REINDEER *run on and prance about stage, imitating movement of reindeer, during following lines.*)

4TH SOLO (*Stepping forward*):

    As dry leaves that before the wild hurricane fly,

(CHILDREN *may whirl across stage to suggest leaves, then return to cots.*)

When they meet with an obstacle mount to the sky,
So, up to the housetop the coursers they flew,
With a sleigh full of toys — and St. Nicholas, too.
(*Sleigh bells are heard, and* REINDEER *exit.* 4TH SOLO
steps back.)

1ST SOLO (*Stepping forward*):
And then in a twinkling, I heard on the roof
The prancing and pawing of each little hoof,
(*Pounding sounds are heard.*)
As I drew in my head and was turning around,
(PAPA *turns to face audience.*)
Down the chimney St. Nicholas came with a bound:
(ST. NICHOLAS *enters through fireplace opening, as
cloth for backdrop is pushed aside.* ST. NICHOLAS
strides to center. He has pack of toys on his back.
PAPA *and* MAMMA *watch.*)
He was dressed all in fur from his head to his foot.
(ST. NICHOLAS *looks all about him.* CHILDREN *peek out
from under covers, then creep out of bed to watch.*)
And his clothes were all tarnished with ashes
and soot:
(*Dusts himself off*)
A bundle of toys he had flung on his back,
(*Hoists pack as if to make it more comfortable*)
And he looked like a peddler just opening his pack.
(ST. NICHOLAS *takes pack off back and rests it on
floor, as* 1ST SOLO *steps back, and* 3RD SOLO *steps
forward.*)

3RD SOLO (*Quickly*):
His eyes, how they twinkled! his dimples, how
merry! (ST. NICHOLAS *rubs cheeks.*)
His cheeks were like roses, his nose like a cherry;
His droll little mouth was drawn up like a bow.
(*Purses his lips*)

And the beard on his chin was as white as the snow.
(ST. NICHOLAS *strokes his beard.*)

The stump of a pipe he held tight in his teeth,
(*Takes pipe from pocket and puts it into his mouth*)

And the smoke, it encircled his head like a wreath.
(*Makes circle in front of himself and then over his head, as if following smoke.* 3RD SOLO *steps back.*)

2ND SOLO (*Stepping forward*):

He had a broad face and a little round belly
(ST. NICHOLAS *pats his belly with both hands, as he pantomimes laughter, and jiggles up and down.*)

That shook, when he laughed, like a bowl full of jelly.

He was chubby and plump — a right jolly old elf:

And I laughed when I saw him (2ND SOLO *laughs.*), in spite of myself;

A wink of his eyes and a twist of his head,
(ST. NICHOLAS *follows with appropriate gestures throughout.*)

Soon gave me to know I had nothing to dread.

He spoke not a word, but went straight to his work,
(ST. NICHOLAS *picks up pack and goes to fireplace where he puts pack on floor and begins to take toys from pack. He puts them into stockings hanging from mantel.*)

And filled all the stockings: then turned with a jerk.
(ST. NICHOLAS *turns.*)

And laying his finger aside of his nose (*Does so*),

And giving a nod (*Nods*), up the chimney he rose.
(ST. NICHOLAS *exits through fireplace opening and disappears behind backdrop.* PAPA, MAMMA, *and* CHILDREN *hurry to window and look out.* 2ND SOLO *steps back.*)

3RD SOLO (*Stepping forward*):

> He sprang to his sleigh, to his team gave a whistle,
> > (*Sounds of sleigh bells and whistle are heard.*)
> And away they all flew like the down of a thistle.
> > (3RD SOLO *holds up imaginary thistle and blows on it.*)

4TH SOLO (*Stepping forward*):

> But I heard him exclaim, ere they drove out of sight,

ST. NICHOLAS (*Calling, from offstage*):

> "Happy Christmas to all, and to all a good-night!"
> (SOLOS *step forward and take bows with rest of cast. Christmas music may be played in background. Curtain closes.*)

THE END

Santa Changes His Mind

By Anne Sroda

Mr. and Mrs. Elf and their family need a bigger igloo, but they can't afford it — until Mrs. Elf takes matters into her own hands. . . .

Characters

MR. EDWARD ELF
MRS. ELIZABETH ELF, *his wife*
EDITH ⎫
         ⎬ *their daughters*
ELAINE ⎭
SANTA CLAUS

SCENE 1

TIME: *Morning in mid-November.*

SETTING: *The crowded igloo home of the Elf family, at the North Pole. Four sleeping bags with pillows are arranged around a center "fireplace." Small table with four chairs is upstage of the bags, leaving little space to walk. Low doorway is up center. There is a coffee cup on floor near doorway.*

AT RISE: EDITH *sits on a newspaper on a chair, eating her breakfast.* ELAINE *sits on her sleeping bag, brushing her hair.* MRS. ELF, *wearing a bathrobe, is sweeping floor.*

363

MR. ELF (*Looking around igloo*): Where can it be? Where did I put it?

MRS. ELF: What are you looking for, Edward?

MR. ELF: My newspaper! I can't find my newspaper!

MRS. ELF: Did you bring it in?

MR. ELF: Of course I brought it in!

MRS. ELF: Then it must be here. Girls, have you seen Papa's newspaper? (EDITH *pulls it out from under her.*)

EDITH (*Reading masthead*): *The Daily Elf?*

MR. ELF (*Disgustedly*): Of course, *The Daily Elf!* Where did you find it? (*He takes paper from her.*)

EDITH: I was sitting on it.

MR. ELF: You were sitting on it? Why would you sit on it?

EDITH (*Shrugging*): Somebody left it on my chair.

MR. ELF: That doesn't mean you're supposed to sit on it! (*He looks around again.*) Oh dear, where did I put it?

MRS. ELF: What did you lose now?

MR. ELF: My cup of coffee! I just had it a minute ago.

MRS. ELF: How could you lose a cup of coffee? (*She sighs.*) Girls, have you seen Papa's cup of coffee? (EDITH *stands up and looks at her chair.*)

EDITH: I'm not sitting on it. (*She sits down again.*)

MR. ELF (*Walking around*): That's the trouble with this place. You put something down, and it disappears. (*He steps on* ELAINE'*s pillow.*)

ELAINE: Papa! You're walking on my pillow!

MR. ELF: Oh dear! (*He steps into fireplace.*)

EDITH: Papa! You're stepping into the fireplace!

MR. ELF: Oh, my! (*He steps out again.* MRS. ELF *suddenly throws down broom.*)

MRS. ELF: It's too small! It's just too small! (*All look at her in surprise.*)

MR. ELF: What's too small, Elizabeth?

MRS. ELF: This igloo! It was fine when we were newly married, but it's simply not big enough for a whole family!

MR. ELF (*Looking around*): It isn't?

MRS. ELF: Of course it isn't! If we lived in a larger igloo, you wouldn't be losing things all the time. There would be a place for everything.

MR. ELF: But, Elizabeth, you know we can't afford a larger igloo. My job at Santa's factory doesn't pay well enough.

MRS. ELF: I know. That's why I'm going to get a job.

MR. ELF: Get a job? You?

MRS. ELF: Why not?

MR. ELF: Because the only place around here to work is at Santa's factory.

MRS. ELF: Then I'll work at Santa's factory.

MR. ELF: Elizabeth, you know Santa won't hire a lady elf.

MRS. ELF: Maybe I can make him change his mind.

MR. ELF: Not a chance! Do you know who applied for a job as sleigh packer last year?

MRS. ELF: Who?

MR. ELF: Santa's wife, Mrs. Claus.

MRS. ELF: Did she get the job?

MR. ELF: No. Santa told her to go home and clean the house. He said that factory work is only for men.

MRS. ELF (*Indignantly*): Of all the nerve!

MR. ELF: He's right, you know. (*Boasting*) I'd like to see a woman do my job!

MRS. ELF (*Thoughtfully*): So would I!

MR. ELF: It takes a lot of skill to assemble toy trucks, you know.

MRS. ELF: Are you telling me that your job would be too hard for a woman?

MR. ELF: That's right! She couldn't do it.

MRS. ELF: I see. Hmmm. . . . (*She looks toward door, left.*)

MR. ELF: What do you see?

MRS. ELF: Your cup of coffee!

MR. ELF (*Looking around*): Where?

MRS. ELF: In the doorway.

MR. ELF (*Looking in doorway*): By golly, there it is! (*He picks up cup and sips from it.*) Ugh! It's cold.

MRS. ELF: I'm not surprised.

MR. ELF: It's time for me to leave for work, anyway. (*He crosses to kiss* MRS. ELF *on the cheek, then absentmindedly puts newspaper on seat of chair.*) You may as well forget about applying for a job at the factory, Elizabeth. Santa would never hire a woman. (*He crawls out the door, left.*)

MRS. ELF (*After he is gone*): I'm afraid you're right, dear, but I've already thought of that. (*She removes her robe. Underneath, she is wearing an elf suit just like* MR. ELF's. *She takes an elf hat from hook on wall and puts it on, tucking her hair under it.*)

ELAINE: Mama! What are you doing with Papa's clothes?

MRS. ELF (*Smugly*): Wearing them!

EDITH: You look just like Papa.

MRS. ELF: Do I look enough like him to be his brother?

EDITH: Papa doesn't have a brother.

MRS. ELF: He does now, girls. Say hello to your Uncle. (*Thinks*) Your Uncle Ezekiel Elf!

ELAINE: Uncle Ezekiel?

EDITH: I know! You're going to get a job at Santa's factory!

MRS. ELF: Right! I'll be the best truck assembler that factory ever had! (*Girls applaud happily.*) Now, grab your coats, and good old Uncle Ezekiel will walk you

to school on her way — I mean, his way — to work.
(ELAINE *and* EDITH *take coats from sleeping bags and
follow* MRS. ELF *out igloo door, as curtains close.*)

* * * * *

SCENE 2

TIME: *Late afternoon, a month later.*

SETTING: *Same as Scene 1. Mrs. Elf's robe is neatly
folded on her sleeping bag.*

AT RISE: ELAINE *and* EDITH *are sitting at table, doing
homework.* MRS. ELF, *still in men's clothing, sticks her
head in doorway.*

MRS. ELF: Is the coast clear?

EDITH: Yes, Mama. Papa's not home yet. (MRS. ELF
crawls in and stands up, panting.)

MRS. ELF: I don't know how long I can keep this up,
running all the way home. (*She removes hat and hangs
it on hook.*)

ELAINE: Mama, you've been working at Santa's factory
for a month. Why hasn't Papa recognized you?

MRS. ELF: He never had a chance. I keep my head down
when he's around, and I talk (*In deep voice*) like this!
(*Girls laugh. Sound of sleigh bells is heard from offstage.*)

EDITH: Mama! Someone's coming!

SANTA (*From offstage*): Ho, ho, ho!

MRS. ELF: It couldn't be!

EDITH: Do you suppose. . . ? (ELAINE *kneels and looks
out door.*)

ELAINE: It's Santa Claus! (MRS. ELF *grabs robe from
sleeping bag and puts it on over her clothes.*)

MRS. ELF: Oh, dear. He isn't supposed to come until
Christmas Eve!

ELAINE (*Calling outside*): Santa, you aren't supposed to
come until Christmas Eve!

MRS. ELF: Elaine! (*She runs to door and calls.*) Santa, come right in. (SANTA *crawls in and stands up.*)

SANTA: Ho, ho, ho! Don't worry, I'll come back on Christmas Eve, but today I have some business with Ezekiel Elf.

MRS. ELF (*Eyes widening*): Ezekiel Elf?

SANTA: Yes, Ezekiel. Is he here?

MRS. ELF: Well . . . not exactly.

SANTA: Not exactly? What do you mean? (MR. ELF *enters through door.*)

MR. ELF (*Seeing* SANTA): My goodness, what a surprise! Welcome to our igloo, Santa Claus. (*He shakes* SANTA*'s hand.*)

SANTA: Why, thank you, Edward.

MR. ELF: What can I do for you?

SANTA: I have come to see your brother, Ezekiel.

MR. ELF: My brother, Ezekiel? (MRS. ELF *and girls wince.*)

SANTA: Yes, I have a nice bonus for him. (*Takes envelope from under his belt and holds it up.*)

MR. ELF: My brother, Ezekiel?

SANTA: Why yes, and you should be proud of him. Since your brother started at the factory a month ago, he has broken all production records for toy truck assembly.

MR. ELF: My brother, Ezekiel?

SANTA: Now, it shouldn't be that unbelievable. He's a hard worker. I'd like to present him with this bonus of two hundred dollars.

ELAINE (*Jumping up and crossing to* MRS. ELF): Take it, Mama. It's yours!

EDITH (*Following* ELAINE): Yes, Mama, you earned it!

MR. ELF (*Suspiciously*): Elizabeth! Do you know anything about this?

MRS. ELF (*Giving a sickly smile*): Well . . . maybe.

Mr. Elf: Elizabeth!

Mrs. Elf (*Sighing and removing her robe*): All right, then, I'll confess. I'm Ezekiel Elf.

Mr. Elf: What!

Santa (*Astounded*): You? But you're a lady elf!

Mrs. Elf (*Nodding*): Usually.

Mr. Elf (*Sitting on chair with the paper*): Are you the one who set the toy-truck assembly record?

Mrs. Elf (*Shrugging*): I was only doing my job. The job I used to have, that is.

Santa: What do you mean, "used to have"?

Mrs. Elf: Aren't you going to fire me, now that you know I'm not a man?

Santa: With a work record like yours? Are you kidding?

Mrs. Elf: Do I still have a job?

Santa: You certainly do! And here's your bonus. (*He hands her envelope.*) From now on, any lady elf who wants one has a job waiting.

Mrs. Elf: Santa, you're wonderful! Will you stay for supper?

Santa: I'd like to, but I want to hurry home to tell Mrs. Claus the good news.

Elaine: What good news?

Santa: That she can start tomorrow as a sleigh packer. (*To* Mr. Elf) There's no reason why a lady can't pack a sleigh, is there, Edward?

Mr. Elf: I guess there isn't.

Santa: Goodbye, then, and Merry Christmas! (*He crawls out door.*)

Mrs. Elf (*Calling after him*): Merry Christmas to you, too, Santa. (*Girls hug her.*)

Elaine: Congratulations, Mama!

Edith: Mama, I'm so happy for you!

Mr. Elf: Elizabeth!

Mrs. Elf (*Timidly*): Yes, dear?

Mr. Elf: I said that a woman could never do my job, remember?

Mrs. Elf (*Puzzled*): Yes, dear.

Mr. Elf: Will you accept my apology?

Mrs. Elf (*Happily*): Yes, dear! (*She crosses to him and kisses him on the cheek.*) Now, let's look at some ads for larger igloos. I have the down payment right here. (*She holds up envelope.*) Where's the newspaper?

Mr. Elf (*Glancing around*): I don't know. Where is the newspaper?

Elaine: Oh, dear, where is that newspaper? (*They all look at* Edith.)

Edith: Don't look at me! I'm not even sitting down. (*They all look at* Mr. Elf, *who is still sitting. He sheepishly reaches down and pulls newspaper from beneath him.*)

Mr. Elf (*Shrugging*): Well . . . somebody left it on my chair! (*They all laugh and begin to look through newspaper. Curtain.*)

THE END

A Christmas Tale

By Shirley C. Oberacker

In this choral recitation and pantomime, Santa meets his springtime counterpart. . . .

Characters

THREE CHILDREN
TWELVE BOYS AND GIRLS, *for choral recitation group*
EASTER BUNNY
SANTA CLAUS

TIME: *The night before Christmas.*
SETTING: *One side of stage is left bare, for choral recitation group. The other side of the stage shows the interior of a house, with a fireplace, decorated Christmas tree, three beds, and a stool. There is an exit near the fireplace.*
AT RISE: BOYS AND GIRLS *in choral recitation group stand at one side of stage.* THREE CHILDREN *stand beside beds on other side of stage.*
1ST GIRL (*Stepping forward*):
>This is a story you won't believe —
>But it really did happen on Christmas Eve! (CHIL-
>DREN *hang decorations on tree.*)

1ST BOY (*Stepping forward*):

> We were all nestled down in our wee little beds (CHILDREN *get into beds.*)
>
> And those cute little sugar plums danced in our heads.

2ND GIRL (*Stepping forward, as others do when they recite*):

> When all of a sudden came a knock on the door (*Sound of a knock is heard from offstage.*)
>
> And we all jumped up to see what for! (THREE CHILDREN *get up and open imaginary door.*)

2ND BOY:

> We opened the door and to our surprise,
>
> There stood a big rabbit before our eyes! (EASTER BUNNY *enters, carrying basket of red and green eggs.*)

3RD GIRL:

> We said to the Bunny, "Isn't this the wrong date?
>
> You're either too early, or a wee bit late!"

3RD BOY:

> Said the Bunny to us, so calm and serene,
>
> "I had Easter eggs left over all painted red and green.

4TH GIRL:

> "And I didn't want to waste 'em, 'cause wasting food's a sin,
>
> So I saved 'em up for Santa, and hopped right in!" (EASTER BUNNY *sets basket by fireplace.*)

4TH BOY:

> Just then we heard a clatter from the roof and fireplace. (*Banging noise is heard from offstage.*)
>
> 'Twas our old friend Santa with his jolly-looking face! (SANTA *enters from behind fireplace, carrying pack. He looks around, then fills stockings.*)

5TH GIRL:

> He filled all the stockings with his shiny new toys,
> And he "Ho, ho, ho'ed" for us girls and boys!
>> (SANTA *gives a jolly laugh.*)

5TH BOY:

> Santa said to Bunny — "Hi, Pete, what's new?"
>> (BUNNY *and* SANTA *wave.*)
> Then he spied the eggs, and he split in two!

ALL:

> He laughed till he cried as he sat on a stool, (SANTA
> *sits on stool.*)
> And he said to the Bunny, "Man, you're cool!"

6TH GIRL:

> "Because you saved your eggs for the girls and boys,
> On next Easter Sunday, I'll deliver my old toys!"

6TH BOY:

> Then Santa laid his finger on the side of his nose
> And quick as a flash up the chimney he rose! (SANTA
> *exits through fireplace.*)

ALL:

> The old Easter Bunny hopped over there too.
> He said "See you next Easter!" and away he flew.
>> (EASTER BUNNY *exits through fireplace.*)

GIRLS:

> How quiet we stood — it was hard to believe
> That all of this happened on Christmas Eve!

BOYS:

> So take our advice as to all we say —
> For extra gifts that will really pay,

ALL:

> Hang your stockings again on next Easter Day! (SAN-
> TA *and* EASTER BUNNY *re-enter and entire group
> sings an appropriate Christmas song.* SANTA *may in-
> vite audience to sing with cast. Curtain.*)

THE END

Santa's Alphabet

By A.F. Bauman

Making a game out of loading the sleigh, Santa and his elves try to think of a gift for every letter in the alphabet. . . .

Characters

Santa Claus
Mrs. Claus
26 Elves, *girls and boys*
Little Elf

Time: *Christmas Eve.*
Setting: *The living room of Santa's house at the North Pole. There are two chairs center, and a decorated Christmas tree in one corner of the stage. Shelves line side and rear walls, and hold various toys, including the ones individually mentioned throughout the play. There is a fireplace painted on backdrop, with a long mantel, or shelf, over it. A sleigh is at stage right, partially hidden by curtain. Sleigh is front view only, cut from cardboard. There are strings attached, so that it can be drawn offstage. A box is hidden behind sleigh to hold toys.*

At Rise: Santa *and* Mrs. Claus *are seated in chairs.*

Mrs. Claus: Here it is Christmas Eve, Santa, and for once you're ready for your trip ahead of time. Maybe you can take a nap before you leave.

Santa: Oh, no, dear, I couldn't possibly sleep now — I'm too excited.

Mrs. Claus: Uh-oh. When you get excited, it always means trouble. I hope you don't get one of your last-minute ideas. Remember the time you wanted to leave a twenty-pound turkey at each child's home?

Santa: Yes, I remember. My sleigh was so heavy the reindeer couldn't get off the ground.

Mrs. Claus: Yes, and you lost a lot of time unloading all those turkeys before you could leave. So, I hope there won't be any last-minute surprises this year, Santa.

Santa: No, no, dear. I'll use this extra time to check my list again. (*Calls*) Elves! Where are those elves? (*The first eight* Elves *enter.* 1st Elf *carries scroll.*)

Elves (*Ad lib*): Here we are, Santa! Coming, Santa! (*Etc.*)

Santa: Is my schedule ready?

1st Elf: Yes, sir. (*Looking at scroll*) First stop for you is Alice Anderson. Her ABC book is ready.

2nd Elf: The next stop is Barbie Baxter. Her doll is in your sleigh.

3rd Elf: The third stop is Carol Carver. Her bike is all ready to go. We're really ahead of schedule this year, Santa.

Santa (*Musing*): Hm-m-m! Wait a minute! Hold every-thing, Elves. You put the children's names in alpha-betical order this year, didn't you?

4th Elf: You're right, Santa! (*Looking at scroll*) Let's see, after Carol Carver comes Danny Dawson.

5th Elf: After Danny is Eddie Evans!

6th Elf: Then comes Fran Forman!

7TH ELF: G is for Ginny Gibson!

SANTA: That gives me an idea. Elves, what do you say
we have a little fun before I leave on the trip?

MRS. CLAUS: Uh-oh. One of Santa's ideas. What is it this
time?

1ST ELF: Yes, Santa, what do you have in mind?

SANTA: Here's my idea: I want to give each child I visit
a gift that begins with the first letter in his or her
name. That shouldn't be too hard, should it?

ELVES (*Ad lib*): Hard? Not at all! It's a great idea. Let's
get right to work. (*Etc.*)

MRS. CLAUS (*Warningly*): Now, Santa, remember those
turkeys!

SANTA: My dear, this won't be hard. Besides, getting the
gifts together will be different and fun. Not just the
same old business of filling orders. Christmas will be a
little more special.

1ST ELF: I have an idea. (*Motioning to mantel*) Let's put
up all the letters of the alphabet on the mantel. When
we get a special gift ready for the child whose name begins with a certain letter, we can take down that letter.

8TH ELF: You're right! That way we'll know what special
gifts are left to concentrate on until each child has his
own gift.

4TH ELF: I'll go get the letters. (*Exits.*)

2ND ELF: This will really be fun.

3RD ELF: Santa, this is a neat idea!

MRS. CLAUS: It may be a neat idea, but I just hope you
get all these things done on time. (*Looking at watch*)
You have only twenty minutes, Santa.

SANTA (*To* MRS. CLAUS): Now, dear, my elves are very
organized. There won't be any problems.

MRS. CLAUS: All right, Santa, I'll leave you and the elves

to your work. I have lots to do, myself — the turkey needs stuffing, and I haven't even started to make my special Christmas pies! (*She bustles out.* 4TH ELF *runs back onstage, carrying cardboard letters, followed by* LITTLE ELF *and all* ELVES, *who sit cross-legged on floor, or stand.*)

4TH ELF: I have the letters, Santa. And I brought along some elves who want to help. (9TH *and* 10TH ELVES *help* 4TH ELF *arrange letters in order on mantel.*)

9TH ELF (*Motioning to letters on mantel*): We've put all the letters in order, Santa.

10TH ELF: And the first two gifts are ready.

SANTA: My, how organized you all are. I think we're going to enjoy packing my sleigh this year.

11TH ELF (*Removing letter A from mantel, going over to shelves, getting gift.*): Here's the alphabet book for Alice Anderson. A stands for alphabet. That was easy. (*Goes to sleigh, puts book in box behind sleigh. During following dialogue,* ELVES *take turns, in order, removing appropriate letter from mantel, going over to shelves to get gift, and putting it in sleigh as they speak their lines.*)

12TH ELF: Here's a boat for Barbie Baxter.

SANTA: Good start. Now the letter C is next. That must be for Carol Carver.

LITTLE ELF (*Enthusiastically*): I know! I know! A kite for Carol!

13TH ELF: No, silly, kite starts with a K. We can save the kite for Kenneth Kelly.

LITTLE ELF (*Sheepishly*): Girls like kites, too. I'm just trying to help.

14TH ELF: How about a candy cane for Carol?

SANTA: A fine idea!

15TH ELF: I'll go get the candy cane for Carol.

16TH ELF: Danny Davison is next. I think he'd like a dump truck.

SANTA: Good work! Now, what letter is next? (*Looks at letters on mantel.*) Oh yes, of course — E.

17TH ELF: That's Eddie Evans, Santa.

18TH ELF: How about an electric engine for Eddie? I'll go get it.

LITTLE ELF (*Looking at mantel*): F is next, and that's Fran Forman.

19TH ELF: Let's give Fran some fingerpaints.

SANTA: Good idea — she'll like that. What about Ginny Gibson?

LITTLE ELF (*Enthusiastically*): I have it! A jump rope for Ginny!

20TH ELF: No, silly, jump rope begins with a J. (LITTLE ELF *walks over to chair, sits, and puts his chin between his hands, elbows on knees. He looks dejected.*)

SANTA (*Going to* LITTLE ELF *and patting him on shoulder*): That's all right, Little Elf. You're just trying to help. Why don't you go get a granny gown for Ginny.

LITTLE ELF (*Brightening up*): Gee, thanks, Santa! I'll get it right away!

21ST ELF (*Looking at H on mantel*): A hammer would be a good idea for Harry Henderson's tool chest.

22ND ELF: And a pair of ice skates for Ingrid Irving!

LITTLE ELF (*Removing J from mantel*): Now I can get that jump rope for Janie Jackson!

23RD ELF (*To* LITTLE ELF): How about getting that kite for Kelly, too?

LITTLE ELF: O.K. One kite, coming up! This is so much fun.

SANTA: Yes, I don't know when I've had such a good time packing my sleigh. Now, who's next?

24TH ELF (*Looking at mantel*): Linda Lowery is next. She reads a lot.

25TH ELF: I think she'd like a library card. That begins with L.

26TH ELF: Michael Morgan is next. I know just the thing for Michael — marbles!

SANTA: Good, good. Now, what do we have for Nancy Nelson? I know that she likes to sew a lot. Little Elf, would you go get her a needlepoint kit?

LITTLE ELF (*Delighted*): Sure, Santa.

9TH ELF (*Looking worried*): Oh, boy, now O for Ollie Olson. This one's going to be tough.

SANTA: Say, I remember that Ollie has a collection of stuffed animals. How about a toy owl for him?

10TH ELF: That's it, Santa! An owl for Ollie!

LITTLE ELF (*Going over to letter* P): And a popsicle for Pam Patterson! I'll go get it.

11TH ELF: No, silly, that popsicle would melt before Pam could open it in the morning.

SANTA: Now, now — at least Little Elf thought of something beginning with a P.

11TH ELF: You're right, Santa. I'm sorry, Little Elf.

12TH ELF: How about a puppet for Pam?

SANTA: That would be perfect!

13TH ELF: Oh, no. Get your thinking caps on, Elves. Here's Q for Quincy Quigley.

LITTLE ELF (*Enthusiastically*): I know! I know! A car for Quincy!

14TH ELF: No, no, little Elf. Car starts with C. Quincy starts with Q.

SANTA: Maybe we'd better leave Q and go on to the next letters. We'll think about Quincy in the meantime.

1ST ELF: Good idea! (*Going to mantel*) R for Rebecca Robertson. All I can think of is refrigerator — that begins with an R.

SANTA: Yes, Rebecca already has a dollhouse, and a toy refrigerator is just what she needs for the kitchen.

LITTLE ELF (*Rushing over to mantel*): And for Sam Simmons we can get a city kit — a toy city for Sam to put together!

SANTA (*Stopping* LITTLE ELF *from removing letter*): Not so fast, my little friend. City begins with C, and Sam begins with S. O.K.?

15TH ELF: Let's get Sam a skateboard.

16TH ELF: Good. T is for Terry Thompson. We can give him a toy truck.

17TH ELF: Ursula Unger would like an umbrella.

SANTA: And Valerie Van Ackeren would love a volleyball. She's on the first team this year. Little Elf, would you please get a volleyball for Valerie?

LITTLE ELF (*Enthusiastically*): Sure, Santa. One volleyball for Valerie, coming up!

18TH ELF: I'll bet Willy Welch would like a water gun. O.K., Santa?

SANTA: Sure! A water gun for Willy's fine. I'm sure you agree that a gift for my little friend Xavier will be hard to think up. Let's leave the letter X there and go to Y for Yancy Yarborough.

19TH ELF: That's easy, Santa! A yo-yo for Yancy!

SANTA: Very good! (*Motioning to mantel*) Let's see — we still have Z up there. There's that Q for Quincy, too.

20TH ELF: And the X for Xavier.

MRS. CLAUS (*Entering*): Santa, it's almost time. Are you ready to leave?

SANTA: I need just a few more minutes, dear. (*To* ELVES) What shall we do about Q, X, and Z? Our time's running out! (*Pauses, then slowly takes* Q *off mantel*) I think I know the gift for Quincy. He's a smart little boy and likes puzzles. How about a quiz game for Quincy?

ELVES (*Together*): Hurray! A quiz for Quincy!

21ST ELF: I'll get it right away, Santa.

MRS. CLAUS: Santa, you'd better start getting ready. You only have about five more minutes before you must take off in your sleigh. Those reindeer are getting restless.

SANTA: Yes, dear, I know. But we have only two more special gifts to think of, and I can't leave without them.

22ND ELF (*Looking at mantel; with chin in hand*): Z for Zita Zimmerman. Z for Zita Zimmerman. Can't you think of something, Elves?

SANTA: Zita is the little girl who loves the zoo. She goes there every time she can get her parents to take her.

23RD ELF: Then maybe she'd like a zebra. Not a real one, of course, but we do have a couple of stuffed zebras on hand.

ELVES (*Together*): Hurray! A zebra for Zita!

SANTA: Now, something for Xavier. (LITTLE ELF *is pulling on* SANTA*'s sleeve, but* SANTA *doesn't notice.*) We must have one more gift for Xavier. (SANTA *and* ELVES *scratch heads, frown, walk back and forth, etc.*)

24TH ELF: I'm stumped. I can't think of a thing.

MRS. CLAUS (*Looking at her watch*): You're going to be late, Santa.

SANTA: Oh, dear. Elves, we must think faster! (LITTLE ELF *is still pulling on* SANTA*'s sleeve.*)

25TH ELF: None of us can think of a gift beginning with X.

26TH ELF: I'm sorry, Santa.

SANTA (*Finally noticing* LITTLE ELF): Little Elf, do you have any other ideas? None of the rest of us can think of a thing beginning with X, and I certainly don't want to forget Xavier. (LITTLE ELF *whispers to* SANTA.)

SANTA: What's that? I couldn't hear you.

LITTLE ELF: How about an "exylophone"?

SANTA: What's that you're saying, Little Elf?

LITTLE ELF: An "exylophone," the musical instrument you play with little sticks.

1ST ELF: No, silly, that's xylophone. It begins with a Z.

SANTA (*Brightening*): No, Little Elf is absolutely right. The word is xylophone and it does begin with an X. We pronounce the X like a Z. Ho! Ho! Ho! Little Elf gave us the idea for our last gift. (*Patting* LITTLE ELF *on back*) Hurray for you, little friend. Go get us the xylophone. Ho! Ho! Ho!

ELVES (*Cheering*): A xylophone for Xavier! Hurray! Hurray for Little Elf!

SANTA (*To* MRS. CLAUS): Now I can leave. I have a special gift for each of the children and the reindeer are all hitched up. It's time to go up and away! (*Walks behind sleigh, and as sleigh is pulled from offstage,* SANTA *walks alongside and waves.*) Merry Christmas to all, and to all a good night!

ALL (*Ad lib*): Goodbye, Santa! Merry Christmas! Have a good trip! (*Etc. Curtain*)

THE END

Three Little Kittens' Christmas

By Joyce S. Christmas

A new twist to the familiar story of the three little kittens, who lose their Christmas mittens. . . .

Characters

INKY
GINGER } *three little kittens*
DUFFY
MOTHER CAT
MR. KATZ, *an old cat*
TABBY, *a selfish cat*
LILY, *a new cat in town*
KITTEN CAROLERS

TIME: *Christmas Eve.*

SETTING: *Home of the three little kittens and the street where they live. A decorated Christmas tree with three gaily wrapped packages under it is downstage, right. At back are three houses, represented by archways or door frames. If desired, curtains may remain closed for opening of scene, with only Christmas tree visible.*

AT RISE: INKY, GINGER *and* DUFFY *excitedly pull* MOTHER CAT *onstage from right.*

INKY: Please, Mother, let us open our Christmas presents tonight.

MOTHER: No, Inky, Christmas Eve is too early to open presents.

GINGER: But we can't wait until morning. We're too excited!

DUFFY: Ginger is right! We want to see our presents now, before we go out caroling.

MOTHER: All right, you eager little kittens, you may open them now. (*They rush to tree, find their packages, and open them.*)

INKY (*Holding up white mittens*): Oh, Mother dear, what lovely white mittens! (*Puts them on*) They are perfect for me.

GINGER (*Showing orange mittens*): And these beautiful mittens are just the right color for me. (*Puts them on*)

DUFFY (*Showing red mittens*): My mittens are best of all! (*Puts them on*)

KITTENS (*Hugging* MOTHER): Thank you, thank you!

MOTHER: Now, take good care of your new mittens, and when you have finished caroling, you may bring all your friends home for a taste of Christmas pie. (*Sound of children singing a carol is heard from off left.*) I hear the Kitten Carolers now. (KITTEN CAROLERS *enter left and walk slowly across stage, singing a carol.* INKY, GINGER *and* DUFFY *run to meet them.*)

INKY (*Waving to* MOTHER): Goodbye, Mother.

GINGER: We'll be home early.

DUFFY: To eat some pie! (MOTHER *waves to them, then exits as they join* CAROLERS. NOTE: *Curtains may now open, revealing three cats in their houses:* MR. KATZ *sitting in a chair, his back to the audience;* TABBY *sitting on the floor, playing with toys; and* LILY *sitting at a table writing. Or if curtains are already open, the three may enter quietly and take their places.*)

GINGER (*To* CAROLERS): Here we are!

INKY: See what we have! (*Showing mittens*) Lovely new mittens!

DUFFY: Just look at mine. (*Kittens take off mittens and pass them around.*)

1ST CAROLER: How pretty they are!

2ND CAROLER: I like Ginger's best. (*Puts them on, admires them*)

GINGER: Be careful of my mittens!

INKY: Our mother would be cross if anything happened to them.

2ND CAROLER: Here, I haven't hurt them. (*Hands mittens to* GINGER. *Others hand back mittens they have been admiring.* INKY, GINGER *and* DUFFY *take the mittens, but do not put them on again.*)

3RD CAROLER: Come on, we're wasting time.

DUFFY: Yes. Where shall we go first to sing?

1ST CAROLER: We could go to old Mr. Katz's house.

GINGER: But he's a mean old cat. He doesn't like kittens.

INKY: He always chases us away from his house.

2ND CAROLER: Then maybe he needs a little Christmas spirit — we'll try to change his mind with song.

INKY: We can try. Let's go. (*They go to* MR. KATZ'S *house, stand in a semicircle and sing "Jingle Bells." After a few lines, Mr. Katz jumps up and hobbles toward them, shaking his cane.*)

MR. KATZ: Shoo! Scat! Go away, you noisy kittens. Leave an old cat in peace.

DUFFY: We were just caroling, sir. Everyone does it on Christmas Eve.

MR. KATZ (*Shaking cane*): Never mind what everyone does. Keep off my property, or I'll have the law on you! (*He starts toward them, and all except* INKY *run downstage.*)

INKY: Oh, please, sir, don't do that. We meant no harm. We only wanted to bring you a little Christmas cheer.

MR. KATZ: I said go away, and I mean it. (*He starts toward* INKY, *who drops mittens without noticing while running to join others. As* MR. KATZ *turns to go back to his house, he sees them and picks them up.*) Those careless kittens! One of them has lost his mittens. Christmas cheer — bah! (*He goes to his house and sits, holding mittens as* CAROLERS *gather around* INKY.)

GINGER: What a cross old cat Mr. Katz is!

DUFFY: What did you say to him, Inky?

1ST CAROLER: Did he shout at you?

INKY: I told him we only wanted to make him happy, but he didn't seem to care.

DUFFY: Never mind. We'll go somewhere else.

3RD CAROLER: Let's go to Tabby's house.

DUFFY: He's sure to have lots of new Christmas toys.

GINGER: He's not very friendly, you know, and he never wants anyone to play with his toys.

4TH CAROLER: Maybe a Christmas song will make him friendlier. (*They go to* TABBY'*s house and sing "Santa Claus Is Coming to Town."* TABBY *stops playing and comes to meet them.*)

TABBY: What are you doing here?

DUFFY: We're singing carols, Tabby. Would you like to come with us?

TABBY: Don't be silly. I have too many new toys to play with. I can't come out on a cold night like this to sing foolish songs.

INKY: They are not foolish songs. They are lovely Christmas songs.

GINGER: Please come with us.

TABBY: No, I told you, I'm much too busy with my toys.

DUFFY (*Enviously, looking at toys*): Would you mind if we look at all your nice presents?

TABBY: Well, you can look — but don't you dare touch a single one. They're all mine. (CAROLERS *gather around toys and exclaim and point excitedly.* DUFFY *starts to pick up a toy.*) I said, don't touch! (DUFFY *steps back, dropping his mittens.*)

GINGER: This is no fun. Let's go. (*Reluctantly they leave and come downstage.*)

DUFFY (*Calling back*): You certainly don't have any Christmas spirit, Tabby. (CAROLERS *go downstage.* TABBY *sees* DUFFY*'s mittens, picks them up, then tosses them aside.*)

TABBY: One of those silly kittens has lost his mittens. (*Looking toward* CAROLERS) I'm tired of Christmas spirit. (TABBY *sits, looks at toys, then sits back, unhappily.*)

INKY: No one seems to have any Christmas spirit tonight.

1ST CAROLER: Let's try once more.

DUFFY: Who is left?

2ND CAROLER: There is still that new cat in town.

3RD CAROLER: Lily is her name. She's from far away.

GINGER: I don't want to sing for her. She's a stranger — a foreign-looking cat.

INKY: I think we should go to her house anyway. Maybe she has no friends here to be with on Christmas Eve. (*They go to* LILY*'s house and sing "We Wish You a Merry Christmas."* LILY *stops writing and comes to greet them.*)

LILY: A Merry Christmas to you, kittens. How nice it is that you have come to sing for me. I have been very lonely in this new town.

GINGER: We're glad you like our song.

LILY: And now I have something for you, my new friends. (*She goes to table and gets a plate of cookies.*) Here are some sweets for you. (*As they take candies,* GINGER *drops mittens.*)

MOTHER (*Calling from offstage*): Inky, Ginger, Duffy! Time to come home.

DUFFY: Oh! There's our mother calling. We must go home.

INKY (*As they all run toward Christmas tree*): Thank you, Miss Lily! (LILY *waves to them, then sees* GINGER*'s mittens. She picks them up and carries them to her house.*) One of those nice kittens has lost her mittens. I'll find out where they live so that I may return them. (*She sits again at desk.*)

GINGER (*As they reach home*): Here we are, Mother. All ready for some pie. (MOTHER CAT *enters, pushing a tea wagon on which is a large Christmas pie.*)

ALL: Here comes the pie!

MOTHER: My nice little kittens and all the carolers may have a piece of pie — if you'll sing a carol for me.

1ST CAROLER: All right. (*They sing an appropriate carol. As they do,* MR. KATZ, TABBY, *and* LILY *all come to the front of their houses to listen.*)

MOTHER (*As they finish*): That was lovely. Now you may have some pie. Inky, Ginger, Duffy, put away your new mittens so they won't be soiled. (INKY, GINGER *and* DUFFY *look at each other in dismay, then begin to cry.*)

INKY: My mittens are gone!

GINGER: Mine, too!

DUFFY: And so are mine! (*They hold up their bare paws.*)

MOTHER (*Angrily*): You naughty kittens, you've lost your mittens! Then you shall have no pie. (INKY, GINGER *and* DUFFY *cry harder.* MR. KATZ *comes from his house, holding* INKY*'s mittens, followed by* TABBY *with* DUFFY*'s mittens and* LILY *with* GINGER*'s.*)

MR. KATZ: Excuse me for disturbing you, Mrs. Cat. I believe these mittens belong to one of your kittens.

INKY: My mittens! Hurrah! Now I can have some pie.

MOTHER: Thank you, Mr. Katz. And won't you have a piece of pie, too?

MR. KATZ: Well . . . yes, I'd like that. You know, the carol singing seems to have given me the Christmas spirit. I haven't felt so good in years.

TABBY (*Joining them*): Me, too, Mr. Katz. (*Holding up mittens*) Duffy, aren't these your mittens?

DUFFY (*Excitedly, taking mittens*): Oh, yes! Thank you, Tabby. Look, Mother, here are my mittens.

MOTHER: How nice. Tabby, would you like some pie, too?

TABBY: Thanks. And remember, Duffy and all of you, you can come to my house and play with my new toys, any time. (LILY *comes forward as* MOTHER *starts to serve* TABBY *and others.*)

LILY: A good evening to you. I have found these mittens and believe they belong to one of you.

GINGER: Oh, joy! My mittens. Now I can have some pie!

MOTHER: Welcome, Miss Lily. I'm glad you could join us. I meant to call on you when you first moved to our neighborhood, but I have been busy getting ready for Christmas.

LILY: I am happy to be here, with some new friends at Christmas time.

MOTHER (*Passing pie to* CAROLERS *and others*): Now that my naughty kittens have found their mittens, we can all have some pie. (*Hands plate to* INKY) This is for you, Inky. (*To* GINGER) Here is a piece for Ginger. (*Handing plate to* DUFFY) And one for Duffy. (*They all taste pie.*)

MR. KATZ: Delicious, Mrs. Cat. (*To* CAROLERS) Now, how about another song to go with this wonderful Christmas pie?

ALL (*Ad lib*): Yes. Let's sing. (*Etc.*)

GINGER: I would rather have another piece of pie.

INKY: Hush, Ginger, you greedy kitten. We'll sing first and eat later.

DUFFY: Is everyone ready? (*All nod and line up, including* MR. KATZ, TABBY, *and* LILY. *They sing "We Wish You a Merry Christmas," or other appropriate song. At conclusion, curtains close.*)

THE END

The Shoemaker and the Elves

By the Brothers Grimm
Adapted by *Alice Very*

Generosity is rewarded as the Shoemaker and his wife learn who has been helping them make tiny shoes. . . .

Characters

THE SHOEMAKER
THE SHOEMAKER'S WIFE
LITTLE BOY
LITTLE GIRL
ELVES, *4 or more*

SETTING: *The Shoemaker's shop, a few days before Christmas.*
AT RISE: SHOEMAKER *sits hammering shoe.*
SHOEMAKER (*Sighing*):
 Rap-a-tap-tap!
 I've only a scrap
 Of leather to use
 To finish these shoes.
(SHOEMAKER'S WIFE *enters, ringing dinner bell.*)

WIFE:

>Ring-ding-ding!
>Supper's hot.
>All we've got
>Is in the pot.

SHOEMAKER:

>What is there to eat?
>I hope it is a treat.

WIFE (*Sighing*):

>Just buttermilk and whey,
>The same as yesterday.

SHOEMAKER (*Hammering again*):

>Rat-a-tat-tat.
>Who wants to eat that?

WIFE:

>You'd better enjoy
>Whatever you get.
>It could be much worse,
>So don't you fret.

>(LITTLE BOY *enters, barefoot.*)

LITTLE BOY:

>Shoemaker, shoemaker,
>Make me some shoes.
>Christmas is coming,
>There's no time to lose.

SHOEMAKER (*Sighing*):

>I wish I could help you,
>But I'll have to refuse.
>There's not enough leather
>For a whole pair of shoes.

LITTLE BOY (*Picking up leather scrap*):

>But I've no shoes at all,
>And my feet are quite bare.
>There's enough leather here
>For one *little* pair.

SHOEMAKER:

> I'll do what I can,
> Now you take your leave.
> I hope they'll be ready
> Before Christmas Eve.

(LITTLE BOY *exits.*)

WIFE (*Yawning*):

> Now let's go to bed
> And hope a new day
> Will see all our troubles
> Fly far, far away.

(SHOEMAKER *and* WIFE *exit. Lights grow dim and then brighter, as moon shines through window — a blue light bulb may be used.* ELVES *enter through window, capering and dancing.*)

ELVES (*Jumping from window; together*):

> Hop, skip, and jump!
> Down with a thump!

1ST ELF (*Picking up leather scrap from bench*):

> Look what I found —
> A piece of soft leather!

2ND ELF (*Holding up tools*):

> Let's cut out the shoes
> And sew them together.

(ELVES *work, "producing" finished shoes that have been concealed under bench.*)

3RD ELF (*Hammering*):

> Hammer the nails in —
> Tick-tack-too!
> That's the way
> To make a shoe!

4TH ELF:

> Now for the other —
> Nice and neat,

Small enough for
Tiny feet.
(ELF *puts on shoes and dances.*)
ELVES (*Dancing; together*):
Heel, toe,
Over we go!
Heel, toe,
Away we go!
(ELVES *put shoes on workbench and dance out through window. Lights brighten.*)
WIFE (*Peering into room through doorway*):
What was that?
SHOEMAKER (*Peering in from doorway*):
Why, what's the matter?
WIFE:
Little feet
Went pitter-patter!
SHOEMAKER (*Looking around*):
No one's here.
WIFE:
Just look again.
It sounded to me
Like little men.
SHOEMAKER (*Suddenly seeing shoes on bench*):
What have we here —
A pair of shoes!
(SHOEMAKER *and* WIFE *come into room. He walks around, looking closely at doors and windows, and under furniture; shaking his head*)
There's something queer
Going on in here.
How could this pair
Of shoes appear?

(LITTLE BOY *and* LITTLE GIRL *enter; both are barefoot.*)

LITTLE BOY (*Going toward bench*):

    I'm back, Mr. Shoemaker.

    Are my shoes all done?

SHOEMAKER:

    Yes, ready to help you

    Have lots of fun.

    (*Hands* LITTLE BOY *the shoes*)

    How do you like them?

    Do they fit?

LITTLE BOY (*Putting on shoes and stretching foot out to display shoes*):

    They seem to be perfect

    And don't pinch a bit!

    (*Takes coins from pocket and hands them to* SHOEMAKER)

SHOEMAKER (*Smiling*):

    I can buy more leather now,

    And even trim a Christmas bough.

LITTLE GIRL (*Softly, to* LITTLE BOY):

    Tell the man I need shoes, too.

SHOEMAKER:

    I'll gladly make a pair for you!

    (*Gives money to* WIFE)

    Please buy more leather

    At the store.

WIFE (*Smiling, going toward door*):

    We'll have a better Christmas

    Than ever before! (*Exits*)

LITTLE BOY:

    Watch me jump and hop and run.

    (*Jumps and hops, and runs*)

    I just never had more fun.

LITTLE GIRL:

>I'll skip and hop
>With my new shoes.
>I must go tell
>My friends the news.

LITTLE BOY (*Marching toward door*):

>Now I'm marching,
>Stamp, stamp, stamp!
>Left foot, right foot,
>Tramp, tramp, tramp.

>(*He and* LITTLE GIRL *march around.*)

LITTLE GIRL:

>I can hardly wait
>To get my shoes.
>Come, let's go
>And spread the news. (LITTLE GIRL *marches off.*)

LITTLE BOY (*As he follows her off*):

>Left foot, right foot,
>Tramp, tramp, tramp! (*Exits*)

WIFE (*Entering, carrying a piece of red leather*):

>Here's the leather —

SHOEMAKER:

>Why, you bought red!
>Just like the stripes
>On a Christmas sled!

WIFE (*Handing leather to him*):

>I recall
>When I was small
>I loved red shoes
>Best of all!

>(*To* SHOEMAKER)

>Leave the leather
>In full sight,
>And see what happens
>In the night.

(SHOEMAKER *puts red leather on workbench.*)
SHOEMAKER:
 We'll stand there (*Points*)
 Behind the door,
 And wait to see
 Who does my chore.
(SHOEMAKER *and* WIFE *hide behind door.* ELVES *enter through window.*)
1ST ELF:
 Skippity hop,
 Over the top.
 (*Climbing over sill*)
 Up on the windowsill,
 Here's where we stop!
(ELVES *jump down from sill into room, go to workbench, sit down, and begin to work.*)
2ND ELF (*Picking up scissors and cutting leather*):
 Snip, snip, snip!
 (*Picks up large needle and starts to sew*)
 Stitch, stitch, stitch!
 Soon we'll make
 These good folk rich.
3RD ELF (*As he sews, in sing-song voice*):
 Shoe the horse
 And shoe the mare,
 But let the little
 Colt go bare.
4TH ELF (*Working, in sing-song voice*):
 Shoes for the master,
 Shoes for the dame,
 And shoes for the little girl,
 Just the same.
1ST ELF (*Sewing*):
 Jack, be nimble
 With the thimble.

2ND ELF:

> Don't you fumble;
> Don't you stumble;
> So the shoemaker
> Will not grumble.

3RD ELF (*Sewing*):

> Make the slippers
> Fine and neat;
> Perfect for
> Such dainty feet.

1ST ELF (*Holding up finished red shoes*):

> Done in time for Christmas Eve.
> Come, it's time to take our leave.

4TH ELF (*As they dance about*):

> Now we're off
> To play and ramble,
> On Christmas Eve
> Through snow and bramble.

ELVES (*Dancing; together*):

> Heel, toe,
> Over we go!
> Heel, toe,
> Away we go!
> Once to the left,
> Once to the right,
> Out of the window
> And so good night!

(ELVES *dance out.* SHOEMAKER *and* WIFE *come out from behind door.*)

SHOEMAKER (*Picking up shoes*):

> Heel — toe!
> What do you know!
> How did the little ones
> Learn to sew?

WIFE (*Puzzled*):

Yet, how can it be,
That these little elves,
Have hardly a stitch
Of clothes for themselves?

SHOEMAKER:

They must be freezing
From their heads to their toes.
Why don't we make them
Some Christmas clothes?

WIFE (*Enthusiastically, as she picks up scraps of cloth from workbench*):

Here are some bits of cloth —
Just scraps —
But there's enough
To make them caps!

SHOEMAKER:

Is there enough for jackets, too?

WIFE (*As she works at sewing*):

Oh, yes, I'll make them
In red and blue.

(*Both work away busily, sewing cloth.* LITTLE BOY *and* LITTLE GIRL *enter.*)

LITTLE GIRL (*Seeing red shoes on workbench*):

Are these shoes mine,
All bright and red?

LITTLE BOY:

Just right for Christmas,
As I said.

SHOEMAKER (*Smiling, to* LITTLE GIRL):

Now put on your shoes
And dance about lightly.

(LITTLE GIRL *puts on shoes;* LITTLE BOY *pays* SHOEMAKER.)

LITTLE BOY (*Dancing around with* LITTLE GIRL):
> Hoppity, skippity,
> Airy and sprightly!

SHOEMAKER:
> Stay here and watch,
> If you'd like to see,
> How little elves work,
> Quick as one, two, three!

WIFE (*Holding up small caps and jackets*):
> What will they say,
> Do you suppose?
> When they come and find
> These fine, new clothes?
>
> (*Puts clothes down on bench*)

LITTLE BOY:
> There'll be gifts for Christmas
> All around.

SHOEMAKER (*Smiling and starting toward door*):
> May good will aplenty
> For all abound!

(WIFE, LITTLE BOY, *and* LITTLE GIRL *follow* SHOE-MAKER *behind door. After brief pause,* ELVES *enter through window.*)

ELVES (*Singing together as they jump down*):
> Susy, little Susy,
> What's that in the hay?
> Oh, that's my little goosey —
> Goes barefoot all day.
> The shoeman has leather,
> But none for a goose.
> And so my little goosey
> Must go without shoes.

1ST ELF (*Holding up jackets*):
> Just look at this!

2ND ELF:

>What have you there?

1ST ELF:

>Little jackets
>
>For us to wear.

>(1ST ELF *hands jackets to other* ELVES, *and they put them on.*)

4TH ELF (*Picking up caps from workbench*):

>And there are caps here
>
>For us, too!

>(*Handing them to other* ELVES)

>One for you, and you, and you.

>(ELVES *put on caps.*)

3RD ELF (*Preening*):

>We're all dressed like gentlemen.
>
>We won't have to work again.

ELVES (*Dancing about and singing together to tune of "Deck the Halls"*):

>Now's the time for fun and frolic
>
>With new clothes to see the Yuletide in.
>
>We will not be melancholic,
>
>Tra la la la la, la la la la!

1ST ELF:

>We should protect
>
>This man and wife,

ELVES (*Together, as if casting a spell*):

>They shall not want
>
>For the rest of their life.

>(ELVES *exit through window opening. After brief pause,* SHOEMAKER, WIFE, LITTLE GIRL *and* LITTLE BOY *come out from behind door.*)

SHOEMAKER:

>How good they are,
>
>These little elves.

To think of others
And not themselves!

LITTLE BOY:

We'll wear your shoes
In every weather,
And bring you coins
For more soft leather.

(*Jumps around happily*)

LITTLE GIRL:

I'll wear red shoes
For work and play.

(*She dances about.*)

With a ho ho ho,
And a heigh heigh heigh!

WIFE (*Happily*):

At Christmas time
For now and ever
We'll have good fortune
In each endeavor.

(*All join hands and dance about.*)

ALL (*Singing together, to the tune of "Deck the Halls"*):

Let us not be melancholic,
Fa la la la la, la la la la,
Christmas is for fun and frolic,
Fa la la la la, la la la la!

(*They exit, as curtain falls.*)

THE END

Up a Christmas Tree

By Aileen Fisher

Music adds spice to this playlet, and there are some unusual — and welcome — Christmas gifts. . . .

Characters

MRS. TEMPLE
MR. TEMPLE
BONNY ⎫
DONNA ⎬ *their children*
WALLY ⎬
DICK ⎭

TIME: *Several days before Christmas.*
SETTING: *The Temple living room. There are doors at right and left.*
AT RISE: MRS. TEMPLE *is sitting in a chair, sewing, and* MR. TEMPLE *is sitting on the couch, reading a newspaper.*
NOTE: *This skit is a miniature "musical comedy," written to the rhythm of the verse and chorus of "Jingle Bells." The lines may be sung, or, if desired, recited as poetry.*

MRS. TEMPLE (*Singing to tune of "Jingle Bells," or reciting*):
> They asked what gifts we'd like,
> With Christmas Eve so near.

MR. TEMPLE (*Laughing*):
> I trust you said a bike,
> Or roller skates, my dear.

MRS. TEMPLE:
> I answered no such thing.
> I told them all, what's more,
> The nicest gift they each could bring
> Was not sold in a store.

MR. *and* MRS. TEMPLE (*Together*):
> Christmas gifts, Christmas gifts!
> We shall not deny:
> What we really want the most
> Our children cannot buy!

(MR. *and* MRS. TEMPLE *go out left. In a minute,* BONNY *and* DONNA *enter right. They seem puzzled.*)

DONNA:
> I asked Mom several times.

BONNY:
> And I asked Daddy, too.

DONNA:
> I said we'd saved our dimes
> To buy them something new.

BONNY:
> But Mother shook her head.
> And slyly winked her eye,
> And said, "Give us a gift, instead,
> That's not the kind you buy."

BONNY *and* DONNA (*Together*):
> Christmas gifts, Christmas gifts,
> Mother must know best.

But we're "up a Christmas tree"
Because we cannot guess!
(*They sit on couch and appear to be deep in thought.*
WALLY *and* DICK *come in from right.*)
WALLY:

Mom said both she and Dad
Knew something they would like

DICK:

She said they'd both be glad
If we could guess it right.

WALLY:

It's nothing we can *get.*

DICK:

I'm surely stumped, aren't you?

WALLY:

I wonder what it is . . . (*Suddenly*)
I'll bet
It's something we can *do!*

(BONNY *and* DONNA *join the boys.*)
ALL (*Together*):

Christmas gifts, Christmas gifts!
Parents must know best.
But we're "up a Christmas tree" —
We *wish* that we could guess!

(*They all begin to pace the floor, thinking hard. Some-times they are so long in thought that they bump into each other.* MR. *and* MRS. TEMPLE *peek in at the door left, and watch, but the children are too concerned to notice them.*)

WALLY (*Stopping suddenly so that the others stop, too; excitedly*):

I know! I'll write a pledge
Not to tease you anymore.
I'll sign it at the edge
And be courteous once more!

(MRS. TEMPLE *nods to* MR. TEMPLE.)

BONNY (*Eagerly*):

    I'll write a promise, too.

    And I will not get cross

    Instead of getting mad or blue

    I'll be my very own boss.

(MR. TEMPLE *nods to* MRS. TEMPLE.)

WALLY *and* BONNY (*Together*):

    Christmas gifts, Christmas gifts!

    How can we go wrong?

    If we give what can't be bought,

    And give it all year long!

DICK:

    I know! I'll write a rhyme!

    I'll promise, cross-my-heart:

    Instead of wasting time,

    I'll always do my part.

(MR. *and* MRS. TEMPLE *nod to each other.*)

DONNA:

    And I will be like you:

    I'll start to practice thrift.

    I'll save my time and money, too . . .

    And that will be my gift.

(MR. *and* MRS. TEMPLE *nod, smile happily, and tip-toe out left.*)

ALL (*Together*):

    Christmas gifts, Christmas gifts!

    It won't be a cinch —

    Sticking to our promises.

    But we won't budge an inch!

WALLY:

    Let's fix our pledges now.

BONNY:

    Let's make them Christmas-y.

DICK:

Let's draw a holly bough.

DONNA:

Or paint a Christmas tree.

WALLY (*Going out right*):

Our folks will be amazed!

BONNY (*Going out right*):

And glad, I'll bet my hat.

DICK (*Going out right*):

They ought to be a little dazed.

DONNA (*Going out right*):

To get such gifts as that.

MR. *and* MRS. TEMPLE (*Re-entering):*

Christmas gifts, Christmas gifts!

Aren't our children smart?

All those things we wanted most . . .

They knew them all by heart!

(*Curtain*)

THE END

A Christmas Carol

By Charles Dickens
Adapted by *Adele Thane*

Miserly Ebenezer Scrooge sat alone and friendless on Christmas Eve, when a ghost from his past appeared with a dire warning. . . .

Characters

EBENEZER SCROOGE
BOB CRATCHIT, *his clerk*
FRED, *Scrooge's nephew*
COLLECTOR FOR CHARITY
MARLEY'S GHOST
GHOST OF CHRISTMAS PAST
EBENEZER SCROOGE, *as a schoolboy*
FAN, *his sister*
YOUNG SCROOGE, *as an apprentice*
DICK WILKINS, *a fellow apprentice*
MR. FEZZIWIG, *their boss*
MRS. FEZZIWIG
BELLE, *young Scrooge's fiancée*
GHOST OF CHRISTMAS PRESENT
MRS. CRATCHIT, *Bob's wife*

PETER
BELINDA
MARTHA   } *Cratchit children*
NED
SALLY
TINY TIM
GHOST OF CHRISTMAS YET TO COME
FIDDLER
BOY
CAROLERS, *extras*

SCENE 1

TIME: *Christmas Eve, in the 19th century.*

SETTING: *London. The business office of Scrooge and Marley. In the right wall is the door that opens to the street. Upstage of the door there is a clothes tree, holding Bob Cratchit's hat, and Scrooge's muffler, hat and overcoat. At center is a flat-topped desk for Scrooge, with a stool behind it. On the desk is a pile of ledgers, pen and inkstand, a ruler, a metal cash box with money in it, and a lighted candle. Set against the wall is Bob Cratchit's high clerk's desk and stool. This desk also has a lighted candle, ledgers, pen and inkstand. A casement window is downstage of clerk's desk, and potbellied stove is upstage between the two desks. Coal hod and shovel are beside stove.*

AT RISE: SCROOGE *and* BOB CRATCHIT *are working at their desks.* BOB *has long white muffler wound around his neck.* CAROLERS *offstage start singing,* "*God Rest Ye Merry, Gentlemen.*" SCROOGE *rises impatiently, goes to street door and flings it open.*

SCROOGE (*Shouting off right*): Hey! Stop that singing! Stop it, I say! Keep quiet out there! (CAROLERS *stop singing.* SCROOGE *closes door and returns to desk, mut-*

tering.) Police ought to shut those people up. Singing around in the street as if they had no proper business. (*Counts money in cash box, standing with his back to* BOB, *who gets down off stool, blowing on his hands and rubbing them together*)

BOB: Weather seems to be getting colder.

SCROOGE (*Without turning around*): Cold? Humbug! It doesn't feel cold to me. (BOB *goes to coal hod and lifts out shovel, making a grating noise.* SCROOGE *whirls on on him.*) What are you doing with that shovel?

BOB (*Timidly*): I thought I'd put another coal on the fire — if it's all right.

SCROOGE: It's not all right, and you know it. If you persist in burning up my coal like tinder, you will have to find another position!

BOB: But my hand is so cold I can hardly write.

SCROOGE: Warm it at the candle. (*Closes and locks cash box.* BOB *replaces shovel in coal hod, sits at desk and holds hands over candle. Door bursts open and* FRED *enters briskly.*)

FRED (*Cheerfully, removing his hat*): Merry Christmas, Uncle! God save you!

SCROOGE: Bah! Humbug!

FRED (*Laughing*): Christmas a humbug, Uncle? Surely you don't mean that.

SCROOGE: I do! (*Scornfully*) Merry Christmas! What reason have you to be merry? You're poor enough.

FRED: Come, then. What reason have you to be sad? You're rich enough.

SCROOGE: Bah! Humbug!

FRED (*Coaxingly*): Don't be cross, Uncle.

SCROOGE: What else can I be, when I live in such a world of fools? A pox upon Merry Christmas! What's Christmas to *you* but a time for paying bills without money;

a time for finding yourself a year older, but not an hour richer. If I had my way, every idiot who goes about with "Merry Christmas" on his lips should be boiled in his own pudding, and buried with a stake of holly through his heart.

FRED: Oh, really, Uncle!

SCROOGE (*Mockingly*): Oh, really, nephew! Keep Christmas in your own way, and let me keep it in mine.

FRED: Keep it! But you don't keep it at all.

SCROOGE: Let me leave it alone, then. What good has Christmas ever done *you*?

FRED: Why, Uncle, it has done me a lot of good. It is the only time I know when men and women seem to open their shut-up hearts freely — and though it has never put a scrap of gold or silver in my pocket, I believe it *has* done me good, and *will* do me good, and I say (*Thumping* SCROOGE*'s desk*) — *God bless it*!

BOB (*Applauding*): Splendid, sir, splendid!

SCROOGE (*Turning to* BOB *with a vengeance*): Let me hear another sound out of *you*, Bob Cratchit, and you'll keep *your* Christmas by losing your situation! (*Sarcastically, to* FRED) You're quite a powerful speaker, Fred. I wonder why you don't go into Parliament.

FRED (*Soothingly*): Don't be angry, Uncle. Come, dine with us tomorrow.

SCROOGE (*Angrily*): I'll dine with the devil first.

FRED: I want nothing from you; I ask nothing of you. Why can't we be friends?

SCROOGE (*Returning to his work*): Good afternoon.

FRED: I am sorry, with all my heart, to find you so resolute. But I have made this visit in honor of Christmas, and I'll keep my Christmas humor to the last. So a Merry Christmas, Uncle! And a Happy New Year!

SCROOGE (*Thundering*): Good afternoon!

FRED (*Waving to* BOB *with his hat*): Merry Christmas to you, Bob!

BOB: The same to you, sir! God bless you! (FRED *opens door to exit;* COLLECTOR FOR CHARITY *is standing outside, consulting notebook.*)

COLLECTOR: How do you do, sir? Scrooge and Marley, I believe? (FRED *nods and gestures toward* SCROOGE. COLLECTOR *enters.* FRED *exits, closing door.* COLLECTOR *speaks to* SCROOGE.) Have I the pleasure of addressing Mr. Scrooge or Mr. Marley?

SCROOGE (*Impatiently*): Mr. Marley has been dead these seven years. He died seven years ago this very night.

COLLECTOR: I have no doubt his generosity is well represented in his surviving partner. My credentials, sir. (*Lays card on desk;* SCROOGE *brushes it aside without looking at it.*) Mr. Scrooge, at this festive season of the year, we all want to make some slight provision for the poor and destitute. Many thousands are in want of common necessities; hundreds of thousands are in want of common comforts.

SCROOGE (*Putting down pen*): Are there no prisons?

COLLECTOR: Plenty of prisons.

SCROOGE: What about the union workhouses and treadmill? Are they still in operation?

COLLECTOR: They are. I wish I could say they were not.

SCROOGE: Good. I was afraid from what you said that something had stopped them in their useful work.

COLLECTOR: I would hardly call them useful! As I say, Mr. Scrooge, a few of us are trying to raise a fund to buy meat and drink for the poor. We chose this time because it is the time when want is felt most keenly. (*Picking up pen from desk*) What shall I put you down for?

SCROOGE (*Snatching pen from* COLLECTOR*'s hand*): Nothing.

COLLECTOR: You wish to be anonymous?

SCROOGE (*Slamming pen down on desk*): I wish to be left alone! (*Rising*) I don't make myself merry at Christmas, and I can't afford to make a lot of idle people merry. I help support the prisons and poorhouses — they cost enough. Those who are badly off must go there.

COLLECTOR: Many would rather die than go there.

SCROOGE: If they would rather die, they had better do it and decrease the surplus population. Besides, this has nothing to do with my business. (*Turns to desk*)

COLLECTOR (*Reproachfully*): You ought to make it your business to help your fellow man.

SCROOGE (*Testily*): It's enough for a man to understand his own business and not interfere with other people's. Mine occupies me constantly. Good afternoon. (*Sits at desk*)

COLLECTOR (*Going to door, then turning*): If Mr. Marley felt as you do, I fear his ghost is not resting in peace. Good afternoon. (*Exits*)

SCROOGE: Bah! Humbug! (*Looks at watch and speaks grudgingly to* BOB) You might as well go, it's five minutes past time. Get along.

BOB: Yes, sir. (*Closes ledgers, blows out candle, goes to clothes tree for hat, then stands twirling it nervously in his hands.*)

SCROOGE: Well, what are you waiting for?

BOB: About tomorrow, sir.

SCROOGE: You'll want all day tomorrow, I suppose?

BOB: Yes, sir, if it's quite convenient.

SCROOGE (*Rising, banging ruler on desk*): It's *not* convenient, and it's not fair! If I were to deduct something from your salary, you'd think yourself ill-used. And yet, you don't think *me* ill-used when I pay a day's wages for no work.

BOB (*Pleadingly*): Christmas is only once a year, sir.

SCROOGE: A poor excuse for picking a man's pocket every twenty-fifth of December! Very well, take the day off — but be here all the earlier the next morning.

BOB (*Eagerly, as he goes toward exit*): Oh, I *will*, sir! Good night Mr. Scrooge — and a Merry Christmas to you! (*Hurries out, closing door*)

SCROOGE (*Crossing to lock door*): There's another one, Bob Cratchit, with fifteen shillings a week, and a wife and family, talking about a Merry Christmas. They'll drive me to distraction. (CAROLERS *start singing "The First Noël" offstage.*) Carolers, carolers! Will they never leave a man in peace? (*Sits at desk and resumes work.* CAROLERS *fade. Candle flickers, lights dim. Sound of clanking chains is heard off right, faint at first, then growing louder.* SCROOGE *looks up, listening, then shakes head.*) Humbug! (*Suddenly door flies open.* MARLEY'S GHOST *appears in the doorway, pale, heavily bound with chains that drag behind him.* SCROOGE *gives a start, looks toward door, then quickly shakes his head.*) Humbug, I say! That door is locked! (MARLEY'S GHOST *enters dragging chains, and as* SCROOGE *turns again to look he advances to clothes tree, where spotlight comes upon him.* SCROOGE *slides off stool and slowly approaches* GHOST. *In a nervous voice*) Who — who are you?

MARLEY'S GHOST (*Speaking in a deep, forbidding voice*): Ask me who I *was*.

SCROOGE: Who *were* you, then?

MARLEY'S GHOST: In life I was your partner, Jacob Marley.

SCROOGE (*Drawing away*): Jacob Marley! What do you want with me?

MARLEY'S GHOST: Much. (*Pause*) Don't you believe in me?

SCROOGE (*Boastfully*): I don't.

MARLEY'S GHOST: You can see me, can't you?

SCROOGE: I think I can.

MARLEY'S GHOST: Why do you doubt your own senses?

SCROOGE: Because a little thing affects my senses — a slight disorder of the stomach — a bit of undigested beef, a blot of mustard, a crumb of cheese. (*Cackling at his own joke*) There's more of gravy than of the grave about you, whatever you are. (MARLEY'S GHOST *raises a frightful cry and shakes his chains.*)

MARLEY'S GHOST: Silence! (SCROOGE, *suddenly terrified, falls on his knees.*)

SCROOGE: Mercy, oh mercy!

MARLEY'S GHOST (*In a booming voice*): Do you believe in me or not?

SCROOGE (*Terrified*): I do, I must! But why do you walk on earth? And why do you come to me?

MARLEY'S GHOST: It is required of every man that the spirit within him should walk abroad among his fellow men. If that spirit does not go out in life, it is condemned to do so after death. It is doomed to wander through the world. Oh, woe is me! (*Wails dismally, lifting chains high and flinging them heavily to the floor*)

SCROOGE (*Rising fearfully*): You are chained — tell me why.

MARLEY'S GHOST: I wear the chain I forged in life. I made it link by link. I girded it on of my own free will. Is its pattern strange to you?

SCROOGE: I've never seen anything like it before.

MARLEY'S GHOST: That's strange. You wear such a chain yourself. (SCROOGE *looks anxiously about him on the floor.*) It was as long as this chain of mine seven Christmas Eves ago. You've made it longer since.

SCROOGE (*Clasping his hands in supplication*): Oh, no! Jacob, say something to comfort me.

MARLEY'S GHOST: I have no comfort for you.

SCROOGE: But you were always a good man of business, Jacob.

MARLEY'S GHOST: Business! Mankind was my business. I did nothing to help my fellow man. Oh, woe is me! (*Wails again and shakes his chains*)

SCROOGE: Is something hurting you?

MARLEY'S GHOST: I suffer most at Christmas time. Hear me, Ebenezer. My time is nearly gone. I am here to warn you. You may yet have a chance to escape my fate.

SCROOGE: You were always a good friend to me, Jacob.

MARLEY'S GHOST (*Relentlessly*): You will be haunted by three Spirits.

SCROOGE (*Faltering*): Is that the chance you mentioned, Jacob?

MARLEY'S GHOST: It is.

SCROOGE: Then I think I'd better not take that chance.

MARLEY'S GHOST: You have no choice. (*Starts walking backward, step by step, toward door*) Expect the Ghost of Christmas Past when the bell tolls one. Expect the Ghost of Christmas Present when the bell tolls two. Expect the Ghost of Christmas Yet to Come when the bell tolls three. (*Pauses in doorway*) For your own sake, Scrooge, remember what has passed between us. Farewell. (MARLEY'S GHOST *disappears in the darkness off right, dragging his chains.*)

SCROOGE (*Rushing to doorway*): Jacob, wait! Help me! Jacob! (*Falls on knees. Bell tolls one. Live or recorded music of "Lo, How A Rose E'er Blooming" is heard offstage, and continues under following dialogue. Spotlight comes up on* GHOST OF CHRISTMAS PAST, *a ruddy-faced youth wearing white tunic with golden belt, a shining crown, and carrying holly branch, standing left center.* SCROOGE *rises, sees* GHOST, *and walks hesitantly toward him.*)   Are you the spirit whose coming was foretold to me?

1ST GHOST (*Softly, gently*): I am.

SCROOGE: Who and what are you?

1ST GHOST: I am the Ghost of Christmas Past.

SCROOGE: Long past?

1ST GHOST: No, your past. Come and walk with me.

SCROOGE (*Shrinking back*): No, no, I can't!

1ST GHOST: It is your only hope of being saved. (*Taking* SCROOGE *by the arm*) Come, we have far to go.

SCROOGE (*Remonstrating*): It's bitter cold outside.

1ST GHOST: What does it matter? Nothing can wither your cold spirit. We will move swiftly through the air. (*Points to casement window, left, and as he points, it opens magically.* NOTE: *Shutters are pushed open from offstage.*)

SCROOGE (*Pulling away*): Through the air? I am mortal, I will fall!

1ST GHOST: Bear but a touch of my hand there (*Touching* SCROOGE*'s heart*), and you shall be upheld in more than this. Come! (*As* 1ST GHOST *and* SCROOGE *start walking toward window, lights dim to blackout. Curtain closes to sound of whistling wind.*)

*   *   *   *   *

SCENE 2

SETTING: *This scene is played in front of curtain. Schoolroom. School desk and bench are center.*

AT RISE: *Sound of whistling wind fades as spotlight comes up on* 1ST GHOST *and* SCROOGE, *down left.* SCROOGE *is on his knees, clinging to* 1ST GHOST.

SCROOGE: Help, help, I'm falling!

1ST GHOST: Stand up! You're on the ground now. You haven't lost your feet. Stand up, I say!

SCROOGE (*Getting up, looking around, then walking about, nervously*): Where are we?

1ST GHOST: You've been here many times before. (*Spotlight comes up on* EBENEZER SCROOGE *as a schoolboy, seated at desk, his head on his arms, sobbing softly. He does not notice others.*)

SCROOGE: Why, it's my old school. Everybody has gone home for the Christmas holidays.

1ST GHOST: Not everybody. A solitary boy is left there still.

SCROOGE: I know him all too well — my lonely self. Poor boy!

FAN (*Off right, calling*): Hello! Is anybody here? (*Enters, calling*) I'm looking for my brother, Ebenezer Scrooge.

EBENEZER (*Rising*): Fan!

FAN (*Seeing him*): Ebenezer! (*Runs to him and hugs him*) I've come to take you home!

EBENEZER: Home? Is Father dead?

FAN: No, he sent me in a carriage to get you. He's much kinder than he used to be. We're to be together all the Christmas long. (*Taking his hand*) Hurry, let's go! I'm so excited I can hardly talk! (*They run off, right. Spotlight fades out on schoolroom, up on* SCROOGE *and* 1ST GHOST, *down left. During following dialogue, desk and bench are moved to right, representing* FEZZIWIG'*s warehouse.*)

SCROOGE: That was the only happy Christmas I ever had at home. My sister died several years later.

1ST GHOST: She left a child, didn't she? Your nephew, Fred. What have you done for him? Have you loved him dearly for your sister's sake?

SCROOGE (*Ashamed*): Take me away, I don't want to remember any more.

1ST GHOST: You have no choice. I am here to show you the Christmas Past. (*Lights come up full.* YOUNG SCROOGE *and* DICK WILKINS, *both in shirtsleeves, are seated at desk, writing in ledgers.*) Do you know this place?

SCROOGE: Know it! Of course, I do. It's Fezziwig's warehouse — I was apprenticed here. (FEZZIWIG *enters, carrying small Christmas tree and stand.*)

FEZZIWIG (*Jovially, to* YOUNG SCROOGE *and* DICK): Yo ho, there, Ebenezer Scrooge — Dick Wilkins! No more work tonight. It's Christmas Eve. Clear away, my lads, and let's have lots of room here!

SCROOGE (*Excitedly*): It's old Fezziwig! Bless his heart, it's Fezziwig alive again! And there's Dick Wilkins. He was very much attached to me, was Dick. (YOUNG SCROOGE *and* DICK *move desk off right, but leave bench on stage.* FEZZIWIG *sets Christmas tree left stage.* MRS. FEZZIWIG *enters, right, with holly wreath which she hangs on stage curtain.*)

MRS. FEZZIWIG: Merry Christmas, Mr. Fezziwig.

FEZZIWIG: Ho, there, Mrs. Fezziwig! Christmas comes only once a year. Worth waiting for — worth celebrating — worth remembering. (YOUNG SCROOGE *and* DICK *re-enter, struggling into their coats.* CAROLERS *come down aisles of auditorium, singing "Deck the Halls," and go onstage.* FIDDLER *enters, right, with fiddle and bow, stands on bench and begins to play appropriate dance tune. Recorded music may be used.* CAROLERS *dance, as* YOUNG SCROOGE *and* DICK *clap their hands, and* MR. *and* MRS. FEZZIWIG *link arms and dance in circle.* SCROOGE *watches with apparent pleasure, clapping his hands and tapping his foot in*

time to music. The dance ends with CAROLERS, YOUNG
SCROOGE, DICK, MR. *and* MRS. FEZZIWIG *and* FIDDLER
dancing up aisles and out at rear of auditorium.)

SCROOGE: Those were happy times, spirit. And how grateful we all were to old Fezziwig for those Christmas Eves.

1ST GHOST: Yet Mr. Fezziwig didn't spend more than a
few pounds on the whole party.

SCROOGE: What difference does that make? The happiness he gave us was quite as great as if he had spent
a fortune.

1ST GHOST: How did you ever forget these things in your
later years? (*Pause*) My time grows short. One shadow
more from your past. (*Spotlight comes up on* BELLE,
standing center.)

SCROOGE (*Crying out*): Belle! The girl I was to marry!

1ST GHOST: Listen again to the words she spoke on that
fateful Christmas Day when she released you from
your promise of marriage.

BELLE (*Removing ring from finger*): I return your ring,
Ebenezer. Another idol has displaced me, a golden
one. I've seen your love of gold grow like a mighty
passion until nothing else matters to you. Our contract
is an old one, made when we were both poor. I release you from it, with a full heart, for the love of
him you once were. May you be happy in the life you
have chosen. (*Spotlight on* BELLE *fades out.*)

SCROOGE: Spirit, why do you delight in torturing me?
Show me no more!

1ST GHOST: Listen. (*Bell tolls twice.*) My time is up.
Another spirit comes. Farewell. (1ST GHOST *exits left.
Spotlight comes up right, revealing* GHOST OF CHRIST-
MAS PRESENT, *who wears simple green robe, a holly
wreath on his head, and carries a horn of plenty as a
torch.*)

2ND GHOST (*Cheerily, in a hearty voice*): Look upon me, and know me better, man! I am the Ghost of Christmas Present. Will you come forth with me, Ebenezer Scrooge?

SCROOGE (*Crossing to* 2ND GHOST *meekly*): Spirit, conduct me where you will. If you have anything to teach me, let me benefit by it.

2ND GHOST: Come then, let us visit Bob Cratchit's home. (2ND GHOST *gestures toward stage curtain with his torch; glitter falls from torch, and sound of tinkling bells is heard from offstage. Curtain opens, and* 2ND GHOST *and* SCROOGE *stand down right to watch the action.*)

* * * * *

SCENE 3

SETTING: *The kitchen of the Cratchit home. Setting is same as Scene 1, except that office window frame down left has been removed to make an exit. A fireplace is left. Center is large table covered with red-checked tablecloth, plates, glasses, etc. Chairs and stools for eight are placed around the table.*

AT RISE: MRS. CRATCHIT *and* BELINDA *are putting the finishing touches to the table, which is set for dinner.* PETER *is at the fireplace, blowing up the fire with bellows.*

MRS. CRATCHIT (*Looking at clock on mantel*): Whatever is keeping your dear father and Tiny Tim? And Martha wasn't as late as this last Christmas Day. (*Door flies open, and* NED *and* SALLY *rush in, followed by* MARTHA, *wearing bonnet and shawl.*)

SALLY: Mother, here's Martha!

NED: There's *such* a goose for dinner, Martha! Hurrah! (NED *and* SALLY *rush back out.*)

MRS. CRATCHIT (*Kissing* MARTHA): Bless your heart, Martha, how late you are!

MARTHA (*Hanging bonnet and shawl on clothes tree*): We had a lot of work to finish at the shop last night, Mother, and then we had to clean it this morning.

MRS. CRATCHIT: Sit down, my dear, and rest. (MARTHA *starts to sit in chair at table but stops as* NED *and* SALLY *run in from outside.*)

SALLY: Hide, Martha, hide!

NED: Father's coming with Tiny Tim! Let's surprise him!

SALLY: Hide in the pantry! (NED, SALLY *and* MARTHA *hurry out, down left.* BOB CRATCHIT *enters, galloping, with* TINY TIM *on his back, holding a crutch.*)

BOB: Clear the way for the fastest horse in London town!

TIM: Whoa there, whoa!

BOB (*Lowering* TIM *to floor and glancing about room*): Why, where's our Martha?

MRS. CRATCHIT: She's not coming, Bob. (PETER *and* BELINDA, *at fireplace, nudge each other and giggle.*)

BOB: Not coming — on Christmas Day! (*Disappointed*) It just won't be Christmas without Martha.

MARTHA (*Entering, running to* BOB, *and hugging him*): Here I am, Father! I was only hiding. We wanted to tease you. (*Hugging* TIM) Why, Tim! How is my little brother?

TIM: I threw a snowball as far as Peter — almost.

PETER: Come and smell our pudding, Tim. (PETER *and* BELINDA *exit down left with* TIM.)

MRS. CRATCHIT: How did Tim behave in church, Bob?

BOB (*Hanging hat and muffler on clothes tree*): As good as gold, and better. Coming home, he told me that he hoped all the people in church saw him, because he was a cripple. He thought it might help them to remember on Christmas Day who it was that made lame beggars walk and blind men see.

MRS. CRATCHIT: Bless his heart, he does think of the strangest things. (*Calling off left*) Children, come to dinner! (*Cratchit children race in,* PETER *carrying bowl of punch, which he sets at* BOB's *place, right end of table. There is much talking and moving of chairs as everyone gets into place around table.* BOB *ladles out punch into mugs and glasses.*)

BOB: I propose a toast. (*Raising his glass*) To Mr. Scrooge, the founder of the feast.

MRS. CRATCHIT (*Putting down her glass*): Founder of the feast, indeed! I wish I had him here! I'd give him a piece of my mind to feast upon, and I hope he'd have a good appetite for it!

BOB: My dear, the children! It's Christmas Day.

MRS. CRATCHIT: It should be Christmas Day, I'm sure, when one drinks the health of such an odious, stingy, hard, unfeeling man as Mr. Scrooge.

BOB (*Mildly*): My dear, Christmas Day.

MRS. CRATCHIT: I'll drink his health, Robert, for your sake and the day's, but not for his! (*Raising glass*) Long life to him! A Merry Christmas and a Happy New Year! He'll be very merry and very happy, I have no doubt!

BOB: A Merry Christmas to us all, my dears. God bless us!

TIM: God bless us, every one!

BOB (*Picking up carving knife*): And now — the goose! (*All cheer. Blackout. Curtain closes. Spotlight comes up on* SCROOGE *and* 2ND GHOST, *down right.*)

SCROOGE: Spirit, tell me — will Tiny Tim live?

2ND GHOST: I see a vacant chair in that poor room — a crutch without an owner, carefully preserved. If these shadows remain unaltered by the future, Tiny Tim will die.

SCROOGE: No, no! He must *not* die!

2ND GHOST: You can do nothing to change the past, nothing to alter the present. But there is still the future; perhaps in it lie your hope and salvation. I must leave you now. My life upon this globe is very brief. I go, but another spirit comes. (*Bell tolls three times.* 2ND GHOST *exits, right, as spotlight comes up on* GHOST OF CHRISTMAS YET TO COME, *wearing a black robe with a hood hiding his face, down left.* SCROOGE *crosses to him. Spotlight right stage fades out.*)

SCROOGE (*Awed, clasping his hands*): Am I in the presence of the Ghost of Christmas Yet to Come? (3RD GHOST *nods slowly.*) Ghost of the future, I fear you more than any other specter I have seen. But I know you intend to do me good, so I'll bear your company and do it with a thankful heart. Spirit, if you can see the future, show me what has happened to Tiny Tim. (*Live or recorded Christmas hymn is heard.* 3RD GHOST *points to right stage where spotlight comes up on Cratchits.* MRS. CRATCHIT *sits in armchair, hand to brow, weeping.* MARTHA *sits beside her on arm of chair.* PETER, *on stool, is reading from large book.* BELINDA *stands behind him, looking over his shoulder.* NED *and* SALLY *are seated on floor.*)

MARTHA (*Comforting her*): Don't cry, Mother. Our Tim is happy now. He won't ever need his crutch again.

PETER (*Closing book*): Father is late tonight. I think he walks a little slower than he used to.

MRS. CRATCHIT (*Wiping away tears*): I have known him to walk very fast indeed with Tiny Tim on his shoulder. But then, Tim was very light to carry, and his father loved him so, that it was no trouble — no trouble at all.

BELINDA: Here's Father now. (BOB *enters, giving hat to*

MARTHA. MRS. CRATCHIT *rises and motions for him to sit in armchair.*)

BOB: I have visited Tim's grave today. (*To* MRS. CRATCHIT) I wish you could have gone. It would have done you good to see how green a place it is. But you'll see it often. I promised Tim that we would walk there every Sunday. (BOB *speaks gently to children.*) Children, we mustn't grieve — Tim would not want it so. We shall be closer than ever before. When we remember how patient and mild Tim was, I know that we shall not quarrel among ourselves.

ALL (*Ad lib*): No, never, Father. (*Etc.*)

BOB: Then I am very happy — for him, and for us all. (*Spotlight fades out on Cratchits.*)

SCROOGE: Spirit, are these the shadows of things that will be, or is it possible to change the future? Why show me these things if I am past all hope? (3RD GHOST *turns away.*) Spirit, hear me! I am not the man I was. I will honor Christmas in my heart and try to keep it all the year. I will live in the past, the present, and the future. I will not shut out the lessons they teach. (SCROOGE *kneels and clutches* 3RD GHOST*'s robe.*) Oh, speak to me! Give me some hope. Tell me that I may still have time to change. Speak to me! Speak to me! (*Fast fade to blackout.*)

* * * * *

SCENE 4

TIME: *Christmas day.*

AT RISE: *Ringing of church bells is heard from offstage. SCROOGE is alone in his office, kneeling near his desk, violently shaking his stool.*

SCROOGE: Speak to me! Tell me it is not too late! (SCROOGE *looks about incredulously and slowly gets to his feet.*) Why, this is my stool! (*Sets it down*) And this is my office! How did I get here? Am I dreaming? (*Dancing a few steps*) I feel as light as a feather — as merry as a schoolboy! (*Hears bells ringing outside*) Church bells! What day is this? I must find out what day it is. (*Opens street door and calls out*) Hello, out there! Come in here a minute! Don't be afraid — come in! (BOY *enters hesitantly.*) What's today, my fine fellow?

BOY: Today? Why, it's Christmas Day!

SCROOGE: Christmas Day! (*Leaping into the air*) Hurrah! I haven't missed it after all! My fine fellow, do you know the grocer's down the street?

BOY: I should hope so.

SCROOGE (*Grabbing* BOY'*s hand and shaking it*): An intelligent, a remarkable boy! Do you know whether they've sold the prize turkey that was hanging in the window?

BOY: The one that's as big as I am? It's hanging there now.

SCROOGE: Then go and buy it. (BOY *looks incredulous.*) No, no, I'm serious. Here's the money. (*Gives* BOY *several coins from cash box, then scribbles on piece of paper*) Deliver it to this address in Camden Town. It will be too heavy to carry, so take a cab. And you're not to say where that turkey came from — not a word.

BOY: I won't, sir, thank you, sir. Merry Christmas! (*Runs out*)

SCROOGE (*Calling after him*): Merry Christmas! (*Rubbing his hands together gleefully*) Won't Bob Cratchit be surprised to get that turkey! It's twice the size of Tiny Tim. And he won't know who sent it. How surprised they'll be! (*Church bells peal again.*) Just listen to those bells! Makes me feel good just to hear them. (*Calls through open door*) Merry Christmas!

COLLECTOR (*Coming to door*): Are you speaking to me, sir?

SCROOGE: Of course I'm speaking to you. Come in, come in! (COLLECTOR *enters and* SCROOGE *shakes his hand vigorously.*) How are you? I hope you succeeded yesterday in collecting money for the poor. I'm afraid you don't remember me with much pleasure. Allow me to ask your pardon. (*Getting roll of bank notes from cash box and handing it to* COLLECTOR) Will you have the goodness to accept this?

COLLECTOR: Bless me! Are you serious, Mr. Scrooge?

SCROOGE: If you please, not a farthing less. A great many back payments are included in it, I assure you. Come and see me any time you need help. Will you do that?

COLLECTOR: I will indeed, sir.

SCROOGE: Thank you — thank you a hundred times. Bless you.

COLLECTOR: Bless *you*, Mr. Scrooge, and a very Merry Christmas. (COLLECTOR *exits.*)

SCROOGE (*Skipping to clothes tree*): Merry Christmas, Ebenezer, you old humbug! I'm going to have dinner with my nephew, Fred. He invited me, yes, he did! (*Sings "God Rest Ye Merry, Gentlemen" as he puts on muffler, coat and hat. Exits, singing and dancing. Curtain closes.*)

* * * * *

SCENE 5

TIME: *The next morning.*

SETTING: *Same as Scene 1.*

AT RISE: SCROOGE *is peeking out the half-open street door.*

SCROOGE (*Looking at his watch*): Eighteen and a half minutes past nine. (*Chuckling*) He's late! The day after

Christmas, and Bob Cratchit is late for work. Ah, here he comes now. (SCROOGE *closes door, scurries to desk and busies himself, writing.* BOB *enters hurriedly, whips off his hat, tossing it onto clothes tree, and starts across to his desk nervously.* SCROOGE *looks up, scowling.*) What do you mean by coming to work at this time of day, Bob Cratchit?

BOB: I'm very sorry, sir. I *am* behind my time. It won't happen again.

SCROOGE (*Rising with pretended exasperation*): Now, I'll tell you what, my man. I'm not going to stand this sort of thing any longer. And so (*Clapping* BOB *on the back and laughing*) — I am going to raise your salary! (BOB *staggers, gaping in astonishment.*) A merry Christmas, Bob! A merrier Christmas, my good fellow, than I have given you for many a year! I'll raise your salary and endeavor to assist your struggling family. Tiny Tim shall have the best doctors in London. (*Putting arm around* BOB*'s shoulder*) We'll discuss your affairs this very afternoon, over a Christmas bowl of mulled wine. And I promise you that from this day forth, I will be as good a friend, as good a master, and as good a man as this old city will ever know. May it always be said of me that if any man alive knew how to keep Christmas well, that man was Ebenezer Scrooge.

BOB: May that be truly said of all of us, Mr. Scrooge. (*Clasping his hand gratefully*) God bless you. As Tiny Tim always says, God bless us, every one! (*Live or recorded music of "Joy to the World" is heard from offstage. Curtain closes.*)

THE END

A Merry Christmas

From *Little Women by Louisa May Alcott*
Adapted for round-the-table classroom reading
by *Walter Hackett*

Meg, Jo, Beth, and Amy share a simple and loving Christmas in this dramatization from Little Women.

Characters

NARRATOR
JO
MEG
AMY
BETH
MRS. MARCH
HANNAH
MR. KIMBALL
BOY
WOMAN
MR. LAURENCE

NARRATOR: This is a Christmas story from a book that all the world knows and loves. It's about the lives of four young girls, and the name of it is *Little Women*. Our story begins on the day before Christmas in the year

1862. A heavy snow falls quietly, cloaking the little town of Concord, Massachusetts, with an extra layer of whiteness. Set back from the road to Lexington stands the March family house. In the comfortable old parlor are four young ladies. Sprawled on the floor, looking into the fireplace, is tomboy Jo.

JO (*In a complaining voice*): Christmas won't be Christmas without any presents.

NARRATOR: Meg, the eldest and prettiest, looks at her old dress.

MEG (*Sighing*): It's so dreadful to be poor!

NARRATOR: And Amy, the youngest, looks up from her knitting.

AMY: I don't think it's fair for some girls to have plenty of pretty things and other girls nothing at all.

NARRATOR: To this, Beth, the quiet one, adds her comment.

BETH: Never mind. We have Father and Mother and each other.

NARRATOR: The open fire crackles brightly. In the hallway, the old clock laboriously ticks away two minutes. Finally, Meg speaks.

MEG: The reason Mother suggested no presents this Christmas was because it's going to be a hard winter for everyone. She thinks we shouldn't spend money for pleasure when our men are suffering so in the army.

JO: We each have a dollar, and the army wouldn't be much helped by our giving that. I don't expect any presents, but there is a book I'd like so much. What would you like to spend yours on, Beth?

BETH: Some new music.

AMY: I would like a nice box of drawing pencils.

JO: Mother didn't say anything about our money, and I'm sure she doesn't wish us to give up everything.

AMY: What do you mean, Jo?

JO: I say, we should each buy what we want, and have a little fun. I'm sure we work hard enough to earn it.

MEG: I know I do — teaching those tiresome children nearly all day.

JO: You shouldn't complain, Meg. How would you like to be shut up for hours, reading to and waiting on a fussy old lady?

BETH: I hate washing dishes and housework. It makes me cross.

AMY: Suppose you had to go to school with impertinent girls, who laugh at your dresses and label your father if he isn't rich.

Jo (*Laughing*): If you mean "libel," say so, and don't talk about labels, as if Papa was a pickle bottle.

MEG: Don't peck at one another. We have enough worries.

JO: Christopher Columbus! We're only making fun of ourselves.

AMY: Jo, don't use such slang expressions. It's not lady-like.

JO: I hate to think I have to grow up and be Miss March and wear long gowns and a prim expression. If I were a boy, I could be in the army with Papa. Instead, I have to stay home and knit, like a poky old woman.

MEG: Jo, you're too wild, and, Amy, you're too prim.

BETH: And what am I, Meg?

MEG: You're a dear, Beth. (*Briskly*) Enough talk, now. Mother will be home in an hour. Amy, get her slippers. Jo, you light the lamp.

AMY: Marmee's slippers are quite worn. She should have a new pair.

BETH: Why don't I get her a pair with my dollar?

AMY: No, you shan't, Beth. I'm going to buy them.

JO: I'm the man of the family now Papa is away, and *I* shall provide the slippers.

AMY: And I shall give her — oh, dear, what will I give her?

JO: Why don't we each give her something she needs most? We'll put the gifts on the table and bring her in to see them tomorrow morning.

MEG: We've forgotten one thing.

AMY: What's that, Meg?

MEG: Tomorrow is Christmas and we haven't bought a thing.

AMY: But we've just made up our minds to buy presents for Marmee.

BETH: Oh, and now it's too late.

JO: Indeed, it's not! I have the solution. We'll put on our wraps, hurry to Mr. Kimball's store, buy our gifts, and hurry home before Marmee arrives. On your feet, everyone. Off we fly.

NARRATOR: The girls were quickly into their coats and out of the house, reaching Mr. Kimball's store just as he was closing for the day.

KIMBALL (*Heartily*): Well, well! What a surprise! The March girls! You just caught me in time. I was about to lock up.

JO: You can't until we've bought our gifts, Mr. Kimball.

BETH: We're in a dreadful hurry.

JO: I want to buy a pair of slippers for my mother.

BETH: And I want to get her two linen handkerchiefs.

AMY: I'd like a bottle of cologne — a specially elegant bottle.

MEG: And have you a warm pair of gloves, Mr. Kimball?

KIMBALL (*Laughing*): What if I told you I didn't have these articles?

AMY: Then we'd take our trade elsewhere.

KIMBALL: I can't allow that to happen, not in my store. Step right this way, young ladies.

NARRATOR: The girls quickly made their purchases, and were home before their mother returned. As the clock struck seven, the March family was just finishing their dinner.

HANNAH (*Speaking with a slight brogue*): Will you and the girls be wantin' anything else, Mrs. March?

MRS. MARCH: Thank you, no, Hannah. We've eaten all we should.

AMY: Besides, I'm sure there's nothing else left to eat.

JO: Here, here, enough of that. Hannah, as man of the house, I give you permission to clear the table.

HANNAH: I won't be needin' any permission for that, Miss Jo. It's a duty I have starin' me in the face every night.

MRS. MARCH: If you girls will follow me into the parlor, I have a surprise for you.

AMY (*Eagerly*): What is it, Marmee?

BETH: Is it something we'll like?

JO: Don't spoil it by asking questions.

MEG: Marmee, you sit here by the fire.

MRS. MARCH (*Sighing with relief*): Ah, thank you. Now, where were we?

AMY: Don't tease us.

MRS. MARCH: Here is your surprise.

JO: A letter.

MRS. MARCH: From your father.

JO: Hoorah!

MEG: Nothing wrong, I hope.

MRS. MARCH: He's quite well.

BETH: What does he say?

MRS. MARCH: I'll read you the part that he wrote especially for you girls.

MRS. MARCH: "As for my dear girls, give them all my love and a kiss. Tell them I think of them by day, pray for them by night, and find my best comfort in their affection at all times. A year seems very long to wait before I see them, but remind them that while we wait we may all work, so that these hard days need not be wasted. I know they will remember all I said to them; and I know they will conquer themselves so beautifully that, when I come back to them, I may be fonder and prouder than ever of my little women."

AMY: I *am* a selfish girl, but I'll try to be better.

MEG: We all will. I'm vain of my looks and hate to work hard, but won't any more, if I can help it.

MRS. MARCH: I'm sure you mean that, Meg.

BETH: Poor Papa! Spending Christmas all alone in an army camp.

JO: Never mind! Next Christmas he'll be here with us by the fire.

MRS. MARCH: Do you remember how you used to play Pilgrim's Progress when you were little girls?

MEG: Indeed we do.

JO: You used to tie bags on our backs for burdens and give us hats and sticks and rolls of paper.

MRS. MARCH: You'd travel through the house from the cellar —

BETH: The cellar was the City of Destruction.

MRS. MARCH: And up and up you'd go to the housetop to what you said was the Celestial City.

JO: What fun it was — especially passing through the Valley where the hobgoblins were.

AMY: I don't remember much about it, except that I was afraid of the cellar and the dark entry.

MEG: If I weren't too old for such things, I'd rather like to play it over again.

MRS. MARCH: We're never too old for this, Meg, because it's a game we are playing all the time in one way or another. The longing for goodness and happiness is the guide that leads us through many troubles and mistakes to the peace which is a true celestial city.

JO: You mean it's . . . life itself?

MRS. MARCH: Yes, Jo. So suppose you see how far you can go before your father comes home.

AMY: Where are our bundles?

MRS. MARCH: Each of you has her burden, except, maybe, Beth.

BETH: I have my burden to carry. Mine is dishes and dusters, and envying girls with nice pianos, and being afraid of people.

AMY: What a peculiar burden to carry. (*The others laugh good-naturedly.*)

MEG: Let's do it. It is only another name for trying to be good.

JO: We were in the slough of despair tonight, as it says in the book, and Mother came and pulled us out.

MEG: But like the pilgrims in the book, we'll need our roll of directions.

MRS. MARCH: Perhaps on Christmas morning you'll find your guide books. (*Quickly*) Now, don't ask any questions. It's going to be a quiet Christmas for us, what with no stockings hung from the mantel and no presents.

AMY (*Mysteriously*): Perhaps it won't be so quiet after all.

MRS. MARCH: What do you mean, Amy?

JO (*Quickly*): Nothing at all, Marmee.

MRS. MARCH: Hannah says the four of you went out just before I came home. I hope you haven't been up to any mischief.

MEG: No, Marmee. It was to perform an errand we'd almost forgotten.

MRS. MARCH: It may be a none-too-bright Christmas Eve for us, but at least we're warm and quite happy — happy enough to sing. Beth, do you feel like playing?

AMY: I'll sing soprano.

JO: No, you sing the alto part.

NARRATOR: And so, they all joined in the singing of Christmas carols until it was time to go to bed. Their Christmas Eve slumber was filled with pleasant dreams, and anticipation of the happiness and joy of Christmas.

JO (*Yawning deeply*): Ohhh! Sleepy. Still gray out. It's . . . it's . . . (*Sudden realization*) Why, it's Christmas morning! (*Excitedly*) Meg, wake up. Wake up!

MEG: Hm-m-m! Leave me 'lone.

JO: Merry Christmas, you sleepyhead.

MEG (*Suddenly waking up*): Oh! Merry Christmas, Jo. (*Pause*) Look what's under my pillow! A book!

JO: And there's one under mine.

MEG: Mine's a Bible.

JO: So is mine.

MEG: Look inside of yours. What does it say?

JO: "To Jo — Here is a true guide book for any pilgrim traveling the long journey. Love, Marmee."

MEG: Mine says the same thing.

JO: Marmee gave us a present after all.

MEG: And she has so little money.

AMY: Merry Christmas!

BETH: A very merry Christmas. (*All four ad lib Christmas greetings.*)

AMY: Did you two get Bibles? Beth and I did.

JO: Yes, we did.

MEG: Let's slip downstairs and see if Marmee is there. I'm anxious to see her face when she discovers what we've done.

NARRATOR: Meanwhile, downstairs, Mrs. March and Hannah are looking out at the new-fallen snow.

MRS. MARCH: This is a fine bright day out, Hannah. A real Christmas.

HANNAH: That it is, Mrs. March. Would you like to see what the girls gave me?

MRS. MARCH: A box of sweets! How thoughtful of them.

HANNAH: Indeed it was. (*Sniffing a bit*) I'm so happy I could have myself a good cry. (*Firmly*) But I won't. (*Pause*) Er, Mrs. March, have you looked on the mantel?

MRS. MARCH: No, Hannah.

HANNAH: Then do so at once.

NARRATOR: As Mrs. March goes to look at the mantel, there's a knock on the door.

HANNAH: Now who can that be on Christmas mornin'?

MRS. MARCH: I'll get it.

BOY: Merry Christmas, ma'am.

MRS. MARCH: Merry Christmas to you, little man.

HANNAH: It's one of the lads that lives on the edge of the pine grove.

BOY: My mother asked me to give you this note.

MRS. MARCH: Thank you. Won't you come in?

BOY: No, Mrs. March. I have to go right back home. Bye.

HANNAH: Is it anything bad, Mrs. March?

MRS. MARCH (*Disturbed*): Yes, it is. Poor things. (*Quickly*) Hannah, is the breakfast on?

HANNAH: I'm just about to cook it, Mrs. March.

MRS. MARCH: Well, don't.

HANNAH: What's that, ma'am?

MRS. MARCH: Get the big basket and load it with wood. Hurry, Hannah.

HANNAH: Just as you say, Mrs. March.

NARRATOR: Just then, the girls come running downstairs.

GIRLS (*Ad lib*): Merry Christmas, Marmee. (*Etc.*)

MRS. MARCH: And the same to you, my dears.

BETH: Thank you for our Bibles.

MEG: It was a wonderful surprise.

AMY: I'll always keep mine.

JO: Same with me. Brr! I'm starved. Are we having muffins?

AMY: And buckwheats with maple syrup?

MRS. MARCH: That depends upon all of you.

JO: On us?

MEG: What do you mean, Marmee?

MRS. MARCH: A note was just delivered to me. It's from that poor widow who lives down the road, the one with the six children.

BETH: Her husband was killed in the war, wasn't he?

MRS. MARCH: The same one. They have no wood to burn and nothing to eat. Will you give them your breakfast as a Christmas present?

JO: Christopher Columbus! It won't hurt us to do without breakfast for once in our lives.

MEG: Of course we will.

AMY: May we go with you?

BETH: We can help you carry things.

MRS. MARCH: I knew you wouldn't refuse. We'll make it up at dinner time. After we come back we'll have bread and milk for breakfast, and that'll tide us over.

NARRATOR: They filled a basket with food and firewood for the widow and her family, and set out for their house.

MEG: This is the house, isn't it, Marmee?

MRS. MARCH: Yes, Meg.

JO: Not a bit of smoke from the chimney, and it's so bitter cold out.

BETH: And to think last night we were complaining.

NARRATOR: Mrs. March had to knock several times before the door was opened, and the widow greeted her Christmas morning visitors.

MARCHES (*Together*): Merry Christmas!

MRS. MARCH: We hurried as fast as possible. May we come in?

WOMAN: Do good angels ever need an invitation?

JO: We certainly are peculiar looking angels — dressed in hoods and mittens.

WOMAN: And welcome just the same.

NARRATOR: Mrs. March cooked a fine Christmas breakfast for the poor family, and the girls helped serve them. How thankful the widow and her children were! The March family returned home, tired but filled with the spirit of Christmas.

MRS. MARCH (*Heartily*): Well, that could have been a far worse breakfast.

JO: Bread and milk for breakfast is good enough for anyone.

BETH: Marmee —

MRS. MARCH: Yes, Beth?

BETH: Did you ever see such expressions as those poor children had when you served them those buckwheats and syrup?

MRS. MARCH: The poor dears. I doubt if they've ever had such a fine breakfast.

AMY: How they ate those muffins!

JO: It's just as well you didn't have any, Amy. You're getting too fat.

AMY: I am not.

MRS. MARCH: Jo, I thought you were carrying a burden.

JO: I am, Marmee. Amy, I apologize.

MRS. MARCH: I'm trying to think. It seems to me that just as that boy delivered me the note, Hannah asked me to do something. Now, what was it she said? Something about the mantel . . . looking on the . . . the . . .

JO (*Teasing her*): The floor.

MRS. MARCH: No. On the —

BETH: Ceiling?

MRS. MARCH: Ah, I remember. She said for me to look on the mantel. Why, I don't know. (*Gasp of surprise*) Now, what is this? Four packages!

JO: Don't stare at us. Santa Claus must have left them.

MEG: What could they be? Open them, Marmee!

MRS. MARCH: Now, what have we here? (*Pause*) A pair of gloves! Such warm ones, too. Thank you, Meg.

MEG: I hope they fit.

MRS. MARCH: I'll try them on. (*Pause*) They fit perfectly. And what is this? (*Pause*) Two lovely linen handkerchiefs, which I need so badly. How thoughtful of you, Beth.

BETH: I hemmed them last night.

MRS. MARCH: This one looks like a — now, what can it be?

AMY (*Blurting it out*): It's a bottle of real cologne.

MEG: Amy, you spoiled the surprise.

MRS. MARCH: Not really. Thank you, Amy. I'll wear some on Beth's handkerchiefs. (*Pause*) And this last one. Slippers! Aren't they wonderful, Jo!

JO: Try them on.

MRS. MARCH (*After a pause*): They're a bit large, Jo.

JO: Jingo! I'll say they are. You can wear them right over your shoes. I'll change them for you, Marmee.

MRS. MARCH: The sentiment is there, just the same. I think I'm a very lucky mother. I have my family around me. Yesterday I had a letter from your father. This morning we helped our neighbor, and ahead of us —

Jo: Ahead of us is practically the whole day.

MRS. MARCH: For our Christmas dinner we have a pair of fine, plump chickens.

Jo: And tonight . . . tonight. Meg, you announce the news to Mother.

MEG: Tonight will be the first performance of a new play —

Jo: In four acts.

MEG: Titled "The Operatic Tragedy," written by Miss Josephine March. (*Others applaud.*)

Jo: Thank you.

MRS. MARCH: Have you written another play, Jo?

Jo (*With mock seriousness*): My greatest effort to date. I shall now do part of a scene for you.

AMY: Oh, no. You'll spoil it.

MRS. MARCH: Go on, Jo.

Jo: This occurs in the second act.

BETH: The third act.

Jo: No, the second. I've changed it. The heroine — that's Amy — is being kidnapped by the villain. She screams (*Dramatically*), "Roderigo! Save me! Save me!" (*She screams.*)

HANNAH: Who screamed? What's the matter?

Jo (*Feigning fierceness*): You, Zara, you are a knave. (*The others start to giggle.*)

HANNAH: Now, what's the matter, Miss Jo?

Jo: You are a knave. Stand or I shall shoot you. Ah, now I have you, you rogue. Now you shall perish.

HANNAH: I haven't done a thing wrong.

Jo: But you have. You are wicked, bad, ill-fated. I arrest you in the name of the law. (*All laugh*)

HANNAH: The excitement of Christmas Day has gone to your head, Miss Jo. I'm going back to my quiet kitchen.

NARRATOR: Hannah backed hastily into the kitchen, and soon after there was a loud crash.

HANNAH: See what you've done now, you and your foolish theatrics, Miss Jo. I've just crashed into the second-best set of chinaware.

NARRATOR: The kitchen mishap was soon forgotten, and the March family enjoyed a wonderful Christmas dinner together. After dinner, the girls performed Jo's play, much to the enjoyment of their mother and Hannah.

JO (*In deep voice*): And so, my children, I give you my blessing. May your lives be happy from this point onward. I clasp your hands.

MEG: We owe our lives to you, Don Pedro.

JO: And so the curtain falls, signifying the end of the play. (MRS. MARCH *and* HANNAH *applaud.*)

MRS. MARCH: A very fine performance. Well-written, well-acted.

HANNAH: Indeed, I enjoyed every minute of it.

MRS. MARCH: Some day, Jo, you'll be a famous writer. Now, Hannah, do you suppose these hungry performers could be rewarded?

JO: I should like something exotic.

AMY: No, let's have something to eat.

MEG: I'm ashamed to say so, but I'm hungry.

BETH: But we did have such a lovely dinner.

JO: There must be some old chicken bones we can gnaw on.

NARRATOR: All of a sudden, there was an insistent rapping on the door.

HANNAH: I'll answer it, ma'am.

MR. LAURENCE (*Sharply*): Well, woman, open the door wide enough so I can get in. Thank you.

MRS. MARCH (*Surprised*): Good evening, Mr. Laurence. Merry Christmas.

MR. LAURENCE: Same to you. What about your girls? Haven't they any tongues? Can't they wish me a Merry Christmas, too?

GIRLS (*Together*): Merry Christmas, Mr. Laurence.

MR. LAURENCE: You, woman, what's your name?

HANNAH: Hannah, sir.

MR. LAURENCE: Well, take these bundles. Put them on the table.

MRS. MARCH: Aren't you making a mistake, Mr. Laurence? We aren't expecting anything.

MR. LAURENCE: I suppose not, but here they are. Hannah, here, told my cook about your breakfast party.

MRS. MARCH: Breakfast party?

MR. LAURENCE: Don't deny it. I heard all about how you gave your breakfast away to that poor family down the road. I thought I should do something to make it up, and I have. Well, good night, and Merry Christmas.

JO: He's a regular nor'wester, I'd say.

MEG: Marmee, what do you suppose is in those packages?

MRS. MARCH: I don't know.

AMY: Mr. Laurence has never before been in our house.

BETH: He's awfully proud, and he hardly ever speaks to anyone.

JO: Well, we may as well open them.

MRS. MARCH: I suppose we may.

NARRATOR: They excitedly opened the many packages their surprise visitor had brought, and were delighted by the contents.

MEG: Ice cream!

AMY: Two kinds — pink and white.

MRS. MARCH: Real French bonbons. And cake.

BETH: Fruit — so many kinds!

JO: What's in this other long package? (*Pause*)

GIRLS (*Gasping; ad lib*): Flowers. Hothouse roses. Beautiful. Such long stems. (*Etc.*)

JO: Christopher Columbus! And we always thought old Mr. Laurence was so proud.

MRS. MARCH: He's an odd old gentleman. He knew my father years ago.

MEG: He won't let his grandson mix with anyone.

JO: From now on we'll see that his grandson gets to know us; and old Mr. Laurence, too, for that matter.

MRS. MARCH: It shows you can't judge people by their exteriors. Tomorrow we'll write a note of thanks to Mr. Laurence, and all sign it.

JO: Hear, hear!

AMY: I'll deliver it.

MEG: Well, we'd better start before the ice cream melts.

AMY: I just want pink.

BETH: I'll eat either kind.

MRS. MARCH: Hannah, get some plates and spoons.

HANNAH: Right away, Mrs. March.

MRS. MARCH: And, Hannah —

HANNAH: Yes, ma'am.

MRS. MARCH: Bring a spoon and plate for yourself.

HANNAH: That I will, thank you.

JO (*Calling*): And get some vases for these flowers. Christopher Columbus! Hasn't this been the best Christmas anyone could ask for? Well, hasn't it?

ALL (*Ad lib*): The very best. Wonderful. We're very lucky. (*Etc.*)

NARRATOR: It was a fitting end to a perfect Christmas Day. Tired from their various holiday activities, the four happy girls went off to bed.

MRS. MARCH: Well, I'll go and see if my girls are tucked in, Hannah. It has been a busy day for you, hasn't it?

HANNAH: A busy day for all of us, ma'am.

MRS. MARCH: But a fine day, Hannah.

HANNAH: Just about the best day we could have wished for.

MRS. MARCH: We helped our neighbor and our neighbor helped us. (*Pause*) Yes, the spirit of Christmas has lived here all day, and I hope it will for many years to come. (*Warmly*) Merry Christmas!

MEG, JO, BETH, AMY (*Calling, as if from a distance*): Merry Christmas!

THE END

The Christmas Nutcracker

Based on a story by E.T.A. Hoffman
Adapted by *Adele Thane*

A toy comes to life, in this exciting adaptation of a story that has become a Christmas classic . . . .

Characters

MARCHEN, *10*
FRITZ, *her brother, 12*
JUDGE SILBERHAUS
FRAU SILBERHAUS
DOCTOR DROSSELMEYER
LORD CHANCELLOR
ROYAL ASTROLOGER
ROYAL MATHEMATICIAN
KING PUDGY PODGY
KITCHEN MAID
PRINCESS PIRLIPAT
THE MOUSE KING
NICHOLAS NUTCRACKER
CLOCK, *offstage voice*

TIME: *Christmas Eve.*
BEFORE RISE: MARCHEN *and* FRITZ *enter at the back of*

auditorium, carrying a Christmas garland between them. As they march down the aisle and onto stage, they sing a carol to the tune of the "Miniature Overture" of Tchaikovsky's "Nutcracker Suite." NOTE: *Other selections from this work (live or recorded) may be played throughout the play if desired.*

MARCHEN *and* FRITZ (*Singing*):

Bells in the steeples ring
The merry Christmas music;
"Joy to the world!" they say,
"We ring of joy on Christmas day."

Children around the tree
Sing merry Christmas music;
"Joy to the world!" they say,
"We sing of joy on Christmas day."

(*When* MARCHEN *and* FRITZ *reach the stage,* FRITZ *goes to the opening in the curtain and peeks through.*)

MARCHEN: Fritz Silberhaus! You come away from there this minute! You know Papa told us we weren't to go *near* the drawing room till everything was ready.

FRITZ: I just want to see if Doctor Drosselmeyer has come. He always brings such fine Christmas presents. (MARCHEN *takes* FRITZ's *arm and leads him away from curtain.*)

MARCHEN: I'm sure he has. What do you suppose he brought?

FRITZ: I hope he brought me a big castle with soldiers in red coats. We'll have some battles. (*He pantomimes firing a musket at* MARCHEN.) Bang! Bang!

MARCHEN (*Backing away*): I don't like battles. (*As he persists in firing on her*) Stop, Fritz! (*He stops.*) I should like a garden with rose arbors and a lake with silver swans wearing gold collars. I would feed them chocolates.

FRITZ (*Scornfully*): Swans don't eat chocolates.

MARCHEN: Well, whatever Doctor Drosselmeyer brings, it will be very beautiful. (FRITZ *edges his way to curtain again and quickly peeks through center opening.*)

FRITZ (*Excitedly*): Look, Marchen! The Christmas tree — it's all lit up!

MARCHEN (*Going to him hastily*): Fritz! Stop peeking! (*She tugs at his arm.*)

FRITZ (*Trying to shake her off*): There's nothing wrong with it!

MARCHEN: Papa said we shouldn't!

FRITZ: Let go! (*They are jostling one another when all at once* FRITZ *jumps away from the curtain.*) Here comes Papa! (FRITZ *runs to right and stands there, pretending to be innocent.* MARCHEN *takes a quick step to the left when* JUDGE SILBERHAUS *pokes his head through the curtain.*)

JUDGE (*In a threatening voice*): Who's there? Master Fritz?

FRITZ (*Innocently*): Yes, sir? (JUDGE *sees* FRITZ.)

JUDGE: Never mind, lad. (JUDGE *sees* MARCHEN, *who is standing left of the opening, nervously twisting the garland in her hands.*) So it was you, was it? Marchen, I'm surprised at you. Now go over there (*Points left*) and wait patiently, like Fritz. (*He withdraws.*)

MARCHEN (*Running over to* FRITZ): You mean thing, Fritz, letting me take all the blame!

FRITZ (*Taunting her*): Poor Marchen! (*He snatches the garland and starts to use it as a jump rope.*)

MARCHEN (*Stamping her foot*): Don't, Fritz, you'll break it! Give it to me!

FRITZ (*Tossing the garland to her*): Here you are!

MARCHEN (*Relenting*): Oh, Fritz, we mustn't quarrel on Christmas Eve.

FRITZ: You're right, Marchen. Let's call a truce. (*They shake hands. Sound of music box playing behind curtain attracts their attention.*)

MARCHEN: Listen, Fritz! What a lovely tune. (*Curtain opens.*)

* * * * *

SETTING: *The drawing room of Judge Silberhaus' home in an old German village. A large Christmas tree, lighted and decorated with tinsel, candy canes, and nuts in small paper baskets, is at right. A doll, toy soldiers and other wrapped gifts are under it, as well as a nutcracker in the shape of a man, with movable jaws. A fireplace is at left, with an armchair near the hearth. In the back wall is an alcove with a grandfather clock in it.*

AT RISE: JUDGE *and* FRAU SILBERHAUS *stand together at center, and* DOCTOR DROSSELMEYER *sits in armchair. He wears glasses and has gray beard and powdered hair.* JUDGE *holds Swiss music box, which continues to play.*)

FRAU SILBERHAUS: Merry Christmas, children! (MARCHEN *and* FRITZ *run to the Christmas tree.* MARCHEN *thrusts the garland into* FRAU SILBERHAUS*'s hands as she rushes by her.*)

MARCHEN (*Picking up doll*): A new doll! How beautiful she is!

FRITZ (*Examining soldiers under tree*): Soldiers in bright red coats! Just what I wanted!

FRAU SILBERHAUS (*Crossing to hang the garland over fireplace mantel*): Children, you haven't said Merry Christmas to your godfather.

FRITZ (*As he sets up his soldiers in a line*): Merry Christmas, Godfather.

MARCHEN (*As she goes to* DROSSELMEYER, *who rises to greet her*): Merry Christmas, Godfather Drosselmeyer.

DROSSELMEYER: Merry Christmas, my dear.

FRAU SILBERHAUS (*As she finishes hanging up garland*): I'll go see if the other guests have arrived. (*Exits*)

MARCHEN (*Pointing to nutcracker*): What is that standing under the tree?

DROSSELMEYER: That is a nutcracker. (*Crosses to tree. He walks slowly and is slightly bent over.*)

MARCHEN (*Following him*): A nutcracker?

DROSSELMEYER (*Picking up nutcracker*): Yes. Just watch. (*He takes walnut from tree.*) You put a nut in his mouth like this, and then — (*He snaps nutcracker's jaws together and pretends to crack the nut.*) Crack! The strong jaws of the nutcracker will break the nut open.

MARCHEN: May I have him?

DROSSELMEYER: Well, I gave him to the whole family, but since he pleases you so much, I shall place him in your care.

MARCHEN (*Taking the nutcracker*): Oh, thank you! Fritz, see my nutcracker!

FRITZ: What a funny-looking man! I want to crack a nut. Give him to me. Let's see if he can crack this one! (*Takes large nut from tree*)

MARCHEN (*Handing over the nutcracker with reluctance*): Do be careful or you'll break his teeth. (FRITZ *places nut in nutcracker's mouth and cracks it with great force. He holds nutcracker out and looks at it.*)

FRITZ: Oops! This nutcracker has broken. The nut must have been too big for it. I didn't mean to break it.

MARCHEN: Give him back this instant! (FRITZ *does so and* MARCHEN *rocks the nutcracker in her arms.*) Oh, my poor nutcracker! You've broken his jaw!

FRITZ: He's not a good nutcracker anyway. His jaws are too fragile to crack nuts.

MARCHEN: Go away! You're so mean, Fritz!

JUDGE: Now, children, let's not have any squabbling on Christmas Eve.

FRAU SILBERHAUS (*Entering up left*): Come, everyone. It's time for dinner.

FRITZ: Hurrah! I'm starved! (*He races out up left.*)

JUDGE (*Severely, calling after him*): Master Fritz! Where are your manners? (*He follows* FRITZ *off, shaking his head disapprovingly.*)

FRAU SILBERHAUS: Doctor — Marchen — are you coming?

MARCHEN: In a minute, Mama. I want to put a bandage on nutcracker's jaw. (*She sits in armchair.*)

FRAU SILBERHAUS: Very well, dear, but don't be long. (FRAU *exits.*)

MARCHEN (*Detaining* DROSSELMEYER): Wait for me, Godfather. (*She speaks to nutcracker.*) Poor little nutcracker! Does your jaw hurt dreadfully? (*Takes handkerchief from pocket*) I'll tie it up with my handkerchief. (*She proceeds to do so.*)

DROSSELMEYER: I'll tell you a story about nutcracker after dinner.

MARCHEN: Oh, couldn't you begin the story now and finish it after dinner?

DROSSELMEYER: We mustn't keep your family waiting.

MARCHEN: Just a *little* beginning — *please?*

DROSSELMEYER: I have a better idea. I'll tell the story while we're eating dinner. I should like the others to hear about nutcracker, too — especially Fritz. Then, perhaps, he will think more kindly of nutcracker.

MARCHEN: Yes, yes! — but begin *now!* (MARCHEN *rises from chair and* DROSSELMEYER *puts his arm around her. They walk slowly toward the alcove. There is a general dimming of lights, except on the grandfather clock.*)

DROSSELMEYER: Many years ago, when I was a young man, there lived a king named Pudgy Podgy. (MAR-CHEN *giggles.*) In the king's throne room there was a wonderful clock that never had to be wound and didn't strike the hours of the day. (*They stop before the grandfather clock in the alcove.*)

MARCHEN: How did people know what time it was?

DROSSELMEYER: They knew, all right. You see, I invented that clock and gave it to the king. It *spoke* out the hours and the day and the month. No one had to count the time at all. They just listened.

VOICE OF THE CLOCK (*Offstage*): Three o'clock in the afternoon on the first day of April. Three o'clock in the afternoon on the first day of April. (DROSSELMEYER *and* MARCHEN *listen to the clock, then exit. After a brief pause, the lights come up full as the* LORD CHAN-CELLOR *enters hurriedly down right, in long billowy wig and robe.*)

CHANCELLOR (*Speaking over his shoulder*): Come, come, Royal Astrologer! The king wants to see us. (ROYAL ASTROLOGER *enters down right, wearing long robe and very large pointed hat with suns, moons and stars on it, and holding telescope up to eye.*)

ASTROLOGER: Here I am.

CHANCELLOR: Put down that telescope! There are no stars now. It's only three o'clock in the afternoon. We must get the Royal Mathematician and go to the king. (*He starts to cross left.*)

ASTROLOGER (*Following him*): How is the king today?

CHANCELLOR: Happy as a lark.

ASTROLOGER: What does a happy lark look like?

CHANCELLOR (*Impatiently*): Will you stop babbling?

(LORD CHANCELLOR *pulls the* ASTROLOGER*'s hat down over his head.* ASTROLOGER *continues to chatter, bobbing his head up and down, but only a mumble can be heard.* CHANCELLOR *calls off down left.*) Mathematician! The king wishes to see you. (ROYAL MATHEMATICIAN, *wearing robe with numbers and equations on it, hurries on with his notebook and pencil.*)

MATHEMATICIAN (*Eagerly*): Does he want me to add some figures?

CHANCELLOR: No, I don't think he wants you to add up anything.

MATHEMATICIAN: Oh, dear! How *is* King Podgy today? Stodgy?

CHANCELLOR: No, he's as happy as a lark. (KING PUDGY PODGY *is heard singing a merry tune off right, and he enters dancing a little jig. He wears royal robes, stuffed with a pillow to make him plump, and a crown. His cheeks are painted red.*)

CHANCELLOR, MATHEMATICIAN *and* ASTROLOGER (*Ad lib*): King Pudgy Podgy! You're so happy today! It's nice to see you laughing. (*Etc.*)

KING (*Reciting and dancing*):
> The happiest king in all the world
> Is good King Pudgy Podgy,
> Who used to be so very glum
> And, oh! so very stodgy.
> But now he has declared it treason
> To be sad for any reason,
> And it's sadly out of season
> To be sad. So be glad! Oh, be glad, oh!

(*With a flourish*) I'm as happy as a lark!

ASTROLOGER: How happy is a lark is a lark is a lark — (CHANCELLOR *quickly pulls* ASTROLOGER*'s hat down over his head, and the* ASTROLOGER *continues to mumble "is a lark is a lark" inside.*)

MATHEMATICIAN: Shall I add some figures for you, Your Majesty?

KING: No! Where's the Royal Astrologer?

MATHEMATICIAN (*Pointing to him*): Talking through his hat, Your Majesty.

KING: Unhat him! I want to ask him a question. (MATHEMATICIAN *lifts* ASTROLOGER*'s hat off his face.*) Astrologer, did you or did you not say that the stars would be favorable for sausage making today?

ASTROLOGER: I did, Your Majesty.

KING (*Exuberantly*): Then I shall eat sausage after sausage after sausage in honor of the Princess Pirlipat's twelfth birthday. (*He tosses his crown into the air.*) To fair Pirlipat!

CHANCELLOR, MATHEMATICIAN, *and* ASTROLOGER (*Together*): Fair Pirlipat! (CHANCELLOR *tosses his slipper into the air,* MATHEMATICIAN *his notebook, and* ASTROLOGER *his hat.*)

KING (*Proudly*): Did you know that she was born with a perfect set of teeth, and could crack nuts with them at the age of one month?

CHANCELLOR: I know, sire. When I went to the christening, the Princess bit me. (KITCHEN MAID *enters up left, out of breath.*)

MAID (*Wailing*): Oh, Your Majesty!

KING (*Annoyed*): Yes, what is it?

MAID: I don't know how to tell you.

CHANCELLOR: Speak up!

MAID: It happened just after the sizzling aroma of sausage had spread through the palace. You were aware of it, sire?

KING: Yes, yes! Hurry up! I'm getting hungrier by the moment.

MAID (*Speaking rapidly*): A great army of mice invaded the kitchen. We all had to fight them off.

KING: Heavens! What a narrow squeak! I was afraid the sausages had been eaten up.

MAID (*Wringing her hands*): They have been, Your Majesty.

KING (*In panic*): All of them?

MAID (*Nodding*): Not a grease spot left.

KING: Oh-h-h! (*He moans, staggers, and faints in the arms of* ASTROLOGER.)

CHANCELLOR (*Complaining to* MAID): Now you've done it! He was trying so hard to be happy. (CHANCELLOR *and* MATHEMATICIAN *take* KING *to the armchair.* PRINCESS PIRLIPAT *enters up right.*)

MAID (*Curtsying*): Goodness! The Princess Pirlipat! (*She scurries out up left.*)

PRINCESS (*Alarmed*): What has happened to Papa?

CHANCELLOR: He has had a sudden shock, Your Highness.

PRINCESS: Has he heard about the sausage?

KING (*Suddenly coming to; in a rage*): Heard about it! (*He stands up.*) *Heard* about it! Oh-h! Send for Doctor Drosselmeyer! *He* will know what to do!

PRINCESS: Doctor Drosselmeyer is already here.

KING (*Amazed*): He is? My, that was quick!

PRINCESS: He came to court to bring me a birthday present.

KING: Fetch him! Fetch him!

PRINCESS: Yes, Papa. (*She goes up right and beckons off.*) Doctor Drosselmeyer! (DROSSELMEYER *enters. He no longer has beard and his hair is dark. He walks with a sprightly step.*)

DROSSELMEYER (*Bowing*): What is your pleasure, sire?

KING: Pleasure! I have no pleasure. My sausages have been eaten up.

DROSSELMEYER: I know, Your Majesty. I was in the kitchen when it happened.

KING: You were? Why didn't you do something about it?

DROSSELMEYER: I did, sire. I set my special traps and caught all the mice — except one.

KING: Which one?

DROSSELMEYER: The Mouse King. He alone saw through my scheme.

KING: Bah! What of that? One mouse can do no harm.

DROSSELMEYER (*Shaking his head gravely*): I don't know. I have a feeling that all is not well.

KING: But *I* am well! I'm as happy as a lark! Come, come, Doctor, it's a holiday! Nothing can possibly go wrong. (*Blackout. Thunder and lightning.* MOUSE KING *suddenly appears, wearing a tiny gold crown. A green spotlight shines on him.*)

ALL (*Crying out together*): The Mouse King!

MOUSE KING (*In a loud, shrill voice*):
   Pudgy Podgy, you are due for a fall!
   You've killed my subjects, killed them all!
   I'll have my revenge, and it won't be small!
   Pudgy Podgy, you are due for a fall!

(*Thunder and lightning. Blackout.* PRINCESS *screams, then faints.* MOUSE KING *exits. Lights come up full.*)

KING (*Turning in circles*): Where did he go? Where is he?

DROSSELMEYER (*Kneeling beside* PRINCESS): Your Majesty, the Princess Pirlipat —

KING (*Desperately*): Is she dead?

DROSSELMEYER: No — worse than that!

KING: *Worse?*

DROSSELMEYER: The Mouse King has bitten her. Look! (*He lifts the* PRINCESS' *head. She wears a grotesque mask, similar to the face of the nutcracker, which she has slipped over her face during the blackout.*)

KING: Pirlipat! Why do you look like this?

DROSSELMEYER: It is the revenge of the Mouse King. He has put her under a spell.

KING (*To* CHANCELLOR *and* MATHEMATICIAN): Take her to her room. Oh, my beautiful daughter! (CHANCELLOR *and* MATHEMATICIAN *lift the* PRINCESS *and carry her off up right.* KING *turns furiously to* DROSSELMEYER.) It's all your fault! If you don't restore the Princess to her former beauty, I shall order your execution! (ASTROLO-GER *has been peering through his telescope.*)

ASTROLOGER (*To* KING): Sire, I believe I know the quickest way to restore the Princess's beauty. It is written in the stars.

KING: What do the stars say?

ASTROLOGER: There is a certain nut called the Krakatu.

KING: Krakatu?

DROSSELMEYER: Yes, I have heard of it.

ASTROLOGER: The shell is so hard that even a cannon can pass over it without breaking it. The stars reveal that this nut must be cracked in the presence of the Princess by a young man who has never shaved and always wears boots.

KING: Yes, yes, go on!

ASTROLOGER: This young man must present the nut to the Princess with his eyes closed, and with his eyes still closed, take seven steps backward without stumbling. Such is the prophecy of the stars.

KING (*To* DROSSELMEYER): Doctor, you must find this Krakatu nut and the young man, and bring them both to the palace.

DROSSELMEYER: But what if I should fail?

KING (*Drawing himself up to his full height*): You must not fail! (*Blackout. Thunder and lightning.* MOUSE KING *appears again in the green spotlight.*)

MOUSE KING:

> You may search throughout the land,
> The Krakatu is not at hand!

KING (*To* DROSSELMEYER): Be off, Doctor, before the Mouse King defeats us again! (DROSSELMEYER *hurries out up right.*)

MOUSE KING:
He may search throughout the land,
The Krakatu is not at hand.
(*Thunder and lightning. Blackout. There is a brief pause, during which music from "The Nutcracker Suite" may be played. As the music fades, a spotlight comes up on the grandfather clock.*)

VOICE OF THE CLOCK (*Offstage*): Three o'clock in the afternoon on the twenty-fourth day of December. Three o'clock in the afternoon on the twenty-fourth day of December. (*Lights come up full, revealing* ASTROLOGER *standing right, peering through his telescope. At left,* MATHEMATICIAN *is busily adding up figures in his notebook.* KING *enters up left and goes to* ASTROLOGER.)

KING: You don't see Doctor Drosselmeyer up there anywhere, do you?

ASTROLOGER: No.

KING: Oh, dear!

MATHEMATICIAN (*Coming over*): How does the Princess look today, your Majesty?

KING: Uglier than ever. She does nothing but crack nuts with her teeth.

MATHEMATICIAN: Sh-h-h! Here she comes.

KING (*Turning away*): I can't look at her.

MATHEMATICIAN: Neither can I. (*He turns away.*)

ASTROLOGER: Neither can I. (*He pulls his hat down over his face.* PRINCESS *comes in, eating a nut.*)

KING (*Without looking at her*): Sit down, my dear. (*She sits in armchair, puts nut in her mouth and pretends to crack and eat it.* KING *watches, shakes head.*) Dear me. I don't think I'll eat any sausages for supper tonight. My appetite is ruined.

CHANCELLOR (*Running in up right*): Your Majesty, Doctor Drosselmeyer is back!

KING: No!

DROSSELMEYER (*Entering*): Yes!

KING (*Embracing* DROSSELMEYER): Returned at last! (*He turns to* PRINCESS.) My sweet daughter, Doctor Drosselmeyer has come back with a cure for you. (PRINCESS *responds by cracking another nut and eating it.* KING *holds out his hand to* DROSSELMEYER.) Give it to me.

DROSSELMEYER: Give you what, your Majesty?

KING (*Impatiently*): The Krakatu nut. Didn't you find it?

DROSSELMEYER: Yes, sir, I found it.

KING: What about the young man?

DROSSELMEYER: He is without.

KING (*Alarmed*): Without boots?

DROSSELMEYER: No, Your Majesty — he *waits* without.

KING: Have him brought in at once.

CHANCELLOR (*To* MATHEMATICIAN): Bring the young man in. (MATHEMATICIAN *exits up right.*)

KING: Where did you find the nut?

DROSSELMEYER: I searched everywhere — in the mountains, in the forest, by the ocean. I finally found it in a jungle in the tropics. (MATHEMATICIAN *ushers in* NICHOLAS NUTCRACKER, *a boy of twelve or thirteen wearing shiny boots and a sword.*) This is the young man, your Majesty — Nicholas Nutcracker.

KING (*Looking* NICHOLAS *up and down*): Hm-m. Does he fit all the qualifications?

NICHOLAS: I do, Your Majesty. I have never shaved and I always wear boots.

KING: Even in bed?

NICHOLAS (*Nodding*): Even in bed.

KING: Remarkable! Anything else?

NICHOLAS: I have good strong teeth. I can crack the hardest nuts.

KING: Nicholas Nutcracker, I promise you a chest of gold if you succeed in making my daughter beautiful again. (*To* DROSSELMEYER) Where is the Krakatu nut?

DROSSELMEYER (*Taking nut from pocket and giving it to* NICHOLAS): Right here, Your Majesty.

KING: Begin, then — begin! (NICHOLAS *puts Krakatu nut in his mouth, places one hand on top of his head, the other on his chin, and pushes slowly. The others, except* PRINCESS, *do this with him in pantomime. There is a loud cracking noise.*) He has cracked it!

DROSSELMEYER: Now, Nicholas, close your eyes and give the nut to the Princess.

NICHOLAS (*Closing his eyes*): Your Highness. (*He holds out the nut to* PRINCESS *with a bow.* PRINCESS *takes it, puts in her mouth, eats it slowly. The others imitate her.*)

DROSSELMEYER: She has eaten the Krakatu nut. (*Blackout. Thunder and lightning.*)

ALL (*Ad lib*): Oh, no! What's happening? (*Etc. After a moment, the lights come up.* PRINCESS PIRLIPAT *is still in chair, but mask has been removed.*)

KING (*Overjoyed, leaping about*): She's beautiful again! The spell of the Mouse King is broken! Nicholas, my boy! (*He rushes to* NICHOLAS, *who has not moved.*)

DROSSELMEYER (*Grabbing* KING): Wait a minute, Your Majesty! There's more to be done. Nicholas must walk backward seven steps.

KING: Of course! Seven careful steps, my boy.

CHANCELLOR: Don't stumble.

MATHEMATICIAN: Don't trip.

ASTROLOGER: Seven steps, Nicholas. (NICHOLAS *starts walking backward. All count, raising their voices on each successive step.*)

ALL (*Together*): One. Two. Three. Four. (NICHOLAS *starts to sway.*)

DROSSELMEYER: Easy, Nicholas.

KING: No one breathe. I'll have the head of the first man who breathes. (NICHOLAS *steps again.*) You are breathing, Astrologer.

ASTROLOGER: I can't help it. (NICHOLAS *takes the sixth step.*)

ALL: Six. (NICHOLAS *is about to take the seventh step when there are flashes of lightning and a great crash of thunder. Blackout.* MOUSE KING *appears in the green spotlight.*)

MOUSE KING: Hah! Who dares defy the power of the Mouse King's magic?

ALL (*Together*): The Mouse King!

MOUSE KING: Now you, Nicholas Nutcracker, shall wear the nutcracker face of Princess Pirlipat — until some lady, young and fair, says she loves you for yourself, sincerely. (*Thunder and lightning. Blackout. Lights come up.* PRINCESS *is cowering in the* KING's *arms.* NICHOLAS *has fallen to the floor.*)

CHANCELLOR: Nicholas has fallen!

DROSSELMEYER: The Mouse King upset him just as he was about to take the seventh step.

ASTROLOGER: Look at him! It's the curse of the Mouse King! (NICHOLAS *gets to his feet. He wears the mask* PRINCESS *wore before.*)

DROSSELMEYER (*To* PRINCESS): Princess, help Nicholas. Say you love him. Break the spell of the Mouse King.

PRINCESS (*Coldly*): That is not the young man who gave me the nut. That is a hideous creature. Turn him out of the court! (*She flounces out haughtily up left.*)

KING (*Running after her*): Pirlipat! My dear! Come back! Help the young man! (KING *exits up left, followed by* DROSSELMEYER, CHANCELLOR, MATHEMATICIAN *and* ASTROLOGER, *all calling to* PRINCESS. NICHOLAS *stands alone.*)

NICHOLAS (*Boldly*): Watch out, Mouse King! I swear that some day your life shall pay for this face! (*He pulls out his sword and holds it high. Blackout, during which* NICHOLAS *exits. Music. After a pause, the lights come up, revealing* JUDGE *and* FRAU SILBERHAUS, MARCHEN, *and* FRITZ *seated around fireplace.* DROSSELMEYER, *with gray beard and powdered hair, is standing center in the militant attitude of* NICHOLAS NUTCRACKER *at the end of the preceding scene.* MARCHEN *holds the nutcracker.*)

DROSSELMEYER (*Repeating* NICHOLAS'*s closing speech*): Watch out, Mouse King! I swear that some day your life shall pay for this face! (*He breaks the pose.*) That is the story of the nutcracker.

FRAU SILBERHAUS: What a fine story it is! (*She stands.*) But now it's time we were all in bed. Come, Fritz, Marchen. (FRITZ *goes out up right, stretching and yawning, with* FRAU SILBERHAUS.)

JUDGE (*To* DROSSELMEYER): You are to have your old room, Doctor. You know where it is. Good night and Merry Christmas. (*He exits up right.*)

MARCHEN: Godfather?

DROSSELMEYER: Yes, Marchen?

MARCHEN: That wasn't *really* the end of the story, was it? There ought to be more about the nutcracker and the Mouse King.

DROSSELMEYER: There *is* more, my dear. But I can't tell you about it, because it hasn't happened.

MARCHEN (*Puzzled*): Hasn't happened?

DROSSELMEYER (*Smiling at her*): No, not yet. Good night, Marchen.

MARCHEN: Good night, Godfather. (DROSSELMEYER *exits up right.* MARCHEN *speaks to the nutcracker cradled in her arm.*) Poor nutcracker! *I* wouldn't have done as the Princess did. *I* wouldn't have deserted you, because I really love you for yourself, sincerely. (*She puts the nutcracker under the tree, out of sight.*) Good night, dear nutcracker. (*Suddenly she is startled by a shrill laugh.*) Who's there? (*Laugh is repeated.*) Who is laughing? (MOUSE KING *appears up left and advances into the room.*)

MOUSE KING: Do you think you can protect the nutcracker from my vengeance?

MARCHEN (*Frightened*): Go away, Mouse King!

MOUSE KING: I'll give *you* an ugly face, too!

MARCHEN: Nutcracker. Help! Save me!

MOUSE KING: He can't save you! He is only a toy!

MARCHEN (*Desperately*): Nutcracker! Nutcracker! (NICHOLAS NUTCRACKER *leaps from behind the Christmas tree. He wears a white bandage around the jaw of his nutcracker mask.*)

NICHOLAS: Stand back, Marchen! This will be a fight to the finish!

MARCHEN: Oh, my brave Nutcracker! You must defeat the wicked Mouse King! (NICHOLAS *and* MOUSE KING *square off with drawn swords.* MARCHEN *gasps in fright as she watches. Up and down the room they fight, then exit up left, still fighting. There is a dreadful squeak off left, followed, a moment later, by the entrance of* NICHOLAS, *his sword in one hand, the* MOUSE KING's *crown in the other. His nutcracker mask is gone.* MARCHEN *runs to him.*) Oh, Nutcracker! You've won!

NICHOLAS: Please accept this trophy of victory from one who would serve you until death. (*With a flourish, he presents* MOUSE KING's *crown to* MARCHEN.)

MARCHEN (*Taking it with a curtsy*): Thank you.

NICHOLAS: And now, dear Marchen, if you will excuse me, I must go to my people.

MARCHEN (*Curiously*): Your people?

NICHOLAS: The toys. I am their king. (*He exits right, passing the tree. As* MARCHEN *stands looking after him wistfully,* DROSSELMEYER *appears in the alcove upstage.*)

DROSSELMEYER: Marchen! Why aren't you in bed yet?

MARCHEN: Nutcracker and the Mouse King had a duel and Nutcracker won! Look! Here is the Mouse King's crown.

DROSSELMEYER: This is a magic crown, Marchen. If you put it on, you will be Queen of the Toys. (*He sets crown on* MARCHEN's *head.*)

MARCHEN: Is the story all told now, Godfather?

DROSSELMEYER: Yes, my dear.

MARCHEN: But you weren't here to tell it. You don't think it was a dream, do you?

DROSSELMEYER: Who can say? To dream is but to wake from sleep — to wake is but to fall asleep to dream. And children dream wonderful things on Christmas Eve. Come. It's time for you to go to bed. (DROSSELMEYER *puts his arm around* MARCHEN *and they walk out slowly. The lights dim down to a single spotlight on the clock.*)

VOICE OF THE CLOCK (*Offstage*): Twelve o'clock midnight on the twenty-fourth of December. Twelve o'clock midnight on the twenty-fourth of December. Merry Christmas! (*Curtain*)

THE END

The Second Shepherd's Play

Adapted by *Faye E. Head*

Twice the shepherds came to a cradle, once to search for a lost lamb, and then to bring gifts to a Child . . .

Characters

1ST SHEPHERD, *a middle-aged man*
2ND SHEPHERD, *a young boy*
3RD SHEPHERD, *an old man*
MAK
GILL, *his wife*
JOSEPH
MARY
ANGEL

The Second Shepherd's Play, first performed about 1450, is the best known of the Medieval English *miracle* or *mystery* plays. It was one of the plays in the Wakefield cycle (also known as the Towneley cycle) and, typically, deals with the story of the Nativity in a style that combines both humorous and deeply religious elements. This combination of farce and seriousness was often found in these secular Medieval mystery plays, which grew out of dramatizations of episodes in the Old and the New Testaments, originally presented in the church. As these religious dramas became more elaborate and realistic, they moved into the marketplace, with players drawn increasingly from the laity, but the plays continued to be given on religious holidays.

Scene 1

Setting: *A plain near Bethlehem, at night.*

At Rise: *Three* Shepherds *sit on the ground, huddled together against the cold.*

1st Shepherd: These are cold nights and strange as well. I don't think there has been such snowing for many a winter.

2nd Shepherd: The poor little lambs look frozen.

3rd Shepherd: Maybe, but we shepherds and other poor folk are the ones who really feel the cold.

1st Shepherd: Yes, our master is sleeping in a warm bed, like any rich lord.

3rd Shepherd: While we must protect the sheep.

2nd Shepherd: I'm sleepy.

3rd Shepherd: I know, lad; but we must stay awake to watch the sheep.

1st Shepherd: If they don't stray or get caught by wolves, that rascal Mak may try to steal one of them.

3rd Shepherd: And then we would have to pay for the loss.

2nd Shepherd: Mak? Who is Mak?

1st Shepherd: A thief and a villain. No sheep are safe around him. Ours is a hard life.

3rd Shepherd: I have heard it said that the prophets tell of a child who will be born to give peace and joy to poor men like us.

2nd Shepherd: A child? What could a child do for us?

1st Shepherd: Quiet, let him speak.

3rd Shepherd: This child will be like a shepherd to us, and we will be like his sheep, protected and comforted.

1st Shepherd: I have heard such a story, too.

2nd Shepherd: It would indeed be a fine thing to see that child.

3rd Shepherd: Yet who can say whether such things will

be. Even if he does come, what chance have we of see-ing him? But we were talking about Mak. Look! Here he comes.

1ST SHEPHERD (*Calling*): What cheer, Mak? (MAK *enters, wearing a hooded cloak which he holds to hide his face.*)

MAK: Mak? Mak? I don't know what you're talking about. Who is Mak?

2ND SHEPHERD: Listen to him!

MAK: I am a yeoman of the King, a messenger from a great lord. See that you treat me with respect or you'll suffer for it.

1ST SHEPHERD: When you're around, shepherds usually suffer.

3RD SHEPHERD: Watch him. This is some trick to steal a sheep.

MAK: Trick? Trick? Why would I, a simple messenger, play a trick?

3RD SHEPHERD: Don't try to fool us, Mak. We know you.

MAK (*Showing his face*): You're right. It is Mak that stands before you, but I didn't recognize you at first. You're looking well. I wish I could say the same for myself; but hard workers like me feel the cold.

1ST SHEPHERD (*Sarcastically*): *You* a hard worker? That's a joke.

3RD SHEPHERD: You've never worked or done anything honest.

MAK: You're insulting me. Before you say another word, I must have a nap. (*He lies down.*) Such cold nights make me sleepy. (*He lies on ground and pretends to sleep.*)

1ST SHEPHERD: What sort of trick are you up to now? (*To others*) He really is asleep.

3RD SHEPHERD: I still don't trust him.

2ND SHEPHERD: I'm sleepy, too.

3RD SHEPHERD: Why don't you two get some rest? As long as Mak is here, we are safe from him.

1ST SHEPHERD: At least he can't steal our sheep. We'll wake up soon. (1ST *and* 2ND SHEPHERDS *lie down and are soon asleep, snoring.*)

3RD SHEPHERD: Rest. I am older and do not need as much sleep as you two. The night is beautiful, but there is a strangeness in the air. It's as if even the stars are waiting for something to happen. It is cold tonight, and the cold makes — one — very — sleepy. (*His head falls forward as he dozes off.* MAK *gets up cautiously and looks around, making sure the* SHEPHERDS *are asleep.*)

MAK: Ah — all asleep. This looks like a good time for a poor man like me to do a bit of honest work. Let me see. (*He walks first right, then left, peering off into darkness.*) There's a fine fat lambkin that will never be missed if I just borrow it. It will make a tasty meal. (*Puts finger to lips and tiptoes right*) Quietly, now. (*He goes off briefly and returns carrying lamb.*) Now to get home quickly and hide it before they wake. (*He hides lamb under his cloak and slips out quickly. Curtain.*)

* * * * *

SCENE 2

SETTING: *Inside Mak's cottage. Door at left leads outside. There is a rough table at center, a rocker right, and another chair left, next to cradle which is on the floor.*

AT RISE: GILL *sits asleep in the rocker. A loud knock is heard on outside door. She wakes with a start.*

MAK (*From outside*): Open the door, good wife.

GILL (*Still half asleep*): Who makes such a noise at this time of night?

MAK (*From outside*): It is your husband! Open the door quickly, Gill. See what I bring.

GILL (*Grumbling as she gets up and goes to door*): All right, all right, Mak. Don't be in such a hurry. (*Opens the door*) What is it?

MAK (*Entering*): Look here. See what your good husband has provided for you. (*He takes lamb out from under his cloak.*)

GILL: A lamb. Where did you get it? You stole it, I'll wager.

MAK: Mind your tongue, woman. Don't you realize how lucky you are?

GILL: I won't be so lucky when the shepherds come looking for the lamb. I know where you got it, and so will they.

MAK: They are asleep and know nothing. Now let's hide it.

GILL: Hide it? Where can we hide a lamb in this house?

MAK: Let me see. That should be no problem for a clever man like me.

GILL: If you were all that clever, you wouldn't have to steal lambs.

MAK: Quiet. You talk too much. Let me think. If I were a lamb, where would I like to be hidden?

GILL: Wherever you're going to hide it, you'd better make haste.

MAK: I know. We'll put the lamb in that cradle and cover it well. I'll tell the shepherds that we have a new baby in the house. They'll never think of looking there.

GILL: That *is* a clever idea. It might work. (*They put the lamb into the cradle and cover it.*)

MAK: Now, all is well. I must hurry back to the field — to sleep. Take care of yourself and of our — (*With a laugh*) child.

GILL: Be careful. (*He exits. She begins to rock the cradle, as curtain falls.*)

* * * * *

SCENE 3

SETTING: *Same as Scene 1.*

AT RISE: SHEPHERDS *are still sleeping.* MAK *enters, lies down in same place as in Scene 1.*

MAK: They still sleep. They look so peaceful. Now, I will pretend I have never been awake. (*He snores.*)

1ST SHEPHERD (*Waking suddenly*): Wake up, quickly! I have had such a dream. I dreamed that a wolf carried off one of the lambs. (*He wakes* SHEPHERDS.)

2ND SHEPHERD: I will look to see if they are safe.

MAK (*Pretending to wake*): Never mind about that. I have had a dream, too. I dreamed that a new baby was born to my good wife, Gill.

3RD SHEPHERD: That is a strange dream. (*To* 2ND SHEPHERD) Go, count the lambs. (2ND SHEPHERD *exits.*)

MAK: I'm sure it is true . . . dreams often are. I must hurry home to see my new child. Goodbye, good cheer. (MAK *exits.*)

2ND SHEPHERD (*Rushing in*): One of the lambs is gone.

1ST SHEPHERD: That is Mak's work.

3RD SHEPHERD: But you saw him leave just now, and he took no lamb with him.

1ST SHEPHERD: Just the same, I don't trust him. I think we'd better pay Gill and Mak a visit.

2ND SHEPHERD: Come, let's hurry.

3RD SHEPHERD: We will ask the shepherds in the next field to watch our sheep for us. Come. (*They exit. Curtain.*)

* * * * *

SCENE 4

SETTING: *Inside Mak's cottage, same as Scene 2.*

AT RISE: GILL *sits in chair, rocking cradle.* MAK *is seated on the floor, wrapped in a blanket. Sound of knocking is heard on outside door.*

1ST SHEPHERD (*From outside door*): Open up!

MAK: Who is it?

3RD SHEPHERD (*From off*): We have come for our lamb.

GILL: Why come here?

1ST SHEPHERD (*From off*): We know you have it.

MAK (*Opening the door*): Villains! What do you mean making such a noise, when my new child is sleeping!

2ND SHEPHERD: We have lost a lamb. (*The three* SHEP-HERDS *enter.*)

3RD SHEPHERD: Everyone knows this is a good place to look for a lost sheep.

GILL: How can you say such a thing? If Mak or I have taken a sheep of yours, may I — why, may I eat this child of mine.

MAK: Why should I be suspected because you were careless in guarding the sheep?

1ST SHEPHERD: Just the same, we'll search the house.

MAK (*Sitting down*): Suit yourself. I have no sheep of yours. (SHEPHERDS *search the room, as* GILL *continues to rock cradle.*) You all saw me. I was just passing your way and stopped to rest, but I stole nothing.

2ND SHEPHERD: I don't find anything.

GILL: We told you there was nothing.

1ST SHEPHERD: We're sorry we doubted you, Mak.

MAK: You should be.

3RD SHEPHERD: Forgive us, but we were worried about the lamb.

1ST SHEPHERD: That's a fine peaceful child you have there.

GILL: Oh, yes.

MAK: As quiet as a lamb — I mean, as a dove.

GILL: If you have finished looking here, we are very busy right now with the new child.

MAK: Besides, you'll be wanting to get back to your sheep. I hear there are thieves about.

GILL: Goodbye.

MAK: Yes, goodbye. (MAK *and* GILL *get up and try to push* SHEPHERDS *toward the outside door.*) Goodbye.

1ST SHEPHERD: Just a minute! Wait. We must give the baby a present. Here is a farthing for him.

GILL (*Taking it*): Thank you. Goodbye.

3RD SHEPHERD: Come, now let us have a look at him and give him a kiss.

GILL: No, no! You must not disturb him.

MAK: He's sleeping!

2ND SHEPHERD: Let us at least have one look at him. (*He goes to cradle and lifts cover, revealing lamb.*) Look!

1ST SHEPHERD: Why — what a long nose he has!

GILL: That's a fine thing to say about a child.

MAK: And in front of his parents! All children can't be beautiful.

3RD SHEPHERD (*Walking over to cradle*): Let me see. Why, he looks like a lamb!

2ND SHEPHERD: It's our lamb!

3RD SHEPHERD (*Pointing*): Here's the mark on its ear.

MAK: What's this? Heavens, my child has been bewitched. The elves have stolen my baby and put a lamb in its place.

1ST SHEPHERD: We know the name of the elf who did this.

3RD SHEPHERD (*Holding on to* MAK): What shall we do with this thief?

2ND SHEPHERD (*Pulling the blanket off* MAK): He needs a good tossing.

MAK: Let me go! What are you doing?

3RD SHEPHERD: We'll give him a reason to remember this night.

GILL: Stop!

1ST SHEPHERD: Come on! (SHEPHERDS *grab* MAK *and put him on the blanket.*)

MAK: How dare you! Are you mad?

GILL: Monsters! (SHEPHERDS *toss* MAK *in blanket. He and* GILL *scream.* SHEPHERDS *lower blanket.*)

3RD SHEPHERD (*Letting* MAK *go*): Don't ever come near our field again.

1ST SHEPHERD: Perhaps now you'll think before you steal another lamb.

GILL (*Taking* MAK *by the ear*): He certainly will. (*To* MAK) You fool! I warned you.

MAK: But Gill . . .

GILL: Just be quiet. If you ever steal another sheep you'll have to answer to me! (*He squirms out of her grasp, and she chases him off.*)

1ST SHEPHERD: Come. We must get back to the sheep. (SHEPHERDS *exit, carrying lamb in blanket. Curtain.*)

*   *   *   *   *

SCENE 5

BEFORE RISE: SHEPHERDS *are walking along a road.*

3RD SHEPHERD: Poor Mak. Even though he is a thief, I do feel sorry for him.

2ND SHEPHERD: I don't.

1ST SHEPHERD: Listen! Stop! (*They pause and listen, as sound of music is heard from offstage.*)

3RD SHEPHERD: What is it? (ANGEL *enters right, pauses.* SHEPHERDS *stare in awe, and fall to their knees.*)

ANGEL (*Raising her arms*): Fear not: for, behold, I bring you good tidings of great joy, which shall be to all people. For unto you is born this day, in the city of

David, a Saviour, which is Christ the Lord. And this shall be a sign unto you: Ye shall find the babe wrapped in swaddling clothes, lying in a manger. (ANGEL *exits quickly.*)

1ST SHEPHERD: Was I dreaming? Did you see an angel? Did you hear it, too?

2ND SHEPHERD: I did. Look, there in the sky — a star!

3RD SHEPHERD: The prophets say a star will lead us to the child. Come, let us follow it.

2ND SHEPHERD: We must see this child.

1ST SHEPHERD: On the way we'll think of gifts we can bring.

3RD SHEPHERD: Who would think we would be the ones to see this marvel? Come, let us go to Bethlehem to see the child. (*They exit.*)

* * *

SETTING: *A stable in Bethlehem.*

AT RISE: JOSEPH *and* MARY *sit on hay near manger.* SHEPHERDS *enter.* 1ST SHEPHERD *carries basket of cherries.* 2ND SHEPHERD *holds small cage with bird in it.* 3RD SHEPHERD *has a ball in his hand.*

1ST SHEPHERD: Hail to the child.

2ND SHEPHERD: Hail, Saviour.

3RD SHEPHERD: We have followed the star to this place.

JOSEPH: Come closer. Come and look upon the child.

MARY: Do not be afraid. Come nearer.

1ST SHEPHERD (*Crossing to manger*): Why, look how happy he is! Are you laughing, little one?

MARY: He was born to make the world happier.

1ST SHEPHERD (*To baby*): Here, would you like these cherries? (*Putting basket in the manger*)

2ND SHEPHERD (*To baby*): And look, I brought you this bird for a pet.

MARY: See, he smiles at the gift of a bird.

3RD SHEPHERD (*To baby*): We have come far to seek you, lambkin. It makes me sad to see you so poorly dressed.

1ST SHEPHERD: And in a stable.

JOSEPH: There was no room at the inn.

3RD SHEPHERD (*To baby*): I have nothing for you but this ball, but I want you to have it.

MARY: Shepherds, the Father of Heaven has sent us his Son. He will protect you and keep you from woe; and that will be my prayer to him. Now, go forth and spread this news. (*Spotlight shines on manger, music is heard in background.* SHEPHERDS *kneel in awe as curtain falls.*)

THE END

Production Notes

REINDEER ON THE ROOF

Characters: 5 male; 5 female.

Playing Time: 30 minutes.

Costumes: Everyday modern dress. All except Mrs. Stevens wear winter coats as they enter.

Properties: Ornaments, tinsel, reindeer head made of plywood, cloth, paint can and brush, two strings of lights, greens, two Christmas presents, fuses, camera, notebook, pencil, stocking.

Setting: The Stevens living room. An undecorated Christmas tree stands at one side. In upstage wall is a window. On the sill is a large brass candlestick with an unlighted candle. A fireplace with candles on mantel is at left. A basket beside it holds wood. At one side is a small table with telephone and phone book. Easy chairs, tables, lamps, etc., complete furnishings. Door at right leads to hall, and exit at left leads to rest of house.

Lighting: Colored lights can be seen outside window. Lights in house go off as indicated in text, and electric candles are turned on as Mrs. Stevens "lights" them. There is a flash outside as picture is taken.

Sound: Offstage carolers, hammering, doorbell, phone, as indicated in text.

A CHRISTMAS PROMISE

Characters: 3 male; 3 female.

Playing Time: 25 minutes.

Costumes: Modern, everyday dress for all.

Properties: Tuxedo on hanger, white evening gown and sewing basket, packages in Christmas wrappings, brightly-colored shirt, compact, bracelet, perfume atomizer, and suit box containing Santa Claus outfit.

Setting: The Collins living room, decorated for Christmas with a lighted tree, Christmas cards, wreaths, etc. The room is furnished with a sofa, several easy chairs, and telephone on small table. Exits are left and right, leading to front door and to rest of house. At rise, Mrs. Spencer's coat is on a chair.

Lighting: No special effects.

Sound: Telephone, doorbell, and car horn, as indicated in text.

WHATEVER HAPPENED TO GOOD OLD EBENEZER SCROOGE?

Characters: 2 male; 2 female; 10 male or female for TV Announcer, Investment Counselor, dwarfs, Mirror.

Playing Time: 25 minutes.

Costumes: TV Announcer and Investment Counselor wear conservative everyday dress. Scrooge wears top hat, long coat and spectacles. Dwarfs wear beards, eccentric clothing, knickers, etc. Snow White, Prince and Witch wear appropriate fairy tale costumes.

Properties: Hand mirror, papers, pen, etc. for Scrooge's desk, ledger.

Setting: Scene 1: Before Rise, TV studio with table and microphone and two chairs; After Rise, office, with desk and two chairs. Scene 2, factory, with long table and benches at left and desk and chair at right. Scene 3, same as Scene 2.

Lighting: Lights dim, as indicated in text.

Sound: Offstage voice, jingling bells.

RED CARPET CHRISTMAS

Characters: 5 male; 7 female.

Playing Time: 35 minutes.

Costumes: Modern everyday dress. Bessie wears an apron over her clothes. Anita carries a pocketbook.

Properties: Binoculars, newspaper clipping, plate of cookies, packages, strip of red carpet, dress, hanger, glass of punch, handkerchief, folded note.

Setting: The living room of the Hitchcock family. There is a large window at right. The room is furnished with a sofa, coffee table, chairs, television set; other pieces may be added. A rug is on the floor. There is a telephone on one of the tables. Christmas decorations are in evidence.

Lighting: No special effects.

STAR OVER BETHLEHEM

Characters: 8 male; 4 female; male extras.

Playing Time: 30 minutes.

Costumes: The traditional dress of the period. Micah and the Three Wise Men wear more elegant costumes than the shepherds and other characters. Herod's Man should wear an emblem.

Properties: Coins for Micah, coin for Joseph, pitcher for Ann, caskets for Wise Men, doll to represent the Child.

Setting: The yard of the inn near Bethlehem. Downstage center is a bench. The right wall of the stage is the front wall of the inn. In this wall, a door opens into the inn. In the left wall, a portal opens on the highway. The rear wall is the rear of the stable. In this wall, right of center, is a door opening into the stable. A part of the wall should be so built that it can be drawn aside when the tableau of the manger is presented.

Lighting: The tableau at the end of the play should be brightly illuminated.

Sound: Christmas songs as indicated in text.

THE CHRISTMAS STARLET

Characters: 5 male; 6 female.

Playing Time: 30 minutes.

Costumes: Modern everyday dress.

Properties: Knitting materials for Mrs. Sayre, camera for Joe, scrapbook wrapped as Christmas gift.

Setting: The Sayres' attractive living room in Lakeview. Doors at left and right lead into other rooms, and one at upstage center opens

onto the front porch. Up right is a Christmas tree under which presents are piled; down right is a sofa; and, at center, chairs and a table, holding the telephone, some magazines, and a sewing basket. Up left is a bookcase, and, down left, an easy chair.
Lighting: No special effects.

THE TROUBLE WITH CHRISTMAS

Characters: 3 male; 4 female.
Playing Time: 25 minutes.
Costumes: Modern dress for students. Miss Emily wears Victorian costume. Santa Claus wears traditional costume, but it is patched and shabby. He is thin.
Properties: Gift-wrapped package for Miss Emily; glass of milk and plate of cookies.
Setting: A conference room. Down center there is a long conference table with five chairs around it. Up right is a captain's chair with a small table next to it. Up center, against wall, is a larger table. There is a concealed exit behind it. Up left is a pile of Christmas materials, including a small fir tree in a stand, white tablecloth, folding cardboard fireplace, boxes of Christmas tree decorations, candlesticks with red candles, table centerpiece, and five gift-wrapped packages. There is a rocking chair near these objects. Exits are down right and down left, and concealed exit is at rear.
Lighting: Harsh bright lighting, dimming and softening, and spotlight on tree, as indicated in text.

THE CHRISTMAS VISITOR

Characters: 4 male; 3 female; as many Carolers as desired (offstage voices).
Playing Time: 35 minutes.
Costumes: Modern, everyday dress. The Remingtons wear expensive clothes. Laura wears a coat and watch when she first enters, then changes into a long dressing gown. Gerald puts on hat and coat in Scene 1. Sally wears sophisticated pants and blouse. The Boy is bareheaded, and wears a shapeless coat. Graves wears dark trousers and white duck serving coat. He later wears derby and black Chesterfield coat. Mrs. Lester and Jamie wear coats.
Properties: Tinsel star, ladder, wrapped presents (one of them a child's carpenter set with hammer, saw, etc.), cards for Boy and Mrs. Lester, glass of milk.
Setting: The fashionably furnished living room of the Remington apartment in an expensive apartment building in a large city. A large elaborately decorated Christmas tree dominates the room. A couch is at center, and an end table beside it holds a framed picture of Laura, smiling. A stereo is against one wall. The front door is at right, and beside it is a small table with telephone. The door at left leads to the rest of the apartment. A window is in one wall, and if possible, snow is seen falling outside.
Lighting: The room is brilliantly lit in Scene 1 and is dimly lit in Scene 2, and the Christmas tree lights are on. Some of the tree lights go out, as indicated in text.
Sound: Door buzzer, key in lock, telephone, recording of "Away in a Manger" and live or recorded singing of offstage Carolers, as indicated in text.

CHRISTMAS RECAPTURED

Characters: 4 male; 4 female.
Playing Time: 30 minutes.
Costumes: Modern dress. Aunt Mathilda, Charlie and Lucille wear coats when they enter. Charlie wears a sweater.
Properties: Two eggs, purse and bag for Aunt Mathilda, deck of cards; silver necklace.
Setting: The living room of the Stevens' home. There is an entrance downstage right leading to the front door, and another upstage left leading to the rest of the house. Upstage center is a brightly trimmed and lighted Christmas tree with some artificial snow on it. At right is a large easy chair with a table near it, and near the left wall downstage is a sofa with a mirror above it. Other chairs, tables and lamps complete the furnishings. Under the tree and on the tables are Christmas presents, some in boxes, some out. Among them is a cube-shaped box with a crank. On the table near the easy chair are three boxes containing ties, and a large jar of tobacco. On a table upstage center is a stack of handkerchief boxes, one of which contains tickets and handkerchief. On a table near the sofa is a box containing a large, lacy blouse. In front of the sofa is a wastebasket full of Christmas wrappings, and a few pieces are strewn on the floor near it.
Lighting: No special effects, but the lights on the tree should be on.

CHRISTMAS COAST TO COAST

Characters: 9 male; 4 female; as many extras as feasible.
Playing Time: 25 minutes.

Costumes: Modern business suit, overcoat and scarf for John, work clothes for Peggy, appropriate uniforms for Milkman and Delivery Boys, extravagant, flashy clothes for Mrs. Schultz and Miss George, Boy Scout uniform with short pants for Mr. Henries, ordinary suit for Jeffrey Lord, sophisticated outfit with mink coat for Dulcie Baker, work clothes for TV technicians. Extras should wear the costumes appropriate for their parts in "The Twelve Days of Christmas."
Properties: Large potted tree with tag attached, overcoat and scarf, briefcase, water pitcher, letter, telephone, covered bird cage, large crate, large box, egg, several yards of cable, microphones, camera and other photographic equipment, small package, lead pipes, drums.
Setting: A living room, conventionally decorated, with easy chair and draperies hung on large curtain rings. Door at one wing should represent front door; back wall should have a closet door.
Lighting: No special effects.
Sound: Doorbell and telephone rings.

THE VILLAIN AND THE TOY SHOP

Characters: 11 male; 9 female.
Playing Time: 20 minutes.
Costumes: Toys and Fairy Godmother wear appropriate costumes. Three Citizens wear everyday clothes, with hats, scarves, mittens. Town Watchman wears dark coat and hat. The Bankers wear dark suits, vests, mufflers, and derby hats. Glowerpuss wears a dark suit, tall black hat, black cape, and mustache. Joe is dressed in work clothes, with suspenders and sleeve garters in Scene 1; he wears

muffler over these in Scene 3. Carolyn wears a frilly, feminine dress, with a large bow in her hair; she wears a coat in Scene 3. Jeremy wears work clothes in Scene 1; a flannel nightgown, slippers and nightcap in Scene 3. John wears a suit, bow tie, and muffler. Sarah wears a housedress and apron in Scene 1; nightgown, nightcap, and slippers in Scene 3.

Properties: Feather duster, large red handkerchief, briefcase full of papers, large bell, 2 pieces of paper (agreements), pen, suitcase, contracts, magic wand.

Setting: The toy shop. A large window upstage reveals the town of Rosemont. Beneath the window is a shelf for the toys. In Scene 1, there are cardboard cutouts or models of China Doll, Soldier, Calico Cat, Clown, Raggedy Ann, and Humpty Dumpty, on shelf. Up left is the box for Jack. A chair and a small table are down right. The doorway right leads to the rest of the shop; the doorway left leads to the street.

Lighting: Light shining through window; raise and lower stage lights as indicated in text.

Sound: Clock striking, motorcycle, as indicated in text. Appropriate music may be used for the entrances of Carolyn, John, and Glowerpuss. Sound effects and music may be recorded.

SANTA GOES MOD

Characters: 7 male; 5 female; 5 male and female Elves; male and female extras for other Elves, and if desired, additional Reporters can be played by male and female extras.

Playing Time: 20 minutes.

Costumes: Ms. Taylor, Steve, and

Reporters wear everyday, modern dress. Santa wears modern dress at first, then changes into traditional costume. Mrs. Claus wears pantsuit, then changes into old-fashioned dress and apron. Elves wear green tunics and vests with white shirts underneath. Joe and Bill wear uniforms.

Properties: Various toys; pads and pencils for Reporters; clipboards for Elves; portable TV camera, reading CHANNEL 7 NEWS; microphone and clipboard for Ms. Taylor; sacks filled with letters.

Setting: Santa's workshop. There are tables across rear stage covered with Christmas packages, dolls, toy trains, etc. A large sack, partially filled with wrapped packages, is on floor beside table. There is a decorated Christmas tree in one corner of the stage, and a sign reading SANTA'S WORKSHOP on rear wall.

Lighting: No special effects.

Sound: Knock on door.

THE GREATEST CHRISTMAS GIFT

Characters: 5 male; 9 female; 4 male or female for Herald and three leprechauns; as many male and female extras as desired for Townspeople.

Playing Time: 30 minutes.

Costumes: Traditional folk costumes. Boys wear breeches and brightly colored vests. Girls wear long dresses with wide skirts and aprons. Wig-o'-the-Wag wears a witch's costume. Three Leprechauns wear green outfits, with long, white beards which are removed as indicated in text. King wears crown, jewels, and long robe. Prince Kevin wears breeches, a cape, and sword.

Properties: Cane, shawl, briar pipe,

tea kettle, large covered dish, rag and scrub pail, broom, handkerchief, bag of "diamonds," bag of "gold," covered basket of handmade flowers, sheets.

Setting: Scenes 1 and 7: Village square in Killybog Town, Ireland. Some shrubbery and potted plants are down right. Scenes 2, 4, and 6: Main room in Doomsday Castle. Door to outside is up right, with screen beside it. Door at left leads to dungeon. Fireplace with artificial flames is down right. A few pieces of old furniture decorate room. Scenes 3 and 5: Sean Finnegan's cottage. A table and several straight chairs are down left. There is a door at right, with a window beside it.

Lighting: Dim, eerie lighting for Doomsday Castle, to create a menacing effect.

Sound: Offstage clashing of cymbals and fanfare of trumpets, as indicated in text.

SILENT NIGHT

Characters: 4 male; 3 female.
Playing Time: 20 minutes.
Costumes: Father Nostler and Father Mohr wear black. Women wear long dresses; Frau Gruber wears a shawl and Frau Schmidt wears an apron. Gruber and Willy wear simple, dark clothes and may wear Alpine hats. Inge has a long dress and a shawl.
Properties: Paper, guitar in case.
Setting: The living room of the parish house in Oberndorf, Austria. There are several chairs, a desk, tables and other simple furnishings. Exits are at right and left.
Lighting: No special effects.
Sound: Gruber may actually play guitar, or music may be taped.

A NEW ANGLE ON CHRISTMAS

Characters: 13 male; 9 female.
Playing Time: 15 minutes.
Costumes: Everyday winter dress. All wear outdoor clothing except for Joe, Orvil, and Editor who wear office clothes during Scene 1. Santa Claus wears a traditional outfit.
Properties: Note pad and pencil.
Setting: The setting for Scene 1 is a newspaper office. Sign which reads THE STAR is painted on the backdrop over a graph which shows the newspaper's rising circulation rate. JOE KNOW, STAR REPORTER placard is on wooden desk piled with paper and old newspapers. A typewriter is on the desk and a wastebasket, overflowing with crumpled sheets of paper, is next to desk. Additional office equipment is randomly placed around stage. Scene 2 may be played before the curtain or else in a setting which suggests the outdoors. A chair or bench is to the side of the stage.
Lighting: No special effects.
Sound: Music may accompany the singers at the end of the play.

WHAT, NO SANTA CLAUS?

Characters: 1 male; 1 female; 7 male or female elves; two offstage voices for announcers.
Playing Time: 30 minutes.
Costumes: Traditional costume for Santa Claus. Mrs. Claus first wears red dress with white shawl, later changes into Santa suit with cap. Elves wear green suits with red buttons and red stocking caps.
Properties: Big red blanket, white blanket, tea kettle filled with hot water, big box labeled MUSTARD, pack with toys sticking out at top

for Mrs. Santa, basin of hot water, sheet of paper.

Setting: Living room of Santa's house at North Pole. A door at left leads to workshop and rest of house, door at right leads outside. Upstage from door is a window looking out on high drifts of snow. Fireplace upstage center with two big red socks hanging from the mantel. Downstage and left of fireplace is a large easy chair. Upstage in right corner stands a large Christmas tree. Radio is on table upstage. There are comfortable chairs, tables, and Christmas decorations all around. Table at Santa's side has box of tissues, spoon, and several bottles of medicine with big, plainly marked labels reading, COUGH MEDICINE, SNEEZE MEDICINE, and PILLS FOR CHILLS.

Lighting: No special effects.

Sound: Sleigh bells and live or recorded music of "Jingle Bells" as indicated in text.

WE INTERRUPT THIS PROGRAM . . .

Characters: 10 male; 3 female; 19 male or female for Cameramen, Scientists, Computer Technician, Assistant, Elves, and Children; as many as desired for Carolers.

Playing Time: 25 minutes.

Costumes: Master of Ceremonies and Pianist wear school clothes. J. Holly Barberry wears suit with green or red tie, spectacles. Ivy Green has on a red and green pants suit or dress. Two Grenadiers, General Revel, and Two Aides wear uniforms (red if possible) and hats with silver or gold plumes. General Revel has gold epaulettes and Two Aides wear green sashes. Three Scientists, Computer Technician and Assistant wear white lab coats, red or green ties (if boys) or red and green scarves (if girls). Bulletin Boy wears shirt, vest, and trousers, and a green eye shade. Two Elves wear red and green motley and pointed shoes. Santa Claus wears traditional costume. Mrs. Santa Claus wears a red gown, with a mobcap, white wig, spectacles, and a white shawl. Carolers wear outdoor winter clothes. Children of the World have appropriate traditional costumes, or wear school clothes. They carry national flags.

Properties: News bulletins, neck microphones, hand microphone, television camera, small Christmas tree, sky charts, red and green telephones, news desk, chairs, banner reading YOUR HOLIDAY STATION - N-O-E-L, signs reading PRIVATE — TOP SECRET and OPERATION YULEWATCH, swords, test tube, beaker, earphones, microscope, data sheets, music rack, punch-out cards, bubble gum wrapper, benches, international flags, large sack, wrapped gifts, nightcap, shoe tree.

Setting: Scene 1, television station — broadcast news desk, decorated with small Christmas tree and a banner reading YOUR HOLIDAY STATION — N-O-E-L; space laboratories — a computer bank and console up center. Tables and chairs left and right. Sky charts on the walls. Door at left, labeled PRIVATE — TOP SECRET. Scene 2, North Pole — backdrop of Santa's Workshop with northern lights in background. Left and right are tall Christmas trees festooned with snow. There are benches left and right.

Lighting: Flashbulb set off to produce flash of light when rocket lands, as indicated in text.

Sound: Newsroom ticker, computer chatter, cymbal clash, telephones ringing, jingle bells, chimes, whistling, loud bump.

NINE TIMES CHRISTMAS

Characters: 7 male; 4 female.
Playing Time: 20 minutes.
Costumes: The nine children and John the Cobbler are dressed in clean but shabby clothes. At the beginning, several of the girls wear aprons and caps. Later, all the younger children appear in long white nightgowns and tasseled nightcaps. Hard-Heart appears at first in a suit and vest; later, in a long nightgown, cap, and bathrobe.
Properties: Cleaning cloths, dusters, brooms, black moneybag, several pairs of high shoes, cobbler's tools.
Setting: The sparsely furnished sitting room-dining room-workshop of John the Cobbler. Upstage center is a fireplace, with a stool on either side. There is a table upstage left, a workbench downstage right, and an easy chair downstage left.
Lighting: No special effects.

HE WON'T BE HOME FOR CHRISTMAS

Characters: 9 male; 6 female; as many male and female as desired for Elves, and Children in department store.
Playing Time: 25 minutes.
Costumes: The Bensons and other children wear everyday winter dress. Department Store Santa and Santa Claus wear appropriate dress, with white wigs and beards. Elves wear tights and long shirts tied with belt at waist. Western Union Messenger wears uniform.

In Scenes 3 and 4, Mrs. Benson and Benson children wear night clothes.
Properties: Telegram; letter from Santa; pen and receipt for Western Union Man.
Setting: Scene 1 — Grommel's Department Store. There is a chair for Santa at right. This scene may be played before curtain. Shelves of toys may be painted on backdrop. Scene 2 — Santa's workshop at the North Pole. Worktables with toys and tools are placed around stage. File cabinet with papers and folders is at right. There is a telephone on small table at left. Scene 3 — The Bensons' living room. There is a sofa down left. Bare Christmas tree is at right. There are electric lights on tree. Boxes of decorations are on floor beside tree. Chairs, lamp, coffee table complete the furnishings. Scene 4 — Same as Scene 3 except that boxes of decorations have been removed and there are presents under tree.
Lighting: Spotlight and Christmas tree lights, as indicated in text.
Sound: Telephone and doorbell, as indicated in text.

SANTA CLAUS IS TWINS

Characters: 4 male; 5 female; optional extra parents and children.
Playing Time: 25 minutes.
Costumes: Modern, everyday dress. Mack wears a turtleneck sweater of a striking design. He and Freddy put on Santa Claus costumes; Freddy's is old and battered-looking. Perkins wears a police uniform.
Properties: Book on desk, appointment book, Polaroid camera with flash bulb, photograph, frame,

string of lights, small fir tree, two suitboxes with Santa suits and bells; purse and money for Mrs. Sheldon; box of lollipops.

Setting: The recreation room in Donna's home. The back walls may be covered with curtains. A door right leads outside; door left leads to the rest of the house. A desk, telephone and chair are down left, a sofa with coffee table is at left center; a stepladder stands behind the sofa, a highbacked chair is up right. There is a decorated folding screen at right of sofa. There are some chairs against wall at extreme left. On the upstage wall is a sign reading TOYS FOR TOTS, and another above it reading OUR CLUB PROJECT. Beside it is a sign reading HAVE YOUR CHILD'S PICTURE TAKEN WITH SANTA CLAUS.

Lighting: No special effects.

Sound: Telephone, as indicated in text.

THE YEAR SANTA FORGOT CHRISTMAS

Characters: 5 male; 2 female; 4 male or female for elves. As many male and female as desired for German children and English children.

Playing Time: 15 minutes.

Costumes: Santa wears a traditional costume. Mrs. Claus has a long red skirt, white blouse, apron and cap. She wears glasses and a shawl around her shoulders. Elves wear tunics, tights and long, pointed caps with bells at the end. Jean, Billy and Joey wear coats, boots, scarves and caps. German and English children may be in traditional clothing.

Properties: Clipboard and pencil; toys, hammers, paintbrushes, and other tools; plate of cookies covered with a napkin; Santa's pack, containing toys; a large, filled Christmas stocking; a small, real or artificial fir tree.

Setting: Santa's workshop. There are two tables at center, with toys and tools on them. They also hold a sprig of mistletoe and a poinsettia plant. A door and window are at right. A large, throne-like chair is placed at the head of the table, left. Santa's pack of toys is on the floor near one of the tables.

Lighting: No special effects.

Sound: Sleigh bells, as indicated in text.

A VISIT FROM ST. NICHOLAS

Characters: 2 male; 1 female; 19 male or female for 4 Solos, 3 Children, 8 Reindeer, and Dancers (four or more). Extra Dancers may be added, as well as Children and Solos, if parts for all the class are desired.

Playing Time: 10 minutes.

Costumes: Typical Santa Claus costume for St. Nick, with pipe in pocket; night clothes for Children, Mamma, and Papa, including a dust cap for Mamma and a long stocking cap for Papa; antlers for Reindeer; pastel leotards or play clothes for Dancers, to suggest bonbons or candies; red and green costumes for Solos.

Properties: Sack of wrapped gifts; stockings.

Setting: Living room, with fireplace and mantel in rear wall. There is a working window with shutters in wall beside fireplace. Three cots (or more) stand at right, and loveseat with a cushion and couch with pillow stand at left. Exits are left, right, and through fireplace, which has an opening at back with a black cloth backdrop across it.

Lighting: Dim lighting to suggest moonlight at first, as indicated in text.

Sound: Sleigh bells, whistling; live or recorded music.

SANTA CHANGES HIS MIND

Characters: 2 male; 3 female.

Playing Time: 15 minutes.

Costumes: Mr. and Mrs. Elf have green elf suits. Mrs. Elf has green robe over hers when play opens. Elaine and Edith wear green dresses. Santa wears traditional outfit.

Properties: Hairbrush, broom, newspaper, coffee cup, homework, envelope.

Setting: Igloo of Elf family. Four sleeping bags with pillows are arranged around a fireplace at center. Table with four chairs is up center. At left is low doorway through which characters crawl to enter and exit. There is a coffee cup near door. Girls' coats are folded on sleeping bags. Elf hat is hanging on hook on wall. Room should look crowded.

Lighting: No special effects.

Sound: Sleigh bells, as indicated in text.

A CHRISTMAS TALE

Characters: 18 male or female. For choral recitation, parts may be doubled to use a smaller group.

Playing Time: 10 minutes.

Costumes: Traditional for Santa and Easter Bunny; pajamas and nightcaps for 3 children; red and green bow ties, white shirts for choral group.

Properties: Christmas tree, fireplace, chairs (for beds) and blankets for the children in bed, Easter basket with red and green eggs for Easter Bunny, a pack with toys for Santa, 3 stockings hung over fireplace.

Setting: Inside a house. There are 3 beds, stool, Christmas tree, door, and fireplace (used as entrance), at one side.

Lighting: No special effects.

Sound Effects: Knock on door, and clatter, as indicated in text.

SANTA'S ALPHABET

Characters: 1 male; 1 female; 1 male or female for Little Elf; 26 male and female for Other Elves.

Playing Time: About 15 minutes.

Costumes: Santa wears traditional red and white suit with wide black belt; Mrs. Claus wears watch, old-fashioned dress and apron; Little Elf and 26 Elves wear green leotards.

Properties: Long scroll; 26 cardboard letters, each about 5 inches high.

Setting: The living room in Santa's house at North Pole. Two chairs are center, and a decorated Christmas tree stands in one corner. Shelves line side wall, and hold various toys, including the ones individually mentioned throughout play. A fireplace is painted on backdrop, with a mantel, or shelf, long enough to hold 26 cardboard letters of the alphabet, each about five inches high. A sleigh is at stage right, partially hidden by curtain. Sleigh is cut from cardboard, with a front view only. There are strings attached, so that it can be drawn offstage. A box is hidden behind sleigh to hold toys.

Lighting: No special effects.

THREE LITTLE KITTENS' CHRISTMAS

Characters: 3 male; 4 female; 4 or more male or female for Carolers.
Playing Time: 15 minutes.
Costumes: Characters may wear cat masks or makeup. Mother Cat wears an apron. Mr. Katz carries a cane.
Properties: White, red, and orange mittens, toys, plate of cookies, tea wagon with Christmas pie, plates.
Setting: The home of the Three Little Kittens and the street where they live. A decorated Christmas tree with three wrapped packages containing mittens is down right. At back are three houses, represented by archways or door frames. Mr. Katz's house has a chair; Tabby's house has a pile of toys, and Lily's house has a table and chair.
Lighting: No special effects.

THE SHOEMAKER AND THE ELVES

Characters: 2 male; 2 female; 4 male or female for elves. Add extra elves, if desired.
Playing Time: 15 minutes.
Costumes: Elves wear patched and ragged shirts and shorts. Shoemaker wears a long work apron over his pants and shirt. Shoemaker's Wife wears a dress with an apron over it. Little Boy wears pants and a shirt, and is barefoot. Little Girl wears dress, and is barefoot.
Properties: Dinner bell; coins; piece of red leather (oilcloth may be used).
Setting: The Shoemaker's shop. There is a workbench or long table on stage. On it are pieces of red and blue cloth, a piece of leather, tools including hammer, nails, awl, needles, thread, wax, knife, shears, lasts, etc., and an unfinished shoe. Concealed about the workbench there are a pair of shoes to fit Little Boy, a pair of red shoes to fit Little Girl, and red and blue caps and jackets to fit the elves. Exits are door to the outside, at one side of the stage, a window beside door, and door to the rest of the house, on the other side of the stage.
Lighting: Before Elves' entrance, the lights grow dim and then brighten as moon (blue light bulb) shines through the window. As elves exit, blue light goes out and stage lights come on gradually.

A CHRISTMAS CAROL

Characters: 12 male; 7 female; 5 male or female for Ghost of Christmas Past, Ghost of Christmas Present, Ghost of Christmas Yet to Come, Fiddler and Collector; as many male and female extras as desired for Carolers.
Playing Time: 30 minutes.
Costumes: Nineteenth-century dress. Marley's Ghost is made up to look ghastly and he wears suit that looks mildewed. He wears spectacles high on his forehead, and a pigtail is sticking out at the back of his neck. Wrapped around his body are chains that drag behind him. Cash boxes, keys, padlocks and ledgers hang from chains. Ghost of Christmas Past, with youthful face and white hair, wears white tunic with a golden belt and trimmed with summer flowers. He also has a shining crown and carries a branch of holly. Ghost of Christmas Present is dressed in simple, deep green robe, bordered with white fur and with antique

scabbard around waist. He wears on his head a holly wreath with icicles hanging from it, and carries a horn of plenty for a torch. Ghost of Christmas Yet to Come has a black robe with a hood that hides his face. All other characters wear nineteenth century clothes. The Cratchits' clothing is plain and threadbare. Suggestions for costumes can be found in any illustrated edition of "A Christmas Carol."

Properties: Ledgers, ruler, 2 pen-and-ink stands, 2 candles, metal cash box containing coins and roll of bank notes; coal hod and shovel; notebook; calling card; pocket watch; chains weighted with cash boxes, keys, padlocks and ledgers; branch of holly; small Christmas tree on stand; holly wreath; fiddle and bow; ring; torch shaped like horn of plenty, holding glitter; plates, cutlery, mugs and glasses, goose on platter, carving knife, covered vegetable dishes; mantel clock; crutch; punch bowl and ladle; sewing basket and sewing; book.

Setting: Scene 1: The business office of Scrooge and Marley, in London. In right wall is door that opens to the street. Upstage of the door there is a clothes tree, holding two hats, muffler, and greatcoat. At center is flat-topped desk for Scrooge, with a stool behind it. Bob Cratchit's high clerk's desk and stool are set against the left wall. Each desk has pen and inkstand, ledger, and lighted candle on it, and Scrooge's desk also has metal cash box with money in it, and ruler. A casement window is downstage of clerk's desk, and potbellied stove is upstage between two desks. Coal hod and shovel are beside stove. Scene 2: This scene is played before the curtain. School desk and bench are center, representing schoolroom, then moved to right stage, to represent Fezziwig's warehouse. Scene 3: The kitchen of the Cratchit home. Setting is the same as Scene 1, except that office window frame down left has been removed to make an exit. Fireplace is left stage. At center is large table covered with red-checked tablecloth, plates, glasses, etc. Chairs and stools for eight are placed around the table. Scenes 4 and 5, same as Scene 1.

Lighting: Candle flickers; spotlights dim down and come up; blackout, as indicated in text.

Sound: Bell striking when each of Ghosts appears; whistling of wind; live or recorded fiddle music; church bells; live or recorded Christmas carols.

THE CHRISTMAS NUTCRACKER

Characters: 6 male; 4 female; 2 male or female for Royal Astrologer and Mathematician; offstage voice.

Playing Time: 30 minutes.

Costumes: Old-fashioned German clothing for the Silberhaus family and Doctor Drosselmeyer: rather formal dress, with high collars for the boys, long skirts for the girls. Doctor has glasses, gray beard and powdered hair at first, then removes beard and has dark hair. The members of the court of King Pudgy Podgy wear traditional fairy-tale clothing: King wears royal robes stuffed with pillow, and crown, and his cheeks are red; Princess, a pretty long dress and coronet; Chancellor, long robe and billowy wig; Astrologer, long robe and great pointed hat with suns and moons and stars on it: Royal

Mathematician, black robe with numbers and equations on it; Maid, long skirt, blouse, and apron. The Mouse King wears a mouse costume and tiny gold crown. Nicholas wears a page's suit and high boots. There is a nutcracker's mask, which first the Princess and then Nicholas wears.

Properties: Large Christmas garland, music box, toy telescope, notebook and pencil, cardboard swords (for Nicholas and Mouse King), bandage. Nuts, which actors pretend to crack, should be cracked in advance.

Setting: The home of Judge Silberhaus in an old German village. There is a large lighted Christmas tree at right, trimmed with tinsel, toy flutes, candy canes and nuts in small paper baskets. Dolls, toy soldiers, and other wrapped packages are under it, as well as a nutcracker in the shape of a man, with movable jaws (may be made of cardboard). There is a fireplace at left, and near the hearth a large armchair. Set in the back wall is a wide alcove with a grandfather clock in it. (If desired, the clock may be painted on the alcove wall.) There are doors up left and up right in the alcove, and down left and down right.

Lighting: Effect of lightning, if possible, as indicated in the text.

Lights dim and black out temporarily, as indicated. Green spotlight when Mouse King appears; white spotlight to shine on clock.

Sound: Musical selections from Tchaikovsky's "Nutcracker Suite," sound of music box, thunder.

THE SECOND SHEPHERD'S PLAY

Characters: 5 male; 2 female.

Playing Time: 15 minutes.

Costumes: Traditional Biblical costumes. The three shepherds are poorly dressed. Mak wears a large cloak; Gill wears a colorful costume.

Properties: Stuffed (or live) lamb; a strong blanket; 2 shepherd's staffs; a basket of cherries; a bird in a crude cage; a ball; a cradle with cover; traditional manger setting.

Setting: The exterior settings need no properties and could most efficiently be played in front of the stage curtain. Interior settings could be back of the curtain: Mak's cottage — a door, cradle, chair and bench in a poor cottage; the Nativity scene — a stable.

Lighting: The exterior scenes should suggest night. No other special effects needed.

Sound: Appropriate carols, live or recorded, would be effective.